BROTHERS OF THE ACADEMY

BROTHERS OF THE ACADEMY

Up and Coming Black Scholars Earning
Our Way in Higher Education

Edited by *Lee Jones*

FOREWORD BY
Na'im Akbar

STERLING, VIRGINIA

Sty/us

STYLUS PUBLISHING, LLC.

COPYRIGHT © 2000 BY STYLUS PUBLISHING, LLC

Published by Stylus Publishing, LLC.
22841 Quicksilver Drive
Sterling, Virginia 20166-2012

Stylus is a registered trademark of Stylus Publishing, LLC

Library of Congress Cataloging-in-Publication Data

Brothers of the academy: up and coming black scholars
earning our way in higher eduction / edited by Lee Jones;
foreword by Na'im Akbar.—1st ed.
   p. cm.
  Includes bibliographical references and index.
  ISBN 1-57922-027-4 (cloth : alk. paper)—
  ISBN 1-57922-028-2 (pbk. : alk. paper)
    1. Afro-American college teachers. 2. Afro-American
    men—Education (Higher) I. Jones, Lee, 1965– ·

LC2781.5 .B76 2000
378.1'9829'96073—dc21   99-087991

ISBN 1-57922-027-4 (cloth)
ISBN 1-57922-028-2 (paper)

Printed in Canada on acid-free paper
that meets the American National Standards Institute
Z39-48 Standard.

First Edition

10 9 8 7 6 5 4 3 2 1

CONTENTS

PART TWO: NAVIGATING THE ACADEMY

PART THREE: FEATURED SCHOLARSHIP

If a gathering were called of all of the African American men serving in the American academy, very few invitations would probably be necessary and a smaller number of those invited would appear. Though the reasons for this are varied, certainly the most critical reason is how recently African American men have been permitted even to pursue the goal of becoming a scholar, especially in the predominantly European American academic institutions. Even the majority of those who function in Historically Black College and University (HBCU) settings have been required to enter through rites of passage at predominantly White academic settings or into disciplines predominated by their European American colleagues. The first Ph.D. was awarded to an African American man only a little over 100 years ago, and it was followed by an additional century of protest and challenge in order to gain admission to programs that prepared academic scholars. Certainly, the cost and politics of navigating the path of terminal academic degrees continue to make this accomplishment an elusive goal for most African Americans. When we combine these restrictions with the dwindling number of surviving and functional African American men in this society, the limited number of such academicians becomes increasingly understandable.

The other factor that would make this gathering even much smaller than the number of invitations that were extended is the consequence of what happens to the identity of the African American man within the academy. Of the small number who actually enter this sacred ground, even a smaller number are able to preserve their identity and respond to a call for a gathering of African American men. Those factors of socialization that impact the development of academicians manage to obscure the awareness of many of those who endure. They emerge from the academy identified by their profession, their degree, their place of training or employment, and their individual achievements within the confines of their institutions. However, they have grown oblivious to that important historical and social cultural reality that for centuries kept them out of the academy and certainly in some way helped to mold the matriculation and character of each of their experiences within the academy. They have lost sight of who they are.

The men who responded to the call for this volume represent a sample from a very limited pool. They also represent a very special and rare combination of African American men who overcame the odds, endured the process, remembered who they were, and understood the value of such a gathering. Though the majority of these men in academia still operate in HBCU settings, increasing numbers of them are in predominantly White academic institutions. In spite of the tremendous pressures that come from trying to engage in scholarship in culturally alien environments, they responded to this call along with their colleagues in HBCUs. All of these men saw themselves as not only compelled to be witnesses for their own miraculous accomplishments but also to be pathfinders and way-showers for those coming behind them. Despite their rarity and similarity in the consciousness of who they are, they are also very diverse in their interests and involvement. As a quick perusal of the contents of this volume will reveal, these African American academics reflect a wide range of interests, expertise, academic environments, and perspectives. They are far from homogeneous and are definitely not limited in their capabilities. The thing that is significant about this gathering of Brothers is their commonality despite diversity. They are also exemplary of those distinguishing qualities that make African American men successful in the academy and of great value to their communities and to the world.

The first of these commonalties is their resolution of the "double-consciousness" of being "African and American." This dilemma and the maladaptive choices made by so many who fail in joining this brotherhood has been resolved by all of these representatives, because they fully understand their origins and are unapologetically African and American. They find no contradiction between their academic competence and responsibilities and their personification of the rebuttal to the negative stereotypes of African American men in American society. By responding to the call for this project, they affirm their recognition of who they are and invite the world to see them in their proper and self-affirmed identity. The considerable acumen that characterizes each of these contributions reflects the high level of proficiency these men have achieved within the confines and definitions of the European American academy and the comparable academic excellence in HBCU settings. Whether employed in a predominantly White or predominantly Black academic environment, they clearly have competence and mastery in both worlds and have managed to extract the nectar of both (frequently contradictory) realities.

In addition, all of the Brothers of this gathering have a commitment to service. As you read each of their submissions, you will find the level of their commitment to our communities to be all-encompassing. It does not matter whether their proficiency is in science, technology, social science, the law, education, literature, or the arts; they all articulate an agenda that insures their skills will net a return in service to African American communities, in particular, and ultimately to humanity. This is true regardless of the racial and cultural environment in which they work. They are modeling the role of the activist scholar who breaks down the barriers of the traditional ivy tower of academia and insures the continuing relevance of their skills to the advancement of their people. In many ways, they offer an alternative image for their majority colleagues who are often absorbed in parameters of their discipline and restricted by the world of abstractions to the exclusion of relevance and service. They prove that the choice of discipline does not restrict the opportunity for application and social relevance.

All of these Brothers of the academy continue to identify the persistent and pernicious presence of racism within the academy and the society as a whole. They affirm their commitment to engage in combat with this defiant beast of racial injustice. They appropriately bemoan the fact that even at their incontestable level of achievement, they continue to be challenged about their competence and right to be where they are and do what they do. They still face the daily provocation to prove and validate their accomplishments. So a part of the task selected by each of these remarkable men is to engage in the ongoing process of unmasking racism in its many nefarious forms and laying a well-constructed road through these obstacles for generations behind them. They understand that they are recipients of a legacy of people who would not rescind their responsibility to open the way. Even though all of these academicians have penetrated the previously restricted halls of ivy and many of them find themselves in predominantly European American, Caucasian institutions, they realize that their presence is not a solitary accomplishment. These Brothers understand that they are baton carriers in a relay and that the victory of the race requires that every "leg" must be done with excellence to insure that the next carrier will maintain the gained advantage.

So we celebrate the visionary leadership of this project coming from Professor Lee Jones. In many ways, he represents the highest achievement of synthesizing the qualities that unify these exemplary men of the academy. He brings the added quality of the initiative to call this "gathering." He personifies the ultimate danger in the eyes of the oppressor—a formerly oppressed man who got free and will not stop until he has called for a gathering of all that he can find to come join him on the road to self-affirmation and self-determination. Ultimately, this is the theme that these Brothers articulate, and their voices echo the voice that gave the call. Thank you Lee Jones, and thank you to those who heard your call. Thank you also to those fathers who preceded us in prying the doors open and, certainly, to the Providential Higher Power that made it all possible.

Na'im Akbar, Ph.D.
Tallahassee, Florida

Lee Jones

Dr. Lee Jones currently serves as the associate dean for academic affairs and instruction in the College of Education and Associate Professor in Educational Leadership at Florida State University. He is a member of the dean's administrative team. Dr. Jones is responsible for coordinating many functions within the College of Education, including the offices of Clinical Education, Academic Services, and Student Access, Recruitment, and Retention. In addition to his academic and administrative responsibilities, Dr. Jones produces and hosts a television talk show, which reaches over 4 million viewers throughout the state of Florida and parts of southern Alabama and Georgia.

Dr. Jones has received over 175 awards and citations including the Alumnus of the Year Award from Delaware State University, and the Graduate School Leadership Award from Ohio State University. He holds a bachelor of arts degree from Delaware State University, in Drama, Speech, Communication, and Theater. While at DSU he was elected president of the student body. He has a master of arts degree in Higher Education Administration, a master of arts degree in Business and Administration, and a Ph.D. in Organizational Development from Ohio State University. Dr. Jones completed his high school education at Newark, New Jersey's Barringer High School, the third oldest high school in the country.

Known as a prolific orator, Dr. Jones has been in great demand as a speaker throughout the country. He has also been invited to speak in England, Canada, and Puerto Rico. His speeches have received rave reviews and he is consistently requested to appear for repeat visits at numerous engagements. He is a member of Kappa Alpha Psi Fraternity, Inc., National Association for Equal Opportunity, American Association for the Study of Higher Education, American Association for Higher Education, Academy of Human Resource Development, the American Association for Quality Control, and a host of other civic and professional organizations. His motto is, "The bottom line is results, and anything else is rhetoric!"

INTRODUCTION

Lee Jones

The world needs people who do not have a price at which they can be bought; who do not borrow from the integrity to pay for expediency; whose handshake is an ironclad contract, who are not afraid to take risks; who are as honest in small matters as they are in large ones; whose ambitions are big enough to include others; who know how to win with grace and lose with dignity; who do not believe that shrewdness and cunning and ruthlessness are the three keys to success; who still have friends they made twenty years ago; who are not afraid to go against the grain of popular opinion and do not believe in consensus; who are occasionally wrong and are not afraid to admit it. In short, the world needs leaders. . . .

—Joseph Smith

One evening I laid in my bed staring at the ceiling wondering how I would ever get through what seemed like an endless mountain of paperwork and politics en route to obtaining a Ph.D. While I felt my undergraduate alma mater, Delaware State University, had academically prepared me to get through the academic rigors of a Ph.D. process, I had never imagined the politics of achieving what some people call their membership card in the academy. As I stared at the ceiling watching the morning rays creep through the blinds of my bedroom window, I seriously contemplated giving up on my vision to obtain the Ph.D. degree. I was very frustrated about what had become "uncontrollable" politics and depressed by the constant question, often asked by family and friends, about when I would finish the degree. Moreover, I had become very cynical about placing my fate in the hands of a few faculty members.

At the time, I felt that the faculty's only existence was to see me miserable as I attempted the Ph.D. I sincerely wanted to give it all up until I heard a voice tell me, "Practice what you preach, Lee." At the time, I had just begun to accept numerous speaking engagements around the country intrinsically moti-vating college students, civic groups, fraternities, sororities, and so forth. I would tell audiences things like: You have to go for your vision. Never give up your dream. Stay the course! Do not let other peoples' obstacles become your focus. The voice continued to tell me, "Practice what you preach, Lee."

I began to think about the millions of Africans who died in the Middle Passage so that I might have the opportunity to choose what I want as a free man. I thought of people like W. E. B. Dubois, Madam C. J. Walker, Booker T. Washington, Mary McLeod Bethune, Frederick Douglass, Sojourner Truth, and countless others who paved the way so that we might live. I said to myself as I sat up in bed, "You have not earned the right to give it all up." As I continued talking to myself, I said, "You might live until you are 150, and you will never be able to say that you have earned the right to make selfish decisions like giving it all up." It was during this massive revelation that I real-ized all that I am and all that I will ever be is not totally up to me. It has to do with keeping the vision of our ancestors alive, while helping others along the way. It was at this point that I jumped out of bed and began to write down a plan of action for completing my Ph.D.

I decided that I would not let anything get in the way of accomplishing my vision. Later that morning, I decided that I would not go in to work. Instead, I called my mentors around the country and talked about my plan of action. Despite this burst of energy, I was also aware that I must conduct a reality check. I wanted to know what my mentors thought of my plan and if they thought it was manageable. Instead of just deciding that I want a Ph.D., I started to ponder and ask several questions because of this revelation. Why do I feel I want a degree? Do my career goals require me to have a degree? How will I use this degree to assist other people? There was a constant theme that ran through the answers to all these questions. Obtaining a terminal degree was not only something that was in my reach, but also something that I must do for myself and the community I represented. It became glaringly apparent that I had to be steadfast with the task at hand. I realized that I had to take my focus off of the process and place it in the methods I would use to com-plete it. Once I placed all this in perspective and checked my perspective against the wisdom of my mentors, my approach to and motivation for work-ing toward the terminal degree became alive.

As I conceptualize the role of the new African American leader in higher education, I am reminded of what my mentor tells me all the time: "Either you is or you ain't." This "old school" adage, along with my formal and informal education, has helped to guide and focus my energy over the last ten years of my academic life. Witnessing African American academicians like Drs. Jean-nette Cole, Frank Hale Jr., the late Samuel Proctor, James Scott King, J. Herman Blake, Irving P. McPhail, Brenda Jarmon, Linda K. Jackson, Fred Humphries, Anne Pruitt, Al Yates, Cynthia Dillard, and countless others have provided me with the source to commit myself to academic excellence without excuse. Studying the lives of African American educators who have paved the way for us to have a seat at the table reminds us of what a tremendous task we, as the future leaders of the academy, have ahead of us to keep the vision alive. Their tenacity in the face of extreme adversity, their focus to remain diligent in the heat of oppression, and their consistent persistence to conquer the victor's cup are shining examples for all of us to follow during times of challenge. In other words, we, as the "New Jack Leaders of the African American Academy," have a legacy of greatness that has not earned us the right to become comfortable nor complacent with the struggles for academic excellence.

As I travel the width and the breadth of this country, I am often struck by the plethora of African American talent that rests within all facets of our community. I see many highly talented African American faculties, staff, and students anxiously applying the courage and vision taught to us by many who died so that we might live. I observe the richness of our ancestry manifested in ways that make us all proud. Conversely, I see all too often those among us who offer the world's greatest excuses about why we cannot succeed in the higher education. It is no secret that the academy is a microcosm of society and, therefore, is plagued with deep-rooted societal ills, such as racism, sexism, and other covert and overt forms of oppression aimed at maintaining the status quo. Equally prevailing, however, are those African Americans in the academy who have not committed themselves to personal excellence. They represent a small (but often highlighted) few who have tried to take a shortcut to academic success.

Higher education is experiencing yet another metamorphosis of sorts. External and internal constituencies are challenging the mission and the fundamental principles upon which universities operate. Many universities are facing fiscal exigency, and we know from history when America catches a cold, many people of color catch the flu. Therefore, we can ill-afford to be a mere image without substance. We must continue to equip ourselves with the substance and content that will be the guiding force to reach new and greater heights for the yet unborn. At the risk of sounding overly simplistic, many African American educators have overcome greater adversity than we face today. Neither time nor space permits us to profile without a purpose. Our purpose should be inextricably interwoven with a work ethic that directs our daily activity—a work ethic that guides our actions, informs our communication, and strengthens our desire to take control of our lives. The time has passed when we allow others to dictate our daily routine. I offer the following prerequisites for gaining a seat at the table:

1. Develop a plan for maximizing your workday.
2. Engage in strategic networking to assist with your personal and professional growth. Contrary to popular belief, no one reaches the pinnacle of one's success simply because of who one is.
3. Create a personal organizational climate that will allow you time to meet the multiple, and often-competing roles faced in your workday.
4. Discipline yourself to return calls within at least thirty-six hours upon receiving them; and, finally . . .
5. Stop procrastinating and fulfill your commitments.

Although these prerequisites may seem achievable, one would be amazed at the number of people who fall short of accomplishing them. When these prerequisites are not fulfilled, your credibility as a professional can be called into question. Moreover, we represent W. E. B. Dubois's talented tenth and Harriet Tubman's hope for our future. It is necessary that we affirm their vision through our actions. Embracing the aforementioned prerequisites engages one in intrinsic motivation and self-empowerment.

The plea for "The New Jack African American Leaders" in the academy is to not let history repeat itself. We need to build on the positive roads of yesterday, while providing a more intentional agenda for the future. Our leaders of tomorrow need more than a peripatetic style of leadership. We need to call upon our innate strength that offers us personal power to overcome self-defeating attitudes despite the odds against us.

Finally, as we face the changing dynamics in higher education, it is imperative that we create a spiritual base that guides us through this maze of academic hazing. After all, when all is said and done, the bottom line is still results and anything else is simply rhetoric.

Why We Need African Americans with Ph.D.s

During 1997, there were 27,668 terminal degrees awarded in higher education. Only 1,335 African Americans received Ph.D.s, representing only 4.8% of the total Ph.D.s awarded. Even more discouraging is the fact that the number of African American men achieving Ph.D.s has dropped or has remained relatively stagnant over the last three years. In 1995, 490 (1.8%) African American men received Ph.D.s. In 1996, there were 535 (1.9%) and in 1997 there were 527 (1.9%).

Additionally, African American women continue to outnumber African American men in obtaining terminal degrees. During 1995, 1996, and 1997, African American women achieved 819 (2.9%), 780 (2.8%) and 808 (2.9%) terminal degrees, respectively (see Figures 1, 2, and 2a).

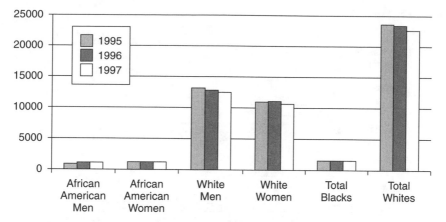

FIGURE 1. Survey of Earned Doctorates (U.S. citizens only).
Source: U.S. Department of Education, National Center for Educational Statistics,
Integrated Postsecondary Education Data System (IPEDS), 1998.

Subfield of Doctorate	Total Doctorate	Black	Percentage Black	White	Percentage White
Total: All fields	30,583	1,476	4.8%	23,789	77.8%
Physical sciences	4,178	70	1.7%	3,163	75.7%
Mathematics	614	7	1.1%	470	76.5%
Computer science	506	4	0.8%	357	70.6%
Physics and astronomy	1,032	17	1.6%	781	75.7%
Chemistry	1,425	33	2.3%	1,071	75.2%
Earth, atmospheric, and marine science	601	9	1.5%	484	80.5%
Engineering	3,275	97	3.0%	2,262	69.1%
Life Sciences	5,836	191	3.3%	4,414	75.6%
Health sciences	1,009	55	5.5%	817	81.0%
Agricultural sciences	627	28	4.5%	477	82.8%
Social sciences (including psychology)	5,349	287	5.4%	4,319	80.7%
Psychology	2,976	152	5.1%	2,464	82.8%
Humanities	4,445	152	3.4%	3,717	83.6%
Language and literature	1,457	36	2.5%	1,218	83.6%
Education	5,531	553	10.0%	4,417	79.9%
Professional/other fields	1,969	126	6.4%	1,497	76.0%
Business and management	859	53	6.2%	678	78.9%

FIGURE 2. U.S. Citizens and Non-U.S. Citizens with Permanent Visas.*
*Includes 3,647 individuals who did not report their citizenship at time of doctorate.
Source: U.S. Department of Education, National Center for Educational Statistics, Integrated
Postsecondary Education Data System (IPEDS), 1998.

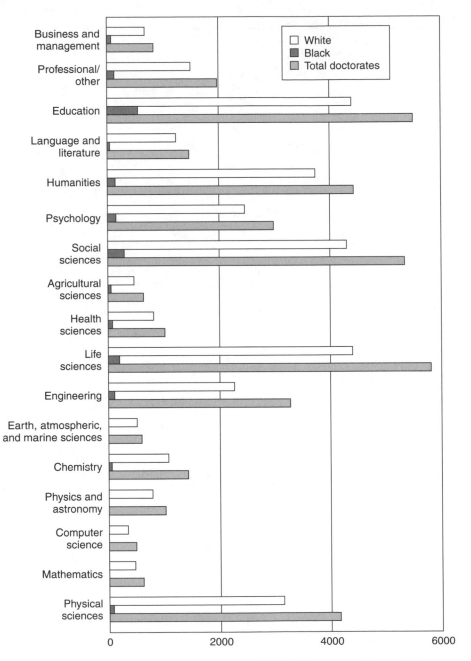

FIGURE 2A   Survey of African American and White Doctorates Earned by Selected Fields.
Source: U.S. Department of Education, National Center for Educational Statistics, Integrated Postsecondary Education Data System (IPEDS), 1998.

More revealing is the number of African Americans who have received Ph.D.s in the education and the humanities. There are less than 800. Figure 2 provides a breakdown of the number of African American Ph.D.s in selected fields.

Moreover, higher education is predicted to experience a significant decline in the number of professors in the academy. Given the number of African American terminal degrees being awarded to African American men, it is imperative that we seek every available means not only to increase the number of African American men going into the professorate but also to retain those of us who are actually teaching in the academy.

Purpose

The purpose of *Brothers of the Academy* is to highlight and showcase African American Brothers who have achieved in their chosen careers despite the odds. This book will not only profile twenty-six African American Brothers of the academy, it will also provide the readers with tangible examples of how these Brothers have progressed in their chosen careers. Additionally, the book will provide twenty-six chapters on specific historical, modern, social, and academic areas affecting African American men in the academy and in society.

Unfortunately, the only visual signs of successful African American males in society are athletes, entertainers, and drug dealers. While I applaud our Brothers who represent the first two groups, it is time that Brothers of the academy are highlighted as well. Further, it is time that society begins to see other images of successful African American men who have earned their way and who are providing some of the most cutting edge research in society—research that will ultimately solve some of America's most pressing issues plaguing African American communities and the larger society. To this end, *Brothers of the Academy* will highlight African American men in higher education who have demonstrated their success as "up and coming" scholars within the academy: The African American New Jack Leaders of Higher Education. Not only will the readers be provided with a glimpse of some of the most thought-provoking and cutting edge scholarship affecting African American men in higher education, but these chapters will also highlight the accomplishments of the Brothers. The major thrust, however, will be to provide insight and information to the young Brothers and Sisters coming behind us.

Content

The book's foreword is written by one of our own—world-renowned psychologist, Dr. Na'im Akbar, professor of psychology at Florida State University and president and owner of Mind Production. Dr. Akbar provides a solid foundation for what is to come in the book. He characterizes the forces that have brought these bright minds together as an "intellectual gathering." He reminds us that having a seat at the intellectual table in higher education is not a right bestowed upon us simply because of our innate talents. Rather, it is a debt owed to the yet unborn for those who died so that we might live. He eloquently states that those who participated in making this book possible are carrying the torch of our forefathers and foremothers to ensure a security for generations to come.

Part One is appropriately labeled "Characteristics of the Academy"—characteristics that are too often in conflict with the intellectual, spiritual, cognitive, and moral foundation of African American men. Paul Green starts us off with a thorough examination of the consistent social, economic, and educational crises facing African American men in society. The first chapter sets the stage for analyzing higher education's role in "perpetuating the crises." Timothy Eatman follows with his chapter as he deconstructs the dominant social structure that disregards the contributions that underrepresented communities have made in education and in society. He provides critical solutions for constructing higher education policy for equity and parity for the Twenty-first Century and beyond. Jerlando Jackson walks us through some of the concrete issues many predominantly White institutions face in trying to diversify the administrative ranks in their institutions. Bryant Marks's assessment of the racial identity and its comparison of Black students attending predominately White and predominately Black institutions provides us a thorough understanding of the role race and economic disparity play within African American communities.

Rodney Hopson treats us to an informative chapter outlining how he has personally transformed his scholarship through his experience by studying and traveling abroad. Through his experiences and ongoing scholarship, he illustrates how to move toward the language and scholarship of freedom and how he has come to terms with being a young Black male in the academy. Larry Rowley captures some of the pressing issues affecting African American male graduate students, particularly at predominately White universities. His informed reflections help us better understand ways to combat the many social issues affecting African American men in the academy. Quickly emerging as one of the touted experts in multicultural education, Tyrone C. Howard provides us with tangible ways to teach and to develop curricula for a multicultural society. This section concludes with a thorough examination of what many call the root cause of the deterioration of race relations in higher education and in society—ethics. J. W. Wiley, in his chapter, "Institutional Ethics: Forty Acres of So-Called Morality and Still No Mule," challenges policymakers in higher education to confront the concept of institutional ethics genuinely and to analyze the code of "morality."

Part Two takes us on a mission of discovery while "Navigating the Academy." Leon Caldwell starts this section with an objective, but very firm, overview of the complex and often misinterpreted view of Black men in society and in higher education. He describes environments that eliminate the African American customs, values, and spirituality as toxic. Juan Gilbert, who represents the less than 5% of African Americans who receive their Ph.D.s in computer science, demonstrates and provides lessons on how to beat the odds when the law of averages is against you. Michael Penn, tells us his story about how he is managing to pursue both an M.D. and a Ph.D.

Willis Lonzer speaks to the almost nonexistent African Americans who are pursuing the hard science degrees. He does an extraordinary job of navigating strategies for those underrepresented students who have an interest in pursuing degrees in the hard sciences. Eddie Moore, one of the most outstanding facilitators on diversity issues, provides a basic formula as higher education continues to grapple with diversity in the Twenty-first Century. Freddie Moore helps us understand the role of mentoring for Black men in higher education. He takes us through a concrete analysis of how to mentor African American men through their educational process—a must read chapter. Le'Roy Reese, an up and coming scholar in Black psychology, assesses the impact of "The American Social Systems on African American Men." Mark Williams, who is pursuing both his M.D. and Ph.D., provides invaluable insight for African American men who need to manage both career and family while matriculating in higher education. Finally in this section, John Carpten, the first African American male to receive his Ph.D. in genetics at Ohio State University, concludes this section with a journey of his academic career, which led him to be one of the top researchers at The National Institute of Health.

The book's final section, Part Three, features a plethora of scholarship from some of the most prolific thinkers in higher education. Troy D. Allen begins this section with a very thorough overview of the ancient Egyptian family and social organization. Troy's analysis of the family order is traced back to ancient Egyptian civilization. Wow! James L. Moore III provides us with a comprehensive approach to the issues confronting African American men in higher education and ways to counsel Black men back to mental health.

Perhaps one of the most pressing social issues affecting African American men today is racial profiling. Brian N. Williams's research in this area captures the rapid phenomenon in great fashion. He highlights the personal costs and societal consequences of racial profiling and examines the effects for African American men. Keith Harrison's research on Black male images in sports is widely read by educators across the country. His chapter examines this issue and its effects on Black male athletes. Charles Ross captures the essence of Black male leadership in his historical analysis of Medgar Evers. He provides a solid foundation on the evolution of Black male leadership in America. Ronald S. Rochon's chapter, "Black Success or White Emulation: Who Shall Sit at the Table to Create Effective Solutions That Empower African American Children?" is considered a classic reflection on African American success in America. Ron challenges us to rethink how we measure success in the African American community. Mark Whitaker provides us with a glimpse of what to expect in the marketplace during this next century. He suggests concrete solutions for transforming American organizations to deal better with the diversity that it faces. Finally, Shuaib Meacham ends the book where it all begins for African American men: Spirituality! His examination of how spirituality directs our work is phenomenal! The book concludes with a model for African American male scholarship in higher education.

Acknowledgments

Finally, I would be remiss if I did not thank the many people who have assisted with this project, for rarely does an effort of this magnitude reach this stage alone. First, I give honor and praise to God, who is the center and the joy of my life. Without God's grace I would not have been able to garner enough energy to construct, edit, analyze, and manage this massive undertaking. I also give much appreciation to the millions of ancestors, many of whom died during the Middle Passage. Without their tenacity, courage, and unyielding commitment to generations yet unborn, we would not be earning our way on the soils of America.

I owe all that I am and will ever be to my parents, the late Carrie and Levi Jones. Although they are not physically with me, I know their presence will be with me always. I will always love you. To my siblings who have endured me as a younger brother over the years, your constant support of my efforts has always been welcome.

To my beloved fraternity, Kappa Alpha Psi Fraternity, Inc., you have been the benchmark for success. Brothers like the late attorney Kevin Sarver, Gary Smith, Fred Parker, Bobby Beale, Ray Nix, Xavier Allen, Zeta Chapter, Juan Gilbert, Marcus Ross, Chris Weathers, Patrick Lee, Dov Clayton, Stephen

Jones, Jeff McCloud, and so many others, have left an indelible impact on my life. You have taught me to strive to achieve in every field of human endeavor.

I give my genuine and sincere thanks to all of the Brothers who started and completed this important and timely book. While there are literally thousands of Brothers who are earning their way in higher education, I send a special thank you to the Brothers who heard and responded to the call to come together once again to send a message to all of Black America highlighting what can happen when we check our egos at the door and develop an institution. I say thank you to Drs. Irving McPhail, James Scott King, Brenda Jarmon, Wendell Rayburn, Frank Hale Jr., Linda K. Jackson, Mike Daniels, Cynthia Dillard, Ernestine Madison, Les Purse, Janet Pichette, Etta Hollins, Bernie Oliver, Anne Smith, Joyce Breasure, Adam Herbert, James Sage, and countless others who have played a significant role in molding me over the last ten years of my academic career. A heartfelt thank you goes to Dr. Jack Miller, who hired me as Associate Dean at one of the finest institutions anywhere in the United States—Florida State University. Dr Miller's belief in my abilities has restored hope that there are people in American higher education who not only believe in equity, parity, and equality, but who manifest this belief in their hiring decisions as well.

I send a much-deserved shout out to my ex-love Ms. Sheri Mustafa. Your care and concern for me arrived during a time when I was thoroughly confused about who I was and perplexed about God's plan for my life. If I knew then what I know now. . . . Kudos to Dr. George Miller for allowing me to pick your brain during many days and nights in your bookstore. I have learned a great deal from you and your wisdom.

There were several times I questioned whether I should continue to lead this important initiative through to fruition. The past, present, and ongoing support of friends like June Jackson, John Ryan, Edward Powell, Chris Weathers, Laura Williams, Jerome Woods, Freddie McSears, Bennie Harris, and countless other associates and friends has sustained this project to its completion. I am indebted to several "mentees" like Jonathan Sprinkles, Carl Latting, Shaletha Mitchell, Khieka Jennings, Lavon McNeal, Anna Green, Michael Owens, Charles Osiris, Thomas Hollins, Jeanette Castellanos, Jose Salvador Gutierrez, Quinton Morris, and countless others who have played a significant part of my motivation as an academician in higher education.

There have been several colleagues over the years who have helped me keep my feet on the ground and head to the sky. People like Tina Love, Joyce Vaughan, Rebecca Parker, Vincent June, Bill Hall, Don Ibezim, Emeka Aniagolu, Saunie Schuster, Raphael Guillory, Milton Lang, Esther Louie,

Edward Vertuno, Bruce Daniels, Ken Tellis, Gwen Johnson, Diana Creamer, Kim Proctor, and Mimi Wolverton.

Words will never be able to express my sincere appreciation to Ms. Yvonne Weems, my Administrative Assistant. Her long hours of work; her attention to details, her willingness to put up with my peripatetic schedule are all constant reminders that we cannot survive in the academy alone. Ms. Weems, you represent the epitome of perfection. To Linda Wilks and Charlene Meeks, your work on this project made it manageable and enjoyable. Your thoughts, wisdom, and care for the substance of this book made it all possible. To Mr. Leon Strayer, my mentee, thank you for taking the time to volunteer as my graduate assistant. Your commitment to the struggle and your innate ability to juggle many tasks provided lots of order and productivity during a time of extreme pressure to meet publication deadlines. To InGee Lee, Wendy Wang, and Nicole Collier, thank you for your diligence and patience. I appreciate your willingness to work with me on this project long after your twenty-hour week had fled. I will always be grateful for your feedback and cooperation. Every professor in higher education should have the benefit of working with such loyal soldiers.

I am forever indebted to Dr. Na'im Akbar for taking the time from his almost unbearable schedule to write the foreword. His wise counsel and mentorship played a significant role in producing this book. You are a Godsend! To Molefi Asante, Frank W. Hale Jr., Cheryl Fields, Tony Brown, Joseph White, Nathan McCall, P. Eric Abercrumbie, thank you for your endorsements. Your incredible reputations lend much credibility to this book. I am appreciative of your feedback and constructive guidance during the early stages of this project.

I sincerely appreciate the personal friendship of John von Knorring, publisher and owner of Stylus Publishing. John's gentle but assertive demeanor provided a healthy working relationship: a relationship rarely experienced between author and publisher. Finally, to the spirits of all those who have come before me, I dedicate this book. Now sit back, relax, and enjoy the teaching and insights of *Brothers in the Academy*!

Asante Sana (Thank You)!

PART ONE

CHARACTERISTICS OF THE ACADEMY

Paul Green

Dr. Paul E. Green is an assistant professor of Urban Politics, Policy, and the Law at the University of California. He taught as a secondary school teacher in the Orleans Parish Public Schools, St. Louis Public Schools and held the position of principal in a secondary alternative high school in Dayton, Ohio. He has a bachelor's degree in Spanish education from Dillard University, a master of education from the University of New Orleans, and a doctorate of philosophy in educational policy and politics from the University of Virginia. His research awards and fellowships include the Walter E. Campbell Scholarship, Nathan E. Johnson Scholarship, California Regents Faculty Fellowship, and the Center For Ideas and Society Fellowship. Professor Green's areas of expertise include the politics, policies, and practices of governmental, institutional, and judicial decision making; social justice, racial and ethnic inequality in lower and post-secondary institutions; and organized resistance at the federal, state, and local levels.

I

AFRICAN AMERICAN MEN[1]
AND THE ACADEMY[2]

Paul Green

The educational system as it has developed both in Europe and America [is] an antiquated process which does not hit the mark even in the case of the needs of the white man himself. If the white man wants to hold on to it, let him do so; but the Negro, so far as he is able, should develop and carry out a program of his own. (Woodson, 1933, p. 68).

Black children: they are the future and hope of Black America. Our struggle to develop their potential must begin with rescuing them from the victimization of the American mis-educational system. (Smitherman, 1980, p. 11)

---

1. Although other races and some groups of females are also suffering an educational crisis, this essay focuses on African American males because their crisis is acute; moreover, any attempt to focus on other subordinated groups would require the length of a book. Education is considered extremely important in the African American community: "Black people have long considered education to be a major solution to the problems of discrimination, oppression, poverty and unemployment which consistently plague the Black community" (Hoover, 1987). "Of all the institutions, excluding the family, which are crucial to the positive development of Black youths, the public school ranks at the top" (Perkins, 1986).
2. Webster's Unabridged Dictionary defines *academy* as a group of authorities and leaders in a field of scholarship, art, etc. who are permitted to dictate standards, prescribe methods, and criticize new ideas. Moreover, *academy* is defined as a secondary or high school, especially a private one. For African Americans, the two definitions are not mutually exclusive due in part to the past and present mission of Historically Black Colleges and Universities (hereafter cited as HBCUs) and the remedial role the institution and the faculty serve in educating often unprepared African American students. In the early 1990s, the development of publicly funded all-male academies for African American males in Detroit, Michigan, and Milwaukee, Wisconsin, signaled a response by African American parents and community leaders to affirmatively address the escalating educational failure, soaring dropout, incarceration, and murder rates of young African American males in America's inner cities.

While discussion of African American men as intellectual scholars in higher education is significant, equally important is the role of the "academy" (all public institutions) in educating[3] rather than schooling children of color, namely African American males (Shujaa, 1994). When asked to identify the most critical problems facing the higher education of African American students in America, one African American leader pointed to the inadequate basic preparation of young people, including both educational and personal development. Another criticism addressed the growing plight of African American youth in the inner cities as "the worst problem not only for the black community but for the whole American community" (Skolnick & Currie, 1997, p. 144). While this chapter illustrates some of the problems plaguing young African American men, by no means is this essay an exhaustive examination of this social, economic, political and cultural phenomenon.

With this in mind, this chapter will examine briefly the continuing crisis of social and educational opportunity facing African American males and the role of the "academy" in perpetuating the problem. To further illustrate this point, the chapter will begin by discussing conceptually the role of social reproduction and cultural capital in undermining social and educational opportunities for the poor and persons of color. The chapter will then address briefly the effects of residential segregation and racial isolation in further limiting the social, economic, and cultural opportunities of African American families and, in particular, young males. In response to the crisis, the importance of role models, mentors, or proteges in the lives of African American males is explored. In addition, the institutional mission of Historically Black Colleges and Universities (HBCUs) in supporting not only the educational and the psycho-social development of African American young men but also the community is examined. The chapter concludes by calling for a reexamination of how the "academy" responds to the escalating problems facing males in our institutions of learning.

Social Reproduction and African American Males

For decades "education" has been considered the primary means for achieving social, economic, political, and cultural liberation not only in the United

---

3. Educating is the process of transmitting from one generation to the next knowledge of the values, aesthetics, spiritual beliefs, and all things that give a particular cultural orientation its uniqueness. Every cultural group must provide for this transmission process or it will cease to exist (Shujaa, 1994, p. 15). Education is a socialization process by which the young learn to develop skills of conceptualization or frameworks to analyze themselves and, in turn, their environment.

States but also in developing nation-states in Africa and Asia. This tradition-alist view, coupled with neo-liberal policies of educational reform, accepts that public institutions of learning are vehicles of democracy as well as social and individual mobility. Hence educators, politicians, and stakeholders assert that the mission of public schools is the development of a democratic and egalitarian society.

Historically, however, public schools (elementary, middle, and secondary) have not contributed to the achievement of equal access or equal opportunity for poor students, let alone students of color. In fact, rather than serve as instruments for liberation for students of color, namely African American males, public schools have served, at best, as agencies of social, economic, political, and cultural reproduction. As Henry Giroux (1988) suggests:

> Public schooling offers limited individual mobility to members of the working class and other oppressed groups, but it is a powerful instrument for the reproduction of capitalist relations of production and the dominant legitimating ideologies of the ruling group. (p. xx)

The reproduction of the proletariat and other oppressed groups by means of public schooling is clearly illustrated in the works of Bowles and Gintis (1976), *Schooling in Capitalist America,* and Shirley Brice-Heath (1983), *Ways and Words.* Using Marxism, Bowles and Gintis (1976) assert that the American educational system is subordinated to and reflective of the production process and structure of class relations in the United States. According to MacLeod (1995), in doing so, they suggest that

> the major aspects of the structure of schooling can be understood in terms of the systemic needs for producing reserve armies of skilled labor, legitimating the technocratic-meritocratic perspective, reinforcing the fragmentation of groups of workers into stratified status groups, and accustoming youth to the social relationships of dominance and subordinancy in the economic system. (p. 12)

In effect, Bowles and Gintis argue that schools socialize the wealthy to assume positions of power in places of authority while conditioning the poor to accept a lower status in the class structure. The result produces major structural differences among schools. For example, schools situated in working-class neighborhoods are more regimented and emphasize rules and behavioral control. In contrast, suburban schools often offer more open classrooms that "favor greater student participation, less direct supervision, more student electives, and, in general, a value system stressing internalized standards of control" (MacLeod, 1995, p. 13). As a result, these organizational variations reflect the differing expectations that sometimes guide the decisions of teachers, administrators, and parents for students from different socioeconomic and sociocultural backgrounds. Such stratification endures within schools through educational tracks that provide different classes of students, emphasizing different values.

Bowles and Gintis (1976) further note that schools also function at an ideological level to promote the attitudes and values required by a capitalist economy. This becomes quite salient when we consider the extent to which educational reforms (such as charters, vouchers, and home schooling), driven by market forces, have influenced the educational access and opportunities of all students, especially students of color (Chubb & Moe, 1986). One example of schools functioning at an ideological level is manifested in policies and practices of tracking students. In brief, children of workers attend schools and are placed into educational tracks, both of which emphasize conformity and docility and prepare them for low-status jobs. On the other hand, MacLeod (1995) states that

> children of the elite are expected to study at their own pace under loose supervision, to make independent decisions, and to internalize social norms, all of which prepares them to boss rather than to be bossed. (p. 13)

Hence, Bowles and Gintis (1976) remark that schools socialize students to occupy roughly the same position in the class structure as that of their parents.

Equally important to this discussion are notions of cultural capital, which Pierre Bourdieu (1977) defines as the general cultural background, knowledge, disposition, and skills that are passed from one generation to the next. Bourdieu and Passeron (1993) write that the methods of cultural and social reproduction remain hidden, because the social practices that safeguard the political and economic interests of the dominant classes go unrecognized as anything other than the only natural or rational explanations (MacLeod, 1995). Hence, schooling is crucial to the reproduction and legitimation of social inequality (MacLeod, 1995). Bourdieu and Passeron (1993) further exclaim,

> Surely, among all the solutions put forth throughout history to the problem of the transmission of power and privilege, there does not exist one that is better concealed, and therefore better adapted to societies which tend to reuse the most patent forms of the hereditary transmission of power and privileges, than that solution which the educational system provides by contributing to the reproduction of

the structure of class relations and by concealing, under an apparently neutral attitude, the fact that it fulfills this function. (p. 178)

According to MacLeod (1995), Bourdieu (1977) believes success or failure in school is often determined by social class. Yet success and failure in school are often disguised in the language of meritocracy, and academic performance is perceived as being the result of innate ability by both low and high achievers. As a result, MacLeod (1995) states, "it implants in those it marginalizes a set of cognitive and evaluative categories that lead them to see themselves as the causal agents of a process that is actually institutionally determined" (p. 16). Therefore, Bourdieu reveals how schooling entrenches social inequality by reproducing class privilege and simultaneously justifying social and economic inequality.

While Bourdieu (1977; 1993) suggests that schools require cultural resources with which only certain students are endowed, Basil Bernstein (1977) extends his argument by looking at the educational costs of different linguistic patterns among children of different social strata. Bernstein's research claims that working-class children generally grow up in homes where common circumstances, knowledge, and values give rise to speech patterns in which meanings remain implicit and dependent on their context. Middle-class families, on the other hand, use elaborated codes to express the unique perspective and experience of the speaker. In short, the meanings of words and phrases are less tied to a local relationship and local social structure and, therein, are made linguistically explicit (Bernstein, in Karabel & Halsey, 1977).

Shirley Brice-Heath's (1983) research into language patterns at home and in the classroom provides additional insight into the significance of linguistic cultural capital. Brice-Heath examines race as well as the relationship among schooling, social class, and language in a working-class American community. In brief, Brice-Heath's research reaches conclusions similar to Bernstein's when she finds that the language used in the home and the language required by the school cause serious problems for working-class and nonwhite pupils (MacLeod, 1995). Not unlike other mechanisms of social reproduction that Bowles and Gintis (1976), Bourdieu (1977), and Bourdieu and Passeron (1993) address, linguistic socialization is an impediment that goes largely unacknowledged. As a consequence, poorer students and students of color blame themselves for failure, whereas more affluent students take their cultural capital as a given and accept full credit for their success (MacLeod, 1995). More importantly, social reproduction theorists reveal in resplendent fashion that formal education actually serves "to certify lower-status youngsters as socially inferior at an early stage and to initiate the process that keeps many of them economically and socially inferior in adulthood" (Yeakey & Bennet, 1990, p. 5).

As discussed above, factors such as race, class, and culture are heavily implicated in academic failure for poor students and students of color. That is, schooling is organized both implicitly and explicitly to promote and sustain the institutions and perspectives of those in power. In doing this, schools engage in policies (school organization and finance, curricula, ability grouping, retention, social promotion, testing) and practices that maintain the systems of cultural capital and social reproduction. Ernie House (1999) in *Race and Policy* states,

> Americans have defined their educational system in such a way as to ensure that African Americans (and other minorities) are treated in an exclusionary way which is to say that they are saddled with an education which is inferior, and this inferior education contributes to whites seeing them as having undesirable attributes and as being unable to govern themselves. (p. 8)

Compounding these dilemmas, students of color, namely African American males, living in isolated and residentially segregated inner-city communities, are less likely to access or participate in college-preparatory courses, let alone remedial and outreach programs in the school or community (Hopkins, 1994; Ross, 1998). In sum, the artifacts of social reproduction and the "cultural capital" within poor African American inner-city communities that children bring into schools has substantially diminished the objective chances of academic success and, therein, has inflamed a crisis of social and educational opportunity for African American males.

Still in Crisis: The African American Male

During the 1980s and early 1990s, advocates, researchers, policymakers, and journalists produced a plethora of reports and literature on the signs of distress among African American males from poor, high-risk families and communities. Some important antecedents were poverty, family dysfunction, and residence in a neighborhood with high concentrations of families also living in poverty, family dysfunction, crime, unemployment, and drugs (Bronfrenbrenner, 1979; Massey and Denton, 1994; Resnick, Burt, Newmark, & Reilly, 1992). Much of the literature depicted the predicament of the African American male in relation to the problems of unemployment, unequal access into institutions of schooling (lower and post-secondary) and escalating numbers of younger African American males entering juvenile and correctional facilities. These facts have been documented in scholarly studies that refer to the African American male as "the vanishing black male" and as being "in crisis."

Prothrow-Stith (1993) remarks that young African American males in prison outnumber those that are in America's colleges: "Approximately one in four African American males between the ages of 20 and 29 is incarcerated, on probation, or on parole[;] . . . only one in five is enrolled in a two or four-year college program" (p. 163). Cornel West (1994) notes:

> the murky waters of despair and dread that now flood the streets of black America . . . the depressing figures of unemployment, infant mortality, incarceration, teenage pregnancy, and violent crime . . . the monumental eclipse of hope, the unprecedented collapse of meaning, the incredible disregard for human (especially black) life and property in much of black America . . . the profound sense of psychological depression, personal worthlessness, and social despair. (pp. 19–20)

A sense of alienation (social, economic, and political) and spatial isolation has long existed in the inner cities of the United States. These themes have been written about by African American writers such as James Baldwin in *The Price of the Ticket* (1985), Richard Wright in *Native Son* (1940), Ralph Ellison in *Invisible Man* (1952), Jonathan Kozol in *Savage Inequalities* (1991), and Nathan McCall in *Makes Me Wanna Holler* (1994). Moreover, these themes of alienation and isolation were central to Douglas Massey's and Nancy Denton's critical work entitled *American Apartheid* (1994). In this seminal piece, Massey and Denton note:

> For America, the failure to end segregation will perpetuate a bitter dilemma that has long divided the nation. If segregation is permitted to continue, poverty will inevitably deepen and become more persistent within a large share of the black community, crime drugs will become more fully rooted, and social institutions will fragment further under the weight of deteriorating conditions. As racial inequality sharpens, white fears will grow, racial prejudices will be reinforced, and hostility towards blacks will increase, making the problems of racial injustice and equal opportunity insoluble. (in Cose, 1997, p. 233)

In *Two Nations: Black and White, Separate, Hostile and Unequal,* Andrew Hacker (1992) in an anecdotal fashion also supports similar notions of alienation and isolation in the American landscape. Hacker (1992) states that in contrast to American society as a whole, many young African American men in

America have been brought up in disadvantaged circumstances, perpetuating an inability to escape their surroundings or envision meaningful futures.

In *Children of the Dream* (1992), Edwards and Polite assert that, "success has always been a relative phenomenon in Black America . . . often measured as much by what has been overcome as by what has been achieved" (p. 3). Majors and Billson (1992) support Edwards' and Polite's thesis that the African American male has tremendous difficulties in his pursuit of success. The researchers addressed the problem of racism in American society, which, they argued, has blocked social, economic, and political opportunities for persons of color. Consequently, some images of a "successful black male" for African American youth in the inner city include individuals who have chosen paths of nonconformity.

Another facet of African American youths' predicament is single-parent homes. Ascher (1991), citing research on single-parent African American homes, stated that the percentage of African American families headed by a woman increased from 22 percent to 44 percent in the years between 1960 and 1995. As recorded from the Morehouse College Community Service Project at Morehouse University in Atlanta, Georgia:

> Half of these children have never visited their father's home. More than forty percent do not see their father at all in a typical year. Only one in five sleep in a father's home in a typical month. In short, more and more of these children simply do not know what it means to have a father. (p. 4)

Ascher further notes:

> high unemployment forces these men into alternative economics. . . . While many are employed irregularly or not at all, others make money by selling drugs or being involved in risky and illegal work. (p. 5)

As a result, institutions that depend on local patronage to flourish have indeed either disappeared entirely (for example, banks, stores, and professional practices) or have sharply reduced their activities and programs, as with churches, block clubs, community groups, and recreational facilities. Means of formal and social control have declined along with these organizations; this has contributed, in turn, to the rising incidence of street crime and to spreading a sense of insecurity that helps increase the deterioration of the neighborhood and, in turn, the community.

In no uncertain terms, the lowering of both the class composition of the inner-city community and thereby its institutions (elementary, secondary, and post-secondary), and of the volume of "cultural capital" that children bring into the classroom from the community has substantially diminished the opportunities of academic success and achievement for African Americans. The high density of under-achieving students undermines teachers' morale and discipline. The prevalence of joblessness weakens the perception of a meaningful connection between education and work and decreases academic aspirations accordingly; this makes it difficult for the school to compete with other available paths to income and status, including illegal ones.

In addition, an important mediation of educational and job success, especially in an economy increasingly oriented toward personal services that require frequent face-to-face interaction and extensive social skills of self-management and communication, is language. Language poses an interesting problem and worrisome implications with the increasing isolation of communities where a Black English vernacular spoken in inner cities is quite common and accepted. For sociolinguist William Labov, the fact that "the majority of inner-city African Americans are diverging from and not converging with the dominant linguistic pattern" (1986, p. 265) is evidence of their deepening contacts within socioeconomic groups and less contact with the language (prescribed English) of the dominant culture. He further views it as the linguistic correlate of "the formation of what has been called 'a permanent underclass' " (Labov, 1986, p. 277).

Consequently, the deepening of linguistic opposition is furthermore becoming less transparent and functions more often than not below the level of social awareness. According to Labov (1986),

> When a child enters school and faces the problem of learning to read and write the standard language, unknown and unrecognized differences in the structural base can interfere with the cognitive process of learning to read and deepen the problem of establishing sound social and emotional relations to the school system. . . . When we look at the divergence of black white vernaculars in the inner city, we see conflict without contact, and therefore conflict without structure. (Labov, 1986, p. 281)

This evidence appears to further support Bourdieu's, Bernstein's, and, more importantly, Brice-Heath's assumptions regarding social reproduction and the role of linguistic cultural capital. In effect, the use of language (Black English or Spanglish) by some residents in poor inner cities of America places them socially, economically, politically, and culturally at a disadvantage. Moreover, Brice-Heath (1983) notes that African American working-class children are not socialized to cope with the language patterns used in school and quickly fall behind, drifting through school into a pattern of academic failure.

Fortunately, in the African American community, this phenomenon of social, economic, political, and linguistic isolation is not a new one. For well over a century, the mission of HBCUs located in predominantly African American urban and rural communities has been to educate, rather than miseducate, and remediate all students regardless of race, color, or creed. The success of this mission has often been accomplished through the use of role models and mentors within the university as well as the surrounding community.

The Significance of Role Models and Mentors

In some inner cities, African American males lack positive male role models. Some theorists believe that the academic failure of African American boys is caused in large part by the paucity of positive male role models, which they need early in their education (Mitchele, 1990; Walters, 1991; Hopkins, 1994; Shujaa, 1994). As Spencer Holland (1993) states,

> Most boys do not have male teachers until the later elementary grades or junior high school, and for inner-city boys this is much, much too late. It is well documented in educational research that many students, especially boys, who fail to complete high school drop out psychologically and emotionally by 3d or 4th grade . . . Creating all-male kindergarten-through-3d grade classes taught by male teachers would provide young black boys with consistent, positive, and literate black role models in the classroom. It would also help overcome many of the negative attitudes toward education that currently hamper black boys' academic achievement. (p. 67)

In an article entitled "Black Youth, Role Models and the Social Construction of Identity," Taylor (1989) and others assert that "choice and commitment are major themes during the adolescent's struggle for identity formation" (p. 157). As the adolescent prepares himself for an adult role in society, he "shops" around for the individual he wishes to emulate. The adolescent at this stage is "in search of identity," and "he seeks someone to follow" (p. 158). Role models provide students "consistent relationships with supportive adults to help them mediate their experiences and thus to learn how to understand

and to control the world around them" (p. 158). Hence, the best role model is one with whom a child closely identifies or a mentor.

The term *mentor* has its roots in classical Greek literature: it means "steadfast" (Ross, 1998). The meaning of *mentor* can be seen in Homer's Odyssey, wherein the Greek poet gave the name *Mentor* to a character who guides and educates Odysseus' young son. Further, the word *protégé* derives its meaning from the French word "to protect" and is, as defined in Webster's Unabridged Dictionary (1998), a person under the patronage, protection, or care of someone interested in his or her career or welfare. The functions of mentors and protégés have been critical socializing tools within the African American community for many decades. In fact, Mahoney (1993) advised that "without support, young men—with the potential to climb out—fall back into a street culture that promises only hopelessness" (p. 5).

Weber (1993), in an interview with Jacqueline Fleming, voiced the importance of mentoring for minority students:

> When students can plug into someone who encourages them, this interaction can be an important part of the college experience and a source of inspiration. . . . Mentoring has also been associated with higher grade point averages. (p. 24)

In addition, a December 1, 1996, New York Times article reported on the present success represented by the University of Virginia's graduation rate for African American students (84 percent). The university has a support system in place, including "peer advisors, faculty mentors, a parents' advisory association, scholarship opportunities and personal touches like a birthday card for every freshman from the dean's office" (Ross, 1998, p. 8). In a more recent New York Times article (August 1, 1999), Michael Winerip states that the continued success of the University of Virginia's recruitment, retention, and graduation of students of color in its undergraduate and graduate programs extends beyond the symbolic levels of interaction of low-income students and students of color co-mingling with faculty and peers. Winerip (1999) writes that Dr. John Casteen, President of the University of Virginia, has made recruitment and retention of poor students and students of color an institutional priority and, therein, a mission of the university.

Similar to programs at the University of Virginia, some predominantly White universities have established successful mentoring programs to enhance the recruitment, retention, and ultimately the graduation of students of color. In short, upon entrance into the university, students are assigned to professors or older students who serve as designated mentors. For example, Cleveland

State University and Ohio University in Athens, Ohio, have created Minority Mentoring programs in the hopes of creating an atmosphere where students of color feel accepted, supported, and encouraged, especially in predominantly White institutions.

Black Colleges versus White Colleges: African American Progress and Achievement

Yet, in spite of the aforementioned recruitment and retention programs at many predominantly White universities and colleges, students of color continue to segregate themselves, programmatically, physically, and socially, in the university and college environment. Rather than accept established canons or dogmas of Western thought, some students of color have chosen academic programs such as ethnic studies (African American, African, Latino, and Asian) as their primary focuses of study. The result has been that a predominant number of students of color are enrolled in ethnic studies courses to the exclusion of their White peers. Further, it is not uncommon to find segregated and ethnically distinct domicile facilities reflective of similar divisions in the social, cultural, economic, and political realities and activities (sorority and fraternity) of students. In a study entitled "Comparative and Predictive Analysis of Black and White College Achievement and Experience," Nettles, Thoeny, and Gosman (1986) found that, "Students need to feel comfortable in their environment, both academically and socially; they need to perceive the college as nondiscriminatory; and they need to feel academically integrated" (p. 293).

In a similar study, "African American College Student Outcomes at Predominantly White and Historically Black Public Colleges and Universities," the findings indicate that African American students who attend HBCUs have benefits beyond what the predominantly White colleges and universities can provide to African American students. According to Allen (1992), the benefits are manifested in

> positive psychological adjustments, more significant academic gains, and greater cultural awareness/commitment than Black students on white campuses. The 'fit' between African American students and higher education seems more favorable on historically Black campuses than on predominantly White campuses. (p. 32)

Allen further observes that the parents of African American students who attend HBCUs have less formal education, fewer prestigious jobs, and less economic means than both African American and White students who attend predominantly White institutions.

Differences in outcome (such as retention, academic achievement, and graduation) exist for African Americans who attend HBCUs versus African American students who attend predominantly White institutions (Allen, 1992). The social-psychological context must be considered in order for African American students to be successful in higher education. Allen comments that on White campuses,

> Black students emphasize feelings of alienation, sensed hostility, racial discrimination, and lack of integration, [but] . . . on historically Black campuses, Black students emphasize feelings of engagement, connection, acceptance, and extensive support and encouragement. (p. 39)

Another obstacle for African American students is the complex task of adjusting to a campus environment different from their own cultural frame of reference. Fleming (1991) observes that

> many Black students will still prefer to attend [black] colleges where the campus ambience supports their personal development without the level of conflict and isolation experienced on many predominantly white campuses. (p. 9)

Fleming asserts that the profile of African American males in attendance at HBCUs let alone at White institutions can be characterized as grim (Ross, 1998). The African American male experiences frustrating incidents that impede his academic drive; the result is "falling grades, diminishing feelings of intellectual ability, declining social adjustment, and losses in perceived energy level . . . [which are] symbolic of their psychological withdrawal" (p. 69).

On the other hand, Fleming's research on the effects of college on African American students reveals that

> Despite some ambivalence surrounding their interactions with teachers, their experience is more strongly characterized by absorption with role models, greater satisfaction with and positive outcomes from the educational experience (including perceived cognition), and gains in assertiveness of self-expression and in dealing with others. (p. 168)

When Fleming was asked to comment on her research regarding African Americans in HBCUs and predominantly White institutions, she stated,

> Now we see that the interpersonal environment has more to do with achievement and development. Students in HBCUs have access to a wider network of relationships that are friendly, that make them feel

as if they belong, and that encourage and inspire them onto greater heights. It is the "people factor" in education that I think has long been ignored and turns out to distinguish the experience of African American students in historically black institutions from that in predominantly white institutions. (p. 21)

In sum, the college experience for African Americans at HBCUs is a cathartic one, in that it is a nurturing environment; faculty members at HBCUs discern students' difficulties and offer to them the social, cultural, and psychological support to achieve and progress. Moreover, through an enduring history of public service, community activism, and advocacy, HBCUs have balanced the missions of research (scholarship) and service (role models, mentors, and protégés) for all students, regardless of color, within the community and the surrounding communities.

Conclusion

As we begin the dawn of a new century, the social ills facing students of color (such as poverty, residential segregation, educational failure, teen pregnancy, HIV/AIDS, gang violence, narcotics, and juvenile homicide and suicide), especially African American males, have by no means dissipated. In fact, the isolation of these young men spatially, socially, culturally, economically, and psychologically from substantive interaction with diverse groups and environments has, in some cases, aided and abetted in the condition of self-destruction. Moreover, punitive federal and state juvenile-justice policies (such as federal sentencing guidelines, mandatory sentencing, and three-strikes laws) as well as the elimination of rehabilitation services (such as drug treatment, counseling, and educational programs) have increased substantially the number of young African American males and now females incarcerated at earlier ages for drug-related or habitual crime offenses. Sadly, the number of young African American men between the ages of 15 and 24 incarcerated in juvenile and penal institutions in the United States is quickly surpassing the number of them in private and public universities and colleges.

That communities of color in inner cities are suffering is not news. Further, the fact that African American males are suffering an educational crisis is equally not a new phenomenon. The all-male academy movement in the early 1990s alerted the nation to the problem of educational failure and the phenomenon of the African American male. In short, in 1993, Mr. Silas Sloan of the Kemet Academy also reminds us that, "teaching Black males is not an educational phenomenon, but what is a phenomenon is why public schools have failed to teach them" (1993 interview in Hopkins, 1994, p. 113).

Harvard Professor of Education, Sara Lawrence Lightfoot illustrates with clarity the essence of a painful and tragic phenomenon and yet a possible a solution when she states,

> a critically important educational success for black and white children lies in the power relationship between communities and schools, rather than in the nature of the student population. Mixing black and white bodies together in the same school and preserving the same relationships and perceptions between schools and the families they serve is unlikely to change the structures, roles and relationships within schools that define the quality of the educational process. The nature and distribution of power among schools, families and communities is a crucial piece of the complex puzzle leading toward educational success for all children. (Bell, 1987, p. 143)

Indeed, the problem is much larger than African American males. In truth, the problem of educational opportunity and success for all persons of color has always been larger than any one group or institution. However, if we are to respect the prophetic words of Carter G. Woodson and the wisdom of Gineva Smitherman, academies (HBCUs and PWIs) must continue to forge and nurture institutional relationships and programs within their institutions and within low-income communities and neighborhoods of color in order to eliminate the mis-education of all children. Educating rather than schooling all children must become a social and institutional imperative.

References

Ascher, C. (1991, June). School programs for African American males and females. *Phi Delta Kappan, 4*, 1–3.

Allen, W. A. (1992). African American college student outcomes at predominantly white and historically black public colleges and universities. *Harvard Educational Review, 62*(1), 26–44.

Baldwin, J. (1985). *The price of the ticket*. New York: St. Martins Press.

Bell, D. (1987, Summer). The case for a separate black school system. *The Urban League Review, 11*(1), 137–145.

Bernstein, B. (1977). Social class, language and socialization. In J. Karabel and A. H. Halsey (Eds.), *Power and ideology in education*. New York: Oxford University Press.

Bourdieu, P. (1977). Cultural reproduction and social reproduction. In J. Karabel and A. H. Halsey (Eds.), *Power and ideology in education*. New York: Oxford University Press.

Bourdieu, P. (1993). *Outline of a theory of a practice*. Cambridge, MA: Cambridge University Press.

Bourdieu, P., & Passeron, J. C. (1977). *Reproduction in education: Society and culture.* London: Sage Publishers.

Bourdieu, P., & Passeron, J. C. (1993). *Reproduction in education: Society and culture* (2nd ed.). London: Sage Publishers.

Bowles, S. & Gintis, H. (1976). *Schooling in capitalist America: Educational reform and the contradictions of economic life.* London: Routledge and K. Paul Publishers.

Brice-Heath, S. (1983). *Ways and words.* Cambridge, MA: Cambridge University Press.

Bronfrenbrenner, U. (1979). *The ecology of human development: Experiments by nature and design.* Cambridge, MA: Harvard University Press.

Chubb, J. E., & Moe, T. (1986). *Politics, markets and America's schools.* Washington, DC: Brookings Institution.

Cose, E. (1997), *Seeing beyond race in a race-obsessed world.* New York: Harper Collins Publishers.

Edwards, A., & Polite, C. K. (1992). *Children of the dream: The psychology of Black success.* New York: Doubleday.

Ellison, R. (1952). *Invisible man.* New York: Random House Publishers.

Fleming, J. (1991). *Blacks in college.* San Francisco: Jossey-Bass Publishers.

Giroux, H. A. (1988). *Schooling and the struggle for public life.* Minneapolis, MN: University of Minnesota Press.

Gordon, E. T., Gordon, W. E., & Nembhrad, J. G. G. (1994). Social science literature concerning African American men. *Journal of Negro Education, 63* (4), 508–530.

Hacker, A. (1992). *Two nations: Black and white, separate, hostile, unequal.* New York: Maxwell Macmillan International.

Holland, S. H. (1993). Fighting the epidemic of failure: A radical strategy for educating inner-city boys. *Viewpoint, 28*(1), 25–28.

Hoover, M. (1987). The politics of education: Illiteracy and test bias. *National Black Law Journal, 64,* 64.

Hopkins, R. (1994). *Educating Black males: Critical lessons in schooling, community and power.* New York: State University of New York Press.

House, E. (1999). Race and policy. *Education and policy archive,* Arizona State University. http//:epac.asu.edu.

Karabel, J., & Halsey, A. H. (1977). *Power and ideology in education.* New York: Oxford University Press.

Kozol, J. (1991). *Savage inequalities: Children in America's schools.* New York: Crown Publishers.

Labov, W. (1986). Language structure and social structure. In S. Lindenberg, J. S. Coleman, and S. Nowak (Eds.), *Approaches to social theory.* New York: Russell Sage Publishers.

MacLeod, J. (1995). *Ain't no makin it: Aspirations and attainment in a low income neighborhood.* San Francisco, CA: Westview Press.

Mahoney, M. E. (1993). *Mentors: The president's report*. New York: Commonwealth Fund.

Majors, R., & Billson, J. M. (1992). *Cool pose: The dilemmas of black manhood in America*. New York: Lexington.

Massey, D., & Denton, N. (1990, September). American apartheid: Segregation and the making of the underclass. *American Journal of Sociology, 96* (2), 329–357.

Massey, D., & Denton, N. (1994). *American apartheid*. Cambridge, MA: Harvard University Press.

McCall, N. (1994). *Makes me wanna holler: A young black man in America*. New York: Random House Publishers.

Mitchell, T. E. (1990, November 8). Project 2000: Gateway to success for some black males. *Black Issues in Higher Education*, 49–50.

Nettles, M. T., Theony, A. R., & Gossman, E. J. (1986). Comparative and predictive analysis of black and white college achievement and experiences. *Journal of Higher Education, 57*(3), 289–318.

Polite, V. C., & Davis, J. E. (1999). *African American males in school and society: Practices and policies for effective education*. New York: NY Teachers College Press.

Prothrow-Stith, D. (1993). *Deadly consequences: How violence is destroying our teenage population and a plan to begin solving the problem*. New York: Harper Perennial.

Raspberry, W. (1989, September 15). All boys classes? The feds say no. *The Washington Post*, p. A1.

Resnick, G., Burt, M. R., Newmark, L., & Reilly, L. (1992). Youth at risk: Definitions, prevalence and approaches to service delivery. Washington, DC: The Urban Institute.

Ross, M. J. (1998). *Success factors of young African American males at a historically black college*. Boston, MA: Bergin and Garvey Publishers.

Shujaa, M. J. (1994). *Too much schooling, too little education: A paradox of black life in white societies*. Newport, CT: Africa West Press.

Skolnick, J. H., & Currie, E. (1997). *Crisis in American institutions*. New York: Longman Publishers.

Smitherman, G. (1980). *Black English and the education of black children and youth*. Proceedings from the National Invitational Symposium on the King Decision. Detroit, MI: Wayne State University Press.

Taylor, R. L. (1989). Black youth, role models and the social construction of identity. In R. L. Jones (Ed.), *Black adolescents*. Berkeley, CA: Cobb & Henry Publishers.

Walters, L. S. (1991, January 18). Black mentors extend a hand. *Christian Science Monitor*, p. 12.

Weber, M. J. (1993). Immersed in and educational crisis: Alternative programs for African Americans males. *Stanford Law Review, 45*, 1099–1131.

Webster's Unabridged Dictionary (2nd ed.). (1998). New York: Random House Publishers.

West, C. (1994). *Race matters*. New York: Vintage.

Winerip, M. (1999, August 1). Making the ask. *The New York Times,* pp. A22–23, 40.

Woodson, C. G. (1933). *The mis-education of the Negro* (reprint). Trenton, NJ: African World Press.

Wright, R. (1940). *Native son*. New York: Harper & Brothers Publishers.

Yeakey, C. C., & Bennet, C. T. (1990, Winter). Race, schooling, and class in American society. *Journal of Negro Education, 59,* 3–20.

Timothy K. Eatman

Timothy K. Eatman is currently a doctoral candidate in the Department of Educational Policy Studies at the University of Illinois at Urbana-Champaign (UIUC). He holds the bachelor of science from Pace University—NYC in early childhood education and the master of education from Howard University, Washington, DC in college student development. His interest in the field of education stems from an "experientially rich" high school experience at the Mt. Pleasant Christian Academy. This school was founded eighteen years ago by his parents and church family and continues to serve families in New York City today.

In addition to pursuing a doctoral degree, Tim works half time for the Committee on Institutional Cooperation as Program Coordinator of the Learning Technology Initiative. In this position, he provides leadership for collaboration among a committee of administrative and technologically oriented representatives from each institution as they seek to impact and develop innovative uses of advanced technologies in teaching and learning in and around the consortium.

Tim enjoys a fulfilling family life with his wife, who is also a doctoral candidate at UIUC, and their three-year-old daughter. He is passionate about the life of the Spirit and his musical life as a songwriter and pianist. The motto "Walk in Victory" summarizes his belief that each day one can achieve success through maintaining a positive spiritual and mental posture and by making steps toward a focused but flexible plan. Greater detail about Tim's interests and involvements can be found on his website at http://eatmanl.isdn.uiuc.edu/tke/.

2

CONSTRUCTING HIGHER EDUCATION POLICY FOR EQUITY AND PARITY IN THE NEXT CENTURY

Timothy K. Eatman

Personal Introduction

Race relations in education and the larger society are of great importance to me, ranking just below the life of the Spirit, commitment to my family, and my passion for music. A recent experience clarified for me the relationship between these interests, my values, and my work.

Recently after attending a conference in northern California I took my first drive down Highway 1. The beauty of the jagged cliffs set against a reddish orange sky buttressed by the ocean waves breaking below was breathtaking.

I parked by the beach and walked up a hill right to the edge of one of the intimidating cliffs. I felt the strength of the winds threatening to push me onto the rocks below, and the violent surge of the waves provoked within me a profound sense of humility. I stepped back in awe, yet my spirit rejoiced at thoughts of my alignment with the One who continually has the power to orchestrate the wind and calm the waves. In the midst of this intense display of nature's strength, I noticed a tiny flower growing from the side of the cliff. The stillness of this contrast evoked within me an overwhelming inspiration— the kind that composers covet—that I did not want to lose before I could get to a piano and attempt to translate the experience. I picked the flower and placed it in my wallet as a reminder of the moment to bring back to part of the experience to my wife and daughter. With a deep sense of happiness and peace I turned from the cliff and descended the hill toward my car.

I saw two men approaching me who were playing with a dog. Still mesmerized by the moment I smiled and commented on the beauty of the scene giving little thought to their being members of another race. Yet they looked away in clear rejection of my overture. Memories of countless similar quiet confrontations on so many college campuses rushed to mind. Confrontations with that silent but certain dominant culture condescension that says, "why don't you just go away?" Was I paranoid to think that the slight was due to the color of my skin? I quickly recognized it for what it was. The lessons my parents taught me about surviving invisibility helped me hold on to bits and pieces of my inspiration through the pain of this encounter. "This is why," I thought. "This is why I do the work that I do." Despite repeated declarations that racial consciousness has ended, injustice, inequity, and division continue to eat at our society like a cancer.

These kinds of social dynamics and their implications for the larger society have drawn me away from absorption in the life of music to devote myself to the study of social justice in higher education. The widespread quotidian consistency of experiences for students of color in higher education should never be minimized (Allen, 1992; Epps, 1972; Feagin, 1992; Steele, 1999).

My calling—the area in which I hope to make my contribution to society— is to examine policy in higher education through a sociological lens. My goal is to identify and articulate opportunities for amelioration, engaging in policy work for the benefit of the entire university community. I hope that I can address these issues with the integrity and composure that these volatile issues require.

Introduction

An ever-increasing sense of strategic planning flooded our society as we approached the new millennium. There is a certain irony in this rally, given the fact that the so-called "Year Two Thousand" (Y2K) bug, probably the most pervasive millennium issue, stems from limited foresight on the part of government and industry programmers in the 1950s with regard to computer operating systems and networks. This irony is in itself instructive and useful as we consider the dynamics of human networks and how they operate in higher education. In my estimation there are at least seven critical similarities between the Y2K bug and what I will call the EQT (short for "equality") bug that has plagued higher education and our entire nation since its inception:

- Y2K relates to computer operating systems, while EQT deals with issues central to our social operating system.

- Both Y2K and EQT stem from narrow thinking.

- Each tends to provoke extreme and irrational reactions within people.

- Both affect everyone in some way, even while there are those who think that neither is of any consequence.

- Both require the attention of leaders and policymakers in our society.

- Creative ideas are needed to fix the problems generated by both.

- The extent or scope of their impact is unknown.

These similarities can be organized around three main themes: a) from what place we have come, b) what the landscape looks like right now, and c) how we get to where we need to go. The purpose of this chapter is to address these themes as they relate to equity issues in higher education and hopefully to contribute ideas that can be useful tools in the resource chest for policymakers in their planning and implementation. I begin by considering the utility of equity and parity within institutional policy. A section designed to place within context the very need for a focus on equity issues in higher-education policy follows. Much of this section is a fairly detailed discussion of some of the most important legal cases and legislative developments that have marked the movement toward justice in higher education. Having set the context, it will then be useful to look at some recent data that provide a snapshot of the inequity that exists and to consider some recommendations.

Institutional Policy
Equity—Parity: Is There a Difference?
Human networks are greatly affected by policy in any institution. A family works or fails to work together in a certain way because of shared values, understandings, standards, and rules outlining "the way things go" in that family. Viable churches and civic organizations have clearly defined missions, ministries, and managers. In no lesser sense, educational institutions stand and sink on the strength of the policy that undergirds the institution. At the core of these networks exists the ever-present human dynamic of self-interest. Humans are generally self-centered beings. Unless compelled otherwise, we tend to choose our own interests and convenience over that of other people or groups. It is no wonder that there is constant tension between those who command the balance of power in a given institution and those who are relegated to submit to that power.

This presents an interesting set of problems at the civic table, especially in regard to education and other social assets that are largely supported by public funds. Black communities, in general, reap a disproportionately small share of the higher-education rewards they help to create with their taxes (Feagin, 1992). Far too often and in too many cases the distribution of resources tends to favor the few in power. The picture of participation by groups that are traditionally underrepresented in higher education (which we will look at in greater detail later) bears this out. Disproportion in terms of the available as well as eligible pool of so-called minority students persists. If we define *equity* as fairness, impartiality, and evenhandedness, then this consistent phenomenon amounts to basic inequity. Something about these kinds of imbalances convicts and accuses those who have come to know the meaning of living above the aforementioned human instincts.

That equity reaches far enough is itself a questionable proposition. The vestiges of segregation and the "separate-but-equal doctrine" that provide the backdrop for American education warn us of the inadequacy of basing educational policy on simple equity standards. The notion of parity is a more reasonable operative. Parity carries with it the image of a state in which two countries, potentially hostile to one another, have equal strategic resources. My experience at the Pacific coast is an example of parity in the way I define it. The men that I "met" there frustrated me on a personal level, but they had no power to withhold or prevent me from enjoying the nature all around; we had equal access to it. I drove there, chose my spot, and decided when to leave according to the desire of my will just like they did. They could not regulate my inspiration, nor I theirs, and as much as they may have abhorred my presence, they could do no more than "make faces" at me (thank God this did not take place on a lonely road in Jasper, Texas). Exercising the same kind of authority, I chose to pity them rather than get wrapped up in the negative energy that they emitted.

As the gravity of the current demographic evolution weighs upon us, I think we will be compelled to forsake the narrowness of exclusionary education models (however subtle the design) and find creative ways to unleash the potential power of education to really improve the overall quality of American life. Establishing interventions that genuinely address the personal needs of students from communities that are traditionally underrepresented in higher education (dominant culture students have long been similarly accommodated) and making transformations to the structural elements that continue to impede them from "securing equal strategic resources" within academe will facilitate this goal. However, this will be the result of focused choices and planning-policy. It will result only when we convince ourselves that it is in the best interest of our society to build a true comprehensive grid of access to quality education.

Higher Education Under Construction
Historical Essentials

I often marvel at the penchant academics have for research, as in identifying critical questions, planning inquiries, measurement, and positive influence. "Construction" as a metaphor does well to capture the essence of this process. This kind of work is long and arduous. It involves intellectual wrestling with difficult issues that occupy large amounts of mental space and often take many years to develop. Yet when it comes to issues of equity and diversity, efforts tend to be so much less fervent; in some ways it seems more like building with Lego blocks than real bricks and mortar.

Clearly the last forty years have seen tremendous advances with regard to social and educational opportunity both within and outside of higher education, but there remains much to be done. We ought not be surprised at the slow pace of advancement. Racial subjugation is like a powerful web that includes structural and psychological aspects, which have been nurtured and reinforced over generations. Willie Lynch (1712), the nineteenth-century slave consultant, forecasted the possible scope of impact that a focused assault on personhood could have on the African victims of slavery. He says, "In my bag, I have a foolproof method of controlling black slaves. I guarantee every one of you, if installed correctly, it will control the slaves for at least 300 years." When we think of the focus and duration of racial subjugation, the time our society has spent at remediation does not even compare. It is only when we divorce ourselves from historical realities that claims can be made about the amount of time that change is taking and about how much money has been spent. This fits nicely in what has become a largely ahistorical society. For this reason, I think it is useful to allow the historical record to remind us where we have been with regard to equity policy in higher education.

Desegregation Policy

One of the nation's most costly and challenging efforts at social change to remedy past discrimination has been desegregation policy. In 1954 many educators and legal scholars were hopeful that the landmark Supreme Court ruling in *Brown v. Board of Education* (1954) and the advent of compulsory desegregation policy could answer the problems of educational inequality. Clearly it has not had this effect. This is, I think, fairly represented by the increasing number of court cases that have granted unitary status to school districts (*Board of Education of Oklahoma v. Dowell*, 1991; *Capachionne v. Charlotte-Mecklenburg Board of Education*, 1999; *Missouri v. Jenkins* 1995), in effect dissolving any responsibility that these schools have to monitor segregation levels in the school. In many cases desegregation has generated more questions than answers. The example of Historically Black Colleges and Universities (HBCUs) is useful here because these institutions have experienced increasingly more insecurities as desegregation policy has been applied in higher education. There have been serious questions raised about the relevance and continued need of existence for this special group of universities.

A fair and intelligent assessment of the matter acknowledges the fact that personal responsibility on the part of individuals and families within the African American community cannot be ignored as a factor in how this dilemma has evolved, especially with regard to academic achievement. True empowerment comes from within. However, this is at best a secondary dynamic; legislative mechanisms, judicial actions, and political pressures have been strategically manipulated by the dominant culture in a pernicious way. Without question, the focused and purposeful oppression of people of color in general and African Americans in particular in American education is the primary source of the dilemma.

A society truly beholden to democratic ideals should be ever cognizant of the fact that if we are to be responsible, the need for remedy grows out of oppression. While there have been tremendous advances that are attributable to desegregation policy, it is unclear if desegregation has been the necessary or appropriate response. Even as we approach the twenty-first century, that prophetic proclamation from W. E. B. Dubois (1953) echoes: "The problem of the twentieth century is the problem of the color line" (p. 54). There is still a dire need to address the pervading inequities in post-secondary education.

Post-Secondary Desegregation

Contrary to popular opinion, efforts to desegregate education in America did not begin with the 1954 Brown litigation or at the primary and secondary levels of public education. In fact, post-secondary education, including graduate and professional schooling, served as the pioneering ground for a focused strategy against desegregation initiated by the NAACP legal defense fund. In southern public higher-education institutions, the long road to desegregation began in 1933 with *Hocutt v. Wilson*. Ultimately, this case hinged on the issue of entrance qualifications. Hocutt was unable to verify his credentials because of the fear of repercussions on the part of his Black undergraduate institution.

Nonetheless, Hocutt brought attention to the grave inequities in graduate and professional programs. This would eventually be a critical inroad to challenging segregation.

It is interesting that a Louisiana case concerning physical transportation on railways would be used as a precedent for subsequent cases about schooling, making it a social transportation of sorts. Decided in 1896, this widely noted case of *Plessy v. Ferguson* was used for the next fifty-eight years by the U.S. Supreme Court to legitimate segregation in public educational facilities. However, it was even earlier policy—The Morrill Land Grant Act of Congress— that set the stage for segregation in higher education.

The Morrill Land Grant Act deserves mention here because of its great importance to the development of some of the nation's largest colleges and research universities. There were two phases of major significance to this act. Morrill I, proposed in 1862, offered each state that would accept the terms land, or land scrip, in an amount equal to 30,000 acres for each member of Congress from that state. The unused land would be sold, with proceeds going toward endowments for the colleges.

Avid interest developed around this proposal, and most states took advantage of this for their White citizenry. Were it not for Alcorn in Mississippi, Claflin in South Carolina, and Hampton in Virginia (one public and two private colleges), not even minimal provisions would have been made for Blacks (Preer, 1982). It is interesting to note this in spite of the fact that Blacks contributed more than their fair share to the public fund. Virtually all of the perks, like agricultural experiment stations in the southern states, were established and maintained at predominately White schools. They received extra support for these kinds of projects.

Supposedly to balance the scales, almost thirty years later and after much clamor, the Morrill Act of 1890, Morrill II, was passed. With a substantially more narrow focus than the first act, it gave financial support to the already existing land-grant colleges and prohibited the payment of funds to states for colleges that made racial distinctions between students for admissions purposes. This prohibition against racial discrimination was subject to provisos that separate colleges for White and Black students would be in compliance only if the funds received were "equitably" divided between them. Because the state legislature or officiating board who would decide how that division would be managed was the very culprit, little was ever equalized. Rigid guidelines of expenditure use were not present in the initial act.

Within nine years of Morrill II, all southern states, Delaware, and West Virginia had established dual systems of higher education. Apparently the federal funds were quite an impetus. Since, simultaneously with the creation of normal schools and land-grant colleges for Blacks, similar institutions for Whites were being established, a general pattern of racial segregation in practice was established at the college level before 1900. The Morrill acts and the land-grant college movement facilitated this pattern.

Preer (1982) has made a critical observation that has been noted as the theme of post-secondary desegregation. She points out that the distinction between institutions based on race served to put the advancement of educational opportunity ahead of the determination of legal rights. Thus, while it was, in fact, the Morrill land grants that paved the way for the large research institutions that are now the pride of this country and the HBCUs that have been so successful in educating the Black intelligentsia, the implementation of this policy established by Congress gave the force and blessing to segregation in higher education.

A significant problem that accompanied this distinction between Black and White institutions was apparent in the early 1900s; land-grant colleges were the only dependable access that Blacks had to post-secondary education. Unfortunately, the same factors that made them accessible, such as low tuition, flexible admissions standards, and compensatory programs, mitigated their status among institutions of higher education. Federal dollars represented the funding stability for these institutions, but this was in exchange for acknowledging the separate status of HBCUs, creating a true political cul-de-sac. Even the NAACP at this time succumbed to the trade-off for the sake of educational opportunity. The NAACP's support of a clause to guarantee funds for separate Black land-grant colleges compromised theoretical purity but recognized educational reality (Preer, 1982). Because of the overt hostile racial climate of the time, it was not realistic to seek legal clarity on constitutionality of separate schools at the expense of educational opportunity.

The Fourteenth Amendment to the Constitution of the United States became an increasingly significant establishment with which the American judiciary was able to measure and weigh the "separate-but-equal" notion posited by the Plessy case. Its interpretation is probably the foremost way in which higher education has been affected by the federal government. Some scholars believe that initially the "separate-but-equal" doctrine reflected the court's understanding that a state furnishing higher education to White residents would be bound to furnish substantially equal advantages to Black residents. However, descriptive statistics are useful in showing that this was not the case.

Charles Thompson, the famed Howard University educator, helps to offer a perspective about this in his 1950 article "The High Court Looks At Jim Crow." In it, he indicates the great disparity in education for Whites as compared to education for Blacks at all levels in the late 1940s. Information taken from the U.S. Office of Education 1945–1946 Biennial report describes what it would take to equalize Black and White schools: "44 percent would have to be added to Negro teachers' salaries, 80 percent to all current expenses, and 420 percent to plant and equipment values" (Thompson, 1950, p. 77). Looking at higher education in particular during this time period, Thompson's research uncovers the reality that in no uncertain terms, separate was not equal.

NAACP-affiliated attorneys Nathan Marigold and Charles Houston developed a plan to use taxpayer suits seeking equalization of expenditures in separate schools as well as qualified African American applicants seeking admission to White state universities as a legal strategy for relief. Space limitations preclude the kind of treatment and detail that these cases deserve; however, these cases were litigated with a focus on chipping away at the shaky principles of educational segregation in general and post-secondary segregation in particular. Probably the most significant gain these cases wrought was that admission was granted to some African Americans. It was perceived by the NAACP legal strategists that higher-education cases would be simpler to litigate than those at primary and secondary schools and that they would have an overarching effect. The elaborate strategies of exclusion elucidated by these cases demonstrated a need to address the issue of educational segregation.

Desegregation at all levels of education was the resounding answer to segregation by the late fifties. But was it the best answer? Despite significant advances in educational opportunity since the advent of post-secondary desegregation, there has been considerable litigation and debate around this issue. In 1970, the NAACP Legal Defense Fund (LDF) sued the U.S. Department of Health, Education and Welfare (HEW) to enforce more desegregation in public colleges under Title VI of the 1964 Civil Rights Act; the case was *Adams v. Richardson* (1973). It may well be considered a sleeper case that forced the judiciary to reexamine the important issues of legality that had been ignored in the cases since the early 1930s. The African American plaintiffs in the Adams case held that because distinct Black and White schools both still existed, the work of desegregation was far from over. They brought to the fore issues the magnitude and complexity of which would hardly be understood until after a federal judge ordered HEW to enforce the law. It was soon learned that there was little agreement on the mandate of the law and that a host of complex issues would have to be negotiated.

HBCU college presidents banded together under the aegis of the National Association for Equal Opportunity in Higher Education (NAFEO) and legally opposed the LDF's position in the Adams case. Their main contribution was with the notion that desegregation could not meet the standards of equal opportunity in higher education. The Federal District Court sided with the plaintiffs in 1972, requiring that the southern and border states comply with the demands of the class-action suit. Each state was required to develop an acceptable desegregation plan. It was the intense legal resistance of the southern states that would require further litigation in the cases of *Knight v. State of Alabama* (1991) and *U.S. v. Fordice* (1992).

The societal fluxes that these cases represent give indication of the difficulty with desegregation policy as a mechanism to ameliorate inequity in higher education. Where the rigidity of law has been found lacking, social scientists contend that theories of social interaction can be useful in assisting us to think about progress or the lack thereof with desegregation. A growing literature is available for one interested in examining these issues (Braddock, 1980; Crain, 1994; Ladson-Billings & Tate, 1995). However, I think it is more useful here to turn our attention to the current picture of higher education.

Higher Education Under Construction
Current Developments—Myriad Myths

Early in the chapter, I proposed seven similarities between the Y2K and EQT bugs. One similarity had to do with the potential both have to provoke extreme and irrational reactions within people. This item has special relevance to equity issues in higher education. The struggle to promote equity in American education has been peppered with events that highlight just how emotionally charged people can become about matters that relate to maintaining the social mobility status quo. A zero-sum-game mentality virtually assures that tensions will abound, especially in a dynamic demographic and ahistorical era that is replete with disparities, which tend to favor members of the dominant culture (Hamilton, 1952). This is also evidenced in the wild assertions that many opponents of affirmative action make about people of color diminishing the quality of an employment or intellectual environment. Seldom do they use any data to support these assertions; rather their arguments hinge on the "fact" that someone they know got beaten out of a job by a "minority."

An example of this in a legal context is evident in *Hopwood v. University of Texas* (1996). One law-review article observes that while the Black students with whom Cheryl Hopwood took issue did score low on admission requirements, a third of the White members of the admitted class also had numbers lower than the Hopwood plaintiffs; yet virtually all of the focus was placed on the "underachieving" Black students. In fact, Hopwood plaintiffs won their victory of principle, but afterward they were denied admission to the law school because their numbers were no better than thousands of other rejected applicants (Law, 1999). Thankfully, sources of data exist that provide an unbiased picture of what the landscape looks like in higher education. This is a useful way to raise questions about these myriad myths.

Some Facts on Student Participation in Higher Education

In a comprehensive analysis of student participation in higher education, Trent et. al. (1999) examined higher-education enrollments, degree attainments, and levels of segregation by sector (Carnegie Classification), segment (public or private), level (undergraduate and graduate), and race over the fourteen-year period from 1982 through 1996. The most obvious and striking feature these data show is an increase in numerical enrollments among all students of color. This is a fact to be celebrated, but it does not shed much light on the heart of inequity that is apparent in current higher-education models. In an effort to uncover those dynamics, the Trent study focuses on patterns and trends within the institutional sector.

The study sets the context by first examining student availability and eligibility pools throughout all levels of education. The data on primary and secondary students is quite revealing in that it gives indication of the deleterious impact that poverty, segregation, tracking, and other factors have on our children at an early age. Availability is understood as the proportion by which people from a specific group are represented in society. Eligibility has to do with the percentage of members in a given category who have satisfied the basic requirements to participate in higher education. Table 1, which presents

Table 1. Total Full-time Undergraduate Enrollment by Race and Year

	1982		1988		1996	
	N	%	N	%	N	%
Black	567,388	9.5	630,318	9.2	800,450	10.9
Latino	314,987	5.2	442,560	6.5	528,157	7.2
N. Amer.	36,700	.6	47,465	.7	70,066	1.0
Asian	157,054	2.6	264,655	3.9	422,212	5.7
White	4,770,129	79.4	5,318,505	77.5	5,137,470	69.9
Total	6,004,445*		6,859,547*		7,351,972*	

*Non-resident aliens are included in the totals.
Source: Adapted from Trent et. al. 1999, "Justice Equality of Educational Opportunity and Affirmative Action in higher Education" (in press).

data for 1982, 1988, and 1996, shows the percentage distribution on undergraduate enrollment for the specified groups. This picture seems to show that all groups except Whites have enjoyed percentage increases—excellent fodder for the proponents of reverse discrimination, but hardly the whole story.

When these numbers are seen in the context of the available and eligible pool for each of these groups, as presented in Table 2, the level of inequity becomes evident. For example, while Latino student representation in 1996 was 7.6 percent of the undergraduate enrollment, these students had an eligible pool of 10.5 percent. For Blacks the picture is similar, as only 11.5 percent of a 13.3 percent eligible student pool enrolled in higher education. It is apparent that Asians and Whites have more than their equitable share of actual participation in the valuable resources that American higher education has to offer.

Table 2. Comparison of Enrolled Full-time Undergraduates to Proportions of College Age (Available) and Eligible Pool by Race, 1996

Race	College Age (18–24) in 1000s	Eligible Pool (HS grads 18–24) in 1000s	Enrolled Full-time Undergraduates
	March 1996 Total	March 1996 Total	Fall 1996 Total
Black	14.3% 3,538	13.3% 2,503	11.5% 800,450
Latino	14.3% 3,525	10.5% 1,980	7.6% 528,157
Native American	.9% 229	.9% 162	1.0% 70,066
Asian/Pacific Islander	4.1% 1,016	4.5% 856	6.1% 422,212
White	66.4% 16,370	70.8% 13,360	73.8% 5,137,470
Total	100.0% 24,678	100.0% 18,860	100.0% 6,958,355

Source: Adapted from Trent et. al. 1999, "Justice Equality of Educational Opportunity and Affirmative Action in higher Education" (in press).

Carnegie classifications are the conventional model of post-secondary institution grouping. They organize colleges and universities together according to selectivity and other attributes, which are relevant to both competition and policy-setting among peer institutions. Research I, Research II, Doctoral, and Masters and Bachelors are the top four categories in the model. The key findings of the Trent study elucidate the persisting disproportion between eligible and actual participation for students of color as well as the value that a certain type of degree has for students.

Among other things, the data show that of the five racial groups included, African American undergraduate enrollment increased at a much lower level of change than all other students of color during the sixteen-year period examined (Figure 1). Of particular importance is the fact that these students had a lower enrollment percentage increase in the Research I sector than for the remaining three sectors (Figure 2). This has resulted in the failure of African Americans to advance toward parity with respect to their population or eligibility pools.

This view of institutional sector and segment is of great importance for several reasons. Most importantly, upper-tier institutions represent the highest quality of advanced learning our country has to offer; they are a valued resource. One reason that they have become such a special resource is because they command focused political and financial attention from the states and the federal government. Research I institutions within the public segment have borne the brunt of recent attacks with regard to the use of race in admission

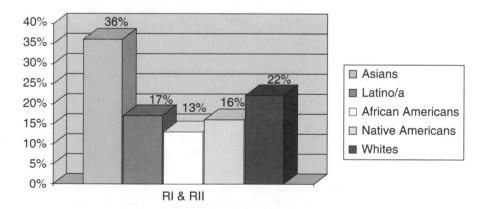

FIGURE 1   Undergraduate enrollment concentrations by race in Research I & II institutions

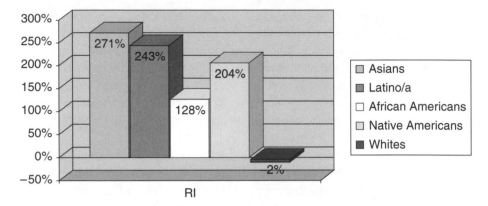

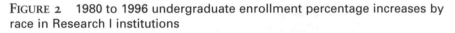

FIGURE 2   1980 to 1996 undergraduate enrollment percentage increases by race in Research I institutions

and other selection decisions. These institutions have long been viewed as important elements in the struggle to increase equity in higher education through graduate degrees for traditionally underrepresented students. Also, increasing research undertakings pinpoint the importance of sector with regard to the organizational networks in higher education and career results (Bowen and Bok, 1998).

This is only a smattering of the key findings, as this study found similar patterns with regard to graduate enrollment and degree attainment. Another interesting set of findings in the Trent study has to do with levels of segregation at these institutions. These analyses show more segregation principally at doctoral, as well as master's- and bachelor's-degree institutions, which have high populations of traditionally underrepresented students. These findings punctuate the tremendous need for policy improvements in higher education.

Higher Education Under Construction
What Say the Leaders?
In January of this year, The National Center for Public Policy and Higher Education (NCPPHE) published a report entitled "Taking Responsibility: Leaders' Expectations of Higher Education," which compiled the results of a mail survey of six-hundred leaders around the country, including professors, higher-education deans and administrators, government officials, and business leaders (Immerwahr, 1999). Twelve main findings emerged from this study. They include areas of consensus and disagreement among the respondents. In light of what the previous data show about student participation in higher educa-

tion, it is interesting to listen to what leaders have to say about the state of higher education in our nation.

Responses show widespread consensus on both the value of higher education and a concern that qualified students never be priced out of a higher education. Consensus among these leaders was also found with regard to what they view as the greatest problems that face higher education, namely student preparedness. They firmly believe that money or structural issues take a back seat to student motivation and responsibility for their own educational advancement. These individuals are convinced that the vast majority of qualified and motivated students can get a college education if they so desire. The main points of disagreement have to do with how higher education is operated and managed, which includes the content of curriculum, the utility of tenure, as well as student funding. With specific regard to equity issues like racial balance, most of the respondents would like to see a more proactive approach, while business leaders prefer to allow for a natural evolution of things.

Recommendations and Conclusion

These are not shocking findings. It follows logically that professors and administrators would believe that the major problems in higher education stem more from student motivation and responsibility rather than work that they are doing. I image that a survey of students would show opposite results. Yet we deserve more from our leaders, and we need to give more to our leaders.

Leaders must extend their apparent appreciation for the value of American higher education into creativity and commitment to address equity issues if we are to experience real change. Strategies are needed to develop a much closer alignment between primary and secondary schools on the one hand and higher-education institutions on the other, with efforts focused at minimizing critical restricting conditions early in the system. Also, developing cross-fertilization–type programs between various sectors of higher education through the use of consortia and alliances between major research universities and HBCU and Hispanic-serving institutions (HSI) may have useful results. Education in our society is too fragmented. We must come to view it as one seamless grid of opportunity for anyone so inclined to pursue it. It is apparent that policy leaders in higher education are largely uninformed about or underappreciative of both the history and current status of racial dynamics in higher education. The consistent patterns of racial and economic imbalance, some of which were presented in this chapter, scream out for attention not unlike the gregarious waves that inspired me during my visit to the Pacific coast.

Our leaders need more research that identifies the subtle dynamics of racial and economic inequity as it relates to the traditionally underserved in education. However, it must be formatted in a way that is both attractive and digestible. Journals like *Black Issues in Higher Education, The Hispanic Outlook,* and *The Chronicle of Higher Education* are excellent examples of media, both in print and electronic form, that present relevant issues with integrity. Creative approaches to issue-dissemination are greatly needed. Modifying the traditional format of academic conferences to include policy makers and influencers outside of academia, for example in the media and the business community, may provide useful results. I believe that there is tremendous opportunity in higher education to leverage business expertise in areas like advertising and forecasting about the implications of improvements with regard to the current demographic trends. It is easy to pick up the tiny flower of student motivation and ignore the structural inequity of enrollment, degree, and segregation issues that hover around us.

Professors, deans, administrators, legislators, and business leaders have responsibility for higher education, but they are not alone. Parents, students, and organizations within the community must assume greater roles. Leaders in the NCPPHE report astutely identified this. While structural dynamics are an important aspect of institutional access, true empowerment comes only from within. The reputation and success that Asian students enjoy provide a good example of the benefits of community empowerment. However, this is in no way foreign to the African American community. Any historical profile of African Americans is remiss if it fails to articulate the remarkable "in spite of" energy that has sustained them through unspeakable oppression in this country. Churches, fraternities and sororities, and other civic organizations need to cast a much wider net to identify needs and implement strategies to educate people in the community about the relevant issues and opportunities within academia.

Recent innovations in technology provide us with powerful tools that can be used to accomplish the great work before us. Perhaps this is yet another similarity between Y2K and EQT. In order to address Y2K issues, programmers are using tools that were created with computer operating systems that were not set up to anticipate the problems. Similarly, focused and purposeful efforts will be necessary to transform academia into an institution that it was not established to be. I am confident that it can be accomplished and am willing to roll my sleeves up to join the work. Are you?

References

Adams v. Richardson, 480 F. 2d 1159 (1973).

Allen, W. R. (1992, Spring). The color of success: African-American college student outcomes at predominantly white and historically black public colleges and universities. *Harvard Educational Review, 62,* 35–37.

Board of Education of Oklahoma v. Dowell, 498 U.S. 237 (1991).

Bowen, W. G. & B., Derek. (1998). *The shape of the river: Long term consequences of considering race in college and university admissions.* Princeton, NJ: Princeton University Press.

Braddock, J. H., II. (1980). The perpetuation of segregation across levels of education: A behavioral assessment of the contact-hypothesis. *Sociology of Education, 53*(3), 178–86.

Brown v. Board of Education, 347 U.S. 483 (1954).

Capachionne v. Charlotte-Mecklenburg Board of Education, 3:97-CV-482-P 1999

Crain, A. S. W. a. R. L. (1994, Winter). Perpetuation theory and the long-term effects of school desegregation. *Review of Educational Research, 64,* 531–555.

Dubois, W. E. B. (1953). *The souls of Black folk.* New York: Blue Heron.

Epps, E. G. (Ed.). (1972). *Black students in White schools.* Worthington, OH: C. A. Jones.

Feagin, J. R. (1992). The continuing significance of racism: Discrimination against Black students in White colleges. *Journal of Black Studies, 22*(4), 546–578.

Hamilton, J. W. (1952). *Ride the wild horses.* Old Tappan, NJ: Fleming H. Revell.

Hocutt v. Wilson, Civil Issue Docket No. 1-188 (1933).

Hopwood v. University of Texas, 78 F.3d 932 (5th Cir. 1996).

Immerwahr, J. (1999). *Taking responsibility: Leaders' expectations of higher education* (National Center Report #99-1). Washington DC: The National Center for Public Policy and Higher Education, and Public Agenda.

Knight v. State of Alabama, 787 F. Supp. 1030 (N.D. Alabama 1991).

Ladson-Billings, G., & Tate, W. F. (1995). Toward a critical race theory of education. *Teachers College Record, 97,* 47–68.

Law, S. (1999). White privilege and affirmative action. *Akron Law Review, 32*(603).

Lynch, W. (1712). *Slave Control.* On-line. http://www.blackspeak.com/speeches/slavecontrol.ht

Missouri v. Jenkins, 495 U.S. 33 (1995).

Plessy v. Ferguson, 163 U.S. 537 (1896).

Preer, J. L. (1982). *Lawyers v. educators: Black colleges and desegregation in public higher education.* Westport, CT: Greenwood Press.

Steele, C. M. (1999, August). Thin ice "stereotype threat" and Black college students. *The Atlantic Monthly,* 44–54.

Thompson, C. (1950). The high court looks at Jim Crow. *Journal of Negro Education.*

Trent, W. T., Owens-Nicholson, D., Eatman, T. K., Burke, M., Daugherty, J., Kathy, N. (1999). Justice, equality of educational opportunity and affirmative action in higher education. In M. Chang, D. Witt, J. Jones, and K. Hakuta (Eds.), *Compelling Interest Examining the Evidence on Racial Dynamics in Higher Education.*

U.S. v. Fordice, 112S. Ct. 2727 (1992).

Jerlando F. L. Jackson

Jerlando F. L. Jackson currently serves as an assistant to the dean in the College of Education at Iowa State University. Mr. Jackson is responsible for assisting the administrative team in preparing reports, assessments, and evaluations required of the college. He is also responsible for coordinating the Student Ambassador's Program, which is an integral part of the recruitment and retention efforts in the college. In addition to his duties at the university, Mr. Jackson serves as an editorial reviewer with *The Journal of College Student Development*, for the "On the Campus" and "Research in Brief" sections.

Mr. Jackson has received numerous honors and awards, including being named a Holmes Scholar, Outstanding Young Man of America, Winner of the paper competition (Education Division) for the National Black Graduate Student Conference for two consecutive years, Who's Who Among American Colleges and Universities, NAACP Most Dedicated Member Award, National Dean's List for three consecutive years, Phi Delta Kappa National Honor Society, Gamma Beta Phi National Honor Society, and Order of Omega Greek Honor Society.

He holds a bachelor of music education degree from the University of Southern Mississippi. He has a master of education degree in higher education administration from Auburn University.

Mr. Jackson is a member of Kappa Alpha Psi Fraternity Inc., Kappa Kappa Psi National Honorary Band Fraternity, National Association for Student Personnel Administrators (NASPA), Iowa Student Personnel Association (ISPA), and the National Association for the Advancement of Colored People (NAACP).

Mr. Jackson has made presentations at numerous conferences and universities throughout the United States. He has several publications to his credit. Among the publications he has authored are: *Scholars of Color: Are Universities Derailing Their Scholarship* (1999), and *How to Increase Minorities at Perfect University* (1996). His motto is "Excellence: Through Achievement and Consistency."

3

ADMINISTRATORS OF COLOR AT PREDOMINANTLY WHITE INSTITUTIONS

Jerlando F. L. Jackson

Administrators of Color at Predominantly White Institutions

Many higher education institutions in the United States have made commendable attempts to deal with the complex issue of administrative diversity. However, other institutions have attempted to use "quick fixes" to deal with this challenge, and most have made little or no progress in making diversity a reality. The internal and external pressures in higher education continue to mandate changes in the values at colleges and universities. Numerous institutions fail to confront the topic of administrative diversity because of the fear and resistance that come with organizational change. While institutions recognize the necessity of bringing more administrators of color to campus, many have not identified the steps needed to develop a supportive climate for this task (Drummond, 1995). The purpose of this chapter is to give an overview on the issue of administrative diversity at predominantly White institutions. In the context of this chapter, the use of the word *administrator* will encompass individuals employed in academic, student, and administrative affairs.

Between 1980 and 1998, there has been little if any change in the status of administrators of color (Chenoweth, 1988; Konrad & Pfeffer, 1991). White males are overrepresented at the high administrative levels, while people of color are overrepresented at the low administrative levels. Most of the changes that have occurred to diversify administrations are due to White women administrators making advancements. Additional progress is attributed to positions being created for people of color that allow them to help their peers.

These positions were created because of affirmative action efforts, which enable institutions to employ and retain administrators of color (Konrad & Pfeffer, 1991). However, this practice has received vast criticism.

Smith (1993) notes that

> Black administrators were hired to pacify the Black community and/or to demonstrate that the hiring institution is an "equal opportunity employer," neither of which is legitimate; the leadership which they could provide based on their knowledge of a given issue is neither accepted nor respected by those who must be influenced. (p. 64)

Looking at the breakthroughs of people of color in key administrative roles is not encouraging enough; although there have been remarkable improvements in several categories, there have been losses in others. Sixteen percent of the administrators at Historically Black Colleges and Universities (HBCUs) are White, while only 2.5 percent of administrators at predominantly White institutions are people of color (Konrad & Pfeffer, 1991).

Why are we faced with the problem of scarce administrators of color? To answer this question, one must examine four key factors. The first factor is that a small number of people of color enter graduate programs. For example, in 1991 African Americans received less than 5 percent of master's degrees awarded. They also receive only 3.8 percent of all doctorates awarded nationally (Crase, 1994). This leads to the second factor limiting the representation of people of color in administration, which is a small pool of candidates. This problem is a direct result of factor one. It is apparent that not enough potential candidates are being produced, which means there is not a substantial number of applicants. The third factor is a lack of quality mentoring experiences for students of color. This prevents the acculturation of people of color into the field of administration. It has been noted that positive role models tend to influence people of color to choose a particular profession. The final factor is the barriers from within the institution. The first barrier indicates that the institution may not be ready to reorganize for diversity. The second barrier deals with a fear of diversity. Finally, the third barrier focuses on the stereotype that people of color are not "psychologically and cognitively competent" to perform administrative duties (Crase, 1994, p. 18).

The literature states various arguments for the need for administrators of color (Davis, 1994; Crase, 1994; Drummond, 1995; Rusher, 1996). One argument proclaims that a presence of administrators of color will increase the success for students of color at the institution. The administrators of color serving as role models are influential in attracting and retaining students of color (Henry & Nixon, 1994). The Commission on the Higher Education of Minorities found that:

> it is necessary to recognize the important functions that minority academics serve as role models; as advisors; as student advocates; as monitors of institutional policies and practices; as dedicated educators committed to educational excellence and equity; as scholars approaching traditional subjects and research questions with new perspectives or laying the intellectual foundations in emerging fields of inquiry; and as ambassadors to the minority community (Drummond, 1995, p. 44).
>
> An administrator of color can add distinct characteristics to a department or office. The characteristics include a leader who can: 1) lead a diverse group; 2) redirect the educational mission to address the needs of a multicultural and diverse community; and 3) focus on making replacements that reflect diversity. (Bowen & Muller, 1996)

If colleges and universities are to increase the quality and representation of administrators of color, then critical concern must be focused on creating campus climates that are more supportive for people of color. To change a climate, the institution must change behaviors that are established by rites, rituals, and rewards of the university. Charles Moody, who was vice provost of academic affairs at the University of Michigan at the time of this quote, states, "The climate [suggests that] whatever minority candidates have isn't needed . . . [it is difficult] for beneficiaries of racism to be able to see racism" (Cited in Anderson, 1991, p. 116). He recommends undertaking an assessment of campus climates from the perspective of students and alumni of color. Moody believes that this method can begin to remove institutional blindness to racist acts. In order for predominantly White institutions to recruit and retain administrators of color, three factors should be considered: 1) the environment, 2) the office, and 3) sources of daily interactions (Davis, 1994).

The Environment
The environment into which a person of color can come must be positive and comfortable. If a person feels out of place, it will affect his/her job performance and satisfaction.

The Office
The office should be very supportive of decisions made by administrators of color. Concurrently, extra attention must be made so as not to exclude administrators of color in matters of the office.

Daily Interaction

The mentoring process provides an avenue for positive daily interaction. Incoming administrators of color can be paired with senior administrators who can provide insight and support. This support might be the added measure that retains the individual at the institution and ultimately in the profession.

As a result, universities should develop programs to promote diversity. Through the implementation of these programs, more administrators of color can be recruited. Universities can use benchmarks from successful faculty-of-color recruitment programs to help develop programs specifically for administrators. A prime example of a program from which benchmark universities are developed is the Metropolitan State College of Denver Project. Metropolitan State College of Denver developed three initiatives during the fall of 1990. These initiatives were designed to increase the number of women and administrators of color, to attract national and international faculty of distinction to the campus, and to retain quality faculty of color. The three initiatives are: (1) Target of Opportunity, (2) Minority Faculty Recruitment Incentive Program, and (3) The New Faculty Mentoring Program (Davis, 1994). A brief description of each program follows.

Target of Opportunity Program (TOP)

This program provides flexible and less time-consuming recruiting and hiring procedures, as well as additional resources for administrators to draw upon in their search for new hires. Essentially, TOP provides assistance with the search and the hiring of: a) women and faculty of color when there is either an underrepresentation of a particular group or when there is a special need for representation of a particular group, b) nationally and/or internationally recognized faculty of color when the opportunity presents itself, and c) women and administrators of color when there is either underrepresentation or a special need for representation within a particular academic unit.

Minority Faculty Recruitment Incentive Program (MFRIP)

This program allows academic departments that are experiencing stable or slow growth in enrollments to recruit minority candidates aggressively. MFRIP also provides support for professional development. For example, faculty interested in pursuing graduate studies leading to a terminal degree or to a different specialization may be supported through this initiative. In this program, the vice president of academic affairs provides incentive awards of $5,000 to any faculty of color accepting promotion to a tenure-track position. There is, however, a limit of one such development award per department. Those faculty who complete their terminal degree requirements and who receive satisfactory evaluations are offered tenure-track positions at the college.

The New Faculty Mentoring Program (NFMP)

This program grew out of a need to develop a cadre of committed, resourceful, and qualified new faculty, especially from the ranks of minority groups such as the physically impaired, women, African Americans, Native Americans, Asian Americans, and Hispanic Americans. The program's objectives are to provide new faculty with a peer support network and to ensure them a smooth progression through the retention, tenure, and promotion processes. The program requires all incoming faculty to be advised of its requirements during recruitment. A university can use programs of this kind to develop a comprehensive model to recruit and train administrators of color.

Konrad and Pfeffer (1991) conducted a study to examine the conditions under which women and people of color are hired as administrators in higher education. The study focused on the factors that encouraged the aspect of hiring. One factor was the enforcement of affirmative-action requirements that increase the hiring of women and people of color. The basis for this factor is the premise that in the absence of affirmative-action enforcement, White males would continue to dominate the job market. Their research suggests that people of color would have a better chance of being hired as administrators in public institutions than in private institutions. This is due to the fact that public institutions are more liable to affirmative-action enforcement than private institutions.

Furthermore, public institutions are more dependent on governmental funding as opposed to private institutions, which are less dependent. The results show that people of color are more inclined to be hired for positions "held by members of their own group in the past" (Konrad & Pfeffer, 1991, p. 150). People of color are more likely to be hired for positions in institutions where people of color are the decision makers. Surprisingly, people of color hired from within an institution are more likely to be put in the position of an administrator. The findings suggest that the best predictor of people of color being hired is the presence of a person of color previously in the position (Konrad & Pfeffer, 1991).

What can administrators do to help increase the presence of people of color in administration? Administrators can begin by creating an open and nurturing environment if they wish to cultivate new and diverse leadership (Bowen & Muller, 1996). First, administrators should urge faculty of color to become more involved in campus issues. Faculty of color should be allowed to test their interest and aptitude for administration by assuming leadership roles such as program coordinator and departmental vice-chairs. Furthermore, when the opportunity arises to fill acting positions on a temporary basis, regard should be given to people of color in occupying the position. Administrators should take this moment to mentor people of color for administrative leadership (Bowen & Muller, 1996).

Henry and Nixon (1994) analyzed employment practices of administrators by type of institution. The institutions that employed the greatest number of women administrators were liberal arts institutions. They employed 577 women administrators who made up 60.5 percent of the total. The largest number of male administrators was found in comprehensive universities, which were the second largest employers of women administrators. More than half of administrators of color (58.3 percent) are employed by public colleges and universities. They made up 41.7 percent of administrators at private institutions. One implication would be that women and people of color will manage better in institutions designed to aid them; private institutions have been the most responsive to women, and the opposite has been true for people of color (Henry & Nixon, 1994).

If universities plan on retaining administrators of color after recruitment, then new strategies need to be developed to ensure long-term retention (Davis, 1994). Campus leadership must show a commitment to cultural diversity. Affirmative-action efforts should not end with the deed of hiring but should continue through the duration of the administrator's term. The president should make his or her support for administrators of color indisputable and should acknowledge their contributions to the university. Higher education's survival depends on its ability to increase and maintain active representation of people of color on their campuses. Higher education can no longer afford the luxury of accommodating just a few; it must also assume responsibility for retaining people of color (Rusher, 1996).

Minority Presidents

The chapter up to this point has focused on the general area of administration at predominantly White institutions. The focus will now be redirected to examine specific issues concerning presidents of color at predominantly White institutions. Having a president of color can enhance the level of integrity and confidence of an institution. The president of color can serve as a role model, leader, and spokesperson for accepted values of the minority and majority population. Thus, presidents of color will be able to maintain linkages among the total population. Presidents of color can communicate the full significance of diversity and provide avenues for institutions to fit the reality of multiculturalism (Bowen & Muller, 1996).

In order to put this issue in perspective, one should examine the profile of the American college president. Madeleine Green (1988) conducted a study to determine the general characteristics of the presidency. She found that the typical president was a married, White male who was 53 years of age. The average president serves for about seven years. However, as presidents of color are newer to the position, the majority of them serve for fewer than five years. Most women presidents tend to never be married or they are divorced. Over three-quarters of all presidents hold doctorate degrees, with 56 percent having Ph.D.s and 22 percent with an Ed.D. Additionally, 40 percent hold doctorate degrees in the field of education. The typical president of color is married, 53.6 years old, and has a Ph.D. in the field of education. Presidents of color are less likely to be employed at doctoral-granting and research institutions.

Conversely, people of color are more likely to head baccalaureate colleges and comprehensive universities. Fifty-three percent of presidents of color were employed at HBCUs. It was also found that the typical woman president is White, 53 years old, and has a Ph.D. in the field of education or humanities. Forty-one percent of women presidents were at baccalaureate institutions, while 31 percent head two-year institutions, and only 4 percent head a doctoral-granting university. The percentage of presidents of color holding Ph.D.s as their highest degree indicates that there is still a need for them to have more credentials than White males. Sixty-eight percent of women presidents and 58 percent of presidents of color held Ph.D.s as opposed to 55 percent of White males (Green, 1988).

The study also examined the different pathways to the presidency. Generally, it was discovered that the route was incremental. Seventeen percent of presidents were recruited from other presidencies, while 42 percent were recruited from vice presidencies. It was also found that university presidents possessed the highest degree of administrative skills. More specifically, 31 percent of presidents at doctoral-granting institutions were recruited from previous presidencies. One-third of presidents moved up from within the institution, while 36 percent were recruited from similar institutions. People of color were more likely to be recruited from within an institution as opposed to being recruited from outside the institutions. However, there is insufficient evidence that affirmative-action efforts have increased the recruitment of people of color for the position of president (Green, 1988).

Many institutions are not facing the facts when it comes to administrative diversity. Some institutions will not open their eyes to the harsh reality. People often reveal their resistance to change through reactions such as an unwillingness to admit weaknesses. Numerous deans and departmental chairs have verbalized that race and gender problems do not come into play in their academic units. This shows the denial expressed by many administrators. In conjunction, few administrators have implemented plans to enhance the quality of the campus experience for their minority counterparts. Many administrators denoted that they did not know what they could do, if anything, to enhance the experiences of people of color (Farmer, 1990). Coupled with that issue is the perception, or misperception, regarding whether administrators of color can be successful and competent leaders.

In conclusion, changing the campus climate for administrative diversity is a difficult task. The job of diversification is complicated because of an array of problems, including the fear impact; many are afraid of losing power, status, and personal prestige. Another problem is the misperceptions about administrators of color being passive, unqualified, submissive, and dependent. Additionally, the problems are further complicated by the limited pool of diverse applicants. Many solutions to these issues have already been proposed, and it is important that we become attentive to all diversity issues. If we do not achieve full participation of minority citizens in all levels of society, we will not be able to function as a nation. We must achieve the goal of diversification to continue being "The Land of Opportunity."

References

Anderson, J. A. (1991). The politics of retention: Rhetoric vs. reality. *Black Issues in Higher Education, 7*(24), 116.

Bowen, R. C., & Muller, G. H. (Eds.). (1996). The power of the presidency. *Achieving Administrative Diversity, 94*, 39–45.

Chenoweth, K. (1988). African American college presidents in decline: Yet the pipeline of Black scholars poised to assume presidential status is growing. *Black Issues in Higher Education, 15*(6), 20–25.

Crase, D. (1994). The minority connection: African Americans in administrative/leadership positions. *Physical Educator, 51*(1), 15–20.

Davis, J. D. (Ed.). (1994). *Coloring the halls of ivy.* Boston, MA: Anker Publishing Company.

Drummond, M. E. (1995). Minorities in higher education leadership positions: A report of eight years of disappointment, 1986–1993. *Black Issues in Higher Education, 12*(2), 43–47.

Farmer, D. W. (1990). Strategies for change: New directions for higher education. *Managing Change in Higher Education, 18*(2), 7–18.

Green, M. F. (1988). A profile of the American college president. *Educational Record, 69*(2), 44–48.

Henry, W. J., & Nixon, H. L. (1994). Changing a campus climate for minorities and women. *Equity & Excellence in Education, 27*(3), 48–54.

Konrad, A. M., & Pfeffer, J. (1991). Understanding the hiring of women and minorities in educational institutions. *Sociology of Education, 64*(3), 141–157.

Rusher, A. W. (1996). *African American women administrators.* Lanham, MD: University Press.

Smith, Y. R. (1993). Recruitment and retrenchment of African American and other multicultural physical educators. *Journal of Physical Education, Recreation & Dance, 64*(3), 66–70.

Texas Higher Education Coordinating Board. (1994). *Access and equity 2000: The Texas educational opportunity plan for public higher education: September 1994 through August 2000.* (ERIC Document Reproduction Services No. ED 378 862). Austin, TX: Author.

Bryant T. Marks

Bryant T. Marks is a doctoral candidate in the social psychology program at the University of Michigan, Ann Arbor. His research interests are in the areas of stereotyping, prejudice, racial identity, and interethnic relations. His dissertation examines the influence of the negative or positive intellectual stereotype on the standardized test performance of African Americans and European Americans respectively. In another line of research, he is investigating the development of ethnic identity, academic identity, racial attitudes, and perceptions of discrimination among African American college students attending Historically Black Colleges (HBCs) and Historically White Colleges (HWCs). He has also conducted a study that assessed 1) ethnic differences regarding the domains upon which individuals base their self-esteem, and 2) ethnic differences in the relationships among these domains. Finally, he has analyzed the manner in which stereotypes, prejudice, and antiracism relates to support of extreme anti-immigration policy and interracial contact in western Europe. Bryant has taught several courses while attending the University of Michigan and has been given several teaching awards from the Department of Psychology and the graduate school. Bryant received a bachelor's degree with honors from Morehouse college where he majored in psychology and minored in economics. He has received academic honors in mathematics, economics, and psychology as well as scholarships from the National Science Foundation and One Hundred Black Men Incorporated. Bryant was born and raised in Queens Village, New York and attended Benjamin N. Cardozo High School in Bayside, New York. His hobbies include spoken word poetry and collecting the musical recordings of John Coletrane.

4

THE MISEDUCATION OF THE NEGRO REVISITED

AFRICAN AMERICAN RACIAL IDENTITY, HISTORICALLY BLACK INSTITUTIONS, AND HISTORICALLY WHITE INSTITUTIONS

Bryant T. Marks

> To educate the Negro we must find out exactly what his background
> is, what he is today, what his possibilities are, and how to begin with
> him as he is and make him a better individual of the kind that he is.
> Carter G. Woodson, *The Mis-education of the Negro*

There is a great debate amongst college-educated African Americans that finds its genesis in the desegregation of higher education in the United States. Ever since the doors of Historically White Institutions (HWIs), and some would argue the doors of opportunity, were opened to African Americans on a large scale there has been an assumption that the quality of the education received at HWIs is superior to that of Historically Black Institutions (HBIs). The root of this sentiment is easily understood. One of the critical factors that led to desegregation was the miserable failure of creating HBIs that were separate from, but equal to, HWIs. Due to federal and local discrimination, HBIs lacked the material and human resources that HWIs enjoyed. Thus, it was assumed that an education from an HWI was of higher caliber—a point eloquently argued by Thurgood Marshall in the *Brown v. Board of Education* case of 1954. Although the resource divide between HBIs and HWIs has decreased over the last few decades, it has not been closed. Consequently, many believe that HWIs continue to provide a more competitive education.

Although compelling on the surface, this argument becomes less convincing when one expands one's definition of *education* beyond that of the process of imparting and receiving information regarding certain classes of subject matter. Taken from the Latin word *educare,* which means to "bring up" or "to rear," to *educate,* then, is to bring out or assist in the development of one's understanding of oneself and the world. Education involves the realization of individual talents and abilities via exposure to various fields of human endeavor; it is the cornerstone of the process of fulfilling one's potential. What is being brought out of students at any particular moment depends, in part, on their current stage of cognitive development. At the initial stages of formal education, the ability to learn and master fundamental principles of several subjects is brought out. Once individuals are cognitively developed enough to reason at an abstract level, their ability to engage in introspection and to evaluate critically that which they have learned and continue to learn should be brought out. It is at this stage, as suggested by Woodson (1933), that the most severe miseducation can occur, for it is at this point that individuals should ruminate about who they are, what they are, and their options and possibilities in various domains.

Miseducation of African Americans often occurs when external forces restrict or impair one's ability to explore the totality of oneself, which, due to isolation from several social and extracurricular activities, is likely to occur at HWIs (Fleming, 1984). Advocates of HBIs often posit that HBIs attempt to lead many of their students out of this state of miseducation that was fostered by entities at individual, cultural, and institutional levels preceding the college years. To this end, HBIs tend to construct atmospheres both in and outside of the classroom that are conducive to self-exploration and personal growth. In short, HWIs are seen as providing a superior education in the purely academic sense, while HBIs profess to provide an education that excels in the facilitation of psychosocial development in addition to academic rigor.[1]

One of the key components of personal development is social identity— the recognition of one's membership in various groups and the significance and meaning assigned to that membership. Whether voluntary (for example,

---

1. Although many people believe that African Americans attending HWIs perform better academically, the findings of several studies suggest otherwise. African Americans at HBIs achieved greater cognitive growth than those at HWIs (Watson & Kuh, 1996; Fleming, 1984). Moreover, African Americans attending HBIs display more positive outcomes than their HWI counterparts in the following domains: personal and social development, critical thinking in science and technology, vocational and career skills, history and cultural awareness, and arts and literature (DeSousa & Kuh, 1996). African Americans attending HBIs also benefited more from school involvement in comparison to both African American and European American students attending HWIs (Watson & Kuh, 1996).

fraternities, clubs, or teams) or involuntary, (for example, gender, family, or nationality), we are all members of several groups. But one of the key social identities of African Americans is their racial/ethnic identity, defined as the attitudes and beliefs regarding the significance and meaning that people place on race in defining themselves (Sellers, Smith, Shelton, Rowley & Chavous, 1998). Because of the significance of race in American society, the manner in which one defines oneself in terms of race as well as the experiences that influence that definition merit exploration. The purpose of this paper is to review the empirical research that has compared the racial identity of African Americans attending HBIs to that of African Americans attending HWIs. Although some of the studies included in this review do not state the names or various characteristics of participating institutions of higher education, HBIs and HWIs are loosely defined as institutions whose populations have historically had enrollments of at least 75 percent African American (HBIs) or European American (HWIs) students.

Requirements for Inclusion

In order to be included in this review, a study had to be published after 1979 in an academic journal, utilize statistically sound surveys based on a formal theory of racial identity, and include twenty or more African Americans from each campus setting. I focused on studies published after 1979 because the shift of African American student enrollment (from HBIs to HWIs) resulting from desegregation was still taking place in the 1970s. In addition, the United States as a whole was still adjusting to the gains of minorities and women following the other significant changes following the civil rights movement. Studies published in academic journals were selected because they are typically critically reviewed and approved by experts before they are published. I cited studies that included surveys based on formal theories of racial identity because the items on these surveys corresponded with the various components of theory, which allows for clear interpretation of the results. Studies with twenty or more students at each campus setting were chosen because samples below this amount may not represent the larger population of African Americans on campus.

African American Racial Identity and Campus Environment

There are many answers to the question "What does it mean to be Black?" Consequently, there are many theories that describe the racial identity of

African Americans.[2] However, only three of the approximately eight major theories of African American racial identity have been utilized in studies that satisfied the aforementioned criteria (see Marks, Settles, Cooke, Morgan, & Sellers, 1999, for a review of racial-identity theories). These theories are *Nigrescence, African Self-Consciousness,* and the *Multidimensional Model of Racial Identity.*

The Nigrescence Model of Racial Identity

In 1971, William Cross published the nigrescence model of racial identity. It has since become one of the most popular stage theories of racial-identity development. Nigrescence is defined as the transformation from a preexisting (non-Afrocentric) identity into one that is Afrocentric (Cross, 1971). The nigrescence model consists of five stages: pre-encounter, encounter, immersion/emersion, internalization, and internalization-commitment (Cross, 1971).

During the *pre-encounter stage,* individuals downplay the importance of race in their lives and focus more on their membership in other groups (for example, religion, social class, or sexual orientation). The second stage of the nigrescence experience is the *encounter stage,* which is characterized by an actual experience that causes individuals to challenge their current feelings about themselves and their interpretation of the condition of African Americans. Often, the experience is one in which the individual faces a blatant racist event. However, there are other instances in which the experience is more positive. In any event, the encounter experience is one that is so foreign to their previous world view regarding race that it forces individuals to rethink their attitudes about race. In the third stage, *immersion-emmersion,* individuals immerse themselves in Black culture (for example, history, literature, language, and music) and feel liberated from Whiteness. They view everything that is Black as good and everything that is White as bad. Despite this immersion into all things Black, individuals have not psychologically committed to a Black identity. The next stage, *internalization,* is described as a psychological change wherein African Americans learn to balance their Blackness with the other demands of personhood (such as other group memberships). The final stage of

---

2. Although the terms *African American* and *Black* are used interchangeably, the author recognizes that African Americans can be seen as an ethnic group while Blacks can be viewed as a racial group. The identity theories reviewed in this chapter reflect the beliefs and opinions of people of African descent and phenotype living in America, which technically makes them ethnic-identity theories. However, the reference groups in various identity theories and measures are either "Black" or "African," which may connote a racial grouping. Semantically, there is no easy solution. For the sake of this article, *racial identity* rather than *ethnic identity* will be utilized.

the nigrescence model is *internalization-commitment*. In contrast to the previous stage, this stage involves commitment to a plan of action, and individuals begin to live in accordance with the new self-images they have developed.

The Racial Identity Attitudes Scale (RIAS) was designed to measure the first four stages of nigrescence (Parham & Helms, 1981). The RIAS consists of 30 items with a five-option response scale ranging from *strongly disagree (1)* to *strongly agree (5)*. Some racial-identity researchers believe that the attitudes that are captured by each stage may actually be present to differing degrees at every stage (Burlew & Smith, 1991; Helms, 1990). Therefore, the RIAS is often used to describe a racial identity profile rather than to categorize people into distinct stages.

Study 1. Cheatham, Slaney, and Coleman (1990) conducted a study in which 130 Black students attending an HBI and 120 black students attending an HWI participated. Participants ranged in age from 16 to 32 years. Both schools were publicly funded, located in the same state in the northeastern United States, and had similar male-female student ratios. Students from these schools were also similar regarding the size of their hometowns, grade point averages, and parents' education (Cheatham, Tomlinson & Ward, 1990). At the HBI, select faculty administered the RIAS to their students during class meetings. Participants attending the HWI were recruited via classes, advertising, counselors, and African American organizations. The survey was administered in various settings and was part of a larger questionnaire.

These researchers did not find campus differences regarding any of the stages of nigrescence. These results also indicated that African Americans attending both types of institutions have low pre-encounter attitudes, moderately high encounter attitudes, moderate immersion-emmersion attitudes, and moderately high internalization attitudes (see Table 1). The results of this study should be interpreted with caution, however, due to several limitations. In addition to the use of only two schools and campus differences in recruitment methods, the researchers did not take into account two key demographic variables—class status and age—which have been shown to influence racial identity (Baldwin, 1981; Jackson, McCullough, & Gurin, 1988). Moreover, before beginning the questionnaire, participants were told that the purpose of the study was to examine and compare African American students' experiences at HBIs and HWIs. This description could have had a significant influence on participants' responses. Some participants may have been motivated to construct a pattern of responses that they believed would allow them and their school to compare in a favorable manner.

Study 2. Nottingham, Rosen, and Parks (1992) administered the RIAS to 102 honor students attending an HBI (freshmen/sophomores = 78 percent;

Table 1. Summary of Average Scores for Each Study Measuring the Stages of Nigrescence at Historically Black Insitutions (HBIs) and Historically White Institutions (HWIs)

	Stages of Nigrescence			
	PRE	ENC	IM/EM	INT
Study 1				
HBI	1.9	3.7	3.0	3.7
HWI	1.8	3.7	3.0	3.7
Study 2[a]				
HBI	2.2	2.0	2.1*	6.1*
HWI	2.4*	1.8	1.8	5.8
Study 3				
HBI	1.7*	3.5	2.6	4.3
HWI	1.4	3.5	2.8	4.5*
Study 4				
HBI	1.9	3.6	3.2	3.6
Fr	1.9	3.7	3.2	3.4
Sr	1.9	3.5	3.1	3.7[b]
HWI	1.8	3.7	3.3	3.8*
Fr	1.8	3.8[b]	3.5[b]	3.8
Sr	1.9	3.6	3.1	3.7

Note. Maximum possible score for each stage is 5 (which indicates strong endorsement of the attitudes related to a particular stage).

PRE = pre-encounter, ENC = encounter, IM/EM = immersion-emmersion, INT = internalization

[a]Although average scores for internalization exceed the maximum possible (5), they are identical to the values reported in the original article.

*Indicates an institution score statistically greater than the other institution score.

[b]Indicates a statistically significant difference between freshmen and seniors within a campus setting at a specific stage.

average age = 18.75) and 100 students attending an HWI (freshmen/ sophomores = 60 percent; average age = 20.11) as a section of a larger questionnaire. Both colleges were located in Texas, and participants had similar high-school rankings and Scholastic Aptitude Test (SAT) scores. Participants were sent a cover letter and the questionnaire packet in the mail. Upon completion, they mailed these items back to the researchers. Twenty percent of the students attending the HBI and 25 percent of the students attending the HWI completed and mailed the survey.

Statistical analyses indicated that participants at the HBI had lower pre-encounter, higher immersion-emmersion, and higher internalization scores than their HWI counterparts. There was no difference regarding the attitudes consistent with the encounter stage. There were also no campus differences in the following domains: gender ratio, socioeconomic status, parents' marital status, religious activities, and size of hometown. The limitations of this study include a limited number of participating schools (2), minimal consideration of the role of age and class status, and a larger proportion of upperclassmen in the sample from the HWI. In addition, the low response rates of both schools and the use of honor students at the HWI may limit the extent to which these findings can be generalized to the larger student body.

Study 3. Poindexter-Cameron and Robinson (1997) conducted another study that utilized the RIAS. These researchers gave the RIAS and two other questionnaires to 38 African American females attending a predominantly female HBI (average age = 21.3) and 46 African American females attending a predominantly male HWI (average age = 20.3). Both schools were located in the southeastern United States. Participants were recruited via several male and female college professors, sorority presidents, and sorority advisors on their respective campuses who also served as contact people. Although the authors state that one of the eight contact people was European American, they did not state the occupation/position of that individual. The researchers distributed the questionnaire to education classes and sorority members and encouraged them to participate. Willing participants completed the questionnaires and delivered them to their contact people. The proportion of students who completed the questionnaire at the HBI and HWI was 58 percent and 69 percent respectively.

Data analysis revealed that participants attending the HBI reported higher pre-encounter attitudes and lower internalization attitudes than those attending the HWI. There were no encounter or immersion-emmersion differences between the two groups. Once again, these findings should be interpreted with caution because of various limitations. In addition to the use of only two schools and the disparate gender ratio between campuses, the sample was a subset of the student population (those in education classes and sororities) that restricts the generalizability of these findings. Also, participants' responses could have been influenced by the fact that the contact person, one of which was European American, could look at their responses to the questions once the questionnaire was turned in. Last, it is likely that several of the African American females attending the HWI were participants in a year-long discussion series on Black womanhood. Such an experience could have also influenced their responses.

Study 4. The last study involving a comparison of the racial identity of African Americans attending HBIs and HWIs that included the RIAS was conducted by McCowan and Alston (1998). One hundred and three African American women enrolled in an HBI (53 freshmen, 50 seniors) and 109 African American women enrolled in an HWI (56 freshmen, 53 seniors) participated in the study. Both schools were located in the same southeastern state. Participants were selected from a student list provided by the registrar. Participants attending the HBI were randomly selected from the list and received the questionnaire in the mail. Due to the limited number of African Americans at the HWI, the questionnaire was mailed to all of the women on the list. Also included in the mailing were consent forms that stated the purpose of the study—"to examine the relationship among racial identity, African self-consciousness, and career decidedness in first-year and senior women in both historically Black and predominantly White college environments." Once completed, participants returned the questionnaires to the registrar's office in a sealed envelope. The overall response ratio was 66 percent.

The findings of participants attending the HBI are as follows: seniors had stronger internalization attitudes than freshmen; and freshmen and seniors reported similar pre-encounter, encounter, and immersion-emmersion attitudes. Regarding the HWI: freshmen reported stronger encounter and immersion-emmersion attitudes than seniors. Freshmen and seniors did not differ in their endorsement of pre-encounter and internalization attitudes. When the researchers combined freshmen and seniors within each campus and made across-campus comparisons, they found that participants attending the HWI reported stronger internalization attitudes than participants attending the HBI. Although this study was unique in that it compared freshmen and seniors, which should clarify any institution effects, there were several shortcomings. Like other studies, the researchers drew participants from only 2 schools. Also, participants were aware of the purpose of the study before they completed the questionnaire.

Summary

Overall, the pattern of scores revealed no campus differences on two stages and slight campus differences on two other stages of the nigrescence model of racial identity. The extent to which participants de-emphasized the importance of race in their lives (pre-encounter attitudes) was similar across campus settings in studies 1 and 4, greater at the HWI in study 2, but greater at the HBI in study 3. Thus, these results are inconclusive. There were no campus differences in the degree to which participants challenged their current feelings about themselves and their interpretations of the condition of African Americans (encounter attitudes) in any of the studies. Although study 2 revealed that students attending the HBI were more immersed in their Blackness (immersion-emmersion attitudes) than those attending the HWI, this difference was not supported by the other studies. Consequently, it seems that the immersion-emmersion attitudes of students attending HBIs will be equal to or slightly greater than those of students attending HWIs. Regarding the measure that assessed one's ability to balance one's Blackness with other group identities (internalization attitudes), study 1 revealed no campus difference, study 2 found higher scores at the HBI, and studies 3 and 4 found higher scores at HWIs. Although these scores appear somewhat inconclusive, they suggest slightly higher internalization attitudes among African American students attending HWIs. African American students attending HBIs and those attending HWIs seem to have slightly different racial-identity profiles as described by the nigrescence model of racial identity.

African Self-Consciousness

Joseph Baldwin (aka Kobe Kambon) created a theory that outlined the structure of the Black personality (1981). The core component of this structure that is most akin to racial identity is *African Self-Consciousness* (ASC). ASC is the world view or approach to life of African Americans that is directly influenced by a spiritual essence that is unique to people of African descent. Although Baldwin argues that ASC is biogenetic in that it is connected to the melanin that African people possess, he also states that ASC exists on a conscious level that allows it to be influenced by the experiences of the individual. When the individual is nurtured in an environment that is affirming of African ideals and values, individuals' ASCs become synonymous with their spiritual essences. When the environment is not harmonious with these ideals and values, individuals' ASCs become misaligned and individual variation in ASC can be seen. There are several key beliefs, attitudes, and behaviors that result from the ASC. The extent to which a person of African descent possesses these characteristics provides a measure of his or her ASC. These beliefs and behaviors are: 1) awareness of one's African identity (a sense of collective consciousness) and African cultural heritage including the pursuit of knowledge of self (that is, African history); 2) recognition of African survival and proactive development as one's first priority; 3) respect for and active perpetuation of all things African including African life and African institutions; and 4) a standard of conduct toward all things "non-African," and toward those things, peoples, and so on that are "anti-African."

Baldwin (1985) created the 42-item *African Self-Consciousness Scale* to assess the African self-consciousness of African Americans. The scale measures the four competence dimensions mentioned in the previous paragraph and six expressive dimensions (that is, education, family, religion, cultural activities, interpersonal relations, and political orientation).

Study 4 continued. In addition to administering the RIAS, McCowan and Alston (1998) included the ASC scale in their study. They found that seniors had higher ASC scores than freshmen, and participants attending the HBI were higher in ASC than participants attending the HWI.

Study 5. One hundred students attending an HBI and 125 students attending an HWI participated in a study conducted by Baldwin, Duncan, and Bell (1987). The institutions were located in the same southeastern state. The survey was administered to groups and individually. Participants attending the HBI were recruited through psychology classes. At the HWI, students were selected via Black studies classes and the Black student union. Baldwin and his colleagues found that participants attending the HBI had higher ASC than their counterparts at the HWI. After collapsing across educational settings, they also found that older participants had higher ASC scores than younger students and upperclassmen had higher scores than underclassmen. The limitations of this study are the use of only two institutions as well as a sub-sample of African Americans at the HWI (those attending Black student-union meetings or taking African American studies courses).

Study 6. One of the most recent studies that compared the racial identity of African Americans attending HBIs and HWIs was conducted by Cokley (1999). He administered the ASC scale to 112 students attending four metropolitan-area HBIs (two coed, one all male, and one all female) and 92 students attending two HWIs. One of the HWIs was located in an urban area and the other in a residential district. Each school was set in the southeastern United States. Students attending the HBI were recruited by means of class announcements, while those enrolled in the HWIs were identified via African American organizations and minority-affairs offices. The results of this study indicated that students attending the HBIs had higher ASC than those attending the HWIs. There was no ASC difference by classification or gender. The few limitations of this study include a possible sampling bias at the HWI due to the use of the minority-affairs offices and Black organizations.

Summary

The pattern of scores from the studies utilizing the ASC scale are consistent; students attending HBIs have higher African self-consciousness than their counterparts attending HWIs. That is, the extent to which the world view of African Americans is influenced by the spiritual essence unique to people of

African descent is greater among students attending HBIs than those attending HWIs.

The Multidimensional Model of Racial Identity

The *Multidimensional Model of Racial Identity* (MMRI) was recently introduced by Sellers, Rowley, Chavous, Shelton, and Smith (1997). This model of African American racial identity draws upon many preexisting models of racial identity (Sellers, Smith, Shelton, Rowley & Chavous 1998). The MMRI posits that racial identity is multi-dimensional and that it is important to distinguish between the significance (importance) and meaning of racial-group membership. As presented in the MMRI, racial identity is comprised of four dimensions: *racial centrality* and *racial salience*, which tap into the significance of race, and *racial ideology* and *racial regard*, which describe the meaning of race. Racial centrality is a measure of whether race is a core part of an individual's self-concept over time and across situations. Conversely, salience describes the extent to which an individual's race is a relevant part of his or her self-concept at a particular moment in time, and thus can be influenced by the situation. Racial ideology describes an individual's beliefs, opinions, and attitudes regarding the way that African Americans should live and interact with society.

Sellers and his colleagues propose four ideological philosophies: 1) the *nationalist* philosophy emphasizes the uniqueness of being of African descent; 2) the *oppressed minority* philosophy emphasizes the similarities between African Americans and other oppressed groups; 3) the *assimilation* philosophy emphasizes the similarities between African Americans and the rest of American society; and 4) the *humanist* philosophy emphasizes the similarities among all humans. The fourth dimension, Racial Regard, describes the affective and evaluative judgment of one's race. *Private regard* refers to the extent to which individuals feel positively or negatively toward African Americans and their membership in that group, while *public* regard refers to the extent to which individuals feel that others view African Americans positively or negatively. In order to measure the three stable dimensions of the MMRI (that is, centrality, ideology, and regard), Sellers, Rowley, Chavous, Shelton, and Smith (1997) created the Multidimensional Inventory of Black Identity (MIBI).

Study 6 continued. To develop a more in-depth understanding of racial-identity differences as a function of college environment, Cokley (1999) asked participants to complete the MIBI in addition to the ASC scale. In terms of ideology, he found that students attending the HBIs had higher nationalist scores, lower assimilationist scores, and lower humanist scores than their peers

Table 2. Average Scores of the African Self-Consciousness (ASC) Scale and the Multidimensional Inventory of Black Identity (MIBI)

	ASC	MIBI					
		CEN	PRV-R	NAT	MIN	ASSIM	HUM
Study 4							
HBI	5.32*	—	—	—	—	—	—
Fr	5.22	—	—	—	—	—	—
Sr	5.4	—	—	—	—	—	—
HWI	5.13	—	—	—	—	—	—
Fr	5.11	—	—	—	—	—	—
Sr	5.17	—	—	—	—	—	—
Study 5							
HBI	5.69*	—	—	—	—	—	—
under	5.26	—	—	—	—	—	—
upper	6.12	—	—	—	—	—	—
HWI	5.19	—	—	—	—	—	—
under	5.03	—	—	—	—	—	—
upper	5.34	—	—	—	—	—	—
Study 6							
HBI	5.33*	5.27	5.56	4.33	5.10	4.70	5.09
under	5.23	5.26	5.43	4.12	5.13	4.87	5.24
upper	5.48	5.28	5.74	4.63	5.05	4.48	4.88
HWI	4.88	5.02	5.59	3.72	4.99	5.34*	5.32*
under	4.85	4.91	5.60	3.63	5.10	5.37	5.36
upper	4.92	5.22	5.57	3.87	4.83	5.29	5.24
Study 7							
HBI	—	5.28	6.05	4.67*	4.70	4.55	4.87
HWI	—	5.20	6.38*	4.02	4.82*	5.16*	5.33*

Note. ASC = African Self-Consciousness (maximum score = 8); MIBI = Multi-dimensional Inventory of Racial Identity (maximum score for each dimension = 7); CEN = centrality; PRV-R = private regard; NAT = nationalist ideology; MIN = oppressed minority ideology; ASSIM = assimilationist ideology; HUM = humanist ideology; under = underclassmen (freshman and sophomores); upper = upperclassmen (junior and seniors); Fr = freshmen; Sr = seniors.
*Indicates an institution score statistically greater than the other institution score.

attending the HWIs. There were no campus differences in private regard, public regard, centrality, or the oppressed-minority ideology. After combining both groups, however, data analysis revealed that upperclassmen had lower public regard than underclassmen (see Table 2). That is, upperclassmen, more so than underclassmen, felt that other racial groups' opinions of African Americans were negative.

Study 7. Sellers, Rowley, Chavous, Shelton, and Smith (1997) enlisted the participation of 185 students from an HBI and 111 students attending an HWI in an initial validation study of the MIBI. Both schools were located in the mid-Atlantic United States. Participants filled out the MIBI during group administrations of a larger questionnaire. Although the purpose of this study was to validate the MIBI itself and measure how the dimensions were related to race-related behaviors, the researchers also examined campus-specific MIBI scores. They found that students enrolled in the HBI had higher nationalist scores. However, students enrolled in the HWI demonstrated stronger endorsement of minority, assimilation, and humanist ideologies as well as stronger private regard. There were no campus differences regarding centrality. Public-regard scores were not compared because the scale designed to assess the construct was not reliable. Because comparing the racial identity of students from HBIs and HWIs was not the primary goal of this study, the researchers did not statistically adjust for class status or age. Also, the use of two schools does not allow one to draw broad conclusions regarding students attending HBIs and HWIs.

Summary

For the most part, the results of studies six and seven were similar. Both studies found no campus differences in the extent to which race is a core component of students' self-concept (that is, centrality). Although the participants at the HWI felt more positively toward African Americans (that is, private regard) than participants attending the HBI in study seven, study six revealed no such difference. Also, the extent to which individuals emphasized the similarities between African Americans and other oppressed groups (that is, oppressed-minority ideology) was higher amongst participants attending the HWI in study seven, but equivalent in study 6. It seems, therefore, that students attending HWIs have private-regard and oppressed-minority ideologies equal to or slightly higher than students attending HBIs. Both studies indicated that students enrolled in HBIs emphasize the uniqueness of being African American (that is, nationalist ideology) to a greater extent than those enrolled in HWIs. Finally, both studies concluded that students attending HWIs emphasized the similarities between African Americans and the rest of American society (that is, assimilationist ideology) and the similarities among all humans (that is, humanist ideology) to a greater degree than students attending HBIs. In a nutshell, the racial identity profile as outlined by the multidimensional model of racial identity differs across college settings.

General Summary

The studies reviewed in this chapter utilized surveys that were based on three theoretical approaches to racial identity: William Cross' nigrescence model, Joseph Baldwin's African self-consciousness, and Robert Sellers and colleagues' multidimensional model. The results of each model indicate that the racial identity of African American college students differs as a function of college setting. Indeed, students attending HBIs seem to be slightly more enveloped in their Black culture than HWI students as indicated by the pattern of scores on the immersion-emmersion scale of the RIAS, the overall scores on the ASC scale, and the nationalist ideology scores of the MIBI. Conversely, it appears that students attending HWIs possess attitudes that reflect an acceptance and appreciation of diversity that moderately eclipse those of students attending HBIs as evidenced by the internalization scores of the RIAS and the oppressed minority, assimilationist, and humanist ideologies of the MIBI. However, the results of the centrality subscale of the MIBI suggest that the extent to which race is a core part of one's self-concept does not differ between the campus settings. Also, scores on the private-regard subscale of the MIBI indicate that students attending HBIs and HWIs feel equally positive toward African Americans as a group.

And now, a few caveats. It must be kept in mind that "different" is just that—different. Different does not mean better. There does not seem to be an objective optimal racial identity. However, given certain environments, one racial identity profile may facilitate mental health and goal achievement to a greater extent than another. That is, in certain environments or situations, having a nationalist ideology may prove beneficial (for example, persuading African Americans to patronize Black businesses). In other settings, a humanist ideology may be most effective (for example, persuading companies to decrease environmental pollution). It is not clear what type of racial-identity profile will allow one to meet the demands of the college environment most efficiently. The extent to which these demands differ between HBIs and HWIs is also unclear. Excluding the work of Fleming (1984) and Allen, Epps, and Haniff (1991), there is minimal research that has included African American students from several HBIs and HWIs in a study that utilized various demographic, academic, and psychosocial measures. Although complicated, such studies are critical to the dialogue regarding the costs and benefits of particular college settings. The reader should also note that five of the six reviewed studies involved only two institutions, which differed along several important dimensions (such as size, prestige, location, history, and their status as public or private). If taken into account, these dimensions may shed some light on the specific institutional characteristics that foster various racial-identity profiles. Also, it is not clear if a particular college setting actually changes one's racial identity. While the freshmen-senior comparisons of study 4 suggest an impact of college experience on racial identity, the underclass-upperclass comparisons of studies 5 and 6 do not. Thus, it is imperative that researchers employ techniques that assess the racial identity of the same individuals at different points in their college careers.

Returning to the question of miseducation as described by Woodson, I hesitate to say which setting more effectively makes each student "a better individual of the kind that he is." Such a conclusion has an evaluative connotation that may be context dependent, not easily measured, inconsistent over time, and very subjective. I will submit, however, that those who engage in the debate pitting HBIs and HWIs against each other need to sophisticate their arguments by stating which aspects of racial identity they are addressing as well as how each aspect relates to specific outcomes.

References

Allen, W. R., Epps, E. G., & Haniff, N. Z. (Eds.). (1991). *College in Black and White: African American students in predominantly White and in historically Black public universities.* Albany, NY: State University of New York Press.

Baldwin, J. (1981). Notes on an Africentric theory of Black personality. *The Western Journal of Black Studies, 5*(3), 172–179.

Baldwin, J. A. (1985). *African (Black) personality: From an Africentric framework.* Chicago: Third World Press.

Baldwin, J. A., Duncan, J. A., & Bell, Y. R. (1987). Assessment of African self-consciousness among Black students from two college environments. *Journal of Black Psychology, 13*(2), 27–41.

Burlew, A. K., & Smith, L. R. (1991). Measures of racial identity: An overview and a proposed framework. *Journal of Black Psychology: Special Issue: Incorporating an African world view into psychology: II, 17*(2), 53–71.

Cheatham, H. E., Slaney, R. B., & Coleman, N. C. (1990). Institutional effects on the psychosocial development of African-American college students. *Journal of Counseling Psychology, 37*(4), 453–458.

Cheatham, H. E., Tomlinson, S. M., & Ward, T. J. (1990). The African self-consciousness construct and African American students. *Journal of College Student Development, 31*(6), 492–499.

Cokley, K. (1999). Reconceptualizing the impact of college racial composition on African American students' racial identity. *Journal of College Student Development, 40*(3), 235–245.

Cross, W. (1971). The Negroe-to-Black conversion experience. *Black World,* 13–27.

DeSousa, D. J., & Kuh, G. D. (1996). Does institutional racial composition make a difference in what Black students gain from college? *Journal of College Student Development, 37*(3), 257–267.

Fleming, J. (1984). *Blacks in college: A comparative study of students' success in Black and in White institutions.* San Francisco: Jossey-Bass.

Helms, J. E. (1990). *Black and white racial identity theory, research, and practice.* Westport: Praeger Publishers.

Jackson, J. S., McCullough, W. R., & Gurin, G. (1988). Family, socialization environment, and identity development in Black Americans, *Black families* (2nd ed., pp. 242–256, Sage focus editions, Vol. 41). Newbury Park, CA: Sage Publications.

Marks, B. T., Settles, I. H., Cooke, D. Y., Morgan, L. M., & Sellers, R. M. In Press. African American racial identity: A review of contemporary models and measures. In R. L. Jones (Ed.), *Black Psychology* (4 ed.). Hampton: Cobb & Henry.

McCowan, C. J., & Alston, R. J. (1998). Racial identity, African self-consciousness, and career decision making in African American college women. *Journal of Multicultural Counseling & Development, 26*(1), 28–38.

Nottingham, C. R., Rosen, D. H., & Parks, C. (1992). Psychological well-being among African American university students. *Journal of College Student Development, 33*(4), 356–62.

Parham, T. A., & Helms, J. E. (1981). The influence of Black students' racial identity attitudes on preferences for counselor's race. *Journal of Counseling Psychology, 28*(3), 250–257.

Poindexter-Cameron, J. M., & Robinson, T. L. (1997). Relationships among racial identity attitudes, womanist identity attitudes, and self-esteem in African American college women. *Journal of College Student Development, 38*(3), 288–296.

Sellers, R. M., Chavous, T. M., & Cooke, D. Y. (1998). Racial ideology and racial centrality as predictors of African American college students' academic performance. *Journal of Black Psychology, 24*(1), 8–27.

Sellers, R. M., Rowley, S. A. J., Chavous, T. M., Shelton, J. N., & Smith, M. A. (1997). Multidimensional inventory of Black identity: A preliminary investigation of reliability and construct validity. *Journal of Personality & Social Psychology, 73*(4), 805–815.

Sellers, R. M., Smith, M. A., Shelton, N. J., Rowley, S. A. J., & Chavous, T. M. (1998). Multidimensional model of racial identity: A reconceptualization of African American racial identity. *Personality and Social Psychology Review, 2*(1), 18–39.

Watson, L. W., & Kuh, G. D. (1996). The influence of dominant race environments on student involvement, perceptions, and educational gains: A look at historically black and predominantly white liberal arts institutions. *Journal of College Student Development, 37*(4), 415–424.

Woodson, C. G. (1933). *The Mis-Education of the Negro.* Trenton: Africa World Press.

Rodney K. Hopson

Dr. Rodney K. Hopson is an assistant professor in the Department of Foundations and Leadership at Duquesne University. In 1998, upon completion of his dissertation at the University of Virginia in the Department of Foundations, Leadership and Policy, he completed a year as a Postdoctoral Research Fellow in the Department of Social and Behavioral Sciences at the School of Hygiene and Public Health, Johns Hopkins University. Recently, he was named as Fellow to Pennsylvania Education Policy Fellowship Program for the 1999–2000 academic year. His research interests include social politics and policies, foundations of education, sociolinguistics, and ethnographic evaluation research.

Rodney has recently consulted for Baltimore City Health Department HIV/AIDS Prevention Division and two social service agencies in southwestern Pennsylvania that are developing charter-school proposals for local school districts in the area. He is currently working on manuscripts for publication addressing how language shapes the evaluation of social programs and policies, transformation of higher education in the Republic of Namibia, and public health prevention and intervention policy planning for youth criminality in the United States.

Rodney teaches a number of courses in the Department of Foundations and Leadership to students at both undergraduate and graduate levels. These include: i) Society, Politics, and the Teaching Profession, ii) Philosophical, Historical, Sociological Foundations of Education, iii) Educational Language Politics and Policies, and iv) Introduction to Program Evaluation and Planning.

He most recently participated in the 1999 Teaching with Technology Summer Institute and received a Presidential Scholarship awarded to Duquesne faculty for demonstration of research promise. His service accomplishments include: charter member of the Western Pennsylvania Evaluation Network, local affiliate of the American Evaluation Association, member of the Duquesne University Charter Schools Project Advisory Board, and volunteer health and physical education instructor at Ethnan Temple SDA Christian Elementary School.

Rodney is married to Wabei Siyolwe, and they live in Pittsburgh, Pennsylvania, with their two children, Hannibal and Habiba.

5

TOWARD THE LANGUAGE AND SCHOLARSHIP OF FREEDOM AND RESISTANCE

COMING TO TERMS WITH BEING A YOUNG, BLACK MALE ACADEMIC IN AMERICA

Rodney K. Hopson

The time has come, God knows, for us to examine ourselves, but we can only do this if we are willing to free ourselves of the myth of America and try to find out what is really happening here. (James Baldwin, "The Discovery of What it Means to Be an American" in *Nobody Knows My Name: More Notes of a Native Son*)

Coming to terms with being a young, Black male academic in America is like being perceived as a foreigner in a somewhat xenophobic country. This chapter is as much autobiographical as it is narrative about how my academic work, recent and anticipated, attempts to define my own path and the set of issues that I struggle with as a young, Black male academic in America. While exploring my own maturation in the academy from student to faculty member, I see the academy as an arena of sociopolitical struggle and transformation. The essay insinuates that Black males in the academy need to (continue to) be trailblazers within our own institutions of higher education in order to redefine and reconceptualize how experiences similar to ours find construction and legitimation in the academy.

This essay is laid out in three sections. The first section pays attention to teaching and learning experiences abroad in southern Africa that helped contribute to my approach to using a language of freedom and my resistance within the academy. The transforming nature of my visit allowed me to observe what is happening in the United States in order to develop an agenda for social action and change upon my return. The second section portrays the American cultural politics that surround African American men in our larger society, revealing the negative portrayals and spotlights that continue to face us in our everyday lives. The third section illustrates the conceptual lens in which I view how I come to terms with the challenges and hope to come to terms with being a young, Black male academic in America.

> To take part in the African revolution it is not enough to write a revolutionary song; you must fashion the revolution with the people. And if you fashion it with the people, the songs will come by themselves, and of themselves.
> In order to achieve real action, you must yourself be living part of Africa and of her thought; you must be an element of that popular energy which is entirely called forth for the freeing, the progress, and the happiness of Africa. There is no place outside that fight for the artist or for the intellectual who is not himself concerned with and completely at one with the people in the great battle of Africa and of suffering humanity. (Sekou Toure 1959 address in Rome to the Second Congress of Black Writers and Artists, in Fanon, 1963, p. 206)

It was there in the Republic of Namibia that I had true camaraderie and felt less like a stranger than in the country of my birth. Having recently become independent from South Africa when I arrived in January 1991, the countrymen in this southern African country clearly recognized the enemy during its extensive colonial legacy. Songs, chants, and poems attested to the freedom and struggle, the resistance and defiance of apartheid. I found myself singing and humming the same freedom songs that characterized oppositional culture of the pre-independent era. I sang in English, Oshiwambo, Otjiherero, and whatever language the lyrics were in, sometimes not knowing the literal meanings, but with full vigor and intensity, as if my own forefathers had died during war. We sang songs like,

> Toree thonjembo tu karwe ovita
> (Get all the soldiers so that we can go to war)
> Eta wasoldate, wa soldate vo Namibia
> (Bring the soldiers, the soldiers of Namibia)

(or)

Tara Ovakwaita va Namibia
(Look at the warriors of Namibia)
Namibia, Namibia, oretuveni
(Namibia is our country)
Sama Nujoma weikutura
(Sam Nujoma liberated it)
Namibia, Namibia Oretuveni
(Namibia is our country)

It was easy to identify with the spirit of independence and rebirth in this faraway place, largely because I could relate to their struggle against their oppressors. As I listened to the lyrics of freedom and resistance in this southwest country, I wondered how to take this spirit of Namibian independence and apply it to my own teaching at the Goas (R. C.) Primary School in Karibib. How could I impact, through my English lesson, this tradition of freedom and resistance to these boys, many of whom saw me as speaking the language they dreamed of speaking, the "language of liberation"? How could I, in this remote, semi-desert school community, invoke similar themes that had led to their own independence?

The decision to adopt English as the official language of independent Namibia was hailed as the key to liberation, freedom, and international exposure. It was imagined that the language would not only provide access to "a huge international knowledge-base, but would be a medium for building links with the other black southern African countries" (Caldwell, 1990:11). English was a neutral alternative to Oshiwambo, which was spoken by one third to one half of the population, and Afrikaans, which was not spoken outside southern Africa and remained a recurring symbol of apartheid.

As I reflected upon our own tradition as Americans of African descent, who also struggled and resisted White domination and oppression through song, poems, and spirituals, the answer to my question became clear. I found a language of freedom and resistance through which to communicate that would have more far-reaching results for my students than learning simply how to speak "good" English; I found a way for them to use their English to say more powerful things, such as in the words of Langston Hughes (1959, p. 289):

Remember you dark children in the world out there,
    Remember my pain, my sweat, my despair;
    Remember those years heavy with sorrow,
And make of those years a torch for tomorrow.
    Lift high your banner out of the dust.
    Stand like free men supporting your trust.

Hughes' poem was more than an exercise in learning English for the approximately fifty fifth graders who had to repeat it in front of the class. They had to say it to mean it, while reflecting upon the independence of their country and the hope of the southern African region.

Through the Lens of Freedom and Resistance

In search of freedom and resistance in the academy, I envision a significant part of the challenge involving finding conceptual lenses to explain social phenomena in my (and our) own fields. We, as African American faculty and educationists, make epistemological decisions when we assess what is knowledge in order to determine if a particular piece of information should be included in a syllabus or curriculum, or how our own beliefs are central to and influence classroom methods.

With my academic training in educational evaluation, sociolinguistics, and social policy, my efforts have been interdisciplinary. The basis for much of my work seeks to expose the inherent cultural hegemony that exists in American social institutions and to rethink ways to define methods and approaches that inform and empower groups that have been on the fringes and are marginalized in our society. Thus, I invoke approaches and theories of social and educational thinkers (and doers) who challenge and contest the traditional institutional and pedagogical practices that pervade American education and society.

The experiences in Namibia would be a precursor to my urge to develop a language and scholarship of resistance, struggle, and freedom within the walls of academe. What do I mean? I would certainly be setting myself up for my own academic death if I acquired an attitude of "I have arrived" to signify my faculty appointment. I had historic examples to remind me, from Malcolm X's joke—what do you call a Black man with a Ph.D.? A nigger—to my own experiences being searched by customs officials in Boston and Newark when I returned "home" for personal visits to family, to countless other reminders of how lower and higher education institutions have perpetuated exclusionary racist tactics to prevent Black folk and others from attending.

Rather, my own research interests and theoretical framework had to stem from what de la Luz Reyes and Halcon call "a recognition that we have endured racial discrimination and from a compelling need to lend a dimension of authenticity to the prevailing theories about our communities" (1988, p. 306). It meant that I would have to challenge negative and racist assumptions about our people's values, culture, and language in a scholarly way, unlike the primarily protest practices I had learned as an undergraduate at the

University of Virginia as head of the Black Student Alliance (although these, too, still serve appropriately in many instances). It also meant that I would have to realize that my success in the academy depended on my ability to wrestle with a tradition within the largely White, male-dominated profession that had historically manifested discriminatory policies and racism. De la Luz Reyes and Halcon also use a metaphor—a wolf in sheep's clothing—to describe the inherent racism of institutions of higher learning. Their perspective is based on those of Chicano faculty but could very easily apply to African Americans and particularly to young, Black males.

Jeannie Oakes and Martin Lipton (1999) critique in a similar way the myths and metaphors that shape American schooling, with the hope of revealing structural and societal happenings and creating a more socially just teaching profession and world. They identify two myths—the myth of merit and the myth of progress—and two metaphors: the factory metaphor and the market metaphor. The myth of merit stems from the meritocratic nature of our American society and suggests that "any one can grow up to be the president of the United States," while the myth of progress implies that each generation makes significant advances to understanding how to make sense of the world in which it lives. The factory metaphor suggests that schools inherited factory models of production and standardized methods of doing things to make them more efficient, and the market metaphor implies that schools are arenas for competition in a more global environment. In their description of each, Oakes and Lipton purport that the basic ideologies that help support the commitment to schooling and social reality of education in this country, paradoxically contribute to the legitimacy and inevitability of social and educational inequalities.

Let me expand the discussion of the myth of merit and illustrate how this ideology supports notions of social reproduction and cultural hegemony in schooling, culture, and society. Social reproduction theorists, influenced by the work of Max Weber (1970), Emile Durkheim (1953), and Karl Marx (1976), explore how social relations of capitalist societies are reproduced. Schooling arenas, often believed to be level playing fields where lower, working, middle, and upper classes can compete on equal bases, allow social inequalities to abound while pretending to do the opposite (Giroux, 1983; MacLeod, 1995). Reproduction theorists show that the culture and structure of schooling build mechanisms that constrain lower and working class individuals to advance into the upper divisions of the social class structure (Apple, 1996; Bourdieu, 1977).

MacLeod (1995) uses the concept to describe the perpetuation of social immobility, depressed aspirations, and poverty of two peer groups (one White and the other Black) of an inner-city housing project in a northeastern city by challenging the achievement ideology that dominates mainstream schooling and societal life. He suggests that this reigning social perspective, the achievement ideology, equates success with individual merit and differences and that economic inequality is based on ambition and ability (or lack thereof). While the achievement ideology rewards the "rags-to-riches" stories of individuals like Andrew Carnegie, MacLeod illuminates the voices of the socially marginalized youth to offer an appraisal of the American dream. He writes:

> What of Carnegie's grammar school classmates who labored in factories or pumped gas? For every Andrew Carnegie there are thousands of able and intelligent workers who were left behind to occupy positions in the class structure not much different from those held by their parents. What about the static, nearly permanent element in the working class, whose members consider the chances for mobility remote and thus depair of all hope? These people are shunned, hidden, forgotten—and for good reason—because just as the self-made individual is a testament to certain American ideals, so the very existence of an "underclass" in American society is a living contradiction to those ideals. (pp. 3–4)

Cultural hegemony refers to the procedure whereby ruling classes are able, not only by coercion but by acquiescence and conformity, to exert a general predominance over subordinate classes. This concept was influenced by Antonio Gramsci, an Italian revolutionary journalist and communist intellectual theorist who spoke to the importance of a cultural revolution for the purpose of understanding and defeating Italian fascism at the turn of the twentieth century. According to Gramsci hegemony involves the exercise of a power to frame alternatives, win and shape consent, and contain opportunities so that the granting of legitimacy to dominant groups and classes appear to be natural, normal, and beneficial (Clarke, Hall, Jefferson, & Roberts, 1975). In using the concept of cultural hegemony, Apple (1996) illustrates how today's neoconservatives and neoliberals in the United States control the discourse of groups to assert a uniform and homogenous American identity in schools and in the media.

Using Said's (1994) insights as a basis for understanding cultural politics in education, Apple suggests that neoconservatives and neoliberals have been effective in building hegemonic alliances (that is, of dominant economic and political elites, of largely white working-class and middle-class groups, of economic cultural conservatives, and a portion of the new middle class) to exacerbate social anxieties and fears in certain discourse and rhetoric. He summarizes that oppositional groups are created and highlighted—for example, the us-versus-them schism—as a result of the apparent loss of control of economic and personal security, knowledge and values, "sacred" texts and authority, and other social relationships and manifestations.

> Because so many parents are justifiably concerned about the economic and cultural features of their children—in an economy that is increasingly conditioned by lower wages, capital flight, and insecurity—rightist discourse connects with the experiences of many working class and middle class people . . . The binary opposition of we/they becomes important here. "We" are law abiding, "hard working, decent, virtuous, and homogeneous." The "theys" are very different. They are "lazy, immoral, permissive, and heterogeneous." These binary oppositions distance most people of color, women (i.e. "feminists"), gays and lesbians, and others from the community of worthy individuals . . . the "they's" are undeserving. They are getting something for nothing. Policies supporting them are "sapping our way of life" and most of our economic resources, and creating government control of our lives. (pp. 6–7)

To reiterate, the myth of merit involves the achievement ideology, the reigning perspective that sees American society as fair, open, and full of opportunity. It resounds within the assertion that "any child can grow up to be the president." This myth follows meritocracy and suggests that success is built upon individual action, that if one makes the "right" choices, anyone can succeed. It embodies the "rags-to-riches" story that so many in our country, our classrooms, and our boardrooms believe. Family and class background matter little within the myth of merit. Instead, education is the key for the more ambitious and abler to occupy the top rungs of society.

The contradiction of meritocracy, however, is salient and disturbing. While any child can grow up to be president, most do not. (In fact, as my son revealed to me recently based on his own discovery, "Babadi, there are no Black men presidents. Only White men." He did follow up with the promise that he would be the first and his sister would be the first Black woman president.) And while the rhetoric of equal opportunity, democracy, and prosperity surround the myth of merit, this language does not translate in most circumstances to equal results, freedom, and power. Whereas a swelling Black middle class has emerged as a result of social and educational policies aimed at correcting unequal conditions and repairing the merit ideology, measures such as civil rights, the war on poverty, and affirmative-action legislation are necessary, but woefully insufficient.

Besides a swelling Black middle class, there also has been a comparably swelling Black poor, which encompasses about one third of all Black families. Within Black families, more than half of all Black male adults of working age—between twenty-five and thirty-four—are either jobless or underemployed. The plight of Black men is even more vivid when we notice that while 23,000 received a college diploma in 1993, according to Gates and West (1996, p. 25), 2.3 million were sent to jail or prison.

The American belief that success in school and life follows from individual ability and aspirations not only camouflages the fact that children and individuals from privileged backgrounds are favored in our larger social structure but it also typically blames low-income and other disadvantaged children for their own inadequacies. In reflecting upon the disintegration of social organization in inner-city ghetto neighborhoods and how these neighborhoods are infested with rampant poverty, escalating ethnic and racial tensions, and heightened economic insecurities, William Julius Wilson (1997) highlights how negative racial rhetoric has exacerbated tensions and frustrations toward a segment of our society, much of which is Black and male.

> As the new urban poverty has sapped the vitality of many inner-city communities, many of the messages associate inner-city crisis, family breakdown and welfare receipt with individual shortcoming. Blame the victim arguments resonate with many urban Americans because of their own simplicity. They not only reinforce the salient belief that joblessness and poverty reflect individual inadequacies, but discourage support for new and stronger programs to combat inner-city social dislocation as well. (p. 294)

Hence, it is little surprise that savage inequalities exist in many of our urban schools, as documented earlier this decade by Jonathan Kozol (1991), and that those from privileged locations often see their individual success as a result of their own hard work and those from impoverished locations often see their individual inadequacies as less related to societal and structural inadequacies that exist. Cultural deprivation theory, the theory that purports that differences in educational achievement of Black and White children were mediated by differences in home background, resounds with privileged voices in New York within Kozol's book. In suburban Rye, New York, where a decade ago yearly spending per pupil exceeded $9,000 (compared to over $5,000 in New York City), students had much to say about the nature of their programs and academic achievements at their landscaped campus, which resembled a New England prep school. In response to one of Kozol's questions regarding present educational inequalities in poor and rich school districts, the comments of one privileged student, Jennifer, reveal the cultural deficit theory that still reverberates today: "It has to be the people in the area who want an education. If your parents just don't care, it won't do any good to spend a lot of money. Someone else can't want a good life for you. You have got to want it for yourself" (Kozol, 1991, p. 128). This seemingly harmless perception echoes those of deficit-scholar theorists who still continue to insist that culturally deprived students are disadvantaged due to their own impoverished, inner-city surroundings, and reinforces the meritocratic nature of our American society.

Carol Camp Yeakey's and Edmund Gordon's seminal essay nearly two decades ago paints a picture for how basic American ideologies and notions deserve critique. They provide a backdrop for understanding what is happening to lower-status persons (Native Americans, Blacks, lower-status Whites, and Hispanics) in public schools by reviewing the origins and implications of the dominant theory of educability in this country. Upheld by educators, psychologists, and behavioral and social scientists, the prevailing theory (a derivative of Plato's theory of educability that submits differentiation of social classes through schooling and other manifestations) reveals that "the limits of educability are predetermined by the genes inherited from one's parents at the moment of conception and the approximate level of lifetime ability is measurable in childhood" (1981, p. 108). The implications, as the authors continue, are most revealing: "America's school system is founded on this belief and the schooling of all children is influenced by a theory of intelligence that has demanded the use of intelligence tests, tracking, ability grouping, and labeling distinctions designed to select and sort out" (p. 108).

When viewing the myths and ideologies that shape American schooling, moving toward the language of freedom inextricably involves situating lenses of political action and resistance. In one real sense, it could not be more American for us as Black faculty men to surround ourselves with theories and conceptions of freedom. As Maxine Greene, writes of Thomas Jefferson, for instance, "It should be clear that, as Jefferson saw it, the concept of freedom was associated with a concept of action" (1988, p. 28). In another sense, however, the concept of freedom, paradoxically (as she understands) has meant that Black folk can "alter situations by reinterpreting them and, by so doing, seeing oneself as a person in a new perspective. Once that happens, there are new beginnings, new actions to undertake in the world" (p. 90). For many Black faculty men, reinterpreting freedom is close to that of Frederick Douglass' conception: continual resistance and agitation against oppression.

Conclusions

It is difficult to sit idly in a windowed office facing the central quadrangle, adjacent to the older historic building and chapel, without giving thought to what is happening, as Baldwin purports, concerning the role of schooling as a means toward equal opportunity and elevating social class position. As a Black faculty member, I posit that our struggle to democratize the academy and world lies in language and lenses of freedom. It is through these lenses that social reality and struggle are revealed as manners of looking toward hope for social change and freedom.

References

Apple, M. W. (1996). *Cultural politics and education.* New York: Columbia University Teacher's College Press.

Baldwin, J. (1961). *Nobody knows my name: More notes of a native son.* New York: Dell.

Bourdieu, P. (1977). Cultural reproduction and social reproduction. In J. Karabel and A. H. Halsey (Eds.), *Power and ideology in education.* New York: Oxford University Press.

Caldwell, K. (1990, July 27) Eager to adopt the language of liberation. *The Times Educational Supplement.*

Cole, D. (1999). The color of justice. *The Nation, 269*(11), 12–15.

Clarke, J., Hall, S., Jefferson, T., & Roberts, B. (1975). Subcultures, cultures, and class: A theoretical overview. In S. Hall & T. Jefferson (Eds.), *Resistance through rituals: Youth subcultures in postwar Britain.* London: Hutchinson.

de la Luz Reyes, M. & Halcon, J. (1988). Racism in the academy—The old wolf revisited. *Harvard Educational Review, 58*(3), 299–314.

Durkheim, E. (1953). *The division of labor in society.* New York: Free Press.

Fanon, F. (1963). *The wretched of the earth.* New York: Grove Weidenfeld.

Gates, H. L., Jr., & West, C. (1996). *The future of the race.* New York: Alfred Knopf.

Greene, M. (1988). *The dialectic of freedom.* New York: Teacher's College Press.

Hughes, L. (1959). *Selected poems of Langston Hughes.* Toronto: Plato Press.

Kozol, J. (1991). *Savage inequalities: Children in America's Schools.* New York: Crown.

MacLeod, Jay (1995). *Ain't no makin' it: Aspirations and attainment in a low-income neighborhood.* Boulder, CO: Westview.

Marx, K. (1976). *Capital.* Harmondsworth: Penguin.

Oakes, J., & Lipton, M. (1999). *Teaching to change the world.* Boston: McGraw-Hill.

Said, E. W. (1994). *Culture and imperialism.* New York: Alfred Knopf.

Weber, M. (1970). *Economy and society.* Berkeley: University of California Press.

White, A. F. (1999). Ragtime, my time. *The Nation, 269*(11), 11–12.

Wilson, W. J. (1997). The political economy and urban racial tensions. In J. H. Skolnick & E. Currie (Eds.), *Crisis in American institutions* (10th ed.). New York: Longman.

Yeakey, C. C., & Gordon, E. W. (1981). The policy implications of status variables and schooling. In A. Lieberman and M. W. McLaughlin (Eds.), *Policy making in Education* (pp. 105–132). Chicago: University of Chicago Press.

Larry L. Rowley

Dr. Larry L. Rowley received a bachelor of arts degree in speech communication from Old Dominion University in 1991; he earned a master of education degree in social foundations in 1995 and a doctor of philosophy degree in higher education in 1999, both from the University of Virginia. Dr. Rowley's research incorporates theoretical perspectives of educational foundations (that is, social, historical, and cultural theories) into empirical and interpretive analysis of contemporary higher education issues, policies, and organizations. His research and writing includes projects that examine African American issues in higher education, trends in American and African American intellectual cultures and hierarchies, relationships between urban universities and communities, and social and organizational analyses of higher education institutions. He has recently published research and reviews in *The Journal of Negro Education* and *The Urban Review*. His professional and scholarly affiliations include membership in the American Educational Research Association, the American Academy of Political and Social Science, and the Omicron Delta Kappa national honor society. Dr. Rowley has held research positions at the Sanford Institute of Public Policy at Duke University, at the American Association of State Colleges and Universities, and at the University of Virginia. He has held administrative positions and internships at the Urban Investment Strategies Center at UNC-Chapel Hill, the Piedmont Virginia Community College Neighborhood Center, at the Curry School of Education at the University of Virginia, and at Old Dominion University. Dr. Rowley is married to Dr. Stephanie Johnson Rowley, a developmental psychologist at UNC-Chapel Hill. They have one son, Lawrence Jacob Rowley.

6

AFRICAN AMERICAN MEN IN HIGHER EDUCATION

HISTORICAL, CULTURAL, AND SOCIAL REFLECTIONS FOR MASTERING THE DIALECTICAL CHALLENGES

Larry L. Rowley

> Our educational institutions must graduate to the world men fitted to take their place in real life by their knowledge, spirit, and ability to do what the world wants done.
>
> W. E. B. DuBois
> *The Education of Black People*

Introduction

At their most basic levels, the issues, problems, and challenges of African American men in higher education are extensions of underlying historical, cultural, and social realities. The renowned African American diplomat and scholar Ralph Bunche made the following assertion regarding education, American society, and African Americans:

> Enlightened opinion in present-day America accepts it as axiomatic that education is and should be intimately related to all of the forces at work in our social order. The education of Negroes is inextricably tied up with the group status of Negroes, with their economic condition, their political position, and their cultural relations to other groups. (1936, p. 351)

Bunche, ever the consummate political scientist, knew that the various social and political institutions that collectively make up American education were central to the development of nearly every aspect of American society. In fact, education is not only shaped by society but it also shapes society. As such, Bunche captured the essence of the social foundations of American education. Moreover, he realized that the advancement of African Americans is intimately related to our ability to acquire and maximize the benefits of education. Yet our precarious existential position within American society serves to make our educational advancement as African Americans extremely difficult. Today, over six decades after Bunche made these observations, our educational experiences as African American men in higher education continue to be powerfully impacted by the complex array of historical, cultural, and social developments that have molded the American academy as well as our place in contemporary American society. As we shall see, the mores and traditions of the academy are often somewhat problematic or contradictory to the dispositions, experiences, and outlooks of African American men. As a result, the challenges associated with pursuit of advanced academic degrees and professional positions in higher education by African American men have proven to be rather strenuous and dialectical in nature. These challenges, their foundations, and strategies for mastering them are the focus of this essay.

In keeping with the theme of this volume and drawing upon my graduate training and experiences in social foundations and higher education,[1] this essay is comprised of informed reflections on various dimensions of American higher education that continue to present psychological and social challenges to African American men. The analysis focuses primarily on African American men in graduate school and those embarking upon careers in the academy as either scholars or administrators. The core of the reflections presented is centered around the social-foundations perspective of American higher education as described by Bunche (1936) and derived from the persistent internal conflicts experienced by African American men in both graduate school and professional experiences in American higher education institutions. The ultimate goal of this paper is to reflect on these conditions in a manner that will encourage further scholarly analysis of the issues and, subsequently, collaboration and mentoring among African American men with their colleagues and students in hopes of improving their quality of life within the academy.

---

1. My personal academic and professional experiences have been confined to predominantly White research universities. Therefore, this essay focuses primarily on that academic institutional context.

A Note on Dialectical Challenges

Throughout this essay, I refer to what I am calling "dialectical challenges" of African American men in higher education. Cognizant of the risk of oversimplifying a complex philosophical system, *dialectics* can be defined here as a system of interpretation characterized by propositions of existence (theses) that are continually presented with other contradictory propositions (antitheses) and which can only be reconciled by the synthesis of the two. Once a synthesis is reached, the process recurs again and again. In the case of African American men in higher education, the challenges that we face are inherently contradictory and dualistic. Much of what makes up the culture, traditions, and mores of the American academy come into heightened levels of conflict with parts of our personal, familial, or communal cultures. Yet, if we want to be participants in academic life or to acquire the benefits and privileges associated with advanced education, we must confront and master these challenges. I am by no means the first nor am I likely to be the last African American man to pen reflections on these challenges. Other reflective essays with titles like "A Life of Learning," "The Challenge of a Black Scholar," "The Vocation of the Black Scholar," "The Dilemma of the Black Intellectual," and Harold Cruse's magnum opus *The Crisis of the Negro Intellectual* have contributed to my appreciation of the dialectical challenges of African American men in higher education (Cruse, 1967; Franklin, 1995; Harding, 1974; Hare, 1995; West, 1993).

I have endeavored to encapsulate the core dimensions of these dialectical challenges, as well as appropriate responses to them, within the quotes that serve as an epigraph to this essay. First, as noted by DuBois, we must acknowledge that the raison d'être of higher education institutions is to acquire and pass on to others the "knowledge, spirit, and ability" to make ourselves, our families, our communities, and our world better. We do this by developing our minds and applying our talents to the problems of our people. Secondly, Cruse teaches us that we must come to grips with the reality that we as African American men have historically and systematically been excluded from the privileges of higher learning. This continues to be true today, albeit by different methods and for peculiarly different and unfathomable reasons. As such, if we hope to be true to the "calling of higher education," we are forced to navigate both the culture of the academy as well as the various realities and dimensions of African American culture. Perhaps the most difficult reality to acknowledge is that harsh truth of which Harding (1974) has reminded us, which is that although we are students, scholars, and administrators *within* the academy, our primary responsibilities in large measure lie *outside* of the academy. Finally, as James (1903) has so eloquently put it, in order to maintain the proper perspective, we must be reflective and critical of both our behavioral and experiential processes within America higher education, lest we think too highly or too little of ourselves.

Some Recent Statistical Trends

According to recently published data sources (Nettles & Perna, 1997; Nettles, Perna, & Freeman, 1999), there has been much progress on the part of African Americans in higher education overall. However, the percentage increase in higher education degree attainment by African American men is reflective of some problematic trends. For example, between 1976 and 1994 the increase in percentage of baccalaureate degrees received by African American men (19.6 percent) lagged considerably behind that of African American women (55.4 percent). In graduate-degree attainment, nearly twice as many African American women received master's degrees (13,890) as African American men received master's degrees (7,002). Perhaps most important are the trends in doctoral degree awarded to African American men and the number of faculty positions they occupy. The good news is that the total number of African American doctoral degrees increased by 54 percent between 1987 and 1996. The bad news is that African Americans receive only 3.0 percent of the nation's doctoral degrees. Even more problematic is the fact that only 13.5 percent of African Americans in full-time faculty positions are employed in research universities versus 24.1 percent of White men. Also important for issues of socialization and mentoring, which are discussed later in this essay, is the fact that only 45 percent of full-time African American male faculty, versus 60.8 percent of White male faculty, hold doctoral degrees. These statistical trends are only one aspect of the problem. I would like now to focus on strategies for how to reflect upon these challenges.

Reflecting upon History for Comprehension

It will be immediately evident, upon perusal of this section, that I cannot claim to have mastered the methodological or conceptual skills of a trained historian. Nevertheless, in my intellectual academic sojourn, I have read and benefited greatly from the work of historians. The analyses of various historians have, to varying degrees, strengthened my understanding and interpretation of historical developments in higher education that are relevant to the discussion at hand. In this section I highlight the importance of incorporating the insights of educational, social, and intellectual historians into our efforts to understand and survive the challenges we currently face within American higher education.

As professional scholars and educators, we as African American men stand to gain quite a bit from reading the writings of Black historians who have reflected on the nature and concerns of the academic milieu as it relates to the Black community. For me, the reflections of African American historians such as Harold Cruse, Vincent Harding, W. E. B. DuBois, C. L. R. James, David Levering Lewis, and John Hope Franklin are indispensable instruments for fully comprehending and mastering the dialectical challenges. In his seminal theoretical work, *The Crisis of the Negro Intellectual,* Cruse (1967) argued that while African American intellectuals and scholars ". . . are busy trying to interpret the nature of the black world and its aspirations to the whites, they should, in fact, be defining their own roles" (p. 455). For those of us in higher education, it is impossible to do this without first taking note of the lessons of history. I hasten to note, however, that as we work to construct an arsenal of historical knowledge to assist our comprehension of academe, it would be foolish to limit our pursuits to the writings of African American scholars. The writings of several White historians have been useful to me in my quest to understand academic culture more fully. Historians who have examined the American university (Bender, 1988; Rudolph, 1990; Veysey, 1965), social theory (Burke, 1992), and intellectual life (Bender, 1993; Schlesinger & White, 1963; Levine, 1996) have been particularly valuable. I should point out that almost none of these historical citations were introduced to me as part of the required reading for my graduate course requirements. I have learned that one's real education begins once dissertations are defended or after tenure has been granted. These phases of our higher education experiences should be seen for what they are: apprenticeships in an academic guild. I shall have more to say about the guild-like nature of the academy later. For now suffice it to say that personal reading and reflection on history is crucial for African American graduate students and junior faculty to maximize their understanding of and success within the culture of higher education.

When I entered graduate school in 1994 to pursue a master of education degree in social foundations, I instantly realized that I knew almost nothing about the contextual history of African Americans in higher education. My understanding of the historical sacrifices made by African Americans to acquire higher education was severely limited. By reading history I began to fully appreciate the sacrifices that made it possible for me to get a college degree, work in university admissions, and attend graduate school at one of the nation's best universities. Learning our history enables us to know the proud and determined tradition from which we come. Carter G. Woodson's

Education of the Negro Prior to 1861 (1919) taught me that if Black men were acquiring medical degrees at Bowdoin College as early as 1849, surely I could complete a master's degree in 1995. When John Hope Franklin wrote about leaving Harvard and journeying south "to seek a teaching position and complete my dissertation *in absentia*" (1995, p. 712), history taught me that I could move to Durham, North Carolina with my wife (as she started her career in academe) and still successfully complete my dissertation requirements for the University of Virginia. In other words, when reflected upon with the proper level of criticism and scrutiny, the lessons of history have some very practical and personal uses for African American men in higher education.

From a more intellectual standpoint, historical analyses of higher education and African American history can also enlighten one's mind to the political, cultural, and economic contexts that have shaped our contemporary challenges. Several examples will serve to illustrate my point. Just as the history of Southern race politics continues to impact national politics in the United States, the history of Southern race relations and educational politics is crucial to contemporary American educational politics. Having simply a basic historical knowledge and understanding of the role of the Freedmen's bureau teaches us that federal intervention and policies have a long and justifiable history in the education of African Americans (Anderson, 1988; Logan, 1997). From a cultural historian's viewpoint, the culture wars in the academy, which often focus on race and collegiate curricula, are not new. Instead, they are different versions of the battles over academic freedom, course requirements, and core knowledge that have always been present in American higher education. From this historical approach, these developments can be viewed as normal, healthy developments along the way to our institutions becoming more inclusive of the voices of African Americans and other racial and ethnic groups (Levine, 1996). Knowing that the public service mission of higher education had its foundations in the early nineteenth century provides a historical rationale for what many see today as either unnecessary or unjustifiable (Rudolph, 1990). And finally, social history that examines the institutional lives of non-Black academic intellectuals such as E. R. A. Seligman, Charles A. Beard, Lionel Trilling, and C. Wright Mills proves of high value (Bender, 1993). This type of history instructs us that there have always been difficulties and political dualities for those who endeavor to participate fully in the professional realms of both intellect *and* public life. In a later section of this essay, I will explore this notion utilizing historical biographies of three prominent African American scholars.

These are just a few of the ways in which historical reading and reflection can be useful to those of us who find ourselves in a place where we feel torn in several different directions. In short, history can help us to step outside of ourselves and to understand that we are not the first to have these challenges, whatever they may be. By this type of reflection we are also enabled to keep things in perspective. Ultimately, there are many more benefits to historical reflection by African American men in higher education than can be addressed here. However, as the next section of this paper will illustrate, the history and culture of higher education are very closely related to each other. Therefore, there should be no clear demarcation or sharp distinctions made between the two as we endeavor to utilize the practice of informed reflection to master the challenges we face. Rather, we should approach the issues in a holistic manner that takes into account the fluidity of personal introspection and external observations.

Reflecting upon Academic Culture and Socialization

There are many persistent cultural traditions of the American academy that have proven to be problematic to African American men. The culture and traditions are not necessarily problematic in and of themselves. However, the adverse or unintended outcomes sometimes associated with academic culture should be examined and reflected upon by those who currently work and study within that culture. It will be helpful to take a look at how these cultural traditions have developed. According to Bender (1993):

> Men and women of ideas work within a social matrix that constitutes an audience or public for them. Within this context they seek legitimacy and are supplied the collective concepts, the vocabulary of motives, and the key questions that give shape to their work. These communities of discourse . . . *cultures of intellectual life are* historically constructed and are held together by attachment to a cluster of shared meanings and intellectual purposes. They socialize the life of the mind and give institutional force to the paradigms that guide the creative intellect. (emphasis in original, pp. 3–4)

In other words, the culture of intellectual or academic life entails a shared understanding among its members such that anyone who desires to succeed must be aware of and "play by the rules." In order to do this, one must be properly socialized. This socialization process begins (or should begin) in graduate school. It is in graduate school that one's academic apprenticeship begins. As noted by Wagoner and Kellams (1992), "without the 'academic guild,' there could be no university as we know it" (p. 1674). In the plainest sense of the word, a *guild* is an institution that has hierarchical training and socialization methods.

Arguably, the major cultural tradition of the academy that "gives institutional force" to its guild-like structure is the preeminence of the Ph.D. degree. From its inception "the idea of the Ph.D. fired the imagination of academics" (Storr, 1973, p. 48). It should be noted, however, that the notion and institution of the Ph.D. has also been attacked almost from the very beginning. One of the best-known examples was "The Ph.D. Octopus" (James, 1903). The arduous process of obtaining the Ph.D. or its equivalent should logically include the initial stages of socialization necessary for future success within the academy. The problem, however, is that the "pursuit of the Ph.D." often entails overly high levels of despair, attrition, and mental burnout of doctoral students (Bowen & Rudenstine, 1992). These pitfalls are all too common for graduate students in general. However, the problems encountered in graduate school along these avenues are even more problematic for African American men. The reason for this trend is usually inadequate, inappropriate, or nonexistent socialization to the mores of academic culture.

West (1993) has succinctly observed that, "the African American who takes seriously the life of the mind inhabits an isolated and insulated world . . . not of their own choosing" (p. 67). He has further noted that a decision to become a scholar by an African American today is more difficult than during the days when Black undergraduates were not admitted to the elite White colleges and universities. During the years prior to the sixties, Black students who decided to pursue careers in higher education were initially nurtured in one of the nation's Black colleges. They pursued graduate study in leading White institutions under the tutelage of "liberal, sympathetic scholars, often of renowned stature" (p. 68). That type of arrangement produced many of the most renowned African American scholars of the twentieth century, including W. E. B. DuBois, John Hope Franklin, and E. Franklin Frazier. According to West (1993), however, in contemporary graduate school settings, the conditions are quite different because:

> Ironically, the present-day academy . . . present[s] more obstacles for young blacks than those in decades past. . . . First, the attitudes of white scholars in the academy are quite different from those in the past. It is much more difficult for black students, especially graduate students, to be taken seriously as *potential scholars and intellectuals* owing to the managerial ethos of our universities and colleges (in which less time is spent with students) and to the vulgar (racist) perceptions fueled by affirmative action programs which pollute many black student-white professor relations. (emphasis in original, pp. 68–69)

The absence of proper socialization and mentoring presents a "challenge to ethical teaching" on the part of White professors who are very likely to serve as advisors to African American students in graduate and professional degree programs (Harris, 1990). If contemporary academic culture was amenable to the ethical teaching and socialization of African American students, the benefits would accrue to both the students and the faculty. The faculty member who advises African American students ". . . would be free of the prison of racism and cultural dominance that serves to limit his potential for productivity" and students would ". . . acquire the means to solve effectively professional problems" and ". . . provide professional leadership modeled for the good" (Harris, 1990, pp. 167–168). If the proper socialization to academic culture is lacking, then African American men have less of a chance to succeed. As a result, many of those who actually begin pursuit of academic degrees or careers in higher education do not complete their journeys.

At this point, it is appropriate to reflect more closely upon the importance of mentoring. Mentoring is so crucial to sustaining diversity initiatives in higher education that a series of cross-disciplinary conversations at the annual meetings of the American Educational Research Association has spurred a multivolume series on the topic. The series edited by Henry Frierson, an African American education professor at the University of North Carolina at Chapel Hill, includes a variety of insightful reflections on academic culture and mentoring. In one of the most relevant chapters in volume one, Reginald Wilson, former senior scholar at the American Council on Education, made some poignant observations. He noted that although most studies on academic mentoring focus on its positive impact, there is a need to reflect upon and conduct research on the negative consequences of mentoring, especially for minorities. This type of mentoring, which African American men in graduate school are often likely to encounter, includes 1) lowering expectations in the classroom; 2) advising students to consider majors that are lower than their ability; and 3) reinforcing already low self-concept rather than challenging students to aim higher (Wilson, 1997, p. 178). Each of these forms of negative mentoring can serve to have a profound effect on the career aspirations and academic achievements of African American men in higher education. Wilson (1997) also argued that the preponderance of negative mentoring of minorities occurs in graduate study, postgraduate study, and in entry-level academic positions. As a result, one can easily come to the conclusion that African American male graduate students and junior faculty members are in particularly strong need of good-quality mentoring.

The above aspects of academic culture focus largely upon the actions of faculty members as individuals. However, Moses (1990) has argued that in order to enhance diversity in higher education, there are also some things that must be done at the institutional or structural level. There are several areas in which the structure of academic culture must be adjusted; they include 1) leadership from the top, 2) faculty governance, 3) faculty/student relations, and 4) academic hiring practices (Moses, 1990, pp. 407–408). The dialectical challenges of African American faculty members related to mentoring are as follows: 1) they may be seen by colleagues as neglecting other students if they spend their time cultivating relationships with Black students; 2) they run the risk of not gaining tenure if they spend too much time on mentoring rather than writing and publishing; and 3) they may be seen as "selling out" if they spend time mentoring students who are not Black.

Reflecting upon Our Social Positions and Responsibilities

In this section, I first examine the social positions and responsibilities of African American scholars and then I present a conceptual framework for examining the three primary dimensions of professional life in the academy via brief biographies. I employ three historically prominent African American scholars as prototypical exemplars that serve to vividly illustrate the dialectical nature of the social position of African American men in higher education vis-à-vis their social commitments to improving the overall quality of life in the African American community. As noted earlier, this essay's epigraph alludes to what I see as the ultimate aim of our work as African American men in higher education. From the standpoint of history, the transcendent aim of the African American scholar or administrator should be to further the collective advancement of Black people in American society. This fundamental truth should never be avoided, nor should it be seen as contradictory to the mission of higher education. Somewhat ironically an African American scholar, who in my estimation has most succinctly articulated this imperative, is a woman. Joyce Ladner described the social responsibilities of African American scholars and their compatibility with the aims of the academy as follows:

> I believe the academy has a responsibility to promote social change; that knowledge should be used where possible to solve social problems . . . and that we should not and do not have to sacrifice good scholarship in the process of carrying out our social responsibil-

ities . . . Social problems that face black communities today must be addressed with the resources in higher education. (1996, pp. 20–21)

It is precisely the social responsibilities of academy as articulated by Ladner and other African American scholars that present the major dialectical challenge to African American men in higher education. In our educational and professional pursuits, we must always choose the route that does the most good and the least amount of harm to ourselves and to our people. Since education is itself a dialectical entity, this is often very difficult to do. When one adds to this difficulty the condition of being African American, the job becomes twice as hard. The following observation about the aims of education by Donald Smith recounted in Gbadegesin (1996) serves to further highlight the point:

> Education is the most powerful social force in the history of humankind. It may be used to empower or to enslave, to enlighten or to mystify, to clarify or to confuse, to ennoble or to dehumanize, but education is never neutral. (p. 30)

I believe this assertion to be true, and as a result, a large part of my own personal research and writing agenda has explored the public-service mission of higher education and the social responsibilities of African American scholars (Rowley, 1996, 1999; Rowley & Walker, 1999). I have also spent quite a bit of time studying how other African American scholars have navigated their way through the ever-present maze of dialectical challenges. As both historical and cultural reflections have shown us, the social position of African Americans in higher education necessarily brings with it an imperative for service and social commitment. Since DuBois penned his essay "The Talented Tenth" in 1903, we as a community of African American students, scholars, and administrators have consistently grappled with our social responsibilities in relation to the rest of the African American community (Gates & West, 1996). There has been no consensus, per se, on how best to fulfill that responsibility, but it is comforting to know that we diligently continue to grapple with how to address issues of poverty, racism, and injustice that continue to afflict the masses of our brethren.

Interestingly enough, in my reflections while writing this essay, I was struck by the tremendous historical ramifications of the dialectical challenges that I have been describing. There are no doubt dozens upon dozens of our predecessors who have faced similar challenges. However, three African American scholars in particular will be useful for constructing a framework from which to reflect and to which we might compare our own situations. Each of these men, in various ways, experienced the challenge of being one of very few Black men during his day to be fully engaged in higher education. In similar fashion, each of these gentlemen found himself struggling to determine the course of action for him within higher education that would be most beneficial to his desire to advance the causes of African American people. I will briefly discuss each man's professional positions and dialectical challenges as they related to his personal and professional commitments to African Americans.

W. E. B. DuBois: Scholar/Activist

Although it was only part of the complexity of the man, DuBois is best known to many for his discussion of the "double consciousness" faced by African Americans who wish to lose neither their African identity nor their American identity. Stewart (1983) most clearly analyzed the dimensions of psychic duality of DuBois in his classic review of DuBois's novels. In the conclusion of that article, Stewart called for development of new strategies to address contemporary problems associated with "double-consciousness." This essay's encouragement of historical, cultural, and social reflection is one step in that direction.

More directly relevant to African American men in higher education was DuBois's argument that African American scholars, academic journals, and higher education institutions should be sources of both scholarship and propaganda (DuBois, 1944). In fact, DuBois was at least cognizant of the dual dimensions of African American scholarship when he researched and wrote about Blacks in Philadelphia for the University of Pennsylvania in 1899. In *The Philadelphia Negro,* DuBois was torn between his personal goals for the book and those of the College Settlement Association, which commissioned him to conduct the research. As a result of this dialectical tension:

> . . . it would be necessary to write what amounted almost to two books in one—one that would not be immediately denounced or ridiculed by the arbiters of mainstream knowledge, influence, and order for its transparent heterodoxy; and a second one that would, over time, deeply penetrate the social sciences and gradually improve race-relations policy through its not-immediately, apparent interpretive radicalism. (Lewis, 1993, p. 189)

DuBois, who was quite enamored of academic life, held faculty or research positions at Wilberforce University, the University of Pennsylvania, and twice at Atlanta University. However, after seeing the partial remains of a lynched Black man on display in a store window, he was convinced that the approach of scientific scholarship must give way to racial propaganda. As such, here was a man who in essence went back and forth from the halls of academe to involvement in civil rights and political organizations throughout most of his adult life. However, he always did both in efforts to improve the conditions of Black people and other disadvantaged persons the world over.

John Hope: Administrator/Race Leader

According to Davis (1998), the late John Hope, who served as president of both Morehouse College and Atlanta University, experienced a "clashing of the soul." The dilemmas or dialectical challenges that made up this clashing were twofold. "First, there was the inner turmoil that resulted from attempting to balance . . ." the dual roles of college president and race leader (Davis, 1998, p. xxiv). In this challenge he often lost prominent faculty members and administrators to race-advancement organizations like the NAACP. His second dialectical challenge was that of determining when to be the militant Black leader and when to be the moderate educational leader. The latter was often necessary during the era of Booker T. Washington in order to secure money from White philanthropists for his institutions. This tendency to lean more toward a conservative leadership style on educational issues often put him at odds with some of the leaders of the New Negro Movement, including his good friend W. E. B. DuBois. Despite these dilemmas, rarely, if ever, has his commitment to the education and advancement of African Americans been questioned. This aspect of John Hope's dilemmas is instructive to contemporary African American college presidents who are largely saddled with fundraising but who are also expected to be powerful leadership voices in their communities.

Hope also contended with other dilemmas. These included deciding whether or not he should go into the ministry or pass for White. He chose to do neither. As an African American man who could pass for White, who received a degree from Brown University, and who had taken graduate courses at the University of Chicago, he could likely have done quite well for himself by choosing to take either of those alternate paths. However, his commitment to African American people appears to have been preeminently important in his personal decisions. For this type of personal and professional commitment, he should be respected and held up as an example for those of us who currently labor in the academy.

Horace Mann Bond: Scholar/Administrator

Horace Mann Bond's major dialectical challenge throughout his career was that his desire to work mainly as a scholar was unfulfilled because the tenor of the times in which he lived made it nearly impossible for him to do so. His personal commitments to higher education also served to draw him into positions of academic administration. He served as president of both Fort Valley State College and Lincoln University. Despite beginning his career as a professor, the call of duty kept Bond from committing himself to scholarship full time. As I am certain many scholars-turned-administrators of today will attest, it is extremely difficult to find time to read, conduct research, and to write if one has full-time administrative responsibilities. Yet Bond continued to write on academic subjects and to publish a few items during the times that he served as president (Urban, 1992).

On the final page of his important book on Horace Mann Bond, Urban (1992) presents his summation of Bond by reflecting upon Bond's insightful assessment of Black nationalist scholar Martin Delany, who was one of Harvard University's first three Black medical students:

> [Delany] "acquired an international reputation as a scholar." However, he wound up abandoning these areas of accomplishment, because, according to Bond, "the usual fate of the Negro made it necessary for him to enter the cause of racial polemics and advancement." Ironically, Horace Bond's characterization of Delany and his fate could just as fittingly describe what happened to Bond himself in the final decades of his life. (p. 213)

This assessment of our "usual fate" as African Americans points us once again to those commitments, crises, and dilemmas about which DuBois, Cruse, and Harding have instructed us. In both his academic writings and his role as an institutional leader, Bond worked diligently to ensure that African Americans had the best and most equitable educational opportunities possible. We can learn a lot about being scholars, administrators, or both from each of these men. The examples they set show us the way to reflect and to act in our own positions. Their lives demonstrate three things very clearly. First, there should be no separation between our personal and professional commitments that would undermine our call to service. Second, they show us that the dialectical challenges to us as African American men in higher education, though painful, are intimately related to our levels of commitment to service. Third, there is often significant overlap in higher education among scholarship, activism, and administration, which we must embrace rather than setting up antagonistic oppositions that only serve to divide us and to undermine our collective success and well-being.

Conclusion

There are obviously more challenges to our situations in higher education than I have room to reflect upon here. My only hope is that my efforts to share how I view our positions and how I view our responsibilities will help other Brothers to know that the risks are worth taking and the battles are worth fighting. If we do not do that which needs to be done for ourselves and for our people, it is unlikely that anyone else will. We cannot and should not hope to ever be rid of the imperative commitments to racial advancement no matter how unfair or difficult they may seem. If I am truly honest with the readers of this essay, I must candidly admit that I would not have it any other way. I am encouraged by projects like this book, and I am energized by the drive and determination of countless individual African American men who are equally as committed to moral rectitude, academic integrity, and social commitment. Most of all, I am truly blessed to have had the opportunity to learn and to share.

References

Anderson, J. D. (1988). *The education of Blacks in the South, 1860–1935.* Chapel Hill, NC: University of North Carolina Press.

Bender, T. (1988). *The university and the city: From medieval origins to the president.* New York: Oxford University Press.

Bender, T. (1993). *Intellect and public life: Essays on the social history of academic intellectuals in the United States.* Baltimore & London: Johns Hopkins University Press.

Bowen, W. G., & Rudenstine, N. (1992). *In pursuit of the Ph.D.* Princeton, NJ: Princeton University Press.

Bunche, R. (1936). Education in black and white. *Journal of Negro Education, 5,* 351–358.

Burke, P. (1992). *History and social theory.* Ithaca, NY: Cornell University Press.

Cruse, H. (1967). *The crisis of the Negro intellectual.* New York: Quill.

Davis, L. (1998). *A clashing of the soul: John Hope and the dilemma of African-American leadership and Black higher education in the early twentieth century.* Athens & London: University of Georgia Press.

DuBois, W. E. B. (1944). Science or propaganda? *Phylon, 5,* 1–8.

Franklin, J. H. (1995) A life of learning. In H. Boyd & R. L. Allen (Eds.), *Brotherman: The odyssey of Black men in America—An anthology.* (pp. 705–717). New York: Ballantine Books.

Gates, H. L., & West, C. (1996). *The future of the race.* New York: Alfred A. Knopf.

Gbadegesin, S. (1996). Ethics, education, and community. In J. A. Ladner & S. Gbadegesin (Eds.), *Ethics, higher education, and social responsibility* (pp. 25–43). Washington, DC: Howard University Press.

Harding, V. (1974). The vocation of the black scholar and the struggles of the black community. In Institute of the Black World (Eds.), *Education and black struggle: Notes from the colonized world.* Cambridge: Harvard Education Review.

Hare, N. (1995). The challenge of a black scholar. In H. Boyd & R. L. Allen (Eds.), *Brotherman: The odyssey of Black men in America—An anthology* (pp. 705–717). New York: Ballantine Books.

Harris, Sr., W. M. (1990). Professional education of African Americans: A challenge to ethical teaching. *Business and Professional Ethics Journal, 9,* 159–170.

James, W. (1903). The Ph.D. octopus. *Harvard Monthly, 36,* 1–9.

Ladner, J. A. (1996). Ethics, higher education, and social responsibility. In J. A. Ladner & S. Gbadegesin (Eds.), *Ethics, higher education, and social responsibility* (pp. 15–24). Washington, DC: Howard University Press.

Levine, L. W. (1996). *The opening of the American mind: Canons, culture, and history.* Boston: Beacon Press.

Lewis, D. L. (1993). *W. E. B. DuBois: Biography of a race, 1868–1919.* New York: Henry Holt and Company.

Logan, R. W. (1997). *The betrayal of the Negro: From Rutherford B. Hayes to Woodrow Wilson.* New York: Da Capo Press.

Moses, Y. T. (1990). The challenge of diversity: Anthropological perspectives on university culture, *Education and Urban Society, 22,* 402–412.

Nettles, M. T., & Perna, L. W. (1997). *The African American education data book: Volume I: Higher and adult education.* Fairfax, VA: Frederick D. Patterson Institute of The College Fund/UNCF.

Nettles, M. T., Perna, L. W., & Freeman, K. E. (1999). *Two decades of progress: African Americans moving forward in higher education.* Fairfax, VA: Frederick D. Patterson Institute of The College Fund/UNCF.

Rowley, L. L. (1996). [Review of the book *The Future of the Race* by Henry Louis Gates and Cornel West]. *The Journal of Negro Education, 64,* 464–466.

Rowley, L. L. (1999). *The public service mission of urban and metropolitan state universities: An analysis of mission, policy, and practice.* Unpublished doctoral dissertation, University of Virginia, Charlottesville, Virginia.

Rowley, L. L., & Walker, C. D. B. (1999). An academic ethics of race: W. E. B. DuBois, African-American civic responsibility, and racially relevant scholarship. Paper presented at the second annual Moral Education in a Diverse Society Conference, Durham, NC.

Rudolph, F. (1990). *The American college and university: A history.* Athens & London: The University of Georgia Press.

Schlesinger, Jr., A., & White, M. (1963). *Paths of American thought.* Boston: Houghton Mifflin.

Stewart, J. B. (1983). Psychic duality in the novels of W. E. B. DuBois. *Phylon, 40,* 93–107.

Storr, R. (1973). *The beginning of the future: A historical approach to graduate education in the arts and sciences.* New York: McGraw-Hill.

Urban, W. J. (1992). *Black scholar: Horace Mann Bond, 1904–1972.* Athens & London: The University of Georgia Press.

Veysey, L. R. (1965). *The emergence of the American university.* Chicago & London: University of Chicago Press.

Wagoner, Jr., J. L., & Kellams, S. E. (1992). The professoriate: History and status. In B. R. Clark & G. R. Neave (Eds.), *The Encyclopedia of Higher Education* (pp. 1674–1678). Oxford & New York: Pergamon Press.

West, C. (1993). *Keeping faith: Race and philosophy in America.* New York: Routledge.

Wilson, R. (1997). Negative mentoring: An examination of the phenomenon as it affects minority students. In H. T. Frierson (Ed.), *Diversity in higher education: Volume one: Mentoring and diversity in higher education* (pp. 177–185). Greenwich, CT & London: Praeger Publishers.

Woodson, C. G. (1919). *The education of the Negro prior to 1861.* New York: A & B Books.

Tyrone C. Howard

Dr. Tyrone C. Howard is currently an assistant professor in the areas of language, literacy, and culture and integrated teaching and learning in the College of Education at The Ohio State University. His research interests include the schooling experience of African American students, multicultural education, and social studies education. Dr. Howard completed his doctoral studies in curriculum and instruction at the University of Washington, Seattle, where he was a Spencer Fellow. Dr. Howard also worked with the Center for Multicultural Education and the Southern Law Poverty's collaborative Teaching Tolerance Institute.

Dr. Howard's career path to higher education began in Compton, California, where he was born and raised. Upon completion of his formal schooling years, Dr. Howard attended the University of California, Irvine, where he completed a B.A. in economics, and received his M.A. in education from California State University Dominguez Hills. Dr. Howard's pre-academy experience also includes three years as an elementary school teacher in the Compton Unified School District.

Dr. Howard has received numerous awards over the past decade for his humanitarian efforts, community service, and leadership skills. A member of Alpha Phi Alpha Fraternity Incorporated, Dr. Howard remains involved with a number of projects that are committed to school improvement, academic and social uplift of African American students, and community development.

7

DEVELOPING MULTICULTURAL CURRICULUM IN HIGHER EDUCATION

STRATEGIES FOR THE TWENTY-FIRST CENTURY

Tyrone C. Howard

The ongoing shifts in racial and ethnic demographics in the United States warrant an examination of institutions of higher learning across the country. With current projections estimating that so-called "minority" groups will be a majority of the U.S. population within the next quarter century (Pallas, Natriello, & McDill, 1989), it is critical that the missions, goals, and school curricula in higher education reflect the changing face of the nation. This inevitable transformation arrives at a time when race relations continue to be one of the most divisive issues in the United States. While developing a curriculum in higher education poses many challenges, it provides a unique opportunity for educators to shape future generations of citizens. It is critical to educate future generations to coexist cohesively and productively in a nation characterized by sometimes fractious diversity in an increasingly interconnected and interdependent yet still violent and divided world. Thus, our challenge as leaders in academe is to commit ourselves to the improvement of the schooling experience for all citizens as we approach the twenty-first century.

A significant amount of scholarship has been devoted to the need to reform K–12 curricula and instruction to meet the changing school population (Banks, 1993; Gay, 1990; Nieto, 1992; Sleeter & Grant, 1988). Banks (1993), one of the leading advocates of multicultural education, explains that "multicultural education is an idea, an educational reform movement, and a process whose major goal is to change the structure of educational institutions" (p. 7). The primary reason for renewed curricula in schools has been due to the exclusion of the experiences of people of color, women, and poor people. Thus, multicultural education has attempted to offset the cultural hegemony that many have considered a contributing factor to the underachievement and isolation of many culturally diverse students (Howard, 1998).

Pleas for incorporating multicultural education, antiracist education, and a culturally inclusive curriculum have been met with repeated resistance (Ravitch, 1990; Schlesinger, 1992). Critics of multicultural education have argued that the movement will only divide the nation by providing false accounts of historical events and encouraging ethnic polarization. Other critics claim that the traditional Eurocentric canon is becoming gradually excluded from the core of school curricula. Nonetheless, demographic changes warrant an adjustment in the faculty and programming of all educational institutions. Given the paucity of discussion on how to incorporate multicultural education in college curricula, there needs to be further discussion on how institutions of higher learning can adjust to more ethnically diverse student populations. A college population that is more ethnically and culturally diverse will have different intellectual needs than previous generations of higher-education populations (Solomon & Wingard, 1991). This chapter will address strategies that institutions of higher learning can use to meet the changing student body they will encounter in the new millennium. This chapter will also discuss methods that can be used to develop multicultural curricula in higher education by addressing three areas: (1) the subjectivity of knowledge construction, (2) antiracist education, and (3) a movement toward democratic and cultural pluralism in higher education.

Knowledge Construction

One of the complaints from students of color in higher education over the past thirty years has been the persistence of a monocultural curriculum (Gordon, 1992). Nonmainstream students have claimed that their experiences and contributions to U.S. history have been marginalized or in some cases outright omitted in course content. According to Hu-DeHart (1995), these students have maintained that they "want their college experience to mirror that of their white counterparts—to study the experiences and contributions of their community to U.S. society and culture and to use the resources of the university to help solve community problems" (p. 699). As a result, calls for the alteration of higher-education curricula have been a natural response. During the 1960s, the Black-studies movement was initiated by Black college students who were advocates for the inclusion of the life and history of African Americans to be incorporated into the curriculum (Hu-DeHart, 1995). These calls were preceded by the early Black ethnic-studies movement of the first part of the century that sought to create accurate images of African Americans' life and history and to contribute to the establishment of African American institutions (Banks, 1996). Thus, contemporary disciplines such as "multicultural education" exist due to the tireless works of African American scholars such as W. E. B. DuBois (1935, 1973), Carter G. Woodson (1933), Charles H. Wesley (1935), George Washington Williams (1882, 1883/1989), and countless others. The work of these scholars was critical because it helped to create a new canon of the African American contribution to American society. These works hold invaluable importance due to the centuries of scholarship disseminated by western scholars that depicted African American and other non-White groups as intellectually inferior and as individuals who had no positive impact on the development of western culture (Horseman, 1981). The works of Williams, Woodson, and others were among the first efforts to construct knowledge that challenged century-old paradigms and to provide students with contested claims of the events of U.S. history.

The works of early ethnic-studies scholars have had profound implications for higher education. Most importantly, they have provided a body of work that has laid a foundation for critiquing eurocentric literature and thought. One of the strategies that could benefit higher-education curricula is an acknowledgement of the subjectivity and value-laden constructions of mainstream knowledge. Two integral features of multicultural education are to challenge western history and literature that has marginalized the experiences of nonmainstream groups and to uncover new types of knowledge. Examining various types of knowledge helps students understand how knowledge is produced and the subjective role that humans play in this process (Banks, 1996; Gordon, 1992). Banks (1996) defines the knowledge-construction process as "the extent to which teachers help students to understand, investigate, and determine how the implicit cultural assumptions, frames of references, perspectives, and biases within a discipline influence the ways in which knowledge is constructed within it" (p. 21). The knowledge-construction process is an attempt to challenge the notion that knowledge is an objective, value-free paradigm that is not influenced by human interests. As teachers help students understand knowledge, students can be empowered to recognize their potential to recreate new knowledge from different perspectives.

In response to the various contentions among scholars about the creation of knowledge, Banks (1996) has detailed the canon debate between western traditionalists and multiculturalists. At the center of this debate has been the accuracy of historical events, the human subjectivity that has shaped the perceptions and interpretations of these events, and more importantly the debate on whether to reconstruct these bodies of knowledge in order to provide historical accuracy for current and future generations. Banks has suggested that scholars recognize the influence of human interests, biases, and life experiences in the creation of knowledge. Moreover, he posits that the notion of objective or neutral knowledge is a fallacy that must be challenged. He identifies five types of knowledge: (1) personal/cultural, (2) popular, (3) mainstream academic, (4) transformative academic; and (5) school knowledge that can help teachers and curriculum specialists identify perspectives and materials to construct a more multicultural curriculum.

Banks' call for critiquing the idea of objective knowledge is not the first of its kind. Kuhn (1970) was among the first to challenge the legitimacy of objectivity when he revised the history of science. Kuhn's reflections on the history of science showed the description of the scientific enterprise to be mythical. He argued that paradigms were established by accepted truths among scientists and that paradigmatic shifts occur when "revolutionary" scientists detect flaws in the existing paradigm then construct new knowledge in order to lay the foundations for new paradigm structures to coexist with traditional ones. Thus, multicultural educators and other scholars who conduct research in the area of knowledge construction are serving as contemporary "revolutionary scientists" in an attempt to redefine existing bodies of knowledge around race, gender, culture, and ethnicity. This is exactly the call that leaders within higher education must adhere to—the fact that growing populations of students in higher education have identified existing paradigms flawed with racial, cultural, and ethnic inequities. Thus, there is a call for a paradigm shift to redefine the "core" body of knowledge that constitutes a college curriculum. This redefining of knowledge is critical given the rapidly changing makeup of the United States. No longer can knowledge be viewed monolithically through traditional mainstream ideologies when the concept of "mainstream" is in a state of flux. Tomorrow's "mainstream" will possess a way of thinking, communicating, and being that is drastically different along racial, ethnic, and cultural lines than previous constructions. Therefore, the idea of objectivity in the creation of new knowledge must be acknowledged. Code (1991) has contested the validity of an objective epistemology and has claimed that "the sex of the knower is epistemologically significant because it introduces a subjective factor that pertains to the specific, subjective nature and circumstances of knowers—into the conditions that bear on the nature, possibility, and/or justification of knowledge" (p. 27). Moreover, Code claims that "the term knowledge itself needs to be recast so that it can retain its referential and descriptive scope while relinquishing some of its presumption to objectivity" (p. 27). Code's assertion of knowledge as a subjective construct is an important strand in the research on knowledge construction. She is one of an increasing number of researchers who have called for recognition of the subjectivity of knowledge.

A number of scholars have sought to challenge the construction of knowledge based on the viewpoint of its creator. Banks' (1996) references Teatreault (1993), who has contributed to the definition of knowledge as a social construct claiming that feminist scholars argue about the importance of "positionality" in the construction of knowledge. She refers to positionality as those "aspects of our identity (for example, our gender, our race, our class, our age, and so on) that are markers of relational positions rather than essential qualities. Their effects and implications change according to context" (p. 160). Teatreault argues that valid knowledge requires the knower's acknowledgment of his or her contextual positionality in the construction of knowledge. Teatreault's argument holds important implications for curriculum developers in higher education. One of the more useful strategies that faculty can use to diminish the limited scope of monocultural curriculum is to acknowledge that most of traditional, Eurocentric scholarship has ignored the societal inequities along racial, gender, and class lines at the time of their writings. The emerging scholarship on knowledge construction is critical because it provides the opportunity for socially marginalized groups to understand how various social and racial hierarchies have been constructed. Moreover, knowledge construction allows excluded groups to view themselves as change agents who can construct new knowledge given their own positionality and use this as a means to transform their realities. Knowledge construction is a critical element in social action, and it holds important implications in the reformation of the higher-education curriculum.

Antiracist Education

A second approach that institutions of higher learning can implement to reform curricula is to acknowledge the pernicious effects of racism in U.S. society. To effectively address racism, curriculum designs and instructional practices must lend themselves to analyze the inequities in power and economic status that determine race relations (Brandt, 1986). A plausible effort that could achieve this end would be through antiracist education. Antiracist education posits that higher-education curriculum, programs, policies, and pedagogical practices have all been influenced by racism that permeates throughout U.S. society. Therefore, it is vital to begin a reexamination of the various elements of higher education that deconstruct racial hierarchies and inequities. College curricula serve as an ideal starting point to begin the reconstruction of the role of race and racism in the United States. Botstein (1991) maintains that "a promising but difficult arena for effective action [against racism] is the college curriculum. Not only can racism be combated directly and profoundly, but the horizons of students can be broadened in a way that can retard the spread of prejudice" (p. 89). However, he warns that while this seems the most logical of tasks in the fight against racism in higher education, the willingness and commitment on the part of such institutions may not be apparent. He states that "attacking racism in the curriculum requires attention to the aspirations and principles of liberal education to an extent that few institutions realize or may be prepared to give" (p. 90).

Racism manifests itself in school curricula in numerous ways, through the exclusion and inaccurate portrayal of culturally diverse groups and through the implied superiority of certain groups of European descent (Chan and Wang, 1991; Horseman, 1981). Unfortunately, many traditional canons that mischaracterize non-White groups have gone unchallenged for centuries and have been the source of contention for many students of color. One of the ways to reinvent or "multiculturalize" higher education curricula is to debunk certain accounts of western scholarship that have been the center upon which much of contemporary curricula have been based.

One of the more intriguing accounts of the ways that racial hierarchies were established and subsequently disseminated as scientific knowledge is documented in Horseman's (1981) *Race and Manifest Destiny*. Horseman's important work sheds insight into how western canons, which established and would ultimately become core knowledge for college curricula, were racist in their construction. Horseman's accounts of this creation of knowledge claim that during the early to mid 1700s, a number of European scholars made assertions that humanity was comprised of four varieties—European, American, Asiatic, and African. These writers consistently argued through scientific writing that the European or Caucasian variety of humans was innately superior, and they classified non-European groups as "savage" tribes that were degenerated from the original species (pp. 46–47).

Horseman details the works of university professors such as Christopher Meintingen, who suggested that God "divided mankind into the white and the beautiful, and the black and ugly. Only the first had true courage and love of liberty; the second had character defects leading to lack of gentler feelings" (p. 49). These types of characterizations of African Americans became commonplace in university discourse. Edward Long, another European scholar, extended Meintingen's depiction to further depths by stating that the inferiority of African Americans was obvious based on "the black color, the presence of wool—not hair—the infesting of black bodies by black lice, and the bestial smell" (p. 50). Long's work was considered among the most prominent at the time and was referenced by a number of other writers to authenticate the inferiority of African Americans. These accounts of African Americans were viewed as "accepted truths" from highly trained and qualified scientists and scholars and were subsequently used as the rationale for continued enslavement and subjugation.

African Americans were not the only ethnic group to suffer from the vast dissemination of scientific racism during the eighteenth and nineteenth centuries. Countless American scientists did extensive writing explaining the innate inferiority of many non-White groups. According to Horseman, American Indians suffered major distortions of their life and culture through western scholarship. Dr. Charles Caldwell, a respected physician during the early nineteenth century, wrote extensively about phrenology theories that suggested that American Indians, like Blacks, were mentally inferior due to their smaller brain sizes and were more closely linked to animals than humans. He also contended that the intellectual inferiority of American Indians justified their removal and destruction from the North American continent. Caldwell's works, which were highly influential during the early 1830s, were part of a large body of scholarship during this time that depicted American Indians as "uncivilized savages" who desperately needed Christian indoctrination to overcome their inherent propensity for violence and bestiality.

Additional theories of racial inferiority existed about Mexicans during the 1830s and 1840s. Recognizing the benefit of seizing northern Mexican provinces, American scholars asserted that Mexicans were not equipped to make proper use of their land due to their racial weaknesses. According to Horseman, writers such as Lansford Hastings suggested that "to take lands from inferior barbarians was no crime; it was simply following God's injunctions to make the land fruitful" (p. 211). Hastings, in his portrayal of Mexican emigrant workers, maintained that they

> always pursue method[s] of doing things, which requires the least physical or mental exorcise [sic] unless it involves some danger . . . these wild, shirtless, earless, and heartless creatures, headed by a few timid, soulless, brainless officers, that these semi-barbarians, intend to hold this delightful region, as against the civilized world. (p. 211)

The racial stereotyping that portrayed Blacks and Indians as inhumane also classified Mexicans in a similar light. The multitudes of scholarship degrading non-Whites helped to reify perceptions of various ethnic groups and served as contributions to the establishment of widely held beliefs about various groups today.

While race relations in this country have improved over the past two centuries, it is true without question that racism still exists and continues to influence most facets of today's society. The implications for higher-education curricula about such a reality is that college faculty should be prepared to discuss works such as Horseman's to debate the effects that scientific racism continues to have on contemporary society. So-called scientific scholarship continues to emerge that reiterates a great deal of the racist rhetoric that was a staple for mainstream thinking in previous centuries. The widespread popularity of Hernstein and Murray's (1994) best-selling book *The Bell Curve,* which propounds the "natural inequality" between Whites and Blacks, reflects the continued appeal and interest that many Americans have towards racial doctrines that advocate inherent intelligence along racial lines. In many ways, the work by Hernstein and Murray is merely a contemporary account of the racist scholarship that has been a staple in U.S. education for the past two centuries. This frightening reality should alert us that there continues to be a great deal of work needed in dismantling the so-called "classics," "great books," and other western literature that contains racially offensive and inaccurate content.

Democratic and Cultural Pluralism in Higher Education

The debate over how higher-education curricula should be structured comes down to whose knowledge is considered most legitimate. The purpose of a curriculum is to provide a blueprint or a set of courses required by educational institutions for the completion of a particular degree. As a result, curriculum content tends to embody the values, norms, and biases that are integral parts of the educational discourse of those who design, control, and ultimately implement the curriculum (Darder, 1991). Needless to say, curriculum coordinators and many faculty in higher education have designed curricula that have reflected European middle-class values, much to the chagrin of students whose world views and lived experiences are not consistent with such an orientation.

Given the increase of racial and ethnic diversity in higher education, it is imperative to structure curricula in ways that enable all students to study about their own ethnic heritage and contributions to society, in addition to learning about the lived experiences, contributions, and worldviews of other ethnic groups. Ramirez and Casteneda (1974) have suggested that educational institutions create "cultural democracies," which is a philosophical concept whose objective is to challenge the negative effects of the Anglo conformity ideology that reduces all other cultural forms to inferior or invisible status.

The concept of a cultural democracy is important because it is clear in its intent that one does not have to forsake American values in lieu of one's personal culture. Ramirez and Casteneda (1974) explain that

> an individual can be bicultural and still be loyal to American ideals. Cultural democracy is a philosophical precept which recognizes that the way a person communicates, relates to others, seeks support and recognition from his environment . . . and thinks and learns. [Cognition] is a product of the value system of the home and community. Furthermore, educational environments or policies that do not recognize the individual's right, as guaranteed by the Civil Rights Act of 1964, to remain identified with the culture and language of his cultural group, are culturally undemocratic. (p. 23)

The idea of a cultural democracy is one that not only has social and moral implications but also implications for cognitive development. Research by Kogler and Stueber (1999) suggests that multicultural education advances cognitive development by enabling students to understand different cultural perspectives, to develop a reflexive understanding of themselves, and to represent structures shared by individuals in different experiential contexts. By using theoretical frameworks from the field of cognitive science, Kogler and Stueber argue that the "empathy thesis" requires individuals to make sense of quite irrational actions. In other words, when individuals are able to remove themselves from their own mental schema and attempt to understand the real-life situations and societal obstacles of others and to develop empathy for these experiences, such empathy may enhance cognitive development. They posit that the creation of simulated experiences to understand the "other" in nonlogical contexts implies that every interpretation remains embedded in a specific cultural, historical, and social context and that the projection into the other has to take into account cultural, social, and historical differences.

Conclusion

Using a more multicultural approach to higher education must be viewed as a process that benefits students of color as well as White students. The rationale for a culturally pluralistic curriculum is to help diminish ethnocentrism and reduce prejudice on the part of all students. Students of color have long maintained that they have been required to learn about the lives and histories of European Americans while university curricula have not required students to learn about the histories of culturally diverse groups (Altbach, 1991). As a result, the calls for multicultural requirements in college curricula have become an ongoing debate on many college campuses. While the debate continues at the institutional level, creating a culturally democratic curriculum can still take place on individual levels. Yet individual change has been minimal at best. One of the primary reasons for the lack of individual curricular change in higher education has been due to limited knowledge on the part of faculty members, even those who are sympathetic to change (Fitzgerald and Lauter, 1995). Therefore, it is imperative for universities to incorporate faculty-development programs that help individuals increase their knowledge bases and awareness about non-White groups. In addition, it is critical for institutions to make a sincere commitment to increased hiring of faculty of color. The numbers of Ph.D.s awarded to students of color continues to increase, but faculty of color is still in disproportionately low numbers at most colleges and universities.

Attempts to incorporate multicultural curricula into higher education requires a commitment to diversity from individual faculty members, department chairs, and all of the way up to deans of colleges. To offset the persistence of the monocultural curriculum in higher education, it is vital that scholarship that reflects the life, history, and culture of culturally diverse groups becomes commonplace. Moreover, it is critical that multicultural scholarship not become restricted only to courses that explicitly address diversity. The goal of fully incorporating multicultural education into course curricula will be realized when issues of diversity are thoroughly integrated into courses such as school finance, psychosocial development in young children, math, science and technology in the classroom, and school-policy reform. Each of these areas has implications for diversity, and it should become mandatory for future educators to be cognizant of the ways in which class and culture influence theories, concepts, and knowledge. In closing, it is important that educators confront our society's inescapable reality: diversity. For the past two centuries, the United States has prided itself as a nation of many becoming one, hence the term *e pluribus unum*. We have long considered diversity our strong suit not our liability. However, if we truly value diversity as we claim, our efforts and actions in academe need to reflect that through the creation of curricula and learning environments that recognize, value, and respect the lived experiences, contributions, and cultural backgrounds of all citizens.

> What set worlds in motion is the interplay of differences, their attraction and repulsions. Life is plurality; death is uniformity. By suppressing differences and peculiarities, by eliminating different civilizations

and cultures, progress weakens life and favors death. The ideal of a single civilization for everyone, implicit in the cult of progress and technique, impoverishes and mutilates us. Every view of the world that becomes extinct, every culture that disappears, diminishes a possibility of life.

—Octavio Paz (1967)

References

Altbach, P. G. & Lomotey, K. (Eds.). (1991). *The racial crisis in American higher education.* New York: State University New York Press.

Banks, J. A. (1993). Multicultural education: Characteristics and goals. In J. A. Banks & C. A. M. Banks (Eds.), *Multicultural education: Issues and perspectives* (2nd ed.). Boston: Allyn & Bacon.

Banks, J. A. (1996). The canon debate, knowledge construction, and multicultural education. In J. A. Banks (Ed.), *Multicultural education, transformative knowledge and action* (pp. 3–29). New York: Teachers College Press.

Botstein, L. (1991). The undergraduate curriculum and the issue of race: Opportunities, and obligations. In P. G. Altbach & K. Lomotey (Eds.), *The racial crisis in American higher education* (pp. 89–105). Albany: State University of New York Press.

Brandt, G. L. (1986). *The realization of anti-racist teaching.* London: Falmer Press.

Chan, S., & Wang, L. (1991). Racism and the model minority: Asian Americans in higher education. In P. G. Altbach & K. Lomotey (Eds.), *The racial crisis in American higher education* (pp. 43–68). Albany: State University of New York Press.

Code, L. (1991). *What can she know? Feminist theory and the construction of knowledge.* Ithaca, NY: Cornell University Press.

Darder, A. (1991). *Culture and power in the classroom.* Westport, CT: Bergin & Garvey.

DuBois, W. E. B. (1935). *Black reconstruction.* New York: The Blue Herron Press.

Fitzgerald, A. K., & Lauter, P. (1995). Multiculturalism and core curricula. In J. A. Banks and C. A. M. Banks (Eds.), *The handbook of research on multicultural education* (pp. 729–746). New York: Macmillan.

Gay, G. (1990). Achieving educational equality through curriculum desegregation. *Phi Delta Kappan, 70,* 56–62.

Gordon, E. W. (1992). Conceptions of Africentrism and multiculturalism in education: A general overview. *Journal of Negro Education, 61*(1), 4–11.

Hernstein, R. J., & Murray, C. (1994). *The bell curve: Intelligence and class structure in American life.* New York: The Free Press.

Horseman, R. (1981). *Race and manifest destiny.* Cambridge: Harvard University Press.

Howard, T. C. (1998). *Pedagogical practices and ideological constructions of effective teachers of African Americans.* Unpublished doctoral dissertation. University of Washington.

Hu-DeHart, E. (1995). Ethnic studies in U.S. higher education: History, development, and goals. In J. A. Banks & C. A. M. Banks (Eds.), *Handbook of research on multicultural education* (pp. 696–707). New York: Macmillan.

Kogler, H. H., & Stueber, K. (1999). *Empathy and agency: The problem of understanding in the human sciences.* New York: Westview.

Kuhn, T (1970). *The structure of scientific revolutions* (2nd ed.). Chicago: University of Chicago Press.

Nieto, S. (1992). *Affirming diversity: The sociopolitical context of multicultural education.* New York: Longman.

Pallas, A. M., Natriello, G., & McDill, E. L. (1989). The changing nature of the disadvantaged population: Current dimensions and future trends. *Educational Researcher, 18*(5), 16–22.

Ramirez, M., & Casteneda, A. (1974). *Cultural democracy: Bicognitive development and education.* New York: Academic Press.

Ravitch, D. (1990). Multiculturalism: E pluribus plures. *The American Scholar, 59*(3), 337–354.

Schlesinger, Jr., A. M. (1992). *The disuniting of America.* New York: Norton.

Sleeter, C. E., & Grant, C. A. (1988). *Making choices for multicultural education: Five approaches to race, class, and gender.* Columbus, OH: Merrill.

Teatreault, M. K. T. (1993). Classrooms for diversity: Rethinking curriculum and pedagogy. In J. A. Banks & C. A. M. Banks (Eds.), *Multicultural education: Issues and perspectives* (2nd ed., pp. 129–148). Boston: Allyn & Bacon.

Wesley, C. H. (1935). *Richard Allen: Apostle of freedom.* Washington, DC: The Associated Publishers.

Williams, G. W. (1989). *History of the Negro race in America from 1619 to 1880: Negroes as slaves, as soldiers, and as citizens* (2 vols.). Salem, NH: Ayer. (Original works published in 1882 and 1883)

Woodson, C. G. (1933). *The mis-education of the Negro.* Washington, DC: The Associated Publishers.

J. W. Wiley

J. W. Wiley is the assistant dean of academic affairs and director of the McNair scholars program at Claremont Graduate University (CGU). He directs the university's recruitment effort, diversity office, and its minority mentor program. He is a member of the provost and dean of faculty's administrative cabinet and has chaired CGU's diversity task force. He advocates for students, participates in faculty searches, and advises programs on admissions decisions. Prior to his recent appointment, J. W. held a three-year appointment as special assistant for diversity at CGU. In 1996, J. W. was proposal coauthor and co-coordinator of the 8th Annual National Black Graduate Student Conference hosted by CGU.

J. W. holds an M.A. degree in philosophy from Claremont Graduate School and a B.A. degree from California State Long Beach. Currently he is pursuing his Ph.D. in an interfield discipline of philosophy and cultural studies at CGU. Prior to his graduate studies, J. W. worked for Hughes Aircraft Co., Rockwell International, and McDonnell Douglas Corporation.

J. W. is a member of Alpha Phi Alpha Fraternity Inc., the National Black Graduate Student Association (NBGSA), the Council of Graduate Schools (CGS), the National Association of Graduate Admissions Professionals (NAGAP), Western Association of Educational Opportunity Personnel (WESTOP), and Council of Opportunity in Education (COE, formerly NCEOA).

J. W. is an accomplished writer, lecturer, and poet who also teaches tennis and considers exercise a necessary evil. He identifies himself as an optimist and stays that way with his motto: Perspective is the Objective.

8

INSTITUTIONAL ETHICS

FORTY ACRES OF SO-CALLED MORALITY AND STILL NO MULE

J. W. Wiley

Introduction

In his essay, "The Concept of Race," W. E. B. DuBois (1986) stated,

> I saw the race problem was not as I conceived, a matter of clear, fair competition, for which I was ready and eager. It was rather a matter of segregation, of hindrance and inhibitions, and my struggles against this and resentment at it began to have serious repercussions upon my inner life. (p. 649)

What DuBois saw as unfair competition, segregation, hindrance, and inhibitions still to this day permeates the institutional walls of academia and directly contributes to the devaluing and demise of professional and academic careers. That these injustices affect some more than others is not right, just, or ethical. The fact that institutions are not cognizant of situations like these or choose to ignore them complicates matters even more. It is not enough to promise forty acres and a mule and deliver only the forty acres. Nor is it enough to promise forty acres and a mule and deliver only the mule. While all promises cannot be kept, some should not be made if they are not going to be kept. As a result of this, in the halls of major universities within the United States, there is enough acreage for the seeds of morality to be sown, but nowhere is there shelter available to house those mules.

An extremely volatile, albeit covert, dynamic within academic institutions is the affectation of an ethic that arguably reflects these institutions. For the purpose of this essay, I refer to this dynamic as *institutional ethics*. What this essay will reveal is what I mean by the rubric "institutional ethics." This essay shows how institutional ethics are representative of a unification of the traditional ethical positions called *normative* and *descriptive ethics*. I articulate the inconsistencies within an institutional ethic and its impact on any critical mass of Black Americans endeavoring to achieve a voice within institutional walls. Therefore, I answer questions on how an insufficient institutional ethic thrives and permeates every facet of academia and how the utilization of applied ethics contributes a perspective that aides in the eradication of ethical dilemma.

My articulation of the concept of institutional ethics is an analysis of the morality of academic institutions. I assess, in terms of incorporating Blackness and otherness, what institutions "ought" to do, what their deontological responsibilities are (what their "duty" is), and the validity of their judgment on what, in their so-called rules, are right and wrong. More specifically, I evaluate assumptions on minority behavior vs. the so-called legitimacy of nonminority behavior. I look at the ethics of diversity decisions and ponder nonexistent entities like Black privilege within predominantly White institutions juxtaposed against the reality of White privilege. I examine the rationale and ethical implications of faculty hiring along traditional ethical positions. Finally, I examine the moral injustices heaped on the "other" when expectations of "representing the race" become more paradigmatic than plausible.

Forty-Acre Promises and Their Ethical Implications

Ethicists embrace divergent opinions on what the primary focus of ethical inquiry should be. Ethical investigations usually incorporate assessments and notions of what our duty is in a given situation, what we ought or should do, what is the responsible thing to do, and so on. However, the study of ethics is also concerned with the meaning of moral statements and the plausibility of demonstrating the truth or falsehood within those statements.

Most ethicists can be seen as trilingual. This is largely due to the three primary forms of language that comprise ethics. The language of descriptive ethics informs us about the types of lives people live and the moral choices that are made within those lives. Normative ethics addresses ideas of rightness, justice, choices people make, and the rhyme, reason, value, and rationale involved in those choices. Metaethics is the study of the meaning of moral statements as opposed to the contents of the discourse. So, a statement like one used by DuBois (1986) claiming "Prostitution is world old and inevitable" is endemic of a descriptive statement in that it states an obvious fact (p. 649). "Prostitution should be legalized to better legislate the parameters that surround it" is a normative statement about the merits of societal supervision or governance on an illegal activity. "Prostitution is simply not right" is an example of a statement that a metaethicist would assess by first determining what is implied by the word *rightness* in the statement, whether the rightness or illegality of prostitution can be objectively arrived at, and whether there are any facts involved in the statement.

Rebelliousness against traditionalist notions and capitalist assumptions of what is the greatest or most significant area to research in the field of ethics is more commonplace now than in the past. That may be a result of the reality of disenfranchised groups in this country. Conventional applications of ethics never seemed truly to engage the important issues of marginalized constituencies. Applied ethics, as defined in *Moral Philosophy,* is the study of controversial ethical issues like racism, abortion, or euthanasia (Moore & Stewart, 1994). Applied ethics attempts to determine what general ethical principles apply to these morally relevant issues, which can then help us decide similar questions about our own unique situations (McInerney & Rainbolt, 1994). Applied ethics covers such fields as business, medicine, engineering, journalism, the ethics of intimate relationships, and the ethical dimensions of particular public-policy areas, such as race relations and famine relief. As a part of moral philosophy, applied ethics has flourished over the past two decades and demonstrates the implications of both normative theory for specific moral issues and descriptive ethics for decisions made regarding concrete circumstances.

Black people, Mexican people, and third-world people who are mired in the struggle of owning a piece of the American dream often do not have the luxury of lounging about, staring at the stars. Neither do the collective masses often recognize the subterfuge and nuances of the moral injustices that have been cast upon them from their historical heritage. Of all the different ethical focuses available for people to undertake, only a practical and applied ethic capable of producing a more immediate result would suffice in terms of addressing the transgressions of history. Ethical theory applied to the machinations of an academic institution manifests itself in rewarding revelations for all parties involved.

The ethical implications of an activity like prostitution may be a disconcerting example to enlist as a segue from the introduction of this essay to the core of its context. However, an interesting paradox exists in the parallel of an individual consciously acquiescing to being exploited for profit under the auspices of a so-called benefactor. Bracketing the sexual implications of prostitution, is prostitution not the psychological manipulation of special and not easily attainable services for a price? Accepting that as true, a point of departure between the streetwalker and other social misfits—the abused housewife, the marginal entertainer—and the underrepresented academician can be that society has taken the liberty to designate one of them unacceptable for its sexual impropriety. The abused housewife endures all types of social ills from an abusive husband to ensure that his economic protection does not diminish. Marginal entertainers, desiring that breakthrough opportunity, prostitute themselves by taking jobs that they normally would not take. Academicians also allow themselves to be relegated to opportunities that mortify them personally but, fortunately, allow them to begin paying back those loans.

Beaches are often painted in an array of colors without affecting the interpretation of them as beaches. Classic and ageless stories are told many ways without disturbing the morals of the messages. The crux of this assessment of institutional ethics also needs to be seen one way. It is important to recognize that severe dues often must be paid before success is achieved. Moreover, without those dues, successes or progress often would go underappreciated. This does not mean that events like American Slavery and the Holocaust were necessary to elevate the consciousness and character of Blacks and Jews. However, it does mean that a thin line exists between the world of the housewife bedding down her husband to keep a roof over her head and the heads of her children and the world of a prostitute turning tricks as a means of employment, even though she is reporting to a pimp. Stated more concisely, on some level everyone turns a trick from time to time, but our remuneration can vary widely.

In Search of the Proverbial Mule

Does an academic institution have an ethic to which it must adhere? Should an academic institution have an ethic? I submit that the answer to both questions must be yes. The necessity of an academic institution adhering to an ethic is somewhat mandated by federal law and institutional policy. Directives like those ensuring the adherence of affirmative-action practices force institutions to play by the rules, thereby guaranteeing a certain degree of ethical implementation within academia if these academic institutions desire to continue to receive federal funding.

The yes to the question "Should an academic institution have an ethic?" should not be interpreted as an obvious answer to a rhetorical question.

While the term *should* serves the literal purpose of providing within the statement an auxiliary functionality of obligation, the weight it carries is much
more burdensome. Should an institution project an ethic if it does not intend
to stand by it? Does an institution have an ethic if seventy percent of the faculty does not adhere to or believe in that ethic? What percentage of the faculty must support an institutional ethic before the ethic becomes legitimized
or valid? If fifty-one percent of the faculty supports an institutional ethic, is
it then validated as the institutional ethic of the institution? If the president
and provost of an institution, its prime leadership, strive to establish and
maintain an overriding morality, is that sufficient enough to claim that the
university itself has an ethic?

The answer to all of these questions is subjective at best and fleeting at
worst. The answer is subjective because no matter how dynamic the leadership
is and how supportive the faculty is, in terms of implementing ethical initiatives, the question of ethical behavior can always be answered from a personal
perspective. If the goal of an institution is to develop a reputation for serious
research, the metaethical question then becomes, "What is meant by serious?"
Terms like *serious* are often utilized as implements of control to categorize and
then marginalize those that fall outside of the categorization. Serious research
should not be exclusive of nontraditional research interests of marginalized
groups. There is room for an articulation of nontraditional interests. English
and history programs that endeavor to represent a broad scope of American
studies need to recognize the impossibility of the project without inclusion of
the narrative discourses of underrepresented and marginalized groups like
Black and Latino Americans. Management and philosophy programs need to
understand that the scope of their respective missions is global in terms of
marketing and knowledge and, therefore, must be inclusive of voices that historically have been ignored. Mathematics and science programs need to separate themselves from the illegitimate rationale that there is no method of
including diversity into their curriculum until they have at least taken the initiative to recruit and hire diverse faculty who might be better equipped to
develop a curriculum that reflects, if not appropriates, diverse perspectives.

The answer becomes fleeting when you consider that the institutional
ethic must hinge on the leadership of the institution. It all starts with leadership that is firm in its conviction and is prepared to put its money where its
mouth is. If the president and provost are trusted, well-respected individuals,
then their formulation and direction of the institution's agenda will be implemented from moral ground and directed toward even higher ground. Change
agents can infect others with their enthusiasm and zeal, and it does not take

many. Malcolm X (1964) once said, "But just as the fuse is the smallest part or the smallest piece in the powder keg, it is yet that little fuse that ignites the entire powder keg" (p. 274).

A more significant question is, "What are the elements that contribute to an institutional ethic?" A normative ethic within an institution establishes codes of behavior. A descriptive ethic within an institution articulates these codes. It is the intertwining of these two that forms the fundamental ethic needed to permeate every action within the walls of an institution. However, it is the utilization of applied ethics that specifically allows an assessment to be made about the merits of an institution's ethical implementation. In addition, awareness that an institution is only as ethical as its most unethical practice helps.

DuBois, renowned for his scholarship and his seminal work on racism, was a major contributor to the development of applied ethics. This is evidenced in his articulation of the four classes of reasons usually given in defense of race antipathy. DuBois (1914) identified racism as a function of a survival instinct brought on by something repulsive, a self-defense against undesirable traits of another culture, a method of race development, and a method of group specialization. Essentially what DuBois articulated is that race antipathy is a result of the way we are socialized. This socialization process is consistent with the way we develop our perspectives of value, right, and wrong. DuBois explicated the four classes a bit further by identifying them as "a method of maintaining the European level of culture." It is in the noncognitive, socialized sense that an ethic can become corrupted. The socialization process that everyone undergoes is something about which we often must remind ourselves. DuBois (1986) himself said,

> It is hard under such circumstances to be philosophical and calm, and to think through a method of approach and accommodation between castes. The entombed find themselves not simply trying to make the outer world understand their essential and common humanity, but even more, as they become inured to their experience, they have to keep reminding themselves that the great and oppressing world outside is also real and human and in its essence honest. All my life I have had continually to haul my soul back and say, "All white folk are not scoundrels nor murderers. They are, even as I am, painfully human." (p. 650).

DuBois cautions us to attempt to understand that it is our humanity that contributes more to the fact that we may fall prey to unethical practices. So no one should be too quick to cast dispersions on others. Remember, if not for the grace of God . . .

The Impact of Institutional Ethics
on Communities Within

Within all academic environments are communities clamoring for a voice in the proceedings, a presence at the conference table. At many universities in the country, this appears to be the case and it occurs in many forms. Black and Latino agendas for advancement in an institution find themselves clamoring for the same dollars that have been earmarked to go to another ethnic group. Communities that endeavor to promote an egalitarian agenda in terms of race, class, gender, and sexual orientation find themselves having to develop arguments about why their interests should be the most prevalent concern of the academy.

The fact that at many institutions there is only one person of color on the administrative staff or in a faculty unit only heightens the sense of nihilism for that employee. Consider the fact that in your area of expertise or profession your research is designed to address one specific community. Because you may be Black, you will not have just Black folk approaching you for support, but Mexicans/Chicanos, Asian Americans, and gays and lesbians, because it is assumed that your experiences must have made you sympathetic to the plight of other disenfranchised groups. That is normally an accepted situation. But, assuming you are also an extremely competent professional or professor (which you will have to be even to get the job), then you can anticipate having a constituency of non-underrepresented individuals as well who would like your support or assistance. This actually is a major problem at many universities. A White professor who appears to be very accessible will never have to deal with the proliferation of protégés that approach an underrepresented professor because 1) the White professor is not the only game in town and can afford to say no, 2) The White professional or professor often was not reared in an environment where nonsupport of one of your own is likened to denying your heritage or, even worse, acting like an Uncle Tom.

The Uncle Tom phenomenon, including having the designation attached to you, is taken very seriously within the Black community. While it also has often been used as a mechanism of manipulation, it is entrenched in Black heritage and, when possible, is avoided at all costs. Malcolm X (1964) spoke on it this way:

> A few hand-picked Uncle Tom, handkerchief-head Negroes are given big jobs in Washington, D.C. And then those Negroes come back and try and make us think that the administration is going to lead us to the promised land of integration. And the only ones whose problems have been solved have been those hand-picked Negroes. (p. 281)

It is imperative that institutions recognize that part of their moral responsibility is to anticipate problems like this happening and to do something about them. Both supervisors and academic departmental chairs of traditional departments are smart enough to recognize that having one person representing an entire gender in a work environment can be somewhat disconcerting. No woman wants to be the only woman in the men's locker room. No gay person desires to be the only homosexual in a heterosexual conversation. No person of color needs to be the sole representative for all people of color in an academic institution. The wants, desires, and needs of marginalized and underrepresented people are not necessarily the ethical responsibility of academic institutions. But it is the ethical responsibility of the school to create an environment that is welcoming and accommodating for these Jackie and Jacquelyn Robinsons, an environment that better equips them with the potential to change their respective academic landscapes. If that is not motivation enough, then simply consider this special assistance: I am speaking about simply another version of providing Black people their proverbial forty acres and a mule, Japanese people another apology for the internment, Native Americans overdue compensation for their present invisibility within an American context due to a legacy of lies and broken promises by the American government, and Mexican people access to opportunity instead of being once again treated as foreigners in a region of the United States that was once theirs in which to travel freely.

Moral Obligations of Academic Institutions

Academic institutions have a moral obligation to provide the proper support mechanisms or resources for those existing inside its walls. This translates into students having professors that look like them, new faculty having mentors to help them make the transition into the institution, and administrators having an opportunity to succeed in their jobs. Of course the possibility of students and faculty that resemble each other is not assured. New faculty can have someone mentoring them, but if it is not someone who cares about their success, it is simply someone who is fulfilling an assignment that minimally enhances the possibility of success. Administrators who arrive at an institution having accepted a position framed in a certain light should not have to realize a week into the job that they do not have the budget or the staff they were promised.

With most institutions comprised of predominantly White faculty and White senior administration, the impetus to have a mentor takes on an entirely different flavor for the underrepresented members of the institution. White faculty, students, and administrators come into these environments with a plethora of potential mentors available to them. Whether or not they connect with them is not the issue. The issue is that, more often than not, more than one mentor is available for them. This should not be misinterpreted as a statement for mentoring along racial or cultural lines. There would not be Blacks and other underrepresented groups in the academy today without the many White mentors who contributed to our development. Conversely, just because you and a faculty member share a common color, culture, or creed does not necessitate that he or she will be as passionate about mentoring you as you may be about being mentored. Besides, actually having these resources always available is ideal but not realistic. What is most important is having a plan to obtain these resources constantly.

Behavioral Assumptions—They Do Not Really Need the Mule

Years ago as a neophyte graduate student and recently hired recruitment intern, I overheard comments describing someone as moody. Later I was introduced to an older Black man that I ultimately discovered was the guy about whom the comments had been made. He was one of only two Black males working in an administrative position for the university. My initial impression of him was that he was an individual who truly cared about his students. In addition, as a Black man he was invested in assisting the progression of his people. His people, however, were not just Black people but also marginalized, underrepresented, and third-world people. As I became more integrated into the professional ranks of the university, he became even more of a mentor and friend. However, the stigmatization that had been attached to him by his colleagues never dissipated. To them, he was always gruff, curt, bordering on rude, and always with a chip on his shoulder. Eventually, this older Black male, this role model of mine, left the university, without giving notice and without his Ph.D. Unfortunately, he left while still holding the dubious distinction of being A.B.D. ("all but dissertation"). Some conjectured that his departure was stress related. Some speculated that the death of his mother was the final straw. Others hypothesized a drinking problem. Having inherited some of the responsibilities he once had, I unfortunately could see how he left himself vulnerable. However, as his successor within that same institution, I also saw the possibility that his departure was a result of something else: the burden of being a Black man in American society. Is this a paradox or what privileged people might refer to as African American paranoia? If it is African American paranoia, does that negate the fact that the embodiment of an ethic within academic institutions often does include an element of racism in one of its many forms?

Michael Eric Dyson (1996, pp. 33–36) suggests that the concept of racism should be separated into three categories: race as context, race as subtext, and race as pretext. He defines *race as context* as helping the nation to "understand the facts of race and racism in our society." *Race as pretext* enables an understanding of the function of race and racism in America. It is his concept of race as subtext, however, that is germane to my assessment of institutional racism.

For Dyson, *race as subtext* reveals how arguments have been utilized as a means of mystification or deliberate vagueness regarding racism. It describes the "different forms that racism takes, the disguises it wears, the tricky, subtle shapes it assumes." Dyson states that the understanding of race as subtext helps grasp the "hidden premises," "buried perceptions," and "cloaked meanings" of race as they show up throughout our culture. Race as subtext enables us to see how an institution's inability to incorporate underrepresented people into legitimate positions with legitimate support systems is difficult not to interpret as a "buried perception" or "cloaked meaning" within some type of subtext.

The popular adage "just because you are paranoid doesn't mean you aren't being chased" could not be more appropriate than when experiencing the nuances of "nonmention" that permeate academia. There is the nonmention of significant relationships that benefit you juxtaposed against relationships that others have that benefit them in their careers. This nonmention takes on another dimension when you hear about a conversation that take place in your absence but that identified you as a beneficiary of favoritism or tokenism. There is the nonmention of whether you are qualified for the job by those same individuals that tell you how much respect they have for what you do. There is even the most blatant nonmention, the nonmention of how Black intimidation pervades the very essence of interactions with many of those so-called colleagues. This intimidation is largely due either to an unfamiliarity or to xenophobia that must precede confident, well-educated Blacks. Colleagues of mine have confirmed the existence of both at their respective institutions, the former as a phenomenon and the latter as an epidemic. I propose a theory that the epidemic usually occurs when the phenomenon of unfamiliarity threatens to undermine the sanctity of White privilege.

How institutional ethics accommodate White privilege within an institution has been a topic of discussion for years amongst underrepresented people, primarily because no discussion on the lack of an ethical agenda for marginalized groups can be undertaken without reference to the hegemonic culture.

The extent to which White privilege is taken for granted, however, is astonishing. Many White Americans take umbrage about the privilege their culture, race, and heritage affords them, but the obvious cannot be denied. How many all-Black, all-Latino, or all-Gay or Lesbian senior administrations are there in the United States? I would venture to say, with confidence, that there are zero. It is more likely that you will see a senior administration that all stand at 6'5" before you ever see an all-underrepresented senior administration at any institution that is not historically Black or Hispanic. The privileges emanating from senior administrations are only truly ascertained by those who benefit from them. However, I know firsthand the privileges I have benefited from on those rare occasions when I have had a Black male mentoring me socially, academically, or professionally. Sometimes it is as simple as the immediate concurrence or vicarious feeling of an articulated situation. Sometimes it is as complex as the shared research interests that were inspired for both mentor and mentored by the lived American experience. The question that does not go away, though, is "Why has the phenomenon of an all-Black senior administration at a predominantly White institution never occurred?"

The ethics of the situation are evident. Even a Black president of a predominantly White institution is not going to hire an all-Black senior administration. I doubt if she would even feel comfortable replacing her White staff. The Black president would not subject herself to the scrutiny that she would have to endure. She would not open herself up to the accusations of bias or racism. Yet, while the finger of racism is levied in regard to certain dubious hiring practices, in most cases an eyelash does not bat when the senior administration of academic institutions either all stand up to use the restroom or all know they should be applying suntan lotion on a slightly overcast, eighty-degree day.

The difficulty of ethical choices within academic institutions is not racially exclusive. A Black colleague of mine, faced with a decision to hire someone, was forced to decide between the two remaining candidates, a Black man and an Asian woman, both of whom were outstanding. At the time his entire staff was Black. He was also serving as the director of the diversity office at his university. The implications for him surrounding that hire were problematic. He hired the Asian woman, and she proved herself more than worthy in every respect of her professionalism. With hindsight being 20–20 vision, he could reconcile the choice because you never know how the other candidate would have worked out. However, he was left to deal with the irony of the fact that if she had not been an excellent choice, he would not have hired the best candidate because he was Black. More to the point, he had been co-opted into doing the wrong thing in an attempt to do the right thing. Ultimately this situation deconstructed his perspective on hiring, ethical behavior, and ethical decisions. Even though he had made a diversity hire, the turmoil of the decision ensured that he would not be as quick to judge someone for not diversifying his or her staff when given the opportunity. Some larger questions loom with respect to this decision. Because you are Black, must you be predisposed to choose Blackness over Whiteness or run the risk of being labeled a handkerchief-head Negro? If the answer is yes, then how do we challenge institutions not to hire in their own image?

No certifiable answers are available to the conundrums that exist regarding the relativistic nature of ethical behavior and ethical decisions. On some level every appointment and termination can be questioned for its integrity and merit. But, if we liken ethics to love and power to the ability to actualize potential, institutional ethics reductively becomes an issue of power versus love. Institutions by their very structure and foundation must have power or they will not thrive. However, imbedded within them must also be an element of love. Rev. Dr. Martin Luther King (1967) once said, "What is needed is a realization that power without love is reckless and abusive and that love without power is sentimental and anemic. Power at its best is love implementing the demands of justice. Justice at its best is love correcting everything that stands against love" (p. 289). How love and power are balanced against one another is often demonstrated in terms of respect, both for the person being treated ethically and the person exhibiting the ethical behavior. If all institutions would couch their ethical behavior in terms of treating everyone as if he or she were the person in the mirror, respect would be a given and this essay would have been on another topic.

> Respect the stranger
> whose respect of you isn't nice;
> possibly by your actions he might actually think twice,
> and in that process
> find a vast treasure of wealth
> in the beauty of the feeling
> of respecting himself.
>
> —*J. W. Wiley (1988)*

References

DuBois, W. E. B. (1914). Does race antipathy serve any good purpose? In F. L. Hord & J. S. Lee (Eds.), *I am because we are* (pp. 247–249). Amherst: University of Massachusetts Press.

DuBois, W. E. B. (1986). The concept of race. In W. E. B. DuBois, *Writings* (pp. 625–641). New York: The Library of America.

Dyson, M. E. (1996). *Race rules*. Reading, MA: Addison-Wesley Publishing.

King, Jr., M. L. (1967). Black power. In F. L. Hord & J. S. Lee (Eds.), *I am because we are* (pp. 285–295). Amherst: University of Massachusetts Press.

McInerney, P. K., & Rainbolt, G. W. (1994). *Ethics*. New York: Harper Collins.

Moore, B. N., & Stewart, R. M. (1994). *Moral philosophy*. Mountain View, CA: Mayfield Publishing.

Wiley, J. W. (1988). Respect. In J. W. Wiley, *Searching beyond the rhyme* (p. 7). An unpublished manuscript.

X, Malcolm (1964). Speech on "Black Revolution." In F. L. Hord & J. S. Lee (Eds.), *I am because we are* (pp. 272–284). Amherst: University of Massachusetts Press.

PART TWO

NAVIGATING THE ACADEMY

Leon D. Caldwell

Dr. Leon D. Caldwell is an assistant professor of educational psychology at the University of Nebraska, Lincoln (UNL). He is a native of West Philadelphia, Pennsylvania, and the oldest of three from a mother-headed household. He received his Ph.D. in counseling psychology from Penn State University, where he specialized in multicultural counseling, in December of 1998. As a Division I student-athlete at Lehigh University in Bethlehem, Pennsylvania, he earned his B.A. in economics. Two years later while working as the assistant to the Athletic Director for Academic Support, he earned his master's degree in secondary school counseling also from Lehigh. Leon completed his internship at the counseling center of the University of California, Irvine.

At UNL he teaches in the counseling psychology program and supervises doctoral and master's degree students. Since joining the faculty at UNL he has had three publications and several grants and contracts. This has been made possible partly because of his engagement in the Lincoln and Omaha communities. In addition, he is currently in the process of setting up an international exchange program between UNL, the University College of Education at Winneba, and the University of Cape Coast, in Ghana, West Africa. He plans to begin a summer course through the UNL in the summer of 2001.

Dr. Caldwell's goal for the new millennium is to advance the reascension and revitalization of African-centered psychology in the tradition of our great African American scholars. Leon feels that his life purpose is in contributing to the building of the next cadre of community servants.

Besides the academic life Leon is a fanatic student of African drum and dance. Currently he advises the African People's Union, an undergraduate student organization, and serves on the advisory board for several community organizations. He is also president of Caldwell and Associates, LLC, a culturally competent educational and psychological consulting practice.

Dr. Caldwell has established a line of research in career development, mental health service delivery, school counseling, and counseling interventions for African American males.

9

THE PSYCHOLOGY OF BLACK MEN

Leon D. Caldwell

Black male psychology is at best a complex amalgamation of misinterpretations and at worst a labyrinth of uncertain identities. Historically the psychology of Black males (men of African descent born and/or socialized in the United States) has involved the study of the mind as interpreted with European definitions of intelligence, personality, function, and other constructs. These definitions have unequivocally diminished the humanity of Black men; White racial supremacy must be validated in order to perpetuate oppressive social, educational, and economic systems. The White supremacist definition of *Black psychology* has been so pervasive in these systems that even most African Americans cannot produce an authentic definition of self without referencing White cultural norms.

Herein lies the major sticking point in understanding the psychology of Black men: It is the understanding of identity as not just who you are but who you want to be. As Black men our declarations cannot be masked in White definitions of our psychology. Psychology, the study of the mind, in the European tradition is very limiting. Black men must even redefine the term *psychology* and question its usefulness in understanding their "Beingness" Nobles (1986). Maybe we should advance a discipline in spiritual illumination in order to capture fully an authentic ideal for Black male intelligence, personality, and functioning. My point is simply to suggest that in order to understand the psychology of Black men, we must ask whether we are speaking the same language. If not, are there translations? If so, are they accurate in the description of Black males?

Toxic Environments

There is very little evidence to suggest that higher education or any system of education has profoundly impacted the cultural development of Black males. Moreover, there is very little evidence, anecdotal or otherwise, to suggest that environment (that is, the academy) positively impacts the psychology of Black males. We must admit that despite academic success and even after obtaining the highest credentials of an institution of higher education, we pay a price that often seems unquantifiable but definitely describable. The messages we receive from these toxic environments have an effect on the quality of our life experiences.

The academy represents yet another potentially toxic environment. It is important for us to remember that despite our success and ability to navigate higher-education systems, they were not intended for the African American male. One of the biggest mistakes we make upon entering the academy is the expectation of our experience to be reflected in the institution. To be quite frank, this expectation is absurd. Even Historically Black Colleges and Universities (HBCUs) were not intended for our personal edification as much as for our industrial training and American socialization. The toxicity is inhaled when we arrive on campus assuming that "our" institutions owe us something, when, in fact, they are obligated to provide us with anything but nonauthentic cultural images and definitions.

At this point, I might add that many of us do not even know where to find our own authentic cultural images. It is my contention to suggest that the academy is inherently toxic. To expect that an institution predicated upon western (European) norms and values would be anything less than toxic for men of African descent is naive at best and ignorant at worst. The academy consists of many Brothers who have not figured it out yet. They come to campus wondering why it is a struggle for them to get tenured and promoted up the ranks of professorships and administration. We see it in our Black male students who are just angry. Unfortunately, Black male scholarship is not reflected in the curriculum.

On the other extreme are the African American men who expect their presence and participation in the academy to grant them full rights and immunities regardless of their racial background. For those who have figured it out, they enjoy true liberation. As Brothers in the academy, we need to see how our psychology is connected to our environments; both the ones to which we subject ourselves and those that are imposed upon us can be spiritually and culturally deadening. Without inoculation the toxic nature of those environments can be lethal.

Inoculation

Inoculation is a psychological and social process of expunging our systems of the remnants of toxic environments. We must be mindful that our exposure to these environments has taken place over the years; likewise, we should be patient with ourselves during the inoculation. The first part of the inoculation process is, of course, recognizing the need to be inoculated. True, the material benefits of a life in the academy are plentiful. However, if not taken in a greater social context, they provide an illusion of emancipation. Our first challenge is to understand the environment and how it contributes to our psychology.

Our second task in the inoculation process is understanding which piece of the toxicity we contribute to our own psychology. Dr. Joseph White (1998) suggests there is a need for Brothers to make the distinction between blame and responsibility. This is critical to the process because unless we take some ownership for our own psychology, we can never look toward our own remedies. It has been easy for us to point the finger at the systematic, calculated, and deliberate plan of destruction mapped out by oppressive, White supremacist institutions and policies.

Notwithstanding conspiracy theories, much of this has been well documented and even exposed (for example, Tuskegee Experiment, Coin Tel Pro, the Hoover Papers, and so on). Again, however, this is to be expected from the inheritors of a country that has been based on oppression of other people (that is, the indigenous people of this land now called the United States).

However, we Brothers—yes, even in the academy—contribute to our psychological destruction. We need to take responsibility for our contributions to our own oppression and the oppression of other Brothers. And before we get defensive about this point, we must remind ourselves that this is part of the inoculation process. We need to purge ourselves of the sick images of an infallible Black male academic.

And finally, the inoculation process must be culturally authentic. It must be inclusive of God, spirituality, ancestors, family (including "extended"), community, ritual, study, and worship. Although many of these terms have specific meaning in other contexts, we must begin to understand what these words mean in a context of and for men of African descent. Expunging ourselves cannot be predicated upon European notions of inoculation. We must begin the reclamation of our psychology using terms that reflect our authentic cultural tradition.

The greatest stumbling block toward an inoculation process is ambiguity of what comprises an authentic cultural tradition. There have been many debates from "Afrocentrists" about the point in time in African civilization that we claim as reflecting current traditions. Of course, whenever we have this discussion, there is always one African American who proclaims that he has never been to Africa and does not plan to go to Africa, so its importance in his daily functioning is negligible. (I will not waste time here on people in the terminal stage. Their treatment regimen would be too intense to explicate for this publication, but I want to point out that they do exist.) I believe the important piece here is not to get enveloped in that intellectual debate until you have undertaken serious study. Nor is it beneficial to believe you must have this figured out before you begin the inoculation process. The truth of the matter is that once you begin to uncover some of Africa, at any point in time you will begin to see its connections to the diaspora and its contributions to world civilization. Only after serious study will Africa reveal itself. Meanwhile, the key is to find a tradition that speaks to your spirit and a practice that fits with your life.

Once we have initiated the process of expunging ourselves of the high level of toxic exposure (as a result of the academy), we begin to think about how we can protect ourselves from such toxicity through an immunization process. The inoculated Black male must look to find ways to maintain a psychology that is free of distorted images and definitions of himself. Being purged of an alien definition of identity is not enough (see K. K. K. Kambon, 1998). The only true way to immunize ourselves from the toxicity of the academy is to reclaim a psychology that reflects our true identity.

Immunization

A major thrust behind the immunization process is developing new definitions of personality, intelligence, and other concepts that reflect a culturally authentic identity. Akbar (Hillard, 1998; Nobles, 1986) asserts that the major issue confronting African Americans has been the question of identity. It is my position that the formulation of a culturally authentic identity predicated upon African-centered definitions and concepts of manhood is the only way for Brothers in the academy to protect themselves from the academy's toxicity. Germane to this process is the questioning of our identity—not just who we are but who we want to be.

Thomas Parham discusses the question of identity for people of African descent using three questions posed by Frantz Fanon: Who am I? Am I who I say I am? Am I all I ought to be? These three questions are the foundation for the immunization process. We must begin to move past intellectual formulations to describe our essence and begin to understand its praxis. Addressing these three questions that are central to identity initiates the immunization process. Their importance is not in their profoundness but in the challenge they present. They challenge you to ask not just who you think you are but who you want to be and whether you are fulfilling your potential and purpose. The protection we need to discuss lies in successfully negotiating an identity that is self-derived, self-defined, and self-directed. Only when we have addressed these central questions in a meaningful way shall we experience a truly liberating psychology.

Fanon's central questions pose a psychological confrontation to Black men. At the core, Fanon questions our identity, suggests that we are accountable to ourselves, and proposes our potential. These questions are offered as the cornerstone to a Black male psychology that is liberating, healthy, and culturally authentic.

"Who Am I?"

This essential existential question is one of complexity and frustration for the Black male. So much of our identity has been marred by distortions propagated by oppressive cultural domination that even a Brother of average to above-average intellect and consciousness finds it difficult to articulate an authentic cultural identity. This poses the greatest challenge to the psychology of the Black male. The absence of an authentic cultural identity introduces the presence of a fictional demographic identity, a retro-racial identity, and an unbalanced gender identity. Effectively we assume another's response to the central question of who we are.

The ramifications of this event are numerous. The obvious problem arises when we began to look at the behavior of Black males from the halls of elementary education to the towers of higher education. It becomes obvious when we look at the academic achievement of Black boys in schools and communities that seek to define them, as K. K. K. Kambon says, in "alien self" terms. It becomes clear that many of our young boys are looking for someone who clearly depicts them. And consistently our educational system falsely reinforces that there is a void that reflects their greatness. The search for a self-identity in education has the greatest effect on the psychology of Black men because it is our first interaction with an institution that seeks to destroy us culturally which Miramba Ani (1999) defines as the intentional great suffering of people of African descent at the hands of Europeans in the Western hemisphere.

The crucial element in the search for an authentic cultural identity is in defining what actually is an authentic cultural identity for men of African descent. Many of the best and brightest intellects and scholars have advanced notions for the need for men of African descent to reclaim African systems of "Being." Na'im Akbar, Wade Nobles, Asa Hillard, Ilyana Vanzant, and others have attempted to focus this crucial question in the contexts of Ancient-African, traditional-African, and African spirituality.

For Brothers in the academy, this question becomes essential because we are operating in the belly of a beast—namely, the academy. It becomes essential that we immunize ourselves from the toxic syndrome of academic elitism. We must realize that we are dispensable and disposable despite how great European-Americans make us feel when they laud our work, skill, innovation, charisma, and even dress. As soothing as it is to the spirit to receive validation and recognition, you must ask yourself, "Whose definition of success am I choosing?" Definitions of success should be cross-checked with our response to the basic question of "Who am I?" Your response becomes the measure of your achievements.

The Black male search for an authentic cultural identity in many ways must be a violent revolt against years of indoctrination and socialization that addressed identity as reactive reflection to oppression. The Brothers in the academy must guard against a definition of self and purpose that ties into a values system and reinforcement structure that can be dangerous toward our cultural identity. The psychology of Black men is intricately interwoven into the basic question of identity. Recreating a culturally authentic self lies in questioning our current definition of self.

"Am I Who I Say I Am?"

The second essential question posed by Fanon relates to the issue of consistency. In the aftermath of an ambiguous cultural identity, the African American male is constantly forced to redefine and reformulate who he wants to be. There is the obvious spiritual tension between who we say we are, or how bad we think we are, and who stares back at us in the mirror. The silent rage of the inner voice that begs our spirits to be liberated is not always who appears before the classroom, boardroom, or church house. The psychology of the Black male is also enveloped in the complexity of consistently claiming who it is we want to be and living according to that which we say we are but not knowing exactly what it is that we say we are. Often I think Brothers proclaim who they say they are out of habit. Our identity becomes rooted in accolades, accomplishments, and awards given by others.

Liberated Brothers are constantly checking themselves in the mirror of reality, not for good looks and blemishes but to ascertain if their purpose is being fulfilled. The minute we claim or propose to be part of a material conundrum built by selfish deeds and self-service is when we have been co-opted by an alien cultural definition of manhood. We see this in those academic Brothers who do not support the Black student organizations, Black faculty initiatives, or Black community events, but who can always recite the latest joke from the last dean's-wanna-be social hour.

After addressing the questions of who we are, we then need to ask ourselves, "How well do we live this definition of self?" If, in fact, we claim to be African Americans, then how much of this label are we living? If we claim to be Afrocentric, then how much of this one are we living? This question serves as the barometer by which we measure ourselves and allow ourselves to be measured.

In essence, this question is one of self-inquisition; but more importantly, it implies our responsibility to self-monitor our accountability. See, once you have proclaimed it, you must now own it—you are accountable. This happens to be one of the major issues confronting the educated Black male— the Brother in the academy. How can we go from rhetoric to praxis? As a psychologist—an African-centered psychologist—I am constantly confronted with my own inconsistencies. Even after much study, mentoring, and deliberation, I realize that I am not where I want to be. But it is the confrontation of these questions that pushes me towards perfectibility, or as Dr. Thomas Parham puts it, to be "mo' bettah."

As Brothers in the academy, the issue of accountability is paramount to our psychology. Our collective identity obligates us to check ourselves. Fanon's questions ask us to investigate our accountability. The degree credentials allow social mobility and academic legitimacy, but please do not confuse this with personal and communal accountability. There is a reason that students gravitate toward our offices even though they are not in our classes or in academic programs. If we say we are of African descent but then do not make ourselves available to students and the community, then I ask, are we who we say we are?

"Am I All I Ought to Be?"

Fanon's final question addresses our potential. Traditionally, Black male psychology has been measured and described in the absence of another's values and norms. However, one of the greatest attributes to our identity is in what we could be, the untapped, unearthed raw talent that exists within each of us. This third and final question asks us to consider our unlimitlessness; as asked by Fanon, it requires the Black male to question the parameters of self and other imposed definitions of his identity. Conceptually, this question offers us promise toward reclamation of an authentic cultural identity.

A prerequisite to answering this question is an understanding of the prior two questions. Fanon's final question is even more complex because it requires vision. Vision is the ability to see things that are not there. He introduces the notion that we have options for our identity. However, we must be mindful that these options are a pure reflection of the original question of "Who am I?" My position asserts that old definitions of Black male psychology must be abandoned for a new description of an identity that is culturally authentic. Our mission is to develop and design an identity that is truly consistent with our natural self. But I submit that this can only be done with grass-roots strategies that seek to move us from rhetoric to praxis. Fanon contributes to our task by providing a framework from which to measure movement along a continuum of "Spiritness," as Wade Nobles calls it. If these questions are transplanted from these pages, implanted into our heads, and asserted into our lives, then we are beginning the revolutionary process of truly becoming liberated Brothers in the academy.

Afterthought

It is evident that the psychology of the Black man is not only of conceptual importance but also of practical importance. We Brothers must begin to consider not just environmental constraints posed by the academy and other systems but also self-imposed limitations. Arguably, even though the academy offers numerous opportunities for freedom, we must not forget its toxic nature for men of African descent. This thought piece simply offers a process for Brothers of the academy to understand the need for definitions of success and education to emerge from our own cultural tradition, not in reaction to, retrospective of, nor reflected by others' standards. We must acknowledge the toxic infectiousness of the academy, the need for inoculation, and the process of immunization. This process is necessary if we are to cultivate our spiritual illumination.

References

Akbar, N. (1998). *Man know thyself*. Tallahassee, FL: Mind Productions.

Ani, M. (1994). *Yurugy: An African-centered critique of European cultural thought and behavior.* Trenton, NJ: Africa World Press.

Hillard, A. G. (1998). SBA: The reawakening of the African mind. Gainesville, FL: Makare.

Kambon, K. K. K. (1998). *African/Black psychology in the American context: An African-centered approach.* Tallahassee, FL: Nubian Nation Publications.

Nobles, W. W. (1986). *African Psychology: Toward its reclamation, reascension, and revitalization.* Oakland: Black Family Institute.

Parham, T. A. (personal communication, April 23, 1998).

White, J. L. & Cones, J. H. (1998). *Black man emerging: Facing the past and seizing a future in America.* New York: Freeman.

Juan E. Gilbert

Juan Gilbert is currently a visiting instructor in the Systems Analysis Department at Miami University in Oxford, Ohio. He is also completing his Ph.D. in computer science at the University of Cincinnati. His research interests include human-computer interaction, educational technology, and electronic commerce.

Juan also serves as an internet technologies consultant. He has accepted several contracts from business and education dealing with Web development. He specializes in multimedia and Java technologies. He says, "Consulting keeps me fresh and up to date on the new technologies that are being developed out there . . . this allows me to give my students a real-world perspective on how their classroom experiences can be utilized to position themselves within the job market."

Juan holds a bachelor of science degree from Miami University (Oxford, Ohio) in systems analysis. As a student at Miami University, Juan won an Innovative Thinkers Contest Award, NCR Minority Scholarship Award, the Black Student Action Association Service Award, and several other awards. He also holds a master of science degree from the University of Cincinnati in computer science, which was obtained while he was an employee at the NCR Corporation.

His memberships include the Association for Computing Machinery (ACM), IEEE Computer Society, the Association for the Advancement of Computing in Education (AACE), Black Data Processing Association (BDPA), and Kappa Alpha Psi Fraternity Incorporated. Juan believes that being part of technical societies is a very important part of learning who the key players are in the field.

10

BEATING THE ODDS

AFRICAN AMERICANS IN
COMPUTER SCIENCE

Juan E. Gilbert

Introduction

"Because of deeply entrenched racial discrimination, more Black people have died from lightning than have become professors of computer science" (Williams, 1999). In 1969, the first African American computer science Ph.D. was awarded to Clarence Ellis at the University of Illinois. In 1972, James Monroe obtained the second from Texas A&M. According to the Computing Research Association Taulbee Survey (CRA, 1998), 25 percent of computer scientists in the United States are Black. In 1998, the CRA also reported that only 2 out of 1,217 full professors of computer science in all of North America were Black (see Table 1), and that 10 African Americans were awarded a Ph.D. in computer science out of 867 (2 of the 10 accepted tenure-track faculty positions). People may tell stories, but the numbers do not lie. It is shocking to face the reality of how few African Americans have obtained a Ph.D. in computer science. In the sections that follow, I will tell my story about "beating the odds" in obtaining a computer science Ph.D., and I will offer some recommendations for how other African Americans can do the same.

Before Graduate School

This is the story of my path to a computer science Ph.D. I was born in Hamilton, Ohio, a small city north of Cincinnati, and I attended Harrison Elementary School, a predominantly Black school. I continued my education at

Table 1. CRA—Ethnicity of Professors, 1998

	Assistant	Associate	Full
Nonresident Alien	72 (13%)	4	2
African American, Non-Hispanic	8 (1%)	5	2
Native American or Alaskan Native	1	6 (1%)	5
Asian or Pacific Islander	108 (19%)	228 (24%)	186 (15%)
Hispanic	12 (2%)	11 (1%)	16 (1%)
White, Non-Hispanic	337 (60%)	690 (71%)	969 (80%)
Other (Not Listed)	14 (3%)	8 (1%)	13 (1%)
Subtotal	552	952	1,193
Ethnicity Unknown	7 (1%)	23 (2%)	24 (2%)
Total	559	975	1,217

George Washington Junior High School, a predominantly White school, and Hamilton High School, an even more predominantly White school. As a high school student, I was ranked 21 out of more than 800 students, scored 23 on my ACT, made the honor roll several times, and was named the Scholar Athlete on the varsity basketball team. After being offered athletic scholarships as well as academic scholarships from several universities, the only unanswered question was where I would attend school in the fall of 1987. After much consideration, I decided to attend Miami University in Oxford, Ohio, on an academic scholarship.

Because of my love for science, I was determined to do something scientific with my life and initially decided to major in chemistry. It was not until my sophomore year that I decided to change my major to systems analysis—and doors began to open. I was awarded the NCR Minority Scholarship, which paid for my entire college education and included summer internships. The NCR Corporation was very generous to me during my undergraduate experience.

During the fall of my senior year, I was taking a stochastic systems course with the dean of the School of Applied Science. I sat in the front of the class in the first seat by the door, where I had the embarrassing habit of falling asleep in class. Since the instructor would hand out assignments and notes starting with me, he would have to awaken me before he could pass out the notes. Strangely, one day the instructor made the statement, "Juan, you should consider being a professor. I think you would make an excellent college professor . . . if you get your Ph.D., I will hire you." This was the planting of the seed that has developed into a tree today.

The Graduate School Experience

I accepted the challenge from the dean and performed several hours of research on the lifestyle of computer science professors, including their hours, workload, and salaries. Needless to say, I was very pleased with the information I had retrieved and decided to pursue a Ph.D. degree in computer science. Upon graduation in 1991, I accepted a full-time offer from NCR corporation—strictly a strategic move. At that time, NCR was willing to pay for employees to obtain graduate degrees related to their jobs as long as they remained full-time employees at NCR. Given the opportunity to obtain a master of science degree in computer science for nothing, I accepted the offer from NCR. I attended evening classes at the University of Cincinnati until I obtained my master of science degree in 1995.

Without hesitation, I immediately applied to the Ph.D. program at the University of Cincinnati but was shocked when I was denied admission. I was informed that I needed to demonstrate "more research potential." Determined to pursue a computer science Ph.D., I spoke with a professor at The Ohio State University about requirements for that Ph.D. program. Shortly after our conversation, I applied to The Ohio State University and was granted admission along with a fellowship.

Thus, in 1995, I left the NCR Corporation and the University of Cincinnati to pursue a computer science Ph.D. at The Ohio State University in Columbus, Ohio. After my first year at Ohio State, which was marked with much excitement and commendable performance, my advisor went before the faculty for tenure. He was the only faculty member in my research area, so when he was denied tenure and was forced to leave the university, I felt very alone. My choices were either to change my research focus or apply to a different university. I chose the latter.

I took the GRE, (and earned a 1550 cumulative score), obtained great letters of recommendation, and applied to several different departments. However, because of my GRE scores, all of my applications were denied. I was constantly told, "If you could get your GRE scores up to 1800, we could work with you."

With pure determination, I decided to make a case to get into a computer science Ph.D. program at the University of Cincinnati; but this time I was going to pursue admission differently. I decided to talk to a faculty member personally before sending in my test scores or my application. By talking directly with a faculty member who had a similar research area, I was able to get into the program. If ever there were a case of "Who you know versus what you know," this was it. Since my current advisor and other faculty members decided to accept me as their personal student (as opposed to the department admitting me based on other admission criteria), I was granted admission into the program and was given a fellowship before I ever applied to the program. While I thought that getting into a computer science Ph.D. program was very challenging, completing the program is much more difficult.

Completing the Ph.D.

I entered the Ph.D. program at the University of Cincinnati in 1997. As part of the degree requirements, I had to take a specified number of hours of course work; this is usually the easy part. The real challenge occurs when the course work is done and the Ph.D. qualifying exam must be taken. Every computer science Ph.D. program has a doctoral qualifying exam designed to demonstrate that the student has breadth in computer science. Most students think of it as a weed-out process—if you fail the qualifying exam, you are given a second attempt; if you fail it twice, then the department sends you home. Though most students at the University of Cincinnati fail on their first attempt but pass on their second, I passed the doctoral qualifying exam on the first attempt, a rare occurrence at the university. The qualifying exam is a major hurdle that must be passed, but it is not the last hurdle.

After completing the qualifying exam and my course work, I was then faced with the task of selecting a dissertation topic, defending my topic, and completing the degree. Selecting my dissertation topic was very difficult. Although there are so many things to research, I did not know if my topic would be worthy of the blessing of my committee. Thus, in order to assure that my dissertation topic would be accepted, I decided to publish my research topic prior to bringing it before my committee. Currently, my dissertation topic has been published several times and has received great reviews. I plan to go before the committee within the next few weeks, and by the time this essay is published, I will have defended my dissertation and successfully completed my computer science Ph.D.

Getting a Computer Science Ph.D.
Applying to Graduate School

My story may appear to be unique, but it is a fairly common story. Many African American students receive low GRE test scores like I did. Many African American students may have a difficult time getting into graduate school because of their test scores, because of research experience, and sometimes because of their race. With all of these challenges ahead, how can a young African American student get into graduate school? There are several steps that should be taken to "beat the odds" and pursue a computer science Ph.D.

Self-Motivation

If you want to "beat the odds" and obtain a computer science Ph.D., you have to be self-motivated. You cannot do it for the challenge or the money; you must have a love for the discipline and pure determination. You must first look into the mirror and see yourself as a computer science Ph.D. In addition, "beating the odds" is something that cannot be done on intelligence alone. If your heart is not in it, then it is very likely you will be weeded out somewhere along the process.

Identifying Programs

Applying to every school that has a Ph.D. program is not a good idea. Instead, the proper way to pursue the degree is to identify programs that have the research area of interest to you. For example, my research areas are human-computer interaction (HCI), educational technology, and electronic commerce. Since the University of Cincinnati has a faculty member in HCI, I found a potential program there. Also, when identifying programs, you should identify faculty members in your area of research, a process crucial to gaining acceptance. You should contact those faculty members in your research area and let them know your interest in their program. Also, ensure that the professor(s) will not be coming up for tenure during your program. If you recall, my advisor at Ohio State University came up for tenure and was denied, which left me alone in a graduate program without an advisor. You may find that the faculty members you contact are unpleasant and not willing to assist you in getting into the program. This is a blessing in disguise, for if the faculty members are not willing to assist you during the recruitment process, then they will not be willing to assist you when you are in the program. Therefore, you should drop that program from your list and move on to the next university. When speaking with faculty members, you should mention that your goal is to obtain the master's degree and the Ph.D. degree, which will assure the faculty member that you will be around for a while. Faculty members tend to want Ph.D. students because they will be available for work for a longer period of time.

It is also important for all prospective graduate students to make contact with other graduate students. This can be accomplished by visiting the department's Web page and looking for graduate students' Web pages. You should contact graduate students within your research area and any African American students, if available, which will give you an inside perspective on the department and faculty members. Once again, you do not want to enter a program where you are not wanted, and the more information you can obtain about a department, the better you will be able to make a decision. At some point, you will find a nearly perfect match. A faculty member will recruit you into the department and will accept an initial advisor role with you; you may even get funding from the department and/or the faculty member. Once this occurs, you can begin your journey to "beating the odds."

Working on the Inside

After entering the program and starting your course work, it is time to become a politician. As stated earlier, pure intelligence will not get you a computer science Ph.D; you must become a master negotiator. This will be accomplished by frequently visiting your advisor, talking to other graduate students, talking to the department administrators—basically getting to know as many people as possible. While most students realize that they have to establish a relationship with their advisors, they usually fall short when they do not create other relationships. Other graduate students can provide valuable information concerning other faculty members, the qualifying exams, which faculty members work well together, and so on. In addition, it is in your best interest to establish a great working relationship with your department's administration, for the administrators know everyone in the department and keep abreast of all department activities.

One of the most important observations that every graduate student should make is the working relationships between faculty members. When you establish your committee, the worst thing that could happen is having two faculty members on your committee who do not get along, which potentially could prolong your process indefinitely. During your tenure in the graduate program, you must identify those faculty members who are are accustomed to working together. This can be done by attending other dissertation defenses and by paying close attention to those members who appear in meetings together on a regular basis.

Research, Research, Research

Since an important aspect of obtaining the computer science Ph.D. is research, you will have to demonstrate research potential at some point during your program. I recommend doing this by publishing your research ideas—a painful process if you do not take rejection well. My research ideas were rejected several times, which was a good sign that I was way off base. After refining my ideas and organizing them on paper well, my research ideas have been accepted time and time again.

You can identify conferences within your area of research by looking around your advisor's office for conference invitations and journals that are relevant to your research area. The next step is simply to submit a well-written proposal to the conference before the call deadline. If you do not get in, do not take it personally. Simply refine your ideas and try again; eventually you will get in. After getting your paper accepted, you should extend it and submit it to another conference. At some point, when you are comfortable with your research ideas, submit them to a well-known journal. If the journal accepts your publication, then you know you are on the right track and you have proven yourself worthy to become a computer science Ph.D. The point of publishing your research is to establish yourself as a good computer science researcher and to let those who doubt you know that you are "legitimate."

Assuming you have successfully completed all of your course work, passed the qualifying exam, and defended your dissertation research proposal, after establishing yourself as a legitimate researcher, you will be ready to complete the degree. This is the point where you must complete your dissertation and defend it before your committee, a process with which your advisor will assist you. At this time, you will know more about your research than your advisor, so your advisor's role will change. Finally, when you near completion of your dissertation, you should begin looking for a job. Hopefully, you will consider working within academia.

Conclusions

Statistically speaking, there are probably fewer than 100 African Americans with a computer science, Ph.D., and very few of them have faculty positions. This essay describes my journey to beat these odds. Although my story may appear unique, it is very common for African Americans pursuing a computer science Ph.D., and many will encounter the same roadblocks that I did. After reading this essay, perhaps your journey in beating the odds will not be as difficult. If you are a dreamer and you have the love for science in your heart, consider helping to meet the need for more African American faculty members in computer science.

References

Computing Research Association. (1998). *CRA Taulbee survey of Ph.D. granting institutions.* [On-line]. Available: http://www.cra.org/statistics/.

Reis, R. M. (1997). *Tomorrow's professor: Preparing for academic careers in science and engineering.* Piscataway, NJ: IEEE Press.

Williams, S. (1999). *Computer scientist of the African diaspora.* [On-line]. Available: http://www.math.buffalo.edu/mad/computer-science/computer_science.html.

Michael L. Penn

Michael L. Penn, Jr., is an M.D./Ph.D. student at the University of California, San Francisco (UCSF). He is a graduate of Lowell High School in San Francisco, where he excelled in math and science. Mr. Penn accepted a full scholarship from Morehouse College, where he majored in biology. In 1994, he received his bachelor of science degree graduating with an overall 3.94 grade point average and earning himself a position as the highest-ranking student in the biology department. Mr. Penn is indebted to his alma mater for instilling in him a passion for knowledge and service to humanity. Currently a sixth-year student in UCSF's Medical Scientist Training Program (MSTP), Mr. Penn is the only African American enrolled in this highly competitive program. Rapidly approaching the conclusion of his Ph.D. training, Mr. Penn is immersed in AIDS research in the laboratory of Dr. Mark Goldsmith at the Gladstone Institute of Virology and Immunology. His dissertation research involves understanding the mechanisms by which the Human Immunodeficiency Virus (HIV) deteriorates the immune system. By taking advantage of a sophisticated experimental system (used only by one other laboratory in the world), Mr. Penn and colleagues have reported in a number of published articles why certain strains of HIV are more destructive to cells of the human immune system than others. He and his colleagues hope that their discoveries will lead to improved therapies for HIV-infected individuals. After receiving his Ph.D., Mr. Penn will return to medical school and complete his M.D. Mr. Penn is very thankful for his family, friends, and mentors who have challenged him to be the very proud African American man that he is today and the scholar that he will become.

11

AN M.D. *AND* A PH.D.

ONE MAN'S STORY

Michael L. Penn

In this essay, I describe my continuing evolution as a physician-scientist. In the next several pages, I hope to communicate several important concepts as I tell "my own personal story." First, for aspiring scholars, I will describe those elements that were essential to my academic success and how I arrived at the decision to pursue membership in the "academy." I hope to communicate that to become the ultimate scholar requires the highest standards, discipline, and an intimate knowledge of your innate learning process. Reaching this goal relies entirely upon paying close attention to how your brain naturally processes information. The sooner one defines this process, the sooner one can tailor an approach to learning and thereby reap the benefits of superior scholarship.

I hope that my discovery of my own brain's inner workings will help to unleash the intellectual power that is within all of us. I hope to communicate that success is not a destination; it is a journey. I define it as the journey during which a person learns how to maximize his or her full emotional, intellectual, physical, and spiritual potential. Continuing on this journey requires total dedication

Why Pursue an M.D. *and* a Ph.D.?
Isn't One Degree Enough?

When people learn that I am pursuing both an M.D. and a Ph.D., they often cannot fathom why I would want to spend the next seven to ten years of my life in school. When I decided to accept a position in UCSF's Medical Scientist

Training Program (MSTP), I, too, did not really know why I wanted these degrees. I knew that my experiences and opportunities had somehow led me to this program at UCSF. I also knew that this program was extremely competitive and that MSTP students represented the very best of the applicants to medical school. I was attracted to this level of competition and also wanted to study among the best students in the country. Historically, my best performances have arisen from competition. I have always wanted to be the best, and I saw the MSTP as a way for me to be just that.

Having actively pursued and obtained scholarships that covered all of my tuition and living expenses during college, I was very much interested in pursuing this opportunity to fund my graduate education. Not having educational debt in college afforded me the luxury of studying with complete freedom and intensity, which was a key element of my success in college. The fully funded M.D.-Ph.D. program represented the ultimate educational and financial opportunity. I am an educational opportunist in every sense of the word, and I will very aggressively pursue any educational opportunity that I feel will benefit me. I encourage you to do the same and pursue every opportunity to compete for scholarships that will support your education. Receiving such support not will not only build your confidence but it will also help to create the ideal environment in which to study.

The lure of the M.D.-Ph.D. was so powerful that it distracted me from answering the key question: Why did I want both an M.D. *and* a Ph.D.? The answer to this question was not simple and has taken me years to answer completely. In answering this question, let me first reflect on the evolution of my interest and background in science and medicine.

It is critical to identify your innate learning process. A large part of understanding this process is discovering those subjects for which you have a natural affinity. How does one determine these "affinity subjects"? The answer to this question is unique for each person. I determined that mathematics and science were my affinity subjects, not necessarily because I loved to study these subjects, but because I did not dread studying for them. Academically, I tended to perform best in these areas; math and science required less effort than did other subjects. In my case, the process of elimination helped to reveal my affinity subjects. I ultimately realized that the discrete and logical nature of math and science appealed to my brain. My brain naturally compartmentalizes information and concepts—an ability that is well adapted to acquiring mathematical and scientific information. Consequently, I pursued several opportunities to strengthen my background in these areas. In addition to taking honors and advanced-placement courses in these subjects in high school, I also joined MESA (Mathematics, Engineering, and Science Achievement), an organization that provides minority high school students with college-level courses at UC Berkeley during the summer. This program assessed my academic strengths and weaknesses and designed a curriculum that strengthened my weaknesses and promoted my strengths. Because my strongest subjects were science and mathematics, I was placed in college and graduate-level courses in these subjects. These courses gave me an incredibly strong educational base in science and mathematics.

My involvement with MESA enhanced my life in many ways. It provided me with a fun but intense learning environment and taught me that high-level achievement was a product of hard work and discipline. Its demanding course work forced me to develop study techniques that were efficient and effective. (I will expand on this idea later in this essay.) Perhaps the most important way that MESA helped me was that it expected the very best from me. This program believed in celebrating and encouraging academic achievement. Learning in an environment that celebrated my accomplishments and reinforced and validated my academic efforts left me eager for the next academic challenge. In addition, the minority students and professors who taught these courses were tangible role models who exemplified the fruits of academic excellence. These people truly made a difference in my life, and I hoped someday to help others as they had helped me.

After taking a variety of courses in mathematics, computer science, and biological science, I realized that my strongest interest was in the biological sciences. As a result, I decided that I would major in biology/pre-med in college. African Americans are extraordinarily underrepresented in the basic science disciplines. Ph.D.s earned by African Americans make up less than 6 percent of all those awarded in the life sciences and only 2.3 percent of those awarded in chemistry.

Morehouse College was very committed to changing these disparaging statistics. To encourage more students to consider careers as scientists, my biology department wrote a variety of grants to fund programs that gave students the opportunity to get research experience by working in laboratories at the college. Through the encouragement of several of my professors, I applied to a program sponsored by the National Science Foundation to encourage more minorities to pursue Ph.D.s in the sciences. This program provided me with a full-tuition scholarship and even paid me a few hundred dollars every month for the time that I spent in the lab.

I started this program reluctantly, however, for I had many stereotypic notions about what scientists were like. I imagined them as eccentric and isolated from society. I also believed that science not only attracted people with these qualities, but that it also required that people become social recluses.

Because I was afraid of how being a scientist might change my life, I focused mainly on medicine. By doing research with my professors at Morehouse, I discovered two things: (1) not all scientists are strange and eccentric, and (2) I actually *enjoyed* doing research. The possibility of making such a contribution excited me.

I discovered what was missing during a summer that I spent doing research at the National Institutes of Health (NIH) in Bethesda, Maryland. Interestingly, it was not a particular discovery in the laboratory that convinced me to pursue a Ph.D.; it was a conversation with a *medical patient* whom I had met at the hospital at NIH. It was the end of the summer, and all of the students who had done research on the campus came together to present posters of their work during the summer. I had done a project on a rare genetic, neurological disease called Spinocerebellar Ataxia. I was standing by my poster when a man walked by and happened to notice the word *genetic* in my poster's title. He approached me with great interest and enthusiasm and proceeded to ask what seemed like a million questions about my project. With each successive explanation, he became more enamored with my research.

Although I would like to think that it was because my research was so outstanding, I realized that this patient was excited because he *had* a rare genetic disorder. I learned that he was from North Carolina and had come to the NIH to participate in a study that would help scientists learn more about his particular disease. This man had had many bouts with near-death illnesses associated with his disease, yet he seemed to be the happiest man I had ever met. When I asked him how he was able to keep his spirits so high, he told me that just knowing that physicians and scientists were trying to understand the cause of genetic diseases like his gave him a reason to smile every day and keep fighting for his life. It was at that very moment that I realized that I did not just want to practice medicine. I could now see what a tremendous impact I could make in the lives of others by pursuing both the M.D. and the Ph.D. Medicine satisfied my desire to be a compassionate healer, while science satisfied my desire to make a contribution to understanding human disease through scientific discovery. It was clear at that moment that I would apply to the M.D.-Ph.D. program.

I applied to and was accepted at a number of different schools, but I ultimately chose to attend UCSF. In the years following my arrival at UCSF, it became increasingly clear that my decision to pursue my M.D.-Ph.D. at UCSF was more than just a *choice*; it was an instinctive *response* to my calling in life. As the *only* African-American M.D.-Ph.D. student at UCSF, my voice and my actions have a profound impact. Because of this, I am frequently given the opportunity to advocate for African American student issues.

Another arena where I realized I could make a contribution was through research. Research required ambition, creativity, courage, and perseverance. In general, scientists want to understand fundamental biological processes. The most ambitious scientists often ask very simple questions like, "Why do cancer cells divide uncontrollably?" The beauty of science is that it is open-ended—you have the creative freedom to hypothesize about answers to this question. You can design experiments to test your hypotheses in a variety of ways. Often the answers to such simple questions require more than a lifetime of research. Many scientists spend their entire careers trying to answer a single question! Since the overwhelming majority of scientific experiments fail, one must have the perseverance to keep trying.

In addition, scientific inquiry often requires that researchers learn and master new techniques frequently. Being timid about learning is not conducive to being a scientist. The successful scientist is the one who has the courage to travel into unknown territory and learn something new when necessary. Courage is also necessary when a hypothesis is proven wrong and when one needs to formulate a new hypothesis. I was very attracted to these aspects of science, as they were quite consistent with my personality. I knew that there would never be a dull moment in the lab, and I looked forward to being able to use my creativity in the process of generating scientific hypotheses and using experimentation to test them.

I am now immersed in the laboratory working on my Ph.D. I am trying to understand why people respond to HIV infection in different ways. Some people can live with HIV for many years exhibiting very few symptoms before they progress to AIDS, while others progress to AIDS very shortly after becoming HIV-positive. I hypothesized that different strains of HIV might have different abilities to attack the immune system thereby accounting for these differences. My colleagues and I have proven definitively that there are specific types of HIV strains that have powerful abilities to destroy cells of the immune system, while other strains have very mild effects.

Because I have pursued my true calling in life, I am extremely committed to and engaged by the research that I do. Consequently, I have been able to accomplish a great deal as a graduate student. I have an impressive publication record and will likely finish my Ph.D. at least one year ahead of most of my classmates. I could not have asked for a better graduate experience. I mention these things not to boast but to highlight what an impact my accomplishments have had. Because African Americans are so underrepresented in the biological sciences, it becomes critical that those of us who belong to the academy represent ourselves. My work certainly speaks for itself, but it also may speak for the next Brother who applies to the M.D.-Ph.D. program from

Morehouse or another Historically Black College or University (generally students recruited from these schools are considered potential "risks").

The other contribution that I can make as an African American scientist and member of the academy is to make our community more aware of truths and myths about scientific research. Many folks are still bitter and wary of science and medical research because of incidents like the Tuskeegee Experiment. Although undocumented, this has had a substantial impact on the quality of care that we receive. Because African Americans generally distrust scientists, we do not readily participate in studies that address issues specific to our people. Consequently, there is a paucity of literature on African Americans for virtually every medical illness. We do not adhere to pharmacologic regimens that are essential for our health. As a result, we increase our likelihood of remaining ill.

The Tenets of Superior Scholarship

One of the major hindrances to African American achievement at the college and graduate levels is not having access to all of the keys to success in these arenas. I am not suggesting that we are less capable; I am suggesting that African Americans, in general, do not have the benefit of learned academic behaviors of success that are garnered by growing up around generations of educated people. Being successful in college is often more than just studying hard and making good grades. Many times the difference between surviving and excelling is knowing the right person, knowing the right questions to ask, or being in the right place at the right time. Nearly all of these nuggets of information are unwritten—known only by an elite group of students. My parents were first-generation college graduates and, consequently, made a lot of mistakes because they did not have the benefit of such information. I have been able to learn from my parents' mistakes, capitalize on their successes, and add more golden nuggets of information to my treasure chest. My children will have even more experience and information from which to draw. In this essay and the following list, I have put together many of these unwritten rules and guidelines, which I have gleaned from my colleagues, Black and otherwise, along my journey.

1. The first thing to remember as one embarks upon the journey into academia is that you are Black. Do not ever forget that. It can be both your ace and your handicap. Being an African American interested in science, in particular, is very advantageous. Nearly every scientific organization recognizes the paucity of African American Ph.D.s. As a

result, there is a wealth of scholarship and fellowship opportunities to pursue. In contrast, many scientists automatically question our abilities and resent our presence in the scientific arena. Getting acknowledgement and respect from these people often requires that we are better than their best students are.

2. The next golden nugget of advice is to make friends with the "enemy"—the enemy being White or other majority students. This enemy is not real, only perceived. Many African American students walk through life bitter from experiences similar to those I have described above. They perceive White students as the enemy and do everything in their power to isolate themselves from this group. Any attempt to associate with these students is viewed as "selling out" or compromising one's dignity. In fact, not associating with your colleagues is selling yourself out and compromising the quality of your education. The rigors of higher education require that students form alliances. In addition to potentially gaining access to more "golden nuggets" of information, having intellectual exchange with your colleagues is a key part of the scholarly growth process. It allows you to see how you "measure up" to your classmates. It can broaden your perspective and identify areas that need strengthening. Because I realize that I do not know everything there is to know about graduate school, I will readily ask for the information that I need. Know when to ask for help! Never be too proud to ask for assistance. I choose to think of interacting with my colleagues as an opportunity to grow rather than a decision to "sell out." In fact, the combination of having access to these golden nuggets of information and knowing that you have to work twice as hard as everyone else often results in stellar achievements.

3. Another distinguishing factor between the good graduate student and the great graduate student is being able to sell your talents. Do not be afraid to promote yourself. Many of the most successful people are not always the smartest—just the most courageous. Be an opportunist! I learned this lesson during my summers at the Massachusetts Institute of Technology and the National Institutes of Health. I witnessed eager students vying for the attention of the lab directors in hopes of having an opportunity to demonstrate their proficiency and skill. Some of these students would go so far as to *ask* to be nominated for awards! In many cases, their aggressiveness got them what they wanted. However, most of these students had the credentials to back their requests up. The lesson I learned that summer was that if you spend time being the best student you can be, you should feel free to pursue any opportunity you want.

I would be remiss if I ended with the impression that I am a perfect student. The truth is, my story is the result of significant trial and error. I have had serious difficulties at times and have had to overcome them. I have doubted my abilities and, in some instances, let myself down. What allows me to keep going during these times? I draw strength from many sources. First, I pray that God will give me strength and order my steps appropriately. Second, I seek comfort and support from my family and friends who love me and celebrate my achievements. Third, I recall all of the other times in my life when I have felt exactly the same way and remind myself that I always seem to make it through. Years ago, my mother suggested that I keep a "success log," a running list of all of my accomplishments, small and large. This success log represents a celebration of my achievements. Referring to it helps me not to forget my evolution. It also reminds me of the many gifts I have received and allows me to rise and meet the next challenge. Create your own success log!

Divine Intervention

Writing this essay has afforded me the time to reflect on my life (all 27 years of it!). I hope to identify and highlight those elements that were critical to my current success and those I believe will be essential for my future success. In this section, I will deal with the importance of having a strong spiritual base. My intention is not to convert anyone to Christianity but to highlight how my spiritual connection with God has allowed me to achieve at levels I did not think were possible.

Like most kids, I dreaded going to church, and attending a Lutheran school made religion more like a chore for me. I remember hearing many people in the church tell me that my life was an opportunity to do God's work. Unfortunately, it has taken years for me to understand fully what this statement meant.

As I grew up, I developed a deeper sense of spirituality. I began to see that we have two major choices in life: to live with God or without God. Living without God often leads to a misguided, frustrating, and stressful life of struggling with the incredible task of "controlling" one's destiny; life's challenges then seem overwhelming and impossible.

In retrospect, Morehouse provided the greatest examples of truly blessed men who derived their strength and direction from God. I had the opportunity to learn from many great men while at Morehouse. If I looked closely, I could see God breathing his wisdom and strength into them. Collectively, these men have inspired me to become the very best person and scholar that I can be. I can remember Nima Warfield, Morehouse's 1994 valedictorian, who mentored me and provided a standard of excellence by which I still live. His thirst for knowledge, impeccable academic record, and vision for the African American community inspired me to become a distinguished scholar and a passionate voice for my community (Nima later went on to become Morehouse's first Rhodes Scholar). I remember Dr. David Cooke, my freshman advisor and physiology professor, who recognized my academic talents and challenged me to take more than a full load of courses during my first semester in college. His suggestion taught me to never set limits on what I can accomplish. I remember Dr. Joseph McCray, my laboratory advisor and biochemistry professor, whose pressing questions and challenging courses pushed my critical thinking beyond what I thought possible. Dr. McCray often questioned me about my interest in science. His probing questions challenged me to search deep within myself and discover what *really* motivated me.

I also remember Reverend Kelvin Sauls, my associate pastor, who exemplifies for me the ultimate synergy between mind, body, and soul. He enabled me to understand more completely God's plan for my life and how to stay connected to that eternal energy source called Jesus Christ. These people represent only a handful of the countless angels God has sent to me. When I reflect back to my childhood—when I felt as if God had abandoned me—I smile. God had never abandoned me. I now feel his presence all around me, and if I pay close attention, I can see his plan revealing itself right before my eyes; God is guiding my every step.

Now I praise God every day for the gifts he has given me: a sound mind, a supportive family, encouraging friends and teachers, and the ability to be an inspiration to others. I have the peace of mind to accept those things that are beyond my control and the confidence of knowing that God is my lighthouse leading me through every storm. My spirituality is my best stress-reducer. This state of mind has yielded me far greater success than I could ever have achieved "on my own." I would never have predicted that I would graduate from Morehouse *summa cum laude,* or that I would pursue my M.D.-Ph.D. at UCSF, one of the best medical schools in the country, or even that I would ultimately inspire others to pursue similar career paths. But these things were not for me to predict—these events are all part of God's master plan for my life.

Willis L. Lonzer

Dr. Willis L. Lonzer III is currently a postdoctoral research associate in the Department of Physiology and Biophysics at Case Western Reserve University School of Medicine, Cleveland, Ohio, where he is involved in characterizing the structure and function of membrane protein systems that are targets for novel antibiotics or correlated with some diseases.

Dr. Lonzer hails from Richmond, Virginia, where he graduated from Highland Springs High School in the Henrico Public School System. He holds a bachelor of science degree in chemistry from Delaware State University, where he was the recipient of the University President's Outstanding Leadership award given to a graduating senior who has demonstrated outstanding leadership during his or her enrollment at the university. He also holds the doctor of philosophy degree in chemistry from The University of Akron, where he was a Patricia Roberts Harris Doctoral Fellow. He is a member of the American Chemical Society.

In his community, Dr. Lonzer is a very active member in his church, The House of the Lord in Akron, Ohio. In an effort to serve the greater Akron and greater Cleveland communities, Dr. Lonzer also annually visits a number of public and private schools to promote careers in science, engineering, and medicine. He has also served on the Science Advisory Council for the Arlington Christian Academy.

Dr. Lonzer is an active member of Alpha Phi Alpha Fraternity, Inc., Eta Tau Lambda chapter. He is also a member of the Board of Alpha Phi Alpha Homes, Inc., of Akron and the Akron Black College Alumni Association.

He is married to the former Deborah Sanders, an alumnus of Kent State University who holds BFA and M.Ed. degrees. They have two children: Josiah—age 9 and Ryan—age 4. The Lonzers reside in Akron, Ohio.

12

WHEN CAN'T MEANS CAN

BLACK MEN IN CHEMISTRY

Willis L. Lonzer

Introduction

Although African Americans have made many advances into careers in medicine within the past twenty to thirty years, few have ventured into the sciences, particularly the physical sciences. Furthermore, there are not very many African American Ph.D.s in chemistry, biochemistry, or other biomedical areas. For example, a recent article in *Science,* the national magazine of the American Association for the Advancement of Science, cited that out of a pool of all postdoctoral fellows who are U.S. citizens or permanent residents, only 124 were African American (Mervis, 1999). In the article, the author implies that the problem lies at the beginning of the pipeline. Perhaps society's perception of careers in science—particularly in the African American, Hispanic, and Native American communities—needs to change from one of feeling we are not smart enough or we cannot cut it in the sciences to one embracing the challenges and rewards that accompany such difficult endeavors.

To Be Fed by Ravens

In the book of I Kings (I Kings 17:1–6) the Bible tells of how the prophet Elijah, while alone in the wilderness, was fed bread and meat by ravens that had been sent by God. The symbolism implied from this event recorded in Biblical history points to Elijah's total reliance upon God. Even though the magnitude of this reliance is not the same, I do believe that the student relies upon the professor for "nourishment" that most often goes beyond the textbook.

Chemistry, being an exact science, requires a great deal of intuitive ability to visualize and understand many of the seminal concepts. Since the approach of textbook authors, in general, is not always appealing to the student, he or she finds the need for an interpreter—either a graduate assistant or the professor.

During my time at Delaware State University, one of the Historically Black Colleges and Universities (HBCUs), each chemistry professor was a vital component of the department that gave him or her more "clout" than the majority of university professors. Despite the demands upon them due to higher teaching loads and more administrative responsibilities (such as for laboratory setup), Delaware State chemistry professors were available to their students; they cared about their students' academic and personal development. In addition, we seemed to have an interesting mix of students in the Chemistry Department who excelled in and out of the classroom—what I believe is probably commonplace at most HBCUs. The encouragement of these professors has helped to cultivate the careers of many professionals. I was very blessed to have mentors who took a vested interest in my development.

The first professor to serve as a mentor to me, Dr. Brown (not his real name), was important in directing my academic pursuits. This individual interacted with me independently from our departmental adviser, and I used his advice to balance the recommendations of the departmental adviser. This checks-and-balances system later proved important when selecting and pairing work-intensive courses with those less intensive in nature. But one of the most helpful aspects of Dr. Brown's advisement was his wisdom on course selection. While the core courses such as physics and chemistry are generally the same in all science programs, the electives that one takes in an undergraduate program may later prove to be paramount in one's overall preparation. Having exposure to Dr. Brown, a seasoned African American scientist with a Ph.D. from a top-ten chemistry program who also had a commanding knowledge of the "winds" that are dictating his field of expertise, was an essential resource at Delaware State and a rare jewel considering the size of this HBCU. An individual like Dr. Brown can help the undergraduate in identifying directions of interest and help to enhance the learning experience. This enhancement in the learning experience may be realized through the recommendation of special topics/advanced courses that will provide insight and exposure to tools and essential concepts that are vital to a developing scientist.

A second professor (I will call him Dr. Doe) was my undergraduate research adviser and was a key individual in helping me to develop my research skills. By working as a student researcher in Dr. Doe's laboratory, I was able to gain practical experience and training. Regardless of the area of interest, exposure to the research lab, which develops bench and observation techniques and allows utilization of analytical equipment, will bolster scientific development. In chemistry, the use of internships in industry, government, or summer research at a university provides wonderful work or research experiences that involve application of learned techniques. Oral presentations and formal colloquia as well as a bachelor thesis present an early opportunity to hone communication skills that will be useful later.

Having mentors outside of your academic department can also be a valuable supplement. People in this capacity may serve as advisers on career opportunities that may be nontraditional and can point out leadership and team skill-building opportunities that may prove helpful in the job market later. Moreover, the view from an outside professor may offer more objectivity in helping you to discern who you are and where you want to go.

The "backbone" of a scientist is chiefly comprised of his or her fundamental courses and experiences. For those who were educated following a liberal arts program versus a business training, the undergraduate curriculum offers a unique opportunity to select a variety of courses that will hopefully enhance intellectual development. Within that curriculum, several subareas probably exist, including core courses. For the chemistry or science major, some courses are automatically inscribed on the curriculum, including courses such as organic chemistry, physics, and zoology. The courses, however, that are not always evaluated for their relevance and application tend to be the electives. Since academia and industry today both encounter real problems that require an interdisciplinary approach to begin solving them, science electives are extremely important. With the advent of big areas such as biochemistry, we observe the development of courses that act as connections to other disciplines and their traditional courses (such as inorganic chemistry). Today's elective choices may include such offerings as bioinorganic, bioorganic, and biopolymer courses, and the list goes on. Thus, the student is faced with an interesting but sometimes vexing dilemma: What do I take that will enhance my career? Will I die of boredom in this course? Usually the latter question is resolved soon after the student enrolls and embraces the intriguing challenges offered by the course. The former question, however, has a tendency to stick around much longer, as a student sometimes struggles to make the proper choices.

No matter what the choices, these minor courses are very important in presenting relevant and practical tools for assessing scientific/biomedical issues that researchers face today. Students should take a variety of courses, including those of which they have little or no knowledge. This often helps to broaden their scope of knowledge of the subject and may lead to pleasant returns later in the career-development path.

In addition, every science major should take a few business and social science electives. In today's market, scientists often play roles in marketing and planning products. Courses such as principles of marketing and economics are informative and orient an individual toward a more team-oriented role within an organization. Being a team player is almost essential in today's industry and is a necessary element for advancement. Social science courses such as sociology and psychology are also helpful in exposing people to how human beings act or think at home or at work.

Another important aspect of the undergraduate science experience is research. Having a good research experience can make or break a budding scientific career. Despite Delaware State University's size, it has a diverse and cross-disciplinary base of research on campus. Some labs are oriented toward traditional research paradigms such as botany or organic chemistry, while others are rather biomedically oriented with lab emphases ranging from the molecular biology of Graves disease to the synthesis of antiviral agents.

Even though it does not necessarily entail a great deal of independence, researching at this level allows one the opportunity to immerse his feet into the waters of discovery. An individual can then begin to hone skills of observation and evaluation of data and problems that are involved. It should be noted that while the experiences garnered in the academic course lab are a plus, they often lack the student-mentor relationship and research skill cultivating benefits that most often accompany research lab experiences. Not only does the individual go beyond the seminal principles of one's discipline but one actually begins to embrace or make the research problem his by possessing and evaluating the real-life implications involved. This can manifest itself in various ways, but most importantly, the student realizes an actual problem and attempts to solve it. It is also helpful to gain as much exposure and practical experience with as much research equipment and as many tools and techniques as possible. Gaining experience with techniques such as electrophoresis or magnetic resonance will broaden the student's research perspective and bolster marketability. In many respects, these early experiences represent the proverbial grain of sand that later becomes the lustrous pearl of the oyster.

Transitioning into Graduate School

Depending on the student's major, the final year of college could offer a broad spectrum of experiences and restrictions. Depending on how the course load has been planned, an individual could be faced with a range of scenarios between two extremes: 1) a relatively easy course load and one to two senior-level electives per semester, or 2) the convergence of several painfully demanding courses that will make each semester a rather stressful experience. In any case, courses for the senior year must be selected carefully. This offers an opportunity for the student to demonstrate maturity to the faculty and even more importantly, to the admissions committees of the graduate schools that the student is vying to enter. In conjunction with courses chosen, GRE scores will be important for successful entry into graduate school. It should go without saying that the best grades and GRE scores are desired by top institutions. While some feel that a helpful way to attain strong GRE scores is to utilize a GRE prep course and/or GRE prep booklets, the feelings about the worth of such courses and materials seem to be split. Nevertheless, preparation will prove to be vital for success.

Another important aspect of transitioning to graduate school is the actual selection of an institution. While there are probably many factors, I feel that the following three important steps should be considered:

1. What do I want to do in the future?
2. What is the reputation of the university (pedigree)?
3. Is there strong support for minorities?

Deciding which area to pursue in graduate school can be difficult. Chemistry has been and still is a field that has not been aggressively pursued by African Americans. While the reasons are probably numerous, this should not be a deterrence for pursuing chemistry as a career. In choosing a subdivision of chemistry, the student should evaluate what areas will allow the greatest growth potential. Is this subdivision potentially going to be saturated in the near future, or should it observe steady growth? One should also consider if an academic career is planned. More questions will likely exist that are individually significant, and they will have to be addressed before the student can effectively begin pursuing an advanced degree.

After making the appropriate considerations on the area of study, a decision on the institution remains. The questions that can be used to evaluate a potential institution can vary, of course, but they should at least include the following: How strong is the university's academic and research track record in your chosen area? Does the university offer collaborative or dual programs? How will I pay for this? In addressing the last question, my experience has shown me that graduate or teaching assistantships are generally available for graduate students. As mentioned briefly before, strong minority support programs are quite beneficial to students who are facing the new challenges that graduate school brings. These programs will help the student to network and establish some concrete contacts that will hopefully undergird the transition efforts. In addition, a good program should provide faculty contacts who will provide advisory support and a channel or means of handling potential grievances and/or a scholarship/fellowship resource.

After arriving at the chosen school, the student must choose a research adviser. This is obviously very important because not only will this person help guide you as a developing scientist, but that individual's principles and integrity will directly impact your principles and ideologies. Impacting does not suggest that the student should adopt his or her adviser's philosophies, but they will affect the working conditions in the lab, the attitudes of lab personnel, and ultimately, the student/adviser relationship, which is crucial for this level of research. It is also helpful to know an adviser's positive and negative attributes. A couple of relevant examples are provided in the following paragraphs.

First, the level of commitment that the adviser is willing to give to the student is an important consideration that can be crucial in affecting the student's progress and the length of time he or she spend in the program. This becomes even more critical for a student whose chemistry background is weaker. The personality and work ethic of the graduate student should also be considered when choosing a research adviser. Obviously, a good balance between availability and moderate research expectations will help. I had a research adviser who, because of an extensive travel/lecture schedule and administrative duties, was rarely around. In the long run, it has proven to be positive, but it was very difficult as I went through my graduate program.

Second, how does the adviser treat his or her group? What are the group's attitudes? Are people graduating? At what rate? Collectively, these questions pose the second standard by which a potential adviser should be evaluated. Good working conditions and morale go a long way when considering how much time lab personnel spend together and how these factors impact personal and career development. Advisers who respect their lab personnel often reap the benefits through the lab personnel's hard work. These factors should be helpful in finding good faculty advisers.

There is one obvious truth that must be stated: The Ph.D. in chemistry is grueling! Anyone who chooses to embark upon this journey should think about the risks and benefits before starting a program. Having a family and children can complicate matters even more, so be sure to make time for your family and even some time for yourself whenever possible. The lab should not be your only world; a good balance between lab work and play will make a significant difference.

Where Do We Go from Here?

Upon completion of the Ph.D. in chemistry or any other doctorate, the graduate is now poised to take on new challenges as a new member of the community of scholars. What is next? There are several relevant choices. The first may be a postdoctoral research fellowship, which allows a new Ph.D. an opportunity to broaden his or her research experience by researching in an area that is different from the dissertation project. The experience should allow for opportunities to learn new strategies and techniques and to gain experience with other relevant research topics. The postdoc works in the lab of a principal investigator with whom he or she offers collegial advice and support. The long-term goal of the training mode is to increase the marketability of the postdoc and to build his or her publication record. The postdoc has been referred to as a springboard position that can lead to an industrial or academic position. Postdocs are available in academia and industry. While the academic postdoc typically can go to either academia or industry, the industrial postdoc generally stays in industry. Government labs like the National Institutes of Health also offer postdoctoral positions. Whatever the choice, the name recognition of the principal investigator and the university pedigree are always helpful.

A second option is industry. An industrial Ph.D. scientist will function as a senior-level scientist, typically as a member of a team of scientists that works collectively. This scenario is typical of larger firms but may change according to the size of the company, responsibilities, and so on. The industrial setting, especially in a big pharmaceutical company, offers a thriving environment where many scientific and nonscientific considerations are applicable, thereby causing the industrial scientist to be versatile and market driven. On the other hand, an academic career may be chosen. Teaching can be a very rewarding experience in chemistry. Because it is such an integral part of many science and engineering curricula, teaching chemistry will allow interaction with a broad spectrum of students. While small liberal arts colleges and community colleges do not typically require postdoctoral experience, large research universities do.

Finally, some Ph.D,s choose to follow nontraditional career tracks. Some Ph.D.s are now choosing to teach on the high-school level, while others are going on to medical or law schools. Currently, the role of the M.D./Ph.D. has not been really identified between researcher or physician, but the J.D.s/Ph.D.s typically are practicing, for example, intellectual property law. Still others are pursuing business opportunities such as marketing, sales, and management. As we enter into the new millennium, the opportunities available to Ph.D.s will only be hindered by their career vision. The doors are wide open!

Reference

Mervis, J. (1999). Minority postdocs are rare, independent breed. *Science*, *285*, 1529–1530.

Eddie Moore

Mr. Moore is the Assistant Dean of Students and Director of Intercultural Life at Cornell College in Mount Vernon, Iowa. Mr. Moore developed and maintains a growing Diversity Consulting and Research Team: America & Moore. The team has given interactive and challenging presentations/workshops to students from grade K through post-secondary levels. The presentations/workshops have also been given to parents, community members, organizations and city/state government employees across the nation.

Mr. Moore holds a B.A. in political science from Cornell College. He received his M.A. in education administration from Loras College in Dubuque, Iowa. He is currently pursuing a Ph.D. in education (educational leadership) from the University of Iowa in Iowa City.

Mr. Moore has given several educational and academic presentations, including FINE: First in the Nation In Education; Iowa's Educational Research Foundation; AERA in Montreal in 1999; AESA in Philadelphia in 1998; and as keynote speaker for MLK day in Fort Madison, Iowa in 1999 and in Dubuque, Iowa in 1997. Mr. Moore has organized and facilitated forums and panel discussions about gangsta rap, affirmative action, interracial dating, flag burning, women and minorities in higher education, religion/segregation, and race relations. Recognized for his ability to challenge, educate, and motivate folks into advocates for peace, equity, and justice, Mr. Moore continually strives to provide opportunities and hope to every child across America by being an effective, intelligent, and consistent educator. Mr. Moore maintains an energetic, positive, and caring attitude professionally and spiritually.

13

THE CHALLENGES OF DIFFERENCE AND DIVERSITY

Preparing Iowa for Black, Brown, and International

Eddie Moore

My Brotha, I live in Iowa. No, man, not Idaho, I-O-W-A, the state where the corn grows. Oh, yeah, it gets real cold in Iowa; Jack Frost has relatives there. For sure, for sure, there are a lot of White people there, and jungle fever is everywhere. No, no, no, all those White folks are not mean and racist people. In fact, there are some cool White folks in Iowa. They smile, they say "hi," and they will feed you, too. However, there is one thing I don't like about White people in Iowa: they are quiet, and the best friend of hate is silence.

I have this conversation all the time. I am always explaining to my family and friends why a young, Black, educated, and handsome brother is living in Iowa. "Listen people, Iowa is my calling. This is the place where I will make my small contribution to society." Family, friends, strangers on the streets, colleagues at national conferences, they still can't believe that I have lived in Iowa for a total of 9 years and for the last 4 years consecutively. Folks can't understand it.

In fact, I came to Iowa from Florida in 1985. I came to Cornell College in Mt. Vernon, Iowa, to play football, baseball, and basketball. My mom was so happy to see me leaving my neighborhood. She didn't care if I was going to small-town Kansas; I was out of there. Unfortunately, my community was not a place with many opportunities for a young Black man with just a high-school diploma. In addition to that, crack-cocaine sales and use were increasing. Needless to say, Mom was very concerned for my future and excited about the state of Iowa. I was not sure what to expect, but I was looking forward to playing ball and experiencing a new environment. It was culture shock—and that weather!

Today, I tell folks all the time, Iowa has been very, very good to me. I like Iowa. Yes, it's tough finding a Black barber, a Black-owned restaurant with collard greens, a Black dentist, a Black lawyer, and, in some places, a Black person. Iowa is known as one of the Whitest states in America. The only thing Black in some communities is the coffee they serve in the restaurants. So why do I like it? So why am I here? Sometimes I ask myself that same question, especially in the middle of January. I have been called to Iowa, and Iowa needs me. I am an educator, a diversity consultant, a leader, a role model, and an advocate for peace, equity, and justice (APEJ). My call to Iowa: prepare the state for Black, Brown, and international. This is a story about my work and the people of Iowa.

Across the nation there is an increasing number of Black, Brown, and international folks. As a matter of fact, some statisticians have projected that by the year 2050, White people will be the minority. Some say that by the year 2020, an estimated 115 million Americans will be people of color. The Asian population will have the most rapid growth rate, while Hispanics will add the most numbers. These changes would represent a historic shift in America's racial and ethnic composition and could mean long-range changes in social, political, and economic life (U.S. Census Bureau, 1996).

These facts on difference and diversity can be overwhelming. Some Americans don't even talk about the changes, think about the changes, or know about the changes. Nonetheless, the changes are real, and there is absolutely nothing America, nor Iowa, can do to stop the changes. A mass mailing of postcards or commercials on each network telling people not to come or reproduce in America will not work! Face the facts, America and Iowa. This is how I break it down in my presentations:

> *"Some of you, your parents, and grandparents have never had an experience with a person of color. This will not be true for the future generations. They will live in a more diverse America. My friends, you can't run from me (representing Black, Brown, and international). I'm just like digital cable or the Internet: eventually I will show up in your home. There is nothing you can do about it. The question is:* Are you ready?"

In addition to changing demographics, family changes will affect communities and schools across America. The changes will continue into the millennium. The family has changed in three ways: family size, family structure, and family roles.

Family Size

America was a farming economy. Agriculture was the primary source of income for many families. The average White family used to have between six to ten children who were considered a source of income, a matter of survival. The more kids, the more hands to work and maybe more money. Today in America, technology and the computer industry drive the economy. There are more jobs and career opportunities in technology, and the farms are drying and dying. Kids can be an expensive liability at home, so the average White family now has two to three children. Parents today make more money but work longer hours. There is no time, energy, or need for more children. That is their choice.

A smaller family is not the case for people of color and not by choice. Over the past century, Black, Brown, and international families—particularly Hispanics—have remained strong. Many Hispanics still need larger families to survive, as some still earn farm wages as migrant workers. A larger family provides additional domestic resources and another source of income. The average family of color today has five to eight children, and the population projections for Hispanic families is off the scale.

Family Structure

Today, women claim head of household. Single-parent mothers are demanding and receiving much due respect and recognition. They should be applauded for their efforts. Although the number of teen mothers has fallen, America will have to deal with the larger numbers from the past. Another important change to note is that grandparents have become primary caretakers. Finally, some families are no longer just mom and dad. More gay and lesbian couples are pursuing families through adoption; sometimes the family is created from kids through previous heterosexual relationships. More families have two moms or two dads.

Family Roles

Today, many women are either entering the workforce or starting their own businesses. The role of mom has changed. "Soccer moms" are now working professional mothers. Some women leave the house by choice, but many more seem to be doing so for survival. The days of June Cleaver from "Leave It to Beaver" are long gone.[1]

---

1. These facts came from my class with Dr. David Bills. His class really inspired me to understand the demographic shifts and changes. Thanks, David!

This is a small sample of the differences and diversity across America, including Iowa. Some people are excited by the changes, and some are disgusted. Difference and diversity have been the source of problems and tension across America for a long time. Most of the time, the results of the tension show up in headlines of national newspapers or become featured stories and special reports covered on radio or evening news programs. Every year a major story will break because of ignorance or a lack of respect, understanding, and connection. What worries me is that some Americans often associate the major demographic changes and breaking news stories with larger cities like Los Angeles, New York, Chicago, and Philadelphia.[2]

Nothing can be farther from the truth. In fact, over the last ten years, major stories have broken across the Midwest, especially in Iowa. They include cross burnings, Klan marches, police conflicts, suicides, racist graffiti, and school race riots. Most recently, I personally experienced a racist incident. Campus security and the police were called to the premises because of me. I was harassed, detained, and almost arrested for Studying While Black.[3] Difference and diversity are affecting all of America, especially Iowa. In the past, diversity was not visible in Iowa, but things are changing. The people of Iowa are getting a reality check. Some are overwhelmed and not prepared for the dramatic changes. This is my calling: *Difference and Diversity: Preparing Iowa for Black, Brown and International.* I have targeted two areas: city government and education. The following explains why and how my call is being answered.[4]

Why

City government employees, agencies, and leaders have more opportunities to interact and react to difference and diversity within the community. City offices provide everything from tax collection to welfare. Eventually, just about all of the community has interaction with a city employee or leader. Across Iowa, some communities are seeing a large influx of difference and diversity, mostly via language, race, and ethnic background. However, most city employees, administrators, and business owners are White, middle aged, and local. They have very limited interactions and experiences with people of color or issues of diversity. In fact, I have personally shaken the hands of city

---

2. The school shootings over the last five years have opened some rural and suburban eyes.
3. I wrote a short letter to the editor describing the incident in detail. Please feel free to e-mail me at Emoore@cornell-iowa.edu for the details.
4. The detailed explanation is done as if you are sitting there. Read it as a workshop participant.

employees who have never even had an interaction or conversation with a Black man or any person of color. This does not make them bad people; but the fact is, America is changing, the community is changing, and they are not ready. Some of them don't know what to say to minority community members, and too many worry about what not to say. It is a classic case of integration without preparation. The business owners, community leaders, and administrators have to take the lead in preparing the community for difference and diversity. Have no fear . . .

Educational institutions have an opportunity to influence and educate humanity. They can prepare America and Iowa for difference and diversity, if they are ready. According to Nancy Zimpher (Howey & Zimpher, 1989), the future teacher profile is a monolingual, White female from a low–middle- or middle-class suburban or rural home who wants to teach kids who are just like herself. In fact, some future teachers won't want to work with students of color. Across the nation, most future teachers will be White, while less than 10 percent will be people of color. Welcome to Iowa!

For the last three years, I have taught human relations at the University of Iowa. A majority of the students are White, middle-class females from small-town Iowa with limited diversity experiences. Some are resistant to diversity issues and are bigoted and racist. They remind me of a description given by G. Pritchy Smith, an experienced and respected teacher educator, in a keynote address to the NAME conference (1997):

> My own assessment of today's preservice teachers presently in training is that among them is the largest, most outspoken group of racists I have ever encountered since the beginning of my teaching career at the university level . . .

Some of the teachers want help, as they realize they are not prepared for difference and diversity. They don't know what to do and time is running out. A lot of Iowa classrooms, school districts, and communities are experiencing an influx of difference and diversity. In fact, across the nation, by school year 2000, close to 50 percent of all children coming to school will be students of color. Schools, teachers, and administrators must do something in two areas: *teacher preparation* and *student preparation*. Have no fear . . . Diversity Man is here!

How

My sessions are energetic, educational, and inspirational. I challenge participants but always with respect. I don't beat them up but light them up. There are too many quiet and complacent folks in America, particularly in Iowa. Iowans are very nice people. They are good Christians, hard workers, loving, and peaceful, but they are quiet. The best friend of hate is **silence.** Now is not the time for Americans or Iowans to sit quietly. My goal is to train, prepare, and encourage people to say something. I develop students and adults into advocates for peace, equity, and justice (APEJ). They are strongly encouraged to take action against prejudice, bigotry, racism, sexism, and all other forms of fear and hate.

There are times participants accuse me of attacking or making them feel guilty. My reply is, *"You shouldn't feel guilty! What did you do? Were you there? If you have feelings of guilt, then you have some other unresolved issues to attend to. If someone else attempts to make you feel guilty, then he has some unresolved issues. There is no reason for you to feel guilty about America's past, but you should feel responsible. The Americans before us left very ugly scars, and all Americans have a role to play in the healing process. It will take some work, some pain, and some time. Are you ready?"* The session has five simple steps.

1. Demographics: This is an open discussion and activity about the dramatic shifts in demographics, difference, and diversity. The participants are told all the facts; they see them on overhead, and they examine the effects of the changes across the world, America, and their local community. The numbers scare some people. There are some who feel that diversity will never affect them. They think difference and diversity exist in urban communities. They need to see local changes and know how their families, jobs, community services, education, and tax dollars will be affected. That's when they start to pay attention. The challenge is connecting them to difference and diversity. They need a personal stake in the changing demographics, and I get them to understand, respect, and connect. They need to prepare for a changing America. Are you ready?

2. Self-exploration: After the demographics session, participants are challenged to look inside themselves for the answers. The following section is an overview of the activity, "From Poop to Prejudice: *How does it happen?*" There are three rules: 1) Be honest, 2) Don't be offended, and 3) Remember this stuff; it's time to say something. Think of yourself as being there and participating in the exercise.

Hate is not something people are born with. In fact, when you are born, you know nothing. This is how we all start. Now imagine that you are a car, your favorite car. A BMW, Lexus, Mercedes, Chevy, Ford, Dodge, etc. Hey, we are in Iowa now; if you want to be a John Deere Tractor, you can be a John Deere tractor. Now try to picture the car brand new, fresh off the lot, with that new-car smell. What does your windshield look like? Yes, it's absolutely clean. All of us are born that way. We have no dirty spots on our windshields.

Now try to remember way back, when you were a little child in your community, when your windshield was absolutely clean. You had no negative, preconceived prejudices or biases about individuals or groups of people. You judged people not by the outside, but the inside. Try and remember those days and never forget that all of us were born that way, even the most extreme Republicans, Democrats, racists, bigots, and sexists. Many of us end up hating folks for the strangest reasons. None of us is born with hate; it was given to us, practiced and perfected. Hate is just like singing, dancing, sports, or recreation. If you do it enough, you will get better. Please journey back to your childhood, your neighborhood friends, role models, and community leaders. What or who changed you? Have you changed? How did you change? Why? What has taken you from your purpose?

As you know, eventually windshields get dirty. The dirt comes from friends, family, heroes, coaches, teachers, preachers, and keynote speakers. The TV, radio, music, movies, videos, computers, video games, and Internet play a role, too. Now, just think about all those spots on your windshield.

Of course not all your spots on the windshield are bad spots. We need to learn manners, respect, sportsmanship, hard work, loving, sharing, spiritual growth, and giving. However, there are some bad spots, and the challenge is to find them and clean them off your windshield. Some people need to be challenged and some supported. It may be a painful journey for some, but necessary. The procedure includes my personal story.

The game is about my life and how I was taught to hate. My personal story is told with passion, emotion, anger, and humor. I challenge participants to look deep into their own personal histories. Critical self-examination is necessary for individuals dealing with difference and diversity.

If participants continue to carry negative spots, one of two things can happen. The fist is a crash or headlines and special reports. Usually, big stories involve violence, brutality, discrimination, harassment, and murder. Some people have negative attitudes and beliefs about different groups they have never even met or talked to, and the end result is **CRASH!** The second thing that can happen is having too many people miss out! When a person has preconceived beliefs about another individual or group, he or she never gets to develop a relationship or friendship. That is unfortunate because, in many cases, the person who is misjudged or misconceived turns out to be a great person, the next creative idea, a positive addition to the team, someone who was desperately needed. He never gets the chance to contribute or interact, and some end up missing out! Too many individuals, institutions, organizations,

Americans, and Iowans are missing out. Difference and diversity should bring us together and not keep us apart.

3. Challenge and motivation: The challenge afterwards for participants is to challenge others. People have to stay motivated and focused on oppression and hate at all times. The key is to challenge what is in your power or circle of life. Challenge your family and friends. Motivate and teach your children to challenge the status quo. Challenge yourself and your personal biases and prejudices. We have to work on family, friends, and ourselves. We must continue to teach and encourage conversation, interaction and growth, especially in our young people. That is the challenge for all of us.

4. Practical tools: The question-and-answer part starts now. I want to leave participants with some tools and ideas. The most common questions: 1) How do I clean my personal windshield, and 2) How should I deal with other people who have dirty windshields? Negative self-esteem, self-concept, and self-confidence provide the answer to the first question. Clean up yourself and you clean up your windshield. I share my personal pain and struggle with myself. Many of the problems and difficulties I caused others were a direct reflection of my negative self-concept. I was not able to remove the spots from my windshield until I felt better about myself. The second question boils down to understanding, respecting, and connecting. When you understand the influences affecting the individual with prejudices, biases, and hate, and respect his or her difficulties, you can connect. Understanding and respecting doesn't mean agreeing; it's a process. The behavior and not the environments that created them judge many individuals, especially kids. We have to try to develop a better understanding of the surroundings and make a connection.

5. Critical thought and action: The participants need to understand the importance of thinking critically and taking action. Negative stereotypes and misconceptions don't exist in the critical thinkers; they challenge and examine information. Participants learn the importance of taking action. My mindset for action is Piss-ti-ology. It is a state of mind, a way you conduct yourself when advocating for peace, equity, and justice. My ideology comes from answering the question about being optimistic or pessimistic about the future of race relations and education in America. Now I tell people, "I'm neither just optimistic nor pessimistic. I am piss-i-mistic. It's a touch of optimism, but with an attitude." Everywhere I go across America, especially in Iowa, if there is hate, oppression, discrimination, or harassment present, I will say something and do something. No matter what the costs and by any means necessary, I challenge people about issues of hate. This includes my family, friends, and significant others. I am an advocate for peace, equity, and justice (APEJ).

I wish my ideology could be put in folks' food or drink and that it would grow all over them after they take it. Unfortunately, it doesn't work that way. Piss-i-mism can't be forced upon people; it is a painful process, a mental and spiritual development with great rewards.

There is a lot of work to do in America and across Iowa. A lot of folks have anticipated and prepared for Y2K; however, my focus in the millennium is preparing America, particularly Iowa, for difference and diversity. I want to encourage and motivate community and national leaders to deal with difference and diversity. We must be aware of the changes, prepare for the changes, and come together because of the changes.

In closing, one thing I want readers to know is that Iowa has been very, very good to me. I am happy here and truly believe it is my calling. I am questioned and ridiculed for deciding to stay and work in White America, especially if I say good things about it. I'd better not mention White women. Even so, it is my belief that all of America will recognize me for working with White kids in White America. There are some good things I could be doing in Black communities, talk circles, support groups, business ventures, stock market education, and the list goes on. There are some programs and initiatives already in place in urban communities, and the folks there are going to keep making things happen. However, I often wonder who is working with the White kids. Are these kids dealing with privilege? Do they know what privilege is? Can they understand the importance of peace, equity, and justice? Can they define racism or prejudice? What would be their picture of Black America if they did not meet me? Right now, God has called me to do my work in Iowa. The complex problems and difficulties associated with race and race relations are not going to change because Black folks are saying "Change." We need White folks working for change, and if the children can understand the issues of difference and diversity, they will become advocates for peace, equity, and justice. Ask some of your White friends.

My solution to White privilege and racism is to "Work with the rabbits." It comes from the fable of the tortoise and the hare. The rabbit gets an unfair jump, takes off, and leaves the tortoise way behind. That is how America was started. Some people (White men with money) got an unfair jump and took off, leaving many of us way behind. They controlled the money, the laws, and the educational systems. In the end, the tortoise eventually closes the gap and wins the race. Why? The rabbit stops and chills out. He takes a nap. Only one part of the story is true for America. Many groups have closed the gap on the rabbits. The laws have changed and people have access to jobs, housing, education, and other basic necessities. Some individuals from oppressed groups have made considerable gains, and it may appear as if they have the rabbit in sight.

However, in America, the rabbit isn't resting. The rich are getting richer, and the poor are getting poorer. The real test is power structure. Most of the people in positions of power, earning the most wages and obtaining the best education continue to be white males, and they have dough. My friends, I've been called to Iowa to work on rabbits. I am interacting, teaching, influencing, and changing future stockbrokers, Internet millionaires, farmers, CEOs, senators, doctors, and lawyers. Their kids will eventually inherit the power chips. They may make decisions affecting hundreds, thousands, or millions of people of color. I challenge, motivate, and develop understanding, respect, and connecting in rabbits. My work is long from done. I plan to continue on here in the Midwest, particularly in Iowa. Keep me in your prayers, and look for me in a city or school district near you. I will ask you if you are ready, and I will ask you to keep working on the rabbits! Peace and blessings . . .

References

Howey, K., & Zimpher, N. L. (1989). *Profiles of preservice teacher education: Inquiry into the nature of programs.* Albany: State University of New York Press.

U.S. Bureau of the Census (1996). *Current Population Reports, 1996.* Washington, DC: U.S. Bureau of the Census.

Frederick L. Moore

Frederick L. Moore is a Ph.D. candidate in human genetics at the University of California, San Francisco (UCSF). His research in human reproductive genetics focuses on the DAZ gene, which is one of the major known genetic causes of male infertility. Men who have deletions in this gene have low levels of sperm or no sperm at all. Frederick's objective is to understand the role of the DAZ gene in male germ cell development.

In 1996, Frederick graduated from the University of California at Berkeley with a B.A. in molecular and cellular biology and with honors in genetics. While at UC Berkeley, Frederick worked as a research assistant, gaining biochemistry research experience, and tutored upper and lower division organic chemistry for the Chemistry Scholar's and Biology Scholar's program.

Frederick has received many awards, including the Ford Foundation Pre-doctoral Fellowship, the National Science Foundation Pre-doctoral Fellowship, the Eugene Cota-Robble Fellowship, and the National Organization of Black Chemist and Chemical Engineers Undergraduate Award.

In 1998, Frederick served as president of the Black Student Health Alliance at UCSF. The alliance serves disadvantaged communities through health fairs and encourages minority high school students to pursue higher education in the sciences.

Moore hopes someday to be involved in operating a biotechnology company. He plans to expand his work in creating opportunities for minority students to pursue careers in the sciences through scholarships and fellowships, and exposing young people to mentors and programs designed to stimulate their interest in the mystery and excitement of science.

14

THE ROLE OF MENTORING FOR THE EDUCATED BLACK MAN

Frederick L. Moore

Perceptions of Potential

Do you know your potential? Is it something that you have always known or something that you discovered as you progressed through life? I know my potential. I have always known my potential. I fought hard to believe in my potential even when it was stripped away from me at a young age. When I was in the third grade, somebody assumed that I belonged in the lowest reading group. I knew that I was a good reader, but I had no voice. I was bored. Soon after, I lost my natural motivation to achieve. I learned to live with frustration inside and began to challenge myself in other areas of my life, like sports.

I didn't know it at the time, but English and school would plague me for the next 13 years of my life. When kids are first socialized to the world, they live up to the expectations that society and their families place upon them. The first mentors to which kids are exposed such as family, teachers, and peers, are in their immediate environment. The small window of time in the first four to five years of school can have a dramatic effect on a kid's perception of his or her potential. I wish someone had sat me down and explained that the development of a strong mind will affect every aspect of my life and the lives of my progeny. I wish someone had explained to me that Black people are viewed differently by society and that the first step in taking control of your destiny is a good education. I now realize that my potential was never lost. There were steps I needed to take to "deprogram" the perception of myself left by society and reprogram myself to live up to my potential.

Academic Success

It was a near-fatal car accident after I finished high school that triggered a process of soul searching. I spent a week in the hospital with a broken leg and split forehead. I had all the time in the world to think about my future and the lack of direction in my life. I was working at a grocery store and obtaining below-average grades at a local junior college. I decided to change my environment and join the Air Force Reserves. During the year away from my friends and family, I learned two important things: 1) I didn't like to take orders from anyone who didn't know more than I, and 2) I could achieve above-average grades in my classes if I studied hard. Upon returning home from the military, I had a new attitude about life and school. I decided to major in human genetics because I was interested in why some people's bodies responded faster compared to others during a workout program. I didn't know what classes were required for this major, but I had a strong urge to pursue this study.

The mean on my first chemistry exam was 56. I thought to myself, "If the mean is 56, then I must have scored below the average." I watched my friends go up and receive their exams and return to their seats in despair. When my name was called, I went to pick up my test, and to my surprise, I scored an 86, which was the second-highest grade in the class. At that point in time, I did not know where my potential lay, but I was determined to find it. As I took more science and math courses, I began to gain confidence in my ability to understand information. Yet I always tested myself to make sure my reality wasn't false. Every new course was a challenge to test my abilities, and I began, for the first time in my life, competing with myself in school.

Giving Back to the Community

After finishing my lower-division courses at the junior college, I transferred to the University of California at Berkeley. Though I entered this new environment open to different styles of teaching and testing, I didn't know if I could compete at this level of study. The way I dealt with the new pressure was by focusing on my classes and cutting out extracurricular activities. My first semester of classes went well, and I enjoyed organic chemistry enough to join a chemistry lab. The academic portion of my life was progressing, but something was missing. I decided to join the Big Brothers program after some encouragement from a friend. I felt fortunate about my childhood upbringing, and I wanted to give back to the community. Big Brothers is designed to allow adults to mentor elementary-school kids. The commitment is for a year, and the mentor typically spends five hours a week with his little brother. I was assigned a third-grader named Christopher.

When I first met Christopher, there was an uncertainty in his eye as if he thought that I would enter his life then leave it just as I had entered it. This was not without cause, because Christopher was from a single-parent family and was lacking a positive male role model in his life. Even though I felt a connection with him right away, the first year for Christopher and me was difficult. Boundaries were to be established between us, as in any relationship. I focused my attention on being his friend and not a father figure.

Gaining Christopher's trust challenged me in more ways than one; he kept pushing me away because he was scared of our attachment to one another. For example, at the beginning of each visit, Christopher got into the habit of saying, "Why did you come to see me? Leave me alone." By consistently showing Christopher unconditional love, our friendship flourished. I became a role model that Christopher could trust. College students are perfect mentors: not only can they tutor kids with their schoolwork, but just as important, college students can relate to kids on different levels. It wasn't long ago that a college student may have collected baseball cards or comic books. In recent decades, the young Black community has perpetuated the attitude that excelling in school isn't cool. If young Black males are exposed to educated Black men with whom they share things in common, then a change in this stereotype can occur.

Being involved with kids can teach us about the simple things in life. I realized that hanging out with Christopher, especially when I was under pressure, helped me get my mind out of the adult world; I could relax and enjoy the moment. I was more focused on my task after I spent time with Christopher. Removing myself from the intense world was like a breath of fresh air. It put the balance back into my life and made me whole. I know that some Black college students feel that as they proceed through school, they need to focus on their educations and end goals. They may have good intentions to help the Black community after they have reached a position of power, but the young Black youth need you now. You can make a difference in one person's life and at the same time move forward in yours.

Learning to Listen

Black people can benefit from positive role models at all levels. It's great to have someone who has gone through a situation that is similar to yours, who can help break down the rules of the game. But for myself in the sciences, there were few Black role models present. So I learned how to be mentored by someone when no one of color was around. The first step is to actively seek out advice from different people. Ask people who have succeeded and failed at the situation and compare answers. The idea is to have the largest knowledge base available before you engage in your next endeavor. This exercise will expose you to what people are verbally saying.

Yet there is another way to get more information. When people talk to me, I try to follow their flow of logic. I learn their thought patterns as they think through the process. This is achieved by analyzing the expression patterns and eyes of the mentor. Neurologists have discovered that when humans access different parts of their minds depending on their mode of thinking—visual, audio, or kinesthetic (through feeling)—their eyes move in different directions to retrieve the information. When people think about a process visually, their eyes look up to the left to access the given information. When people process information through hearing, their eyes look straight ahead. Finally, if a person learns a process kinesthetically, his or her eyes will move down to the right to access the information. This technique can be used to connect someone's pattern of thinking to the verbal message. For example, say a chemist is explaining how he or she developed a synthetic route to a particular molecule. You ask the chemist, "How did you know that molecule A would attach itself to molecule B versus molecule C?" The chemist looks down and to the right and tells you how he or she logically figured out the problem. The chemist's logic may not make sense to you if you think about the problem visually. But if you think about the problem kinesthetically, like the chemist, you may begin to decipher how he or she understood the problem. So you ask the chemist, "How do you reference the molecules inside your mind to understand the problem?" The chemist goes on to tell you that he or she pretends that molecule A is moving through the solution interacting with molecule B and molecule C. The chemist tells you that he or she can feel the different positive and negative charges associated with molecule A, and based on the environment of the solution, molecule B is a more favorable reaction. Most people use one or two different thought processes to learn, but some people may use a mixture of all three to solve something complex. By mastering this technique, you begin to decipher which information someone tells you is relevant to your success and how to process it the same way. I believe that if you surround yourself by the best and learn to think like the best, you can become one of the best.

Asking for Help

For some reason men have a harder time asking for help compared to women. Most of the time women make up the vast majority of participants in summer programs, intensive workshops, and tutoring programs. Brothers have to learn how to ask for help. It doesn't make you any less of a man to receive help from someone. One of my favorite lines is, "It doesn't make a difference who helped you learn the information before a test: his name is not on your grade." Be aggressive. No one is going to give you anything in life unless you ask for it. Don't assume that people are naturally going to have your best interests in mind. People are not going to read your mind and give you what you deserve.

Black people have the loudest mouths with no voices. Part of Black people's history in America is being conditioned to be silent. During slavery White people talked about Black people as if they weren't present. Black people had no voice or opinion, and no one wanted to listen to them. If you knew the master was wrong, you had to present your solution indirectly. I believe that Black people still have a hard time voicing their opinions around White people. One reason is that some Black people in America feel that they cannot articulate themselves appropriately. Most Black people live two different lives: one around White America and a different one around Black people. Black people have to master switching their vocabulary between both worlds. This means sometimes not being able to express a thought for a lack of words or risking that people will misunderstand you unless you use the language of your respective discipline. We have to get past this point. In addition, White people tend to form a different opinion about you after they find out you speak Ebonics. If you have a good idea, voice it. If you don't understand something, ask a question. Part of reprogramming your mind for greatness is collectively being exposed to the tools other people use, from both inside and outside of your culture, in order to succeed. Integrate that information into the way your mind naturally thinks, and make a well-informed decision on how to proceed in life.

Freeing Your Mind

What does it take for your mind to be free? My mind wants to be free, but the process takes time and patience. There are different levels of self-awareness and self-assurance through which one has to pass. My mind is scared sometimes to express itself. Can I handle it? Can society handle it? Science is one avenue through which I'm learning to express myself. My attitude is to learn all of the rules of science in order to break all of the rules of science. I let my imagination and creativity dictate what conclusions I draw from a framework of logical and irrational thoughts. The challenge is to not always use logic when figuring out complex problems. I feel that logic can sometimes hinder us from unraveling the answers to problems. Both logical and irrational thoughts are abstract, and we do not understand from where the information comes.

However, if knowledge is revealed, it doesn't have to make logical sense. Our viewpoints and understanding of nature are small; it takes a mind free of bias and inhibitions to take a quantum leap into an unknown process. While developing and sustaining this mindset is challenging, this could be the catalyst to discovering truths about nature of which one can only dream.

Why is it hard for Black people in America to reach a point of mental freedom? Why when a Black person has the attitude that he or she can accomplish anything in life, do others think that person is crazy? Is he or she crazy? I think that person is a hero. Such heroes have already deprogrammed the negative stereotype of Black people left by society and reprogrammed themselves to succeed. My definition of *mental freedom* is the state of being without constraint or worry of societal and personal judgement. It is the realization that no one can stop you from succeeding in life but yourself. It is the understanding that competition with oneself is the only true race to win.

Black people need to set their own standards. Do not measure yourself based on the people around you. What if the people around you are idiots? Setting your own standards means striving for perfection in everything you do. One thing that upsets me is to hear people say that they failed; yet, when I ask them, "Did you try with all of your being?" they answer by saying no. I made an agreement with myself when taking competitive classes at Berkeley to give 110% in whatever I do in life. Therefore, if I failed in the process, I would never have to wonder if I could have done better.

Dealing with the Struggle

Life is hard. Everyone struggles with something in life. There are people who look from the outside in and think that people who possess mental freedom, confidence, and self-awareness glide right through life. Most people react to other people based on their perception of them and how that fits into their ego. To an insecure person, a confident person may seem arrogant or conceited. Some insecure people who haven't yet faced their insecurities are reminded of the fact when a confident person has a favorable experience in a situation that the insecure person cannot handle. Jealousy is another emotion that stems from an insecurity that people cannot control. People who are jealous are aware on a conscious level of their insecurities, and they realize that a secure person possesses something they wish they possessed. Black males who have achieved a certain level of success have to learn how to deal with insecure and jealous people in addition to people who are prejudiced. When Black people are operating at a lower level than the people around them, everyone feels secure. Yet a Black person who begins to develop that mental freedom, self-awareness, and confidence—triggered by the reprogramming process—becomes a threat. People who manifest these feelings may do malicious things to you to steal your joy away. For example, my first year in graduate school I was required to take a class that had an oral final exam. Basically, the class required an independent research proposal on a topic covered in class and a final exam in which two professors would ask you questions based on the proposal and anything covered in lectures that quarter.

Not surprisingly, some students had a hard time with this course due to the nature of the oral exam. I studied the course material adequately and was prepared to take the final exam. In my program, graduate students are required to rotate in different research labs during their first year. The lab rotations are designed to introduce students to the lab of a professor whom they may be interested in joining and to expose students to different research environments. My goal during my first year was to work hard in lab and produce data. As a result, my homework grade in the class was a little below average. One of the two professors, whom we'll name *Professor X,* made an assumption about my ability to pass the exam based on my homework grades. Before the exam started, Professor X reassured me that the teaching committee wanted everyone to pass the class. This comment was striking to me because there was never a doubt in my mind that I would pass the class. During the exam I answered the questions that both professors asked of me. Judging by the types of questions I received compared to others in my class, my exam was challenging. I began to realize during the exam that Professor X was upset that I was answering the questions correctly. The more questions I got right, the more disturbed Professor X became.

After the exam was over, I went to receive my grade from Professor X's office. Professor X told me, "It looks like you pulled it off. You somehow managed to pass the course." Professor X proceeded to tell me my grade in the course and how the teaching committee felt that I should retake the course next year to get a stronger background in the material for future use. Professor X continued insulting my intelligence by telling me that, while I answered the questions, they were not sure "if the information would stick." I later discovered that Professor X lied about my grade in the course; moreover, he lied about the committee's decision that I should retake the course. It was made clear to me later that Professor X had issues with Black people's ability to understand science at the graduate level. My first reaction to this experience was anger. But I realized that if I kept the anger inside, it would accomplish what Professor X had set out to do—take a piece of my happiness and leave me with bitterness.

I was prepared to deal with this situation before I came to graduate school. A Black post-doctoral fellow in the chemistry department at Berkeley mentored me. He explained to me how people would perceive me both before and during my graduate career. He shared with me horrifying stories of deceit from faculty and students, inside and outside of his lab. This person was strong mentally and emotionally, and I drew strength from his stories.

It is not easy to deal with the perception that society has of Black males. How can we use this negative perception to our advantage? Yes, most of the time you have to be twice as good as your counterparts to get the same respect. Yes, you have to endure harsh working environments and weird stares in the elevator. But I would not have it any other way. If you can make it through the difficult situations and survive, you are a stronger person in the end. You are not a victim, but a survivor! Educated Black males who have gone through this system and achieved their Ph.D.s must share their experiences with younger Brothers. Few Black people have parents with Ph.D.s. We do not learn the rules of the academic game from our friends and family. I would rather succeed and be a part of someone else's success than succeed alone.

Changes and the Future

It is hard to be Black in America and not know who you are, because you are faced with your Blackness everyday. Every time you succeed, there is someone to remind you of your Blackness. Be proud of being Black. Every time you succeed, remind people of your greatness. Don't be afraid of letting your true nature come out. Black males in America are still dealing with their manhood, a large part of which was stripped away during slavery. Black males could not provide for their families. They had to sit back and watch their women being raped and beaten. I feel that, today, many Black males from disadvantaged communities try to regain the feeling of lost manhood by having sex with many women. They think the more women they can conquer the more of a man they are. Yet in White America, manhood is defined more by money and power. Advantaged and disadvantaged Black males are still fighting to prove their manhood by White America's standard.

What a man is—particularly a Black man in America—needs to be redefined. We need a definition that allows Black men to help one another grow, a definition that says that whatever level you have achieved in your chosen profession, your manhood is judged by how many other Brothers you have helped to obtain that level or higher. We need a definition that encompasses not the number women with whom you had sex, but how many of your children have a college education. A man not only provides for his family but also provides for his community.

In the future, I envision the next generation of Black scholars taking control of Black people's academic destiny. I envision the creation of an organization called "The Black Scholar Academy," which will focus on developing scholarships, fellowships, and educational programs targeted toward Black youth. I envision mentor camps where Black students can meet and learn from Black scholars, where programs will be designed to begin the deprogramming process and inspire the process of reprogramming to succeed. This academy will bring the most prominent Black scholars together with junior scholars and create a sense of community—the sense that we can make it together. Black scholars need our youth as much as the youth need the Black scholars. I envision a day when it will be an honor to be part of the academy, and young Black students will be recognized in school as junior academy members. I envision the Black Scholar Academy designing videos to be watched in every classroom across the country. The videos will be composed of academy members' inspirational speeches. The central purpose will ensure that every Black child, in any environment in America, will be exposed to positive Black people who have obtained their Ph.D.s. I envision different websites, composed of chat rooms, advice rooms, and informational bulletins on Black Scholar Academy members. There is a role for the educated Black man in mentoring, and there is a common goal: to educate Black people and reactivate the lost power that has been hidden inside of our minds; to begin the healing process of our people as a whole, and to take back our mental freedom. Black people, once again, need to realize that there are no constraints on how high they can rise. If it takes a village to raise a child, then our village will be a haven of Black scholars.

Le'Roy E. Reese

Dr. Le'Roy Reese is a Senior Fellow at the Centers for Disease Control and Prevention's (CDC) National Center for Injury Prevention and Control where he is a scientist in the Division of Violence Prevention on the Youth Violence Prevention Team. In this position, Dr. Reese provides scientific and programmatic leadership in the nation's efforts to reduce youth violence in the United States. Additionally, he has continued to develop his own program of research, which focuses on the reduction of health-compromising behaviors in young people by promoting social, emotional, and behavioral competencies. A related focus of his research is the enhancement of the functioning and protective features of families and communities. A special emphasis of his research examines the impact of marginalization and oppression and its influence on the disproportionate impact of violence in communities of color.

A psychologist by training, Dr. Reese was an assistant professor of psychology prior to joining the CDC and an adjunct professor of African American studies at Chicago State University, one of the largest predominantly Black universities in the United States. While on faculty at Chicago State, he and a colleague co-directed a prevention research team that conducted community- and school-based prevention research with young people and their families. Previously, he has been principal investigator and project officer on two grants from the Office of Minority Health, Department of Health and Human Services, which focused on health promotion among Black children, adolescents, and their families. In addition to these and other professional activities, Dr. Reese maintains a small clinical practice specializing in child and family therapy.

15

THE IMPACT OF AMERICAN SOCIAL SYSTEMS ON AFRICAN AMERICAN MEN

Le'Roy E. Reese

Many have argued that the Black or Afrikan male is an endangered species in the United States, while others have simultaneously celebrated and have actively worked toward that goal. Indeed, there has been no shortage of books, essays, and the like devoted to this subject where the "problem" has been defined, described, and recommendations advanced to rectify the crisis or exacerbate its condition. Of contemporary scholars who have written about this topic in a constructive manner, foremost in my mind are the works of Haki Madhubuti, El-Hajj Malik El-Shabazz (Malcolm X), Wade Nobles, and Na'im Akbar. In different yet critical ways, each of these scholars has provided essential insight into the emasculation of the Black male in the United States, the forces behind these processes, and the overt and covert consequences of this phenomenon.

The problem now, however, is that in light of this body of literature and scholarship, little has been done beyond verbal rhetoric to address in a positive manner the realities that all too many Brothers in this country face. The critical challenge facing Black males is to develop a positive sense and experience of Black manhood as informed and defined by Black culture while simultaneously existing in a society that is threatened and fights any assertion of positive Black masculinity and manhood. In truth, the challenge is not to develop but instead to embrace and reconnect with the spirit of Black maleness and manhood as originally conceived by our ancestors.

Prior to exploring this topic, it is important to define the "emasculation of Black men." While a full thesis on emasculation is beyond the scope of this chapter, it is an essential feature. As directed toward Black men in western societies, it is the active undermining of the cultural integrity of the Black community by limiting the opportunity and ability of Black men to assume their natural positions within their families and communities. This has manifested in "attacks" economically, educationally, politically, in health care, and within our families. Seemingly lost on many in our community is that our cultural and historical legacy dictates that Black manhood, indeed the functioning of the Black community and family, is predicated on the reciprocity between male and female as providers, parents, educators, leaders, and community elders and griots. The sexist and racist nature of the United States undervalues women in general and sees any attempt by non-European males to assume a position of active leadership in their families and communities as a threat. It is a threat because it implies that these same individuals will, at some point, aspire to be leaders outside their immediate communities. In contemporary times, one need only consider the fates of Malcolm X, Martin Luther King, and Medgar Evers to appreciate this reality.

While history is important, briefly I would like to paint the canvas with the modern-day experience of Black men in this country, which is embedded in our U.S. history. From the late 1980s to the present, the number-one cause of death for Black males between the ages of 15 through 34 has been homicide. Imagine being a Black teenager and having to come to grips with the reality that you are more likely to die by a bullet at the hands of someone who looks like you than you are to attend and graduate from college. In addition, recent research by the The Sentencing Project, a think tank focused on the problems of the justice system, found that approximately 30 percent of all Black men in the United States between the ages of 20 and 30 are currently involved with the corrections and court system. Specifically, this research reveals that these young men are either incarcerated, on parole, on probation, or involved in some other type of court-directed supervision. Yes, the Brothers existing in these "academies" are also receiving advanced degrees, the effects of which are far greater than the degrees handed out in the institutions of higher education in this country.

Similarly, while African Americans constitute 13 percent of the population in the United States, African American males make up over 40 percent of the incarcerated population in juvenile and adult prisons. These observations are made at a time when the prison industry is one of the fastest growing sectors of the country's economy. Certainly, it appears that some capitalists have found the cheap and bountiful labor force in the country while simultaneously answering the question, "Where are all the Black men?"

In health care, African Americans generally lead in a manner disproportionate to their representation in the general populace in practically every disease category ranging from heart disease to breast and prostate cancer. For Blacks in the age group 25 through 34, the Acquired Immune Deficiency Syndrome (AIDS) is the leading cause of death overall. Currently, Human Immunodeficiency Syndrome (HIV) infection is growing fastest among Black women, and half of all newborns with HIV are Black. Further, Black men live significantly shorter lives than their male counterparts from other racial and ethnic groups, and they are less likely to seek medical attention if they have access to it, thus facilitating their high rates of disease. Additionally, for those Blacks who seek medical treatment, recent research indicates that their maladies are less likely to be treated as aggressively as those of Europeans Americans, again contributing to high mortality rates for certain diseases. The net result is that for those Blacks not directly impacted by violence or the prison system, they tend to resemble the walking wounded. Finally, the rates of reported hypertension, poor quality of life, mental health, and perceptions of racism as a public health threat are reported by a significant number of Black men.

In education (a term that needs to be examined more closely), Blacks have made important gains in the area of formal education. More African Americans are graduating from high school and attending college than ever before. Yet proportionally, we continue to lag behind other racial and ethnic groups in the United States with respect to formal educational achievements. Beyond the challenges of and need for formal education is the need to examine what Blacks are being educated to do. A compelling argument can be made that many Blacks in this country (and certainly this would seem to be true for Black males) are being educated to work for other people rather than to be leaders in industry, education, and politics. In addition, Blacks—who historically have prospered in an entrepreneurial sense—find in the 1990s, a period of unprecedented economic growth, that while the Black middle class has grown appreciably, there has been only a modest rise in the number of Black-owned businesses.

We have become so overwhelmed by some of the problems described here that we have lost sight of the more pressing problem. We continue to "wait" for these very same institutions to redress these issues in a fair and equitable manner. This is the real dysfunction in our community, as we seemingly have forgotten that the establishment of the United States, its very prominence in the world community, has been predicated on the exploitation of non-European people. As proof one need only consider the history of the indigenous people of this country, our enslavement, and the recent backlash against affirmative-action initiatives as a proposed remedy to the historical marginalization of communities of color in the United States.

Beyond how the institution of formal education is being utilized is the need to redefine what it means to be an educated Black male in this country.

It is here that the seminal scholarship of Carter G. Woodson (1990) and W. E. B. DuBois (1961) is educative. Dr. Woodson, in describing the miseducation of the Black community, challenges us to embrace an epistemology that places Afrikan culture and the best interests of the Black community at the center of the educational process. DuBois, in his *talented tenth* notion, corroborates the importance for education to serve as a catalyst in advancing the status and well-being of the Black community. In fact, each of these visionaries would agree that an education that does not facilitate these objectives is not education at all. Instead, as advanced by Wade Nobles (1986), it is a form of intellectual enslavement or "conceptual incarceration."

Given the scope of the problems and dysfunction that the social systems and institutions described above have facilitated, we are left to ponder what we should do to ameliorate these conditions. Certainly the citizenry of the United States have been socialized to believe that they can, actually that they must, rely on the integrity and equity of the educational, justice, health-care, and political processes, as well as just economic opportunities in order to enjoy the full benefits and "liberation" afforded those living in the United States. Indeed, the pledge of allegiance concludes with, "with liberty and justice for all." One of the greatest delusions that has occurred in this country and continues with incredible effectiveness is the idea that a God-inspired and universal moral sense of justice is being practiced by these social institutions. In view of the problems outlined earlier in this essay, Na'im Akbar's introduction to *Visions for Black Men* (1991) suggests "No rational person who is aware of these facts could with any claim to sanity minimize this situation," which in my view suggests that the important question here has been asked and answered. To depend on a system that in a historical context has based its economic, educational, and political prosperity on the active and inhumane exploitation of the community suggests dysfunction. It is akin to the cycle of violence we observe in another contemptible behavior—that of domestic violence in which the perpetrator of the violence batters psychologically and physically another human, promises he won't do it again, and regains the victim's trust only to later retraumatize the victim and on and on. We must move from victims to nurturers and protectors of our own interests.

In reflecting on the goals of this book, we must not only consider how to create opportunities for more Brothers and Sisters to join us in positions of leadership and scholarship, but we must also challenge ourselves to find ways to stay connected to the whole of the Black community. Despite popular convention, the principal problem for Blacks in America is not whether a taxi will stop and pick us up, but instead whether our children are being educated about themselves, whether they are being prepared to be future leaders, whether they have enough to eat, and whether we are safe in our communities. While the Black middle class has grown considerably over the last decade, the poor among us have gotten poorer and more despondent about their futures. Cornel West (1993), in an important series of essays on race, details the liberal versus conservative political view on the challenges of racial equity, which are defined by structural opportunities and behavioral accountability. While I agree with Dr. West's critique on the pros and cons of these two perspectives, I digress and suggest an additional problem with these positions. The problem is that liberal nor conservative views are informed by the ontological perspective of Blacks; thus, their efficacy in ameliorating the problems facing Black America is limited.

I do not advocate a separatist or nationalist approach to the problems facing Black America and Black males in particular, but instead that we face and take responsibilities for taking care of us. The principal challenge to such an approach is peacefully coexisting in a hostile environment. In *The Wretched of the Earth,* Fratz Fanon (1965) articulates the need for a national consciousness and indirectly challenges the "brothers of the academy" to provide some of this leadership. Specifically, he suggests that at times members of the Black middle class do not understand the need for popular action because of their position in the society and that this represents an unconscious familiarity or desire to identify with the colonizer. We must resist this tendency. As citizens of the United States, it is reasonable to expect that we would be included as full partners in experiencing the "American Dream"; yet in reality, we have been offered a 400-year-old promissory note. Other essays offered in this volume will advance some of the ideas offered here. In the language of our ancestors, the essence of our journey and work is in the transition from an environment characterized by the maafa to an environment characterized by the principles and spirit of maat.

The intent of this essay was not to be some angry diatribe about the evils of western society and its influence on Black males and the Black community. Instead, my goal was to make the case about our collective condition based upon the available scientific data. DuBois in the beginning of the century suggested that the problem of the twentieth century would be the issue of race. It is clear that we have not made sufficient progress as we approach the millennium and that the issue of race is now only compounded by the issue of social class.

The Brothers in this volume must help provide some of the leadership inspired by the courage and cultural integrity necessary to do the important work before us. In so doing, we should not make the mistake that others in this society have: We should not assume that the only wisdom that exists is owned by the voices of those with degrees. Leadership and progress do not occur in a vacuum; they are the by-product, reflected in our understanding of the interrelatedness of our common good and, thus, our interdependence. As such, we cannot afford to lose any of our voices. Like my colleague and Brother Dr. Lee Jones reminds us, "The bottom line is results; anything else is rhetoric."

References

Akbar, N. (1991). *Visions for black men*. Tallahassee, FL: Mind Productions and Associates.

DuBois, W. E. B. (1961). *Souls of Black folk*. New York: Dodd, Mead & Company.

Nobles, W. W. (1986). *African psychology: Toward its reclamation, reascension, and revitalization*. Oakland, CA: Black Family Institute.

West, C., (1993). *Race matters*. New York: Vintage Books.

Woodson, C. G. (1990). *The mis-education of the Negro*. Trenton, NJ: Africa World Press.

Mark A. Williams

Dr. Mark Williams received undergraduate training in biology from the University of Cincinnati. In 1992, he received a bachelor of science degree from the Cincinnati College of Mortuary Science. Graduating summa cum laude, Dr. Williams was class salutatorian and received the Charles O. Dhonau, the Dr. George M. Sleichter, and the Rising Star Awards for outstanding scholastic achievement and excellence in embalming technology.

Dr. Williams is currently an M.D./Ph.D. student at the University of Cincinnati College of Medicine, where he received the Award of High Academic Achievement. To his acclaim are several competitive research fellowships from the Association for Academic Minority Physicians, the Merck Company Foundation, and the famed Howard Hughes Medical Institute. The University of Cincinnati awarded him a Yates Fellowship and Scholarship to pursue his graduate studies. In 2000, he will graduate with a Ph.D. in pharmacology and will pursue a career in academic surgery.

Dr. Williams serves as vice-president of the Board of Trustees for Kingdom Life World Outreach Center (KLWOC). He also serves as the Worship Leader and Director of Music, Worship, and Arts. His devotion to spirituality is paralleled only by his commitment to family. He and his wife, Darice, organize the marriage-enrichment conferences and activities of KLWOC. Together they impart principles of servitude to God and family to their sons, Demarcus and Aaron. Dr. Williams asserts that his greatest accomplishment will be to "finish with the same wife I started with," a goal rarely accomplished by colleagues in academic environments.

16

MANAGING FAMILY AND CAREER

Mark A. Williams

The decision to pursue a graduate degree is seldomly an easy one. Regardless of the area of study, the pursuit of a doctoral degree requires a serious commitment of time, effort, and in many cases finances. This inherently difficult task is complicated further when the decision to enroll in a graduate program affects not only the enrollee but also a spouse and/or children. Graduate school is stressful and demanding. The emotional, physical, psychological, and financial stresses incurred by the student are shared (sometimes equally) by his or her spouse and children. Because of the enormity of the commitment required by graduate school, the decision to enroll in a doctoral program should be made considering the student's current and anticipated familial status.

Give Up All That Money? Are You Crazy?

Often, doctoral studies are pursued after a substantial amount of time has been spent in the workplace. Thus, it is frequently difficult to sacrifice the economic security of the current position for an uncertain promise of success after obtaining the graduate degree. Although there is the promise of increased earning potential and prestige attributable to earning the Ph.D., the fulfillment of the promise must be delayed for more than ten years in many instances. Although many graduate-degree granting institutions provide stipends, the 20 percent of graduate and first-professional students who receive such aid often live abstemiously for 5–7 years with institutional assistantships averaging $7,300 per year (U.S. Department of Education, 1996). Following receipt of the degree, 2 to 6 years may be spent in post-doctoral training still earning less than that which could have been earned immediately after undergraduate training. Considering the average yearly salary for a person holding a baccalaureate degree is over $35,000, this is indisputably a substantial sacrifice to make in the name of higher education (U.S. Department of Health, Education, and Welfare, 1988). Prior to enrolling in medical school, I was employed as a funeral director/embalmer by the largest funeral service provider in Cincinnati, which is also the largest African American owned and operated funeral home in the state of Ohio. I earned a comfortable salary and had tremendous opportunity for advancement to upper management and even partnership. Shortly after becoming licensed, my picture was placed on all of the advertisements for the funeral home. It was a picture of me and the C.E.O. of the company shaking hands with a caption that read "the torch is passed from one generation to the next." I was referred to as the heir-apparent. The prospect for my success in this company was certain. Then came the acceptance letter from medical school. I was now faced with that awful decision of whether to continue in the career that assured me great success or to defer gratification for 7 to 18 years while I pursued training in medicine. Especially because I was now married, this was no easy decision for me. Moreover, we were expecting the birth of our first child. Making matters more complicated, I was offered by my employer a substantial pay increase, a new home, and a new automobile as incentives to stay with the company. These incentives, coupled with the notoriety received by having my "mug" plastered around the city in various advertisements, were quite tempting. How could my wife or I sacrifice these things to endure what would at best be an unpleasant decade of additional sacrifices? Although she affirmed her devoted support for whichever path I chose, this deliberation haunted me for weeks before I decided to enroll in medical school.

Was I out of my mind? Am I crazy? To this day, I ask myself these questions. My response has always been and still is "Maybe!" But to practice medicine has been a lifelong goal of mine that I had the opportunity to pursue in spite of how attractive the distractions appeared. Although the financial reward remains a distant 8 to 10 years away, I have already benefited from the weightier sense of personal accomplishment. It was a decision well made.

Do Not Give Up Everything

Although doctoral training and pursuit of an academic career requires a huge commitment, it is important to remember that you are still an individual with specific desires outside of your career choice. I am sad to report that there are many people in academia who are consumed by their scholastic pursuits. They have *become* their careers, like those in other professions. The totality of their identity is wrapped up in their professional accomplishments. I believe the trend toward self-deprivation and injurious devotion to career begins in graduate school. The misconception that graduate school requires 100 percent of your time and effort has poisoned the minds of many would-be great investigators. As such, the price may have been perceived as too great and the pursuit may consequently have been abandoned. The old adage "all work and no play makes for a boring day" holds true for graduate school and an academic career. While it is necessary to let some things go in order to pursue an academic career, not all things should be sacrificed.

Perhaps you have a favorite pastime of bowling, hiking, boating, fishing, scuba diving, or any number of things. Choose the one or two that mean the most to you and hold fast to them. Realize also that time spent alone with your spouse is as important as time spent alone with your children, which is as important as time spent by yourself. All three are critically important to the well-being of the family throughout the doctoral studies. Therefore, where possible, choose activities that can accommodate your spouse and/or children. I love fishing. Accordingly, there are times when I go fishing alone. Those times when I don't care much about catching fish, I'll take my sons. And on very rare occasions, my wife might take a book along for reading as she relaxes on a boat while I fish. Another activity that is even more accommodating is singing. While I can sing any place, I particularly like singing in church. At church I am the worship leader and chief musician. Although these activities require a lot of time in practice, they are vitally important to me, so I make time for them. I do envision a day when my schedule will not accommodate all of these activities. Until then, the motto carpe diem (seize the day) prevails.

Something Has to Give—School or Family

Within a time span of 18 months, my life changed dramatically. I was married, became a father, and enrolled in medical school—three major life-changing events. Motivated by delusions of inflated grandeur, I felt I could be super-student, super-husband, and super-father concomitantly. Up to this time, my life had been marked by outstanding academic and personal achievements. Why couldn't it continue in the same vein? I had envisioned a world where there were no obstacles that are insurmountable. Although I still maintain this ideal, it was quickly tempered by reality. The obstacle remained conquerable, but I learned that the extent of my success in any area was contingent upon the amount of effort I could afford to commit to the task. By this, I mean that there are only so many tasks that even the greatest of minds and most organized and efficient of people can accomplish simultaneously. There is a limit to the number of butcher knives the world's most accomplished juggler can handle. Medical school helped me to recognize my limit.

One of the most humbling experiences I encountered was realizing that I wouldn't be the top student of my medical school class. I graduated from high school and college summa cum laude and class salutatorian. I fully expected that this level of accomplishment would extend into medical school. To my surprise, there were several hindrances to this possibility. First, in medical school I was among a cohort of students who, likewise, graduated at the top of their classes. By necessity there would be a distribution among even these students—some would attain top honors, while others' grades would be average. Unthreatened by this reality, I felt I would be among the former. However, I overlooked two very important variables—my wife and my son.

After months of trying to be all things to all people in all places, I had exhausted myself near the point of depression. At this juncture, I accepted the fact that something had to give. It would either be my family or my academics. By no means am I suggesting they are mutually exclusive and that a person can't have both. However, I do submit that in order for me to obtain honors in all classes as I had hoped, I would have to sacrifice time spent with my family. Conversely, in order to prepare four-course meals for my family, to be present at every family gathering, and to wake up six times each night to get the baby so my wife could rest, I would have to sacrifice my dreams of top honors in medical school. There necessarily had to be a happy medium, and I had determine what it was for me. "P equals M.D." is an ideal that was frequently heralded by my classmates. This ideal maintained that in order to become a physician, all that was required was to "Pass" each class and the national board exams.

I soon adopted this philosophy and thought I had embraced it completely until I received my first "P," an 82 percent and the equivalent of a "C." This was a painful experience, especially because I had never studied so fervently for an exam and reached only a measure of mediocrity. I perceived that score to be a failure because I had missed the goal I set for myself. After torturing myself sufficiently, I realized that by necessity I had to change my focus, my perspective, my perception. If I continued to look solely at the number of 82 percent or the grade of a "C," I would consistently be extremely disappointed. Alternatively, if I looked at the grade or the score in light of the time I spent with my family, I would quickly become content—dare I say, pleased. I had to determine what was more important to me, the grades (which in the end really don't matter much) or the interaction with my wife and child. Hands down the family emerged the victor. Most students who have the responsibility of a family when they enroll in a graduate program will at some point be met with the same challenge. They will likely have to determine for themselves whether the end goal of obtaining stellar grades is worth the additional sacrifices and hardships placed on the family as a consequence. The one contention I hold is that the only true certainty is that the returns on the investment in your family are much more assured than those gained from investing in a career.

I'll share a story of a friend who in medical school committed countless hours to studying, sometimes even neglecting his wife. He and his wife willingly sacrificed to the extent that it caused marital problems. My friend's expectation, like many other medical students, was that if he did exceptionally well in all of his classes and on the national board exams, he would get the residency program of his choosing upon graduation. So, he studied and he studied. He sacrificed and sacrificed. And it paid off in terms of the grades he received. His transcript was outstanding. It would even appear that he allotted some time for his wife seeing that during his tenure as a medical student, he and his wife had a child. However, there remained an unhealthy balance between school and family.

The most anticipated and celebrated day that occurs in medical school is Match Day. After applying to and interviewing with various residency programs around the country, the student ranks each program in order of favor. Likewise, the residency programs rank the students. A computer-generated match between applicants and residency programs is revealed on the famed Match Day. The day had now arrived when my friend would learn his fate. There was an overwhelming feeling of excitement and anticipation in the air as each student individually went to the front of the auditorium and opened the envelope that disclosed the place of their future home for the coming years. The overriding hope is that the blood, sweat, and tears shed during the preceding four years would reap the program of the student's top choice. Finally, it was time for my friend to discover his fate. With his wife and their adorable daughter, he eagerly approached the front of the auditorium. After what must have seemed like ten minutes to them, he finally opened his envelope. As he read the enclosed match report, his wife ran disappointedly out of the auditorium crying while she clung to her four-month-old baby. My friend, trying to appear enthused with the outcome, announced the location of his residency program; it was not his first choice as he and his wife had expected. I can only imagine the thoughts that raced through both of their minds as they read the report and recalled the many arguments, the countless and uncertain promises that these sacrifices will pay off in the end, the trips to marriage counselors, and the recurring bouts with depression brought about from the stresses of marriage and school. It would appear that the hard work didn't pay off. Of one thing I am certain: If the time and energy he committed to medical school were shared more equitably with the marriage, a healthier relationship would have been there to benefit him far more than stellar grades. Careers come and go. And today marriages come and go, too, but children are a life-long commitment. From my perspective, so are marriages. Any person considering graduate studies must count all of the costs, financial and otherwise. After the decision is made and mutually agreeable, he or she must continue to reevaluate the plan. Sometimes the plan needs revision in order to accomplish the end goal of satisfaction with the pursuit.

Who Flipped the Script?

Despite how infallible the original plan may seem, it may require minor and sometimes major adjustments along the way. It is impossible to fully know and understand the total expense of pursuing a doctorate. Sometimes the script necessarily flips. In the process of reevaluating progress through the doctoral studies, frequently one discovers that the original hypothesis was incorrect or not testable. As such, an alternative hypothesis may have to be proposed. A similar situation may occur when evaluating the state of the marriage and family while obtaining the degree. Routine checkups should be made to ensure that the relationship is still healthy and that the expectations originally set forth are still agreeable. If not, a change in strategy may be necessary—in some cases, this may mean a leave of absence.

The pursuit of the doctorate and the career is not a sprint; it's a marathon. Frankly, it doesn't matter if you finish first or last as long as you finish. When you are married, the course becomes a three-legged marathon. You can't run faster than your partner who is joined to you at the hip. Occasionally, one partner may need to pause for a breather or a drink of water in order to recuperate. It then behooves the other partner to take the break rather than continue on the untenable task of finishing the course.

During doctoral training it is easy to become overly concerned about the amount of time it is taking to complete the training. In fact, it can become a bitter thorn in the side of the student. Consequently, the student may focus on the finish line and forget about his or her partner. Despite his best intentions at the outset of the journey, it may be discovered that your partner wasn't sufficiently conditioned to run the marathon or perhaps he or she sprained an ankle during the course.

Unforeseen circumstances arise over the course of the number of years required for the doctoral and post-doctoral training. Loss of employment, severe illness, birth of children, and the death of family members are a few among many events that arise with the potential of thwarting or deferring the ultimate goal of obtaining the doctorate. Although these are challenges faced by unmarried students as well, the probability of them occurring is at least doubled when a spouse and children are brought into the picture. The possibility of such occurrences should be considered at the onset on graduate studies. Depending on the impact of the event, it may require that the student take a leave of absence to deal with the situation and the family's response.

During my first two years of medical school, my wife experienced four deaths in her family: an aunt, a sister, her step-father (since the age of two years), and her grandmother. Some may carelessly say, "those are her family members, not yours." Indeed they are. However, if my wife hurts, I hurt. If she cannot function at the level of her usual performance for whatever reason, I must take up the slack, particularly with our children. In any marriage worth its weight in salt, the infirmity of one spouse is endured by the other. So it was with ours. Because I was a licensed funeral director and embalmer, I handled the funeral arrangements. In hindsight this may not have been the wisest decision for me personally because of the undue stress it added. But for the sake of my wife and her family and to minimize the expenses, I chose to do these things. After the death of her father, my wife's youngest sister came to live with us—another of those unforeseen circumstances. One reality with which I have become intimately acquainted is that no matter how much you love a person—a spouse, a child, or another—when you take on some level of responsibility for that person, you also take on more stress. In no way does this realization diminish the love you have for that person. It is just important to recognize that most major life events, such as marriage, birth of a child or graduation are paradoxically joyous yet stressful.

As I entered my second year in medical school, I had my share of stressful life events. I realized that I had to take a break rather than plunge ahead on the appointed course. The medical school, like many other graduate programs, allows for familial or personal leaves of absence. Ideally this time could be used productively to deal with personal circumstances and to prepare for the return to the program. For me this involved applying for a research fellowship from the Howard Hughes Medical Institute. I vividly remember proposing to my wife the idea of extending my medical education by an extra year; it wasn't initially embraced as a great idea. Like me, she wanted my medical training to end as soon as possible. How could I even consider extending it another year? It offered two benefits. First, it allowed me to take a break from the rigorous didactic course work of medical school. Second, it provided an opportunity for me to gain exposure to research, a career that I had never before considered. Despite how inviting the benefits were, I determined that if my wife were not in agreement with the extension, I wouldn't pursue it. Fortunately for both of us, she agreed to it.

Over the course of the year, I was rejuvenated and, consequently, our relationship was refreshed. In addition, this year of research, which started out as a personal breather, developed into a career pursuit unto itself. Upon discovering that I enjoyed research, I decided that I wanted to pursue the Ph.D. in addition to the medical degree. This would involve an additional three years of training. Again, the script flipped. This too, had its benefits. Our second child had been born during my year reprieve. If I had continued in the course of medical school, I would have been in a surgery residency working 100 to 120 hours each week with a two-year-old and a five-year-old child. My wife would have been, in essence, a single parent of very young children. This would have been unfair and unduly stressful to her. Additionally, having seen the influence that my presence had on my oldest son during his first three years of life, I wanted to provide the same opportunities for my second child. Back to the bargaining table we went.

Consider that at the onset, my wife and I had anticipated a training course that would take four years. Because of circumstance, an additional year was added. During that year, the original plan was altered due to the birth of a second child and expounded upon because of new-found interests, bringing the final commitment to eight—count them, *eight* years. This excluded the years I would spend in residency, which would be an additional seven to ten years. Eighteen years of sacrifice is what we were facing. Was I out of my mind? More so, was my wife out of her mind for agreeing? A resounding "*no*" is the answer.

I've learned two valuable lessons through these experiences. First, anything worth having is worth working for. This holds true for careers as well as for marriages. You never know where life is going to lead you; you find some of the most precious discoveries when you're not looking for them. In order to take advantage of them, you must be flexible enough to adjust the original plan as necessary to accommodate the revised or modified goal. This may require a focused deferral of gratification.

Second, I've learned to consider my wife as I proceed through the program and through life in general. Unlike my medical school friend, I've committed myself to sacrifice everything else before my wife. There is a scripture in the bible, Ephesians 5:25–27, that has become a principal for my life. It instructs husbands to ". . . love your wives, even as Christ also loved the church, and gave himself for it; . . . that he might present it to himself a glorious church. . . ." I've learned that the more I sacrifice for my wife, the more glorious she becomes. As such, there is no career direction that I have taken or will take without her full support. I frequently shared with my wife that the eight years spent obtaining the M.D. and Ph.D., seven years of residency, and two years in fellowship training are inconsequential in comparison to her. I could be on the precipice of tremendous earning potential when she might request that I abandon my career, or at least defer it, for the sake of the marriage and family. I would be obliged to do so. When I originally made this claim, I was confronted with the emphatic response of disbelief. "Yeah, right," she exclaimed. As a matter of fact, I wasn't so persuaded of it myself. But the more I made the declaration, the more committed to it I became and the more my wife believed in the sincerity of the vow.

Some may argue that to make such a sacrifice is foolish, especially considering the amount of effort placed into obtaining this level of accomplishment. Using the analogy of the three-legged marathon, if I refused to sacrifice the end career goal, I would be crossing the finish line dragging a lifeless body attached to my hip. This is an undesirable outcome in my estimation. Therefore, I am committed to the ultimate goal of finishing the course with the same wife I started with, no matter how long it takes or how much it costs—even if it costs the career itself. The true measure of success is not the acquisition of an established goal. It is, rather, the personal satisfaction and gratification experienced not only at the end of the journey, but also along the way.

Where Is the Passion for the Process?

If there is one thing resonating like a bolt of thunder, I hope it is the admonishment to consider your spouse and family in any and all career decisions. The moment we stand at the altar of matrimony to say the infamous "I do's," we by implication and extension say, "I do make you the highest priority in my life; I do subject the pursuit of my personal, academic and career goals to the ultimate goal of harmonious dwelling in our relationship; I do willingly sacrifice as necessary with the expectation of reciprocation; I do vow that no matter how hectic or chaotic life becomes, I will intentionally spend quality time with you and our children." The responsibility of family carries with it the inherent ability to change a person's entire outlook on life. The things that once seemed all-important suddenly take a lesser position of significance. Somehow, almost magically, if parents dare to explore the bountiful wealth of potential in their offspring, they will suddenly realize that of the many monumental accomplishments they may achieve, those of longest lasting value are the investments made in the lives of their children. This perspective imparts unto the benefactor an invaluable sense of purpose. The ultimate beneficiary of all we accomplish should be those who remain after we're gone—our offspring.

The time I've spent with my children during these years of graduate and medical school training have caused me to realize that what I do as a professional is not nearly as important as what I do as a father. To my five- and two-year-old children, the fact that I obtain honors in every class and heap unto myself countless awards means nothing. The titles and degrees I earn are of little use to them. What matters most to them is "where is Daddy?" "can I play with Daddy?" or "does Daddy even know who I am?" Young children do not understand the concept of deferred gratification nor should they be expected to. They have needs that must be met at the present time not at a later date. Perhaps as children age, our relentless and selfish pursuit of degrees and careers may take on a greater significance. However, I surmise that if the needs of the child are forsaken in the earlier years, the path chosen by dad or mom would not be appealing to the child at any age. Therefore, it is imperative that while we pursue our careers that we make time for our families.

A friend once told me, "Time is like money when you don't have it; you must make it!" We must make time to enjoy our children, to enjoy our spouses, and to enjoy ourselves. Academic life does not necessarily have to be gloom and doom. We must ensure that somewhere along the way, we realize what is really important and maximize our pleasure while we sacrifice. Somehow, we must gain a passion for the process. If single people so choose, they can put fourteen hours each day into studying. I'm not quite sure of why they would, but they have the option. A married person and especially a parent is not afforded such a luxury. Sometimes such long hours are not a luxury but a necessity. Even still, it may not be afforded to the married person or parent. Therefore, a compromise must be made. Instead of spending fourteen hours studying, one should spend twelve hours studying, one hour playing catch with his or her son or daughter, and one hour talking to his or her spouse. In the end, spending the extra two hours studying may not benefit as much as some relaxing activity may.

During medical school, there were times when I desperately needed to study. At some of these times, I desperately needed to be fishing as well. I did both—studied while I fished. Actually it turned out to be more fishing than studying, but nonetheless my mind was refreshed and renewed. I enjoyed myself, with an appropriate but not excessive concern for the time I needed to spend studying. In keeping with this principle, the night before an exam, I would stop studying at around 6:00 P.M. and fire up the grill. It was time to barbecue. A friend thought this was the strangest pre-test activity. However, it was a way for me to enjoy my children and enjoy my wife. Realistically speaking, there are times when graduate students may not be able to "fire up the grill" before an exam. In fact, they may have to burn the midnight oil instead.

However, they should not allow this to become the norm, because they will undoubtedly miss out on the greater good—quality time and interaction with their families. It is sometimes better for them to get a "B" in a course and spend time with their spouses and children than to get an "A" in the course and be estranged from them. As I mentioned before, something has to give. Students should not let it be their families.

As graduate students enjoy their families, they should also enjoy the process of learning. Many academicians reflect back on their graduate school years and conclude that these were some of the best years of their lives. This was the time when they could explore and investigate unencumbered by the mundane stresses of day-to-day professorial duties. They didn't have the concerns of writing grants and the uncertainty of securing funds. They had little if any teaching obligations. Their primary responsibility was to do that which they loved most—learn. Individuals pursuing careers in academia should share one common passion—learning. Discovery is to an academic institution what blood is to the body. Just as blood delivers nutrients and oxygen to all parts of the body, intellectual discovery is the life-supporting element of the institution. Without continued exploration and uncovering of novel truths, inventions, and discoveries, an academic institution is relegated to death. The never-ending pursuit of "why" or "how" is what drives investigators and provides the impetus for continued inquisition. This passion should be capitalized upon by aspiring graduate students. For never again will such an enormous quantity of time be allocated to you specifically for uninterrupted investigation. As students proceed with doctoral studies, they should commit to making the most of the opportunity at hand from the perspectives of academics and family, and they should maximize the benefits their gain from their graduate school experience.

These will ultimately shape the future of their careers and families. They must realize that the sacrifices they make to obtain the doctorate are numerous and costly; however, they should not make the sacrifice so great that they lose those things that are most important to them, particularly their families. Finally, may one additional principle carry them over as they enter their chosen academic career: "Find and keep the passion for the process."

Acknowledgments

I must acknowledge the support and love of my wife, Darice, and my two sons, Demarcus and Aaron. Your unwavering devotion to me has been unparalleled. Your understanding, flexibility, and loyalty have been overwhelming. I often wonder what I could possibly have done to deserve these priceless benefits. I do, however, know how they can be repaid. Reciprocation is the key!

To you I commit my life and my aspirations. You are indeed the highest priority in my life. Accordingly, I will sacrifice all that is necessary for the well-being and health of our family.

I would also like to acknowledge my mother, Mary Williams. You are the most organized and efficient person I know. I thank you for teaching me how to perform multiple activities at once, while maintaining a standard of excellence. To my late father, Charles Williams, I offer thanks for demonstrating on a daily basis the importance of family. You have amply shown me how to place career in its proper perspective.

Finally, in all my ways I acknowledge God, for He directs my path. I have been humbled through these life experiences to realize that apart from God, I can do nothing. But through Him, all things are possible. All praises are given to my Lord and Savior, Jesus Christ!

References

U.S. Department of Education. (1996). *Student financing of graduate and first-professional education, 1995–1996: With profiles of students in selected degree programs, national postsecondary student aid study: 1995–1996*. Washington, DC: U.S. Department of Education, National Center for Education Statistics.

U.S. Department of Health, Education, and Welfare. (1998). *Digest of Education Statistics*. Washington, DC: U.S. Department of Health, Education, and Welfare, Education Division, National Center for Education Statistics. Table 378, p. 378.

John David Carpten

Dr. John David Carpten was born on February 28, 1966, to U.S. Marine Corp Master Sargent George Carpten, Jr. and Hazel Lee Carpten in Honolulu, Hawaii. He was preceded in childhood by a sister, Lisa Victoria Carpten, and a brother, George Carpten. He graduated from Leland High School as an accomplished bassist, most valuable player, 1st team all-conference football player, and an honor graduate.

He attended Lane College, in Jackson, Tennessee, and majored in biology with a minor in chemistry. While at Lane College, John was involved in many campus and community activities. He was a member of the football team, and a member of Kappa Alpha Psi Fraternity, Inc. During the summers of 1985 and 1986, he attended the UNCF Pre-Med summer institute at Fisk University.

After graduating from Lane College in 1988 as valedictorian of his class, he entered graduate school at the Ohio State University in the Molecular, Cellular and Developmental Biology Program. He successfully defended his dissertation in November, 1994.

After applying for jobs and postdoctoral positions, he accepted a staff fellowship at the National Center for Human Genome Research under the direction of Dr. Francis Collins and Dr. Jeffrey Trent. Soon after starting his new position he married Mary Kay Davis on December 22, 1994.

He and Mary Kay have been in Maryland now for five years. They now have a home and have adopted a beautiful twelve-year-old daughter named Kanisha. He currently serves as a senior fellow in the Cancer Genetics Branch of the National Human Genome Research Institute and project leader of the Hereditary Prostate Cancer Project. Dr. Carpten prays that he touches a life everyday . . .

17

BLACK MEN IN GENETICS

John David Carpten

I was born John David Carpten on February 28, 1966, as a gift from God to United States Marine Corp Master Sergeant George Carpten, Jr., and Mrs. Hazel Lee Carpten, formerly Hazel L. Snyder, at the Marine Corp air-base, Koneohe Bay, Oahu, Hawaii. I was preceded in childhood by my sister, Lisa Victoria Carpten (September 15, 1958), and my brother, George Carpten III (March 22, 1962). After a year of preschool, I entered the first grade at Alice Burn Elementary School in Yuma, Arizona.

My parents moved us to Leland, Mississippi, where we lived with my grandmother, Willie Lee Higgins, and my grandfather by marriage, Albert Bernard Higgins. While I enjoyed being near my grandparents, the move was culture shock to me. I went from living in an environment that was less than 2 percent African American to an environment where over 90 percent of the population was African American. In Arizona, all of the homes in our neighborhood were very nice, single-family homes. In Mississippi, most of the homes in my new neighborhood were basic shotgun houses. For those who don't know, a shotgun house is a house where you can look through the front door and see out the back door. But my grandparents had a decent house; no, it was a decent *home*. They provided great structure for us. My grandmother is the purist human being that I've ever met. I can truly say that she's "done it right." I saw God for the first time in her eyes. I think the move was easiest for me because I was the youngest. I soon met new friends in the neighborhood and became well acquainted with the culture of the Deep South.

As I grew up, I began to gain certain interests. The problem was that I wanted to know everything, and I could never focus on one thing. But I always kept God first and foremost in my life. I wanted to be a good student because my brother and sister both were very bright. My brother was great at math and physics, while my sister was very good in language and literature. My father came from a musical family. I remember family reunions in Helena, Arkansas, where my father's family would all sit around the piano and sing gospel music. So naturally all of the children were pretty good musicians. My sister has a beautiful voice, as does my brother. I could hold a note but not gracefully, so I took great interest in playing instruments. I would use cardboard boxes and make drums. Since my parents couldn't afford to buy me an instrument, I joined the school band and played the tuba because it was a school-owned instrument.

I also had a great interest in sports. My brother was on the high-school football team, and I became a ball boy in the 4th grade. This was the best thing to happen to me, because it allowed me to be around the game all of the time. By the time I was 13 years old, I had won every punt, pass, and kick competition that I had entered. I played football for the Leland Middle School team in 7th grade and 8th grade, where I won honors as the best defensive player. I also played Little League baseball consistently well and made most of the local all-star teams.

However, the one thing that was most natural for me was life sciences. I loved the outdoors. Early on summer mornings, I could be found outside, digging to find insects, catching bees and butterflies, and collecting tadpoles and crayfish from Deer Creek. I couldn't get enough. Though I built several insect collections, my mother and grandmother didn't approve. I've always believed that the most important birthday present I ever received was a chemistry set, which I used to win my school science fair.

Just before I entered high school, my parents separated. It was hard at first, especially since my brother had left for college that year. That left only me and my mother in the house, but we managed. I became closer to God at this period in my life. I'll always love my mother for the strength she showed through those years. This was the time in my life when I really needed a man around to teach me, but she did a marvelous job. She was and still is a very strong woman.

I entered high school as an accomplished bassist in the band, a very good football and baseball player, and an above-average student. I went to Milwaukee the summer before my sophomore year in high school and had my first summer job. With the money I earned, I bought a new wardrobe and new shoes. I went to concerts and dances and opened up a lot socially. This also happened to be the summer when I hit my growth spurt and grew at least two inches and gained about 15 pounds. Although I was much more confident when I returned to Mississippi, I always maintained a certain amount of humbleness and humility; I understood that everything I had was given to me by God and that it could all be taken away in a heartbeat.

I played varsity baseball and football my sophomore year. Our baseball team made it all the way to the state championship game. Things really began to take off for me. I made all-state bassist in several honor bands and also went to the state science fair as a sophomore.

Good things carried over into my junior year. I made all-conference in football and played a lot on the varsity baseball team. However, for the first time, tragedy hit my family. My father died of a heart attack around 6:00 A.M. on April 7, 1983. The tragedy was compounded by the fact that after my brother and I had spent the previous weekend with him in Helena, Arkansas, he brought us back and asked my mother if he could move back home after over two years of separation. My mother accepted. She and my dad stayed up the entire night in the living room talking. Early the next morning my brother and I awakened to the sound of our mother screaming. When we walked into the living room half asleep, we both saw my father slumped over in the recliner after suffering a massive heart attack. My brother tried to revive him but to no avail. I was devastated, but the magnitude of the event really didn't hit me until right after the funeral when I said to myself, "I'll never see him again." Even though he had not lived with us for a couple of years, that was very difficult to accept. However, I never faltered because I soon realized that as long as I was alive, my father was alive. That's the law of life and death. I knew what he wanted me to do, so I did it. I excelled in music, sports, and academics.

I made the Mississippi Lions Club all-state band, which is the highest honor for a high-school musician in the state. We traveled to Philadelphia and Washington DC, where we played concerts and marched in national parades during the summer. I also liked playing jazz music and jumped into the original hip-hop scene with a vengeance. I loved Grand Master Flash and the Furious Five, Grand Master Melle Mel, and Ice Tee. I graduated from Leland High School with honors and as the best high-school bassist in the state of Mississippi and an all-conference football player with multiple recruitment opportunities.

College was the next step, and I knew I was going. I had made a promise to myself to become either a professional athlete or a doctor. I was recruited by Ole Miss for football but not aggressively. A local booster took me and two other football players on my team to the Ole Miss vs. LSU game in 1984. I really wanted to play "big" college football. But I decided that I would never attend Ole Miss after sitting in the stands and hearing the crowd get very quiet before they all began to whistle "Dixie." It was one of the scariest things I had ever experienced, because I knew that these were the descendants of the old confederacy. As badly as I wanted to, I just couldn't go to Ole Miss knowing the story of James Evers, who had to be escorted into the university by the National Guard. After football season and during the Christmas holiday that year, one of my high-school coaches told me about Black colleges. Although Mississippi is one of the states with the most historically Black colleges and universities (HBCUs) and although my sister graduated from Mississippi Valley State University, I really didn't know how many Black colleges there were. My coach introduced me to a football recruiter for Lane College in Jackson, Tennessee. The meeting was positive, and although I was courted by other schools during the spring, I had already decided that I would attend Lane College.

Life on a Black college campus was not easy but not difficult. My brother drove me to my college campus, and I was really excited. I did so well on all of the so-called "placement tests" given to all freshmen students to determine their scholastic level that most of the professors wanted me to enter their departments. But I knew I wanted to study biology. Samuel Braxter was the director of the Biological Sciences Department and expressed great interest in me. He was and still is the greatest educator I have known thus far, and I thank God that he was brought into my life. He always had good advice. Although he always pushed me to pursue a career in medicine, he once told me, "If the Pros offer you a chance to play ball, take the money." I have the utmost respect for him. I basically breezed through the academic part of the Black college experience. It was the social part that would prove to be the hardest challenge to overcome.

I met my lifelong best friend in college. Brady A. Cooper was my classmate, and we soon realized that we had the exact same curriculum. Brady was from Chicago, Illinois, and two people could not have come from two more different worlds. We soon saw that we had a lot in common, however. We took every class together and ended up at the Kappa Alpha Psi "smoker" together. We both became members of Kappa Alpha Psi in 1986 and were roommates from our sophomore year in college until I graduated in the spring of 1988. We went through a lot together, carrying each other through the "Black college experience." Brady is now a senior sales representative in charge of international sales for Akzo Chemicals in Chicago. I was the best man at his wedding in 1992, and he now has a three-year-old son, Brad, Jr.

I played football at Lane College and was a starter for all four years. I received all-conference honors all four years, both all-scholastic and football all-conference. In my sophomore year, I began playing baseball and continued as a two-sport athlete throughout the remainder of my college career, all while carrying a full pre-med academic load. I had constant pressure from the department professors to enter medical school. During the summers of 1985 and 1986, I attended the UNCF Pre-Med Summer Institute at Fisk University, where I competed against some of the most talented students from Black colleges all over the country. Although medical school was possible, I knew research was my calling. Just before graduation, I went on a recruitment trip for graduate school at the Ohio State University. I met Dr. Paul Fuerst, who offered me a position as a first-year graduate research associate in the Molecular, Cellular and Developmental Biology Program in the College of Biological Sciences. I graduated from Lane College in 1988 as valedictorian of my class. Although I had a couple of opportunities to play professional football, I took Dr. Fuerst's offer to attend OSU.

Culture shock is not even close to explaining the feeling I had when I finally moved to Columbus, Ohio. I had no friends, no family, and was completely on my own, except for the everlasting comfort of my Lord and Savior. It didn't become evident to me how alone I was until I attended the graduate-school mixer to introduce all of the first-year students to the department. Of course I was the only African American. I soon learned that I was the only African American in the whole department and one of less than a handful in the entire college of biological sciences at the largest single-campus university in the United States. I soon found out why. Many of the professors had a preconceived idea that African Americans simply could not comprehend the information; thus, they could not succeed in this field of study.

I was very interested in the field of DNA research, and no one was going to stop me from learning as much about this discipline as I could. Interestingly, it was a young, first-time assistant professor, Arthur Burghes, Ph.D., who would ultimately give me the opportunity to succeed. I became a member of Arthur's lab and learned a lot about human genetics and diseases that are caused by hereditary factors. I worked with Arthur and other graduate students and members of the Burghes laboratory to discover the gene responsible for causing spinal muscular atrophy, a very severe neuro-degenerative disorder. After more than six years of graduate education, I defended my dissertation research successfully in November 1994. Although I didn't shed a tear at my college graduation, I went into the bathroom in Means Hall after I learned that I had passed, and I cried like a baby.

I can say that I did enjoy some of the time in Columbus. I met a lot of good people, some of whom I consider lifelong friends. I couldn't say this without mentioning the Ross family. One day I was on campus and saw a Brother with a Kappa Alpha Psi jacket on, and I introduced myself. He was an undergraduate student named Ray Nix. He informed me of a meeting that the fraternity was holding that evening. I went to the meeting and during the introductions, one Brother said that he had pledged at Stillman College. Stillman was one of

Lane College's sister schools, and I actually had met some of the Kappa Brothers from the Stillman baseball and basketball teams.

After the meeting, Charles (Chuck) Ross came up to me and introduced himself. Since we both had a Black-college mentality and had a lot of things in common, we quickly became friends. We spent a lot of leisure time together and since he was from Columbus, he introduced me to many people. His younger brother Marcus "Quesi" Ross also became a great friend.

Chuck was actually a master's student in the Department of History, and upon completion of his master's degree, he went to Philadelphia to Temple University to pursue a doctorate in African American history. When he moved to Philadelphia, his younger brother Quesi was completing his bachelor's degree from Hampton University. When Quesi moved back to Columbus to study for the law-school admissions test, he and I became friends. Another Brother that befriended me was Kevin Sarver, a student in the OSU law school. Kevin, Quesi, and I were like the "three amigos." When Chuck moved back to Columbus a year later, the four of us became inseparable. Chuck and Quesi's father was a Black activist in Columbus and always kept us aware of our importance to the community and our obligation to succeed. I grew a lot and had some really good times in Columbus. When we were not studying, we spent a lot of time playing basketball and softball with Chuck and Quesi's childhood friends—Pat Jackson, Eugene Tynes, Jimmy Butler, Carlton and Gary Howard, and others (you know who you are). We also had a great time with other professional students.

Although I moved to Columbus to obtain a doctorate degree, music has always been in my blood. I yearned to have some recording equipment so that I could write songs and produce music. It was a hobby, but I really enjoyed it. I began saving money little by little until I was able to buy some equipment. I would spend hours in music-instrument stores dreaming of buying lots of things. I would write songs and make music tracks all night long. I eventually began making hip-hop tracks for a few local rappers. Through mutual friends, I met Nicolas Mitchell and Chris McLaghlin, who were songwriters and hip-hop artists. We quickly became friends and would spend entire evenings making music. Of course we always wanted to work toward a record deal, but the friendships that we made are almost unbreakable now. To this day, we are great friends and actually consider each other family.

Although I left Mississippi engaged to be married, that relationship started to deteriorate from distance problems, and I began dating in the Columbus area. In 1992, I met Mary Kay Davis, the woman I would soon marry, through a mutual friend. Although we didn't date immediately after we met, I asked her out a month or so later. We fell in love and have been together ever since.

Mary Kay and I come from similar backgrounds, which is probably why we connect so well. Although she grew up in Lima, Ohio, her parents were from the Deep South, so she was raised in a somewhat "southern" household. We actually moved in together about six months after we started dating, and we lived together the remainder of the time I spent in Columbus pursuing my Ph.D.

I began writing my dissertation in the spring of 1994. I then began entertaining job interviews and subsequent offers. As a young graduate student, I had always wanted to pursue a career in industry. I went to a recruitment seminar at Proctor & Gamble in Cincinnati, Ohio, but I wasn't quite sure if I was interested in the type of research programs that were available. My advisor suggested that I look into a fellowship for the National Institutes of Health (NIH) in Bethesda, Maryland. Interestingly, NIH had just set up a new Center for Human Genome Research (NCHGR) under the direction of Dr. Francis Collins and Dr. Jeffrey Trent. I contacted the personnel office and inquired about postdoctoral fellowships opportunities. I received a call from Dr. Trent who was very interested in interviewing me for a fellowship at NCHGR. I interviewed, and although I had not yet defended my dissertation, Dr. Trent offered me a position, and I accepted. Although she was under pressure from friends to stay in Columbus, Mary Kay decided to move to Maryland with me. I began my new job on November 1, 1994, successfully defended my dissertation research on December 1, 1994, and was married to Mary Kay Davis on December 22, 1994.

Mary Kay and I have been in Maryland now for five years. We've made the most of this experience. We now have a home and have adopted a beautiful, 12-year-old daughter named Kanisha. I am the senior fellow in the Cancer Genetics Branch of the National Human Genome Research Institute and project leader of the Hereditary Prostate Cancer Project. I only hope that through my everyday tasks I might do God's work.

In the late 1980s, several human hereditary disease genes were identified, including those that inferred chromic granulomatous disease, Duchene muscular dystrophy, and cystic fibrosis. Technological improvements aided in the discovery of genes responsible for many hereditary diseases thereafter. Under the direction of Dr. Francis Collins, the National Institutes of Health have embarked upon the task of determining the sequence of the entire human genome (the DNA within the cells that make up the body or organism). This is a mammoth effort requiring a collaboration between mega-labs from around the globe. This sequence information will prove invaluable to researchers studying human disease. It will greatly facilitate the basic understanding of disease etiology and also could lead to new and exciting therapeutic discoveries.

Of extreme interest to me is cancer genetics—specifically, prostate-cancer genetics. Prostate cancer is the most common cancer in American men. In 1998, over 200,000 new prostate cancer cases were diagnosed in the United States, and over 40,000 deaths were attributed specifically to prostate cancer. African Americans have the highest prostate cancer incidence of any other ethnic group. Prostate cancer is also a serious disease in other countries, and prostate cancer cases have been on the rise in west Africa.

As a result of several studies, it is now well known and accepted in the clinical and scientific arenas that prostate cancer may have a genetic factor. In other words, men who have an affected father and/or brother are much more likely to develop prostate cancer than age-matched men who don't. Results from these studies also showed that the more affected relatives a man has, the higher his risk of developing prostate cancer. Follow-up studies using simulated genetic analysis suggested that possibly a rare mutant gene could be responsible for the clustering of prostate cancer in families. One major characteristic seen in families at high risk for prostate cancer was an early average age of diagnosis for prostate cancer cases within these families. Data from the National Cancer Database show that the average age at diagnosis for prostate cancer in American men is about 73 years of age. It is now known that high-risk families have an average age at diagnosis of around 65, although this is not universal. This is mainly because of new and advanced methods for diagnosis. In fact, it is believed that the rare mutant gene that confers susceptibility to prostate cancer probably only accounts for less than 10 percent of all prostate cancer but accounts for nearly 50 percent of the early-onset cases. These studies have led to the possibility of identifying prostate-cancer-susceptibility loci, which harbor genes that, when mutated, give rise to prostate cancer in affected family members who could pass the mutant gene on from generation to generation. A similar story has been seen in breast cancer, and several genes have already been identified whose mutant forms infer breast-cancer susceptibility.

Our laboratory performed a genome-wide scan of families at high risk for prostate cancer and revealed evidence of a major prostate-cancer susceptibility on 1q24–q3 1. Prostate-cancer linkage to markers from the 1q24–q3 1 has been confirmed by additional independent data sets, giving strength to the findings by our group. Interestingly, there is significant genetic heterogeneity in prostate cancer, as several other prostate-cancer-susceptibility loci, including Xq27 and 1q42, have been reported by us and others. Our laboratory, among others, is now searching for the actual genes that in their mutated forms give rise to prostate-cancer susceptibility.

In the genetic analysis published by our group, 91 families were used in the study. Of the 91 families, only two were of African American descent. I felt that this is not a good representation, since African Americans have the highest incidence rate in the world. Initial reasons given for the lack of African American families in the study were that African-American families were reluctant to be involved in research studies due mainly to fear and distrust as a result of past deceitfulness by researchers. This is rightfully so. Since then, with the aid of Francis Collins and Dr. Georgia Dunston of Howard University, we have set up a network of recruitment centers headed by mainly African American clinicians and scientists to identify a large cohort of African American families at high risk for prostate cancer. This is a landmark study that is off to a tremendous start and serves as a starting point for the study of other diseases disproportionately affecting the African American community, such as type II diabetes and hypertension. It is my hope that I might play a major role in these efforts.

John Guguam
Igwebuike

Dr. John Guguam Igwebuike was born in Anambra State, Nigeria, during the Nigerian-Biafran War. He and his family came to the United States in 1973. He was raised in Toledo, Ohio.

Dr. Igwebuike holds a B.S.Ed. and B.S.B.A from Ohio State University. Also, he holds an M.B.A. from California~State Polytechnic University and a second master's degree in labor and human resources (M.L.H.R.) from Ohio State University. He earned a Ph.D. in business and education from Ohio State University. In December of 2000, he will receive a doctorate of jurisprudence (J.D.) from Indiana University. All of these degrees will have been achieved by age 31.

In 1996, Dr. Igwebuike founded The Messenger, International, a professional speaking, training, and consulting organization. His personal and professional motto as a speaker, trainer, and seminar leader is: "Not for the reward of the message, but for the truth of the message." To that end, he speaks to a wide spectrum of audiences, including corporations, associations, universities, schools, churches, prisons, and drug-rehabilitation centers.

He is the author of the upcoming book *You've Got Something Special.* This book provides practical strategies for a richer, more interesting, and more creative life. In addition, he is the author of the motivational audiotape series entitled, *Igwebuike's Illustrious Insights.* Presently, he writes a monthly motivational column for *Purpose Magazine,* a national magazine dedicated to helping readers find their life purpose. Finally, he currently lectures and researches at Indiana University.

Dr. John Guguam Igwebuike ranks giving his life to Jesus Christ as his greatest life choice.

18

WHEN TWO ADVANCED DEGREES ARE JUST NOT ENOUGH

John Guguam Igwebuike

Mind is the master-power that molds and makes,
And man is mind, and the more he takes
The tool of thought and shaping what he wills,
Brings forth a thousands joys, a thousand ills:
He thinks in secret and it comes to pass:
Environment is but his looking glass
          —James Allen, *As a Man Thinketh*

Introduction

This essay investigates the general theme, "when two advanced degrees are not enough." It could more generally embrace the theme, "why no amount of education is ever enough." The essay selects dialectical dialogue as the venue for this intellectual inquiry. Dialectics is a Socratic technique for investigating eternal ideas. The hope of this inquiry-by-query approach and the ultimate aim of this essay is for you to formulate your own answers, construct your own solutions, and generate new, additional questions. In this spirit, the essay rejects any hints of pedantry and spurns any pretense for having right answers. I want to emphasize that this essay offers few, if any, answers. For the most part, it asks questions—lots of them. As with so many issues in life, it embraces quandaries and queries and makes hypotheses—mere guesses—as hopeful starting points for creating solutions.

Essentially, the salient question throughout this dialectic is "What can you teach?" By way of introduction, the essay takes you on a hypothetical trek back in time. Various inventions, technologies, discoveries, and creations from antiquity to the present are considered. You are asked to consider which you would be able to teach, invent, discover, or create were you teleported to a particular period of the past. The question "What can you teach?" springs from the proposition that you cannot teach what you do not know. Thus, you are invited to consider the veracity of that proposition based on what you currently know and can therefore teach.

The remaining part of the essay leaves it to you to construct the answer to the general thesis that no amount of education is enough. You will construct answers to the theme and thesis of this essay based on how you are able to answer the question "What can you teach?" In the end, you ultimately must determine whether two advanced degrees or any amount of education are enough.

Finally, it must be admitted at the outset that this essay leads you to the ledge. Specifically, through dialectic dialogue the author takes you to the ledge of what you know in order to consider what you do not know. This approach is best captured by Kahlil Gibran in *A Teacher's Wisdom:*

> The teacher who walks among his or her students gives not of one's wisdom but rather of one's faith and lovingness. If he or she is indeed wise he or she does not bid you enter the house of his or her wisdom, but rather leads you to the threshold of your own mind. For the vision of one person lends not its wings to another person.

What Can You Teach?

Consider this hypothetical situation: Suppose you were teleported to a given period of human history. For instance, you may find yourself in Harlem, New York, during the Harlem Renaissance at the turn of the twentieth century. Or you may find yourself in the backwoods of Maryland among runaway slaves who are fleeing north while being led by a courageous woman named Tubman. Or maybe you discover that you are in a dusty, arid desert where an Egyptian Pharaoh speaks of building several triangular-shaped pyramids as eternal monuments for future progeny. Perhaps your time teleportation finds you among many seated in a resplendent palace among thousands who have sojourned to hear the wealth of wisdom of a young king named Solomon. Perchance your teleportation into yesteryear places you on an expansive southern African landscape currently being ruled by the great Zulu king and warrior, Shaka. For this intellectual exercise, the exact place of your transportation is not of utmost significance. In fact, you can choose whatever past period you wish to visit. What is of key import, however, is the knowledge you bring when you arrive and the ideas, thoughts, and understandings you carry with you to be shared with the ancient forebearers you encounter. The question posed by this essay and most likely by the ancients you meet is simple: "What can you teach?"

The glory of America is its educational system. Those of us living in America today are particularly fortunate to live in the richest, most technologically advanced society that has ever existed. By the time an American student graduates from high school, that graduate has acquired over 25 million bits of information. American citizenship endows us with free education from preschool through high school. America has more knowledge repositories (libraries) than any country that has ever existed. Add the fact that libraries are free, and the conclusion is ineluctable: Learning opportunities abound in America.

Formal education is equally abundant. America has more universities and colleges than any country in the world. For example, each of America's largest 25 cities has more colleges and universities than does any country within the entire continent of Africa. This abundance of educational opportunity did not come without cost. Our foremothers and forefathers could only dream and hope for what you can experience and take advantage of today. Thus, with the wealth of schools, libraries, and educational opportunity to which you are now privy, with the great amount of knowledge you have heretofore acquired, and with the ample opportunity to gain more knowledge, the question again must be asked, "What can you teach?"

For instance, were you teleported into a dilapidated agricultural laboratory during the early 1900s in the rural southern town of Tuskegee, Alabama, to visit a promising young African American scientist at Tuskegee Agriculture and Normal School? Could you show George Washington Carver 300 additional uses for a single peanut in addition to the more than 300 he had already discovered independently? What can you teach?

Could you build a computer from scratch to help track and test Carver's experiments? At the writing of this essay, personal computers have been around less than 20 years. There are now more than twice as many of them as there are people on the planet. In addition, approximately 50 billion embedded chips are currently extant. These ubiquitous microprocessors operate cars, track time, power appliances, light cities, power engines, heat and cool homes, navigate satellites, fly and land planes, and power the same instruments that build these contemporary technological conveniences. Even with the ubiquity of computers and the plethora of computer chips, very few know how to build or design one. But, could you build one? What can you teach?

Could you design the computer chip? Would you know where to dig and excavate to find the rich mineral resource of silicon or copper that is essential to the microprocessor chip? Could you build the communication infrastructure of LANs, servers, and digital wiring for the Internet? Or could you build a telephone and all of its present-day progeny—cellular phones, digital pagers, and satellite communication systems? What about an answering machine?

Next to computer technology, electricity has been hailed as the greatest discovery of the twentieth century. When we throw an electrical switch, we expect things to happen: lights to come on or off, a car motor to surge to life, or a computer to boot up. But what is electricity? How does it work with machinery to bring it to life? Often electricity and many other phenomena like it are taken for granted because the lights come on so easily, the car turns on reliably, and the computer boots up instantly. That notwithstanding, could you show people of past generations how to conduct and generate electricity? For example, would you be able to select which of the thousands of filaments is necessary to make the incandescent light bulb? Or could you show them how to make a simple wire? As you would begin to look for the necessary materials to start, however, you would likely realize that making wire really is not simple after all. What can you teach?

Each year hundreds of thousands of cargo ships are piloted and docked in ports of the United States. Of the numerous items imported, billions of barrels of crude oil are unloaded to be refined into gasoline, heating oil, airplane fuel, petroleum jelly, plastics, and hundreds of other formulations. Could you tell the ancestors where the rich black resource of oil can be found? Could you show them how to pump it from the bowels of the earth to the surface? Would you be able to instruct them on refining techniques to transform crude oil to diesel fuel or gasoline to power the automobile you build for them? What can you teach?

Note that I said, "the automobile *you* build for them." Asked simply, can you build a car? Automobiles have been around in America for nearly a century. Automotive manufacturing and the many ancillary industries it spawned (such as rubber, steel, plastic, glass, textile, and computer) are largely responsible for the standard of living Americans enjoy today. Nearly every American family has at least one automobile, and many have more than two. The automobile is viewed as a necessity for many in America. Yet automotive engineers at Ford, Chrysler, and General Motors are in unanimous agreement that there is not a single human being alive who can single-handedly build a modern automobile from scratch. Thus, out of the present world population of more than 6 billion, not one person alive can build a present-day automobile. The same holds for the modern airplane, ocean liner, submarine, or space shuttle. What can you teach?

Even if you could not build a car, perhaps you could build something for Leonardo da Vinci and his contemporaries. Were you to visit the anachronistic inventor, he would gladly usher you into his workshop. There he would place in your hand hundreds of sketches at which he had labored. Included with the many drawings would be pictures of planes, rockets, and helicopters. Could you help this technological prophet bring his sketches to life? In other words, using the benefits of your years of education and what you now know, could you inform and transform his sketches into fully functioning machines? If not, what can you teach?

Every day we use hundreds if not thousands of inventions, creations, and innovations that have greatly improved our present lives. For example, light amplification by stimulated emission radiation (LASER) is a device that produces a narrow beam of intense radiation. It was developed in California in 1960 and symbolized modern technology in its glory. With it we now have the basis for remote-controlled televisions, radios, stereo equipment, automatic garage door openers, VCRs, wireless phones, and a multiplicity of electronic and digital conveniences. Could you teach how to develop this four-decade-old scientific technology? Or, taking your pick, which of the thousands of present-day advancements could you create? What could you teach?

Modern medicine has brought us to a new plateau of longevity and wellness. The present age is the beneficiary of triple-bypass heart surgery, organ transplants, blood transfusions, DNA testing, genetic cloning, and bone-marrow replacements. The pharmaceutical industry affords a bounty of life-saving and life-enhancing drugs including antibiotics and chemotherapy. CT scans, MRIs, and EKG devices provide a more resolute probe into the causes of sickness. Could you design any of these modern-medical miracles to give enhanced life to the sick of ancient times? At a more basic level, could you synthesize aspirin? Could you formulate the cure for polio, small pox, measles, scarlet fever, tuberculosis, cancer, or AIDS? Would you be able to help Dr. Charles Drew transform his dissertation entitled "Banked Blood" from an inchoate conceptualization of blood plasma preservation techniques into the actual creation of the Red Cross? What could you teach?

Little is known of the miracle of the human heart. Each day the heart pumps gallons of life-giving blood throughout the body. The heart pumps in response to electrical synapses, which occur 103,680 times a day. This amounts to about 38 million electrical synapses a year and to several billion synapses over an eighty-year life span. But how does this vital synaptic life function happen? It is a complete and total mystery. No empirical researcher has yet been able to establish with any plausibility how the synapses occur. All that can be definitively asserted is that sometime around the middle of the fourth month of gestation, a tiny little heart in a tiny little baby begins to beat. Could you explain this little-known mystery?

That there is a connection between all living substances has been demonstrated. Dr. Martin Luther King, Jr. said: "Whatever affects one directly affects all indirectly. We are all links in the great chain of humanity" (King, 1992). Actually, when Dr. King made this assertion, he was particularly referring to human interrelationship. Evidence now shows that there is an interconnection between all living things, and polygraph experiments extend Dr. King's assertion. In a study, for example, polygraph experts demonstrated that houseplants know when the home's occupant has returned home from a shopping trip, for the plants react in their own emotional way. When the owner dumps the recently purchased live shrimp in boiling water in the kitchen, observations indicate that the shrimp seem to faint right before they come into contact with the hot water that will kill them. At that precise moment, the plants throughout the house react violently to the murder atop the kitchen stove. Could you explain the relationship between a homeowner and houseplants, live shrimp to boiling water, or houseplant reactions to fainting, dying shrimp? More generally, could you explain the ultimate interconnection between all organic and inorganic things? All of this is an indirect way to begin to suggest that there is much that we do not know. Unless we know it, we cannot teach it.

That notwithstanding, what can you teach about ending war? Since the dawn of humanity and throughout all of recorded history, there has never been a millennium, century, decade, year, or day when humankind was not at war with itself. At the writing of this essay, forty-eight wars are waging across the globe. Trillions of dollars are being spent to conduct these wars, and millions of men, women, and children are being killed as a consequence. Today's cold fact is that new wars are erupting every day. John F. Kennedy said, "Mankind must put an end to war, or war will put an end to mankind." Facts sadly suggest that humanity is closer to self-destruction and annihilation than to lasting peace. Philosophers and sages have long concluded that the single greatest mystery is modern man. And, as Kennedy suggested, war is putting an end to mankind, because mankind is not putting an end to war. Therefore, armed with the benefit of your present education, can you show society how to put an end to war and, therefore, preserve humanity? Can you teach tenets that will yield lasting world peace? Can you inculcate permanent solutions to violence or advocate a strategy to eliminate hate completely? Can you teach the opposite of hate—love? What can you teach?

The gap between what is known (what you can teach) and what is unknown (what you cannot teach) is vast. Distinguished scientist and inventor Charles Kettering cleverly demonstrated this fact before an audience of engineers. Specifically, he constructed a stage backdrop consisting of a large, shiny sheet of stainless steel measuring thirty feet by fifty feet in area. He took a metal stylus, moved to the corner of the sheet, and made a tiny, almost invisible mark. He focused the audience on the nondescript mark. He then told his audience that the mark he had just made was to represent all that science had accomplished at the present time, while the great, pristine, untouched expanse of the stainless sheet represented what was yet to be discovered.

Actually, Kettering overestimated what science had discovered. Nevertheless, his illustration elucidates a profound point that cannot be overemphasized: There is much to be discovered and learned. The philosopher René Descartes came to the same exhilarating conclusion, saying "all that men know is almost nothing when compared to what remains to be known." Thus, Kettering's graphic illustration of scientific progress, or the lack thereof, in the field of traditional science can also be applied to every other discipline. It applies to the fields of law, education, and business. It relates to the humanities, arts, or social sciences. It pertains to medicine, dentistry, optometry, and physical and occupational therapy. It applies more broadly, yet with equal force, to humanity's social progress, harmonious interrelationship, and mutual respect for one another. Finally, it extends and applies with particular poignancy to each person's progress toward self-awareness, self-understanding, and self-knowledge.

What can you teach? Certainly, an infinite number of scenarios, hypotheticals, and illustrative vignettes could be offered to make the single point: There is so much that is unknown. Thus, the foregoing dialectic exercise elucidates several important considerations as to why no amount of education is enough.

First, the exercise illuminates the fact that humanity is just taking its first, tentative steps toward knowledge. Despite the advance of the present age and all of the explosion of new information it affords, the most that can be reasonably asserted is that we know very little. In reality, we have more questions than answers. We know a lot and have vast libraries, educational institutions, and access to lifetimes of information. But in terms of what can be clearly instructed and sufficiently taught, little is sufficiently known of any of it. In our modern age replete with modern advances, we still do not know enough. The vast storehouse of knowledge, if anything, informs us of how little we actually know about what we already know. And, paradoxically, it instructs that we have much more to learn and informs that there is much about which we do not yet know.

Second, it demonstrates that the dialectic (question-asking) approach can be a valuable teaching and learning tool. Knowledge results from asking questions such as new questions to old problems or old questions to new problems. In addition, knowledge is not the sole provenance of the learned, aristocratic, or privileged. It is the provenance of all who willingly and indefatigably seek it. Once you learn to ask relevant and substantive questions, you are equipped with a potent permanent tool to learn whatever you want or need to know. You need no longer wait to be instructed or taught by others. Instead, if you formulate questions and seek answers, you can learn from and by yourself.

Third, the dialectic exercise highlights the importance of education. The ultimate purpose of education is for you to come to know what you do not know. Education is not mere classroom lectures, quizzes, tests, and homework. Rather, education integrally involves the individual creation of knowledge. The purpose of learning is for you to construct your own meaning, not just absorb and memorize the "right" answers and regurgitate someone else's ideas, opinions, or meanings. It requires you to deconstruct what has been taught in order to reconstruct your own meaning and understanding. This constructivist notion of education impels you to step out on the *ledge* to learn what you do not currently *know*. This is the act that produces *knowledge*.

Fourth, the exercise shows that we are all dependent on each other's knowledge. No one knows every thing. Consequently, everyone is ignorant about something. Veritably, to some questions we can only answer, "I do not know." This lack of total knowledge should give us pause. It recognizes that every day we eat foods, use products, and operate equipment and devices we could not independently grow, create, or design for ourselves. That notwithstanding, we are the beneficiaries of the shared knowledge of others. At the same time, we are all knowledgeable to teach and share something. Thus, we all have the value of a skill, expertise, or idea with which to make a contribution to humanity. Though we cannot teach a multiplicity of things, we can at least teach something. No matter how little, what we can share may be used to make a collective difference in the world.

Fifth, what we do not know can enhance our human relationships. Socrates was thought to be the wisest man of his time; historical evidence confirms that the oracle at Delphi designated Socrates as being the wisest. Yet when Socrates learned of being accorded this mark of distinction, the only answer Socrates could give was that, if he was indeed the wisest man alive, it was because he "knew what [he] did not know." If we, too, are to be our wisest, we will admit that in our social affairs there is much we do not know. For instance, we do not know enough to rush in judgment of others. We do not know enough about the reason for the cry of the low-birth weight baby born to a crack-addicted mother. We do not know enough of the condition that brings the homeless person to beg for money. We do not know enough about the pain that is causing the slow walk of an elderly woman. We do not know enough about the daily mental turmoil of the troubled war veteran. We do not know enough about the persistent pain that keeps the drug addict hooked or the alcoholic addicted. We do not know enough of the love the young person lacks but seeks in vain to find in a gang. We do not know enough about why the prostitute puts herself on parade. We know so little about the psychological, emotional, physical, and mental problems of our fellow Brothers and Sisters. If we will be wise, what we do not know can impel greater patience, awareness, and mutual respect.

Finally, and woven throughout the preceding points (and the entire essay), is the importance of becoming autodidactic. An autodidact is a self-taught individual. Through determination and sheer desire to learn, the autodidact learns what he or she does not know. Hence, the glory of Africans in America is the ability to become autodidacts. With or without opportunities for education, they became self-learners. For instance, the silver-tongued orator Frederick Douglass taught himself how to speak eloquently. Malcolm X drew great dividends by teaching himself how to read and write by copying an entire dictionary from cover to cover. George Washington Carver taught himself and others sophisticated agricultural and crop-rotation techniques. Booker T. Washington taught himself in great measure how to read and write. W. E. B. DuBois was the first African American to graduate from Harvard. Yet this achievement was part and parcel of a self-teaching habit he had begun and sustained from his youth. Beginning from the age of twelve, he read, studied, and wrote for at least six hours every day. He continued this habit of self-study and self-learning without stop all of his life. Marian Anderson taught herself, in large part, to sing in nine different languages. Martin L. King, Jr. spent thousands of hours living and learning the nonviolent methods of Mahatma Ghandi, Henry David Thoreau, and Jesus. He even sojourned to India to become learned in peaceful resistance. We can take a historical cue about the importance of becoming autodidacts and apply it to our modern times.

The ability to become self-taught is within each of us. This affirms the true meaning of education as derived from the Latin word *educare,* which means "to draw forth." Thus, the process of becoming self-taught or autodidactic is a process of drawing forth gifts, intelligence, and knowledge already within one's self.

The present age behooves each of us to become autodidacts. We must teach ourselves to learn independently. Education, schooling, training, and continuing education can lay an excellent foundation. However, the degrees, certificates, and diplomas are not enough. They should attest that we are autodidacts, or self-learners. In the current climate of dynamic information explosion, often what we learn in school will not be transferable years later in the workplace. It will be obsolete. Therefore, becoming and staying autodidactic is a must. No matter what colleges we attend or at which schools we are enrolled, eventually the formal class session must come to an end, and we must go back home—home to ourselves.

Ultimately, we must all become our own teachers. Standard schooling will at most yield standard education. This point cannot be overemphasized. One of the most salient reasons to become self-taught is that there are certain things we would otherwise never learn were we to depend on someone else to research, find, and teach it. For example, our own unique skills, values, beliefs, and spirituality are vital to a worthwhile life. Yet they can only come from within. They can only come through self-teaching, by becoming an autodidact.

Conclusion

No one knows enough to stop learning. The amount of knowledge is growing at an explosive rate. The total storehouse of knowledge accumulated in the last two hundred years of the existence of the United States is now greater than the amount of knowledge gathered in all of previous recorded history. The present age is the age of the information revolution. At the writing of this essay, knowledge doubles every seven years. In the field of medicine, knowledge doubles in less than five years. Thus, it is estimated that 75 percent of all workers will need retraining by the year 2000. The implication of these facts is inescapable: Education must be lifelong. The rate of informational doubling will not abate. And the amount of accumulated knowledge will continue to grow. Likewise, our personal knowledge must continue forever to grow and expand in order to keep pace with the inexorable growth of knowledge.

The good news from psychologists and neurologists is that our ability to learn can remain steady throughout a lifetime, perhaps even increase. Researchers confirm the conclusion that learning can be lifelong. Whereas medical evidence suggests that, on average, our hearing begins to decline at the age of ten, our visual acuity starts to go down from age ten, our eyesight begins to decline by age twelve, and overall physical health begins to deteriorate by about age forty. Our mind power, nevertheless, can continue to grow, develop, increase, and expand throughout all of life. However, just as the body needs stretching and exercising to remain vigorous and to grow, our mind must be stretched and exercised in order to grow and stay vital. Relentless reading, endless education, and ceaseless learning are optimal ways to stretch and exercise one's mind.

Learning is a lifelong process. Viewed correctly, learning is life. Every day commences a new day for learning. Graduation at any level (for example, preschool, kindergarten, elementary, trade school, college, professional, or graduate school) is the beginning of learning. Education in not merely K–12; it is birth through life. Thus, a lawyer need no longer be a law student to be a student of the law. A doctor need not remain in medical school to remain a student of medicine. A dentist need not stay in dental school to stay schooled in dentistry. The same holds for each of the more than 4,000 professions in existence today. No matter the field, we can always learn and grow. To stop becoming educated is to stop growing. And, to stop growing is to start dying— intellectually, spiritually, and mentally. Conversely, to continue to learn, study, and teach what we know is to continue to grow and know all of the days of our life.

No amount of education is enough. With twenty-six years of continuous formal schooling, I have come to the conclusion that even two advanced degrees are just not enough. In fact, even a lifetime of degrees and learning represents but a commencement on the road of knowledge. Perhaps you came to the same conclusion. You need not necessarily be teleported into another dimension of time or space nor be enrolled in a doctoral program faced with a dissertation defense to know and accept what scholars, philosophers, poets, artists, and prophets have pronounced throughout the ages: Education is lifelong.

Reference

Gibran, K. (1995). A teacher's wisdom. *The treasured writings of Kahlil Gibran* (unpublished).

King, M. L., Jr. (1992). I have a dream. In J. M. Washington (Ed.), *Writings and speeches that changed the world*. San Francisco: Harper.

PART THREE

Featured Scholarship

Troy D. Allen

Dr. Troy D. Allen is currently an assistant professor of history at Southern University in Baton Rouge, Louisiana. There he teaches courses in African American history and world civilizations (honors) along with a course on ancient Egypt. He also teaches a joint course between Southern University and Louisiana State University in race relations Dr. Allen advises students, serves as a mentor, and volunteers for various community/social events. He also finds time to volunteer as a baseball and basketball coach at the YMCA.

Dr. Allen is a native of McKeesport, Pennsylvania, a suburb outside of Pittsburgh. He completed his undergraduate work at Point Park College, a small liberal arts college in the heart of downtown Pittsburgh. After receiving his bachelor of arts degree from Point Park, Dr. Allen attended the Ohio State University, where he received his master of arts degree in Black studies, with an emphasis in Black community development. He obtained his Ph.D. from the Department of African American Studies at Temple University, where he had the honor of studying under two of the most prolific scholars in the field of African American studies, Dr. Molefi Asante and Dr. Theophile ObengJa.

Dr. Allen is the author of many articles and also serves on the editorial board of the *Journal of Black Studies*. His work on the ancient Egyptian family has been accepted for publication and is due out in the spring of 2000. Dr. Allen has traveled to both Africa and Europe. Dr. Allen is married to the former Lia White and is the proud father of three children—his sons, Sa'iid and Khephren, and his daughter, Aksosua.

19

ANCIENT EGYPTIAN FAMILY AND SOCIAL ORGANIZATION

Troy D. Allen

Its contribution to human knowledge in the fields of science, astronomy, medicine, philosophy, mathematics, geometry, and engineering leaves most observers of ancient Egyptian civilization in awe (Petrie, 1940). Ancient Egypt was one of the greatest civilizations that has ever existed. Indeed, ancient Egypt's historical greatness seems to be surpassed only by the remarkable endurance of its monuments through time.

Despite its remarkable monuments, it is evident that the greatness of ancient Egypt does not reside in the answer to the question, "How were the pyramids built?"; rather, it resides in the question, "How was their society built?" Clearly, to comprehend the enduring grandeur of ancient Egyptian civilization, one must first understand not merely its technological innovations, which are fascinating, but also its institutions.

Throughout all of human history, a major foundation of all institutions in a society has been the family. The organization of the family underlies the structure of other social institutions (Zonabend et al., 1996). In order to understand ancient Egyptian society as such, we must first know precisely how the ancient Egyptian's family was organized in terms of marriage, kinship, and lineage.

Indeed, there is a problem when it comes to comprehending ancient Egyptian family and social organization. Some Egyptologists state that it was structured along patrilineal lines (Johnson, 1978; Kemp et al., 1983; O'Connor, 1990). Others argue that the ancient Egyptian family was organized along matrilineal lines (Clayton, 1994; Diop, 1974; Erman, 1947; Murray, 1949; Petrie, 1924).

Anthropologists and social evolutionists have consistently used patrilineal family and social organization as an indicator of civilization, while matrilineal family and social organization was declared a measure of "barbarism" (Sanderson, 1990). In fact, this way of looking at the family and social organization was used to justify the imposition of European cultural values on African societies in the name of the three C's: Christianity, civilization, and commerce.

It is very clear that many African societies practiced matrilineal family social organization prior to the time of European invasion (Radcliffe-Brown & Forde, 1950). Matrilineal families and social organization might, in fact, be seen as the dominant mode of social organization in pre-colonial African societies (Diop, 1974). Today the traditional African family and social organization has virtually disappeared under the enormous assault of Western culture (Phillips, 1953).

Since ancient Egypt did not emulate the patrilineal family model of family and social organization, it has become an enigma for those who cannot accept its matrilineal structure. Indeed, for those scholars who solely equate "civilization" with the patrilineal model of family and social organization, Egypt remains their albatross and their foil for denying the African basis of Egyptian civilization. The matrilineal nature of ancient Egyptian society reveals both the continuity between African and Egyptian civilizations and the compatibility between matrilineal social structure and civilization. For Africans looking to rebuild their families, the ancient Egyptian family and social organization could be used as their model.

The organization of the family underlies the structure of other social institutions. Family structure is sociologically controlled, and the family's relationship among members is subject to some regular arrangements. However, the organization of the family varies in different societies (Radcliffe-Brown, 1950). There are several different modes of family structure (Murdock, 1949), and the distribution of such models is not a random affair. Every model of family organization has its own internal logic. In each model there are certain relationships among family members, and every family member has a specific role in relation to others. All roles are designated and defined by kinship terms, which serve as an internal guide to family relationships and organization (Keesing, 1975). Usually, most people include as relatives those who have a common ancestor. When tracing is done through the males, the practice is said to be patrilineal; if the tracing is done through the females, the practice is called matrilineal (Schusky, 1983).

A key component used by Cheikh Anta Diop to support his thesis of an African origin of ancient Egyptian civilization is its matrilineal family and social organization. Diop demonstrates that this type of family grows out of material conditions that favor agricultural food production and a sedentary lifestyle. Diop explains the impact these factors have on the status of women by stating:

> In fact it is only in this framework that the wife can, in spite of her physical inferiority, contribute substantially to the economic life. She even becomes one of the stabilizing elements in her capacity as mistress of the house and keeper of the food. (1990, p. 34)

Also, it is known that during the Old and Middle Kingdoms of ancient Egypt, textile manufacturing was conducted exclusively by women, and they continued to play a large role in it during the New Kingdom. Women clothed their families and were able to trade any surplus they may have accumulated. These factors along with her contributions in food production (agriculture) made women in ancient Egyptian society an economic asset (Fischer, 1989; Lesko, 1987).

The "status" of women is a fundamental criterion that distinguishes ancient Egypt from ancient Semitic civilizations such as Mesopotamia Assyria and Babylon as well as ancient Indo-European civilizations such as Greece and Rome. Diop emphasizes this point with the following observation:

> Moreover this situation has been unchanged since ancient times: the couples to be seen on the African monuments of Egypt are united by a tenderness, a friendship, an intimate common life—the like which is not found in the Eurasian world of this period: Greece, Rome, Asia. This fact, in itself, would tend to prove that ancient Egypt was not Semitic: in the Semitic tradition, the history of the world begins with the fall of man, his ruin caused by a woman (the myth of Adam and Eve). (1978, pp. 127–128)

Marriage is the crucial link between family and social organization. Marriage is defined as a union between a man (husband) and a woman (wife). This union is both economic and sexual, known to other members of society, accepted by them, and considered permanent. Those linked by marriage are termed *affines* by anthropologists. Married couples provide the affinal link that bind two existing families. These links are cemented by the birth of children who then provide the consanguineal (blood) ties. Affinal and consanguineal ties form the basis of the family institution (Zonabend, 1996).

Marriage was the primary institution of social life in ancient Egypt, although no term exists that denotes marriage as such. Marriage in ancient Egypt did not involve a religious ceremony or require a legal certificate, but it appears to have been a private act, albeit with a public ceremony between families that were culturally recognized (Pestman, 1961). This point cannot be understated, because it illustrates the fact that ancient Egyptian family/society was built on consanguineal ties and not a legal basis. Therefore, terms such as *mother-in-law, father-in-law, brother-in-law,* and *sister-in-law* have no authenticity when used to describe the ancient Egyptian family.

Since the ancient Egyptians never codified their laws into specific collections such as the Code of Hammuarabi, it is difficult to ascertain precise knowledge about marriage in Pharaonic Egypt. There are no legislative texts that exist, public or private, that govern family practices. Therefore, in order to obtain an intimate glimpse of family life in ancient Egypt, it is necessary to search through and compare different sources, both iconographic and written texts (Forgeau, 1996).

The iconographic evidence illustrates that the ancient Egyptian family was both monogamous and polygynous in its structure. The monogamous family ranged from married couples without children to married couples with children (one or more) to married couples with children and extended families. The known cases of polygamy in ancient Egypt were found to be polygynous in structure (Simpson, 1974). They could range from a husband with more than one wife or a husband with more than one wife and children to a husband with more than one wife with children and extended family (Allen, 1998). The most important item in regard to polygynous marriages is that in societies where it does exist, family and social organization are both impacted.

The Egyptians used the term *grg pr,* which simply means to "found or establish your household," and a man and a woman became "married" by setting up a house together. Similarly, "divorce" is referred to as expulsion *h3'* or departure *sm,* generally of the woman from the house. The word used to denote husband is *hi,* while the term for wife is *hmt, snt* is sister (a term used from the Eighteenth Dynasty), and *nbt pr* is lady/mistress of the house (Eyre, 1984). Married couples were usually from similar social groups, and the primary function of marriage was to produce children and perpetuate the family.

The ancient Egyptians used only six kinship terms:

it   = father

mwt = mother

sn (t) = brother/sister

s3 (t) = son/daughter

hi   = husband

hmt = wife

However, these six terms do not designate all the possible kinship relations or categories; the ancient Egyptians achieved this by connecting two elementary kinship terms by the genitive *n* (nt) (Willems, 1983). For example, *sn.f n mwt.f* translated literally is "his brother of his mother." The ancient Egyptians used suffix-pronouns such as *.f* ("his") or *.s* ("her") to indicate kinship relations (Gardiner, 1994). The ancient Egyptians used what anthropologists call a *classificatory kinship system* (Schusky, 1983). Classificatory kinship systems are found in the clan or group. Thus, in a classificatory system, ego (or the speaker) reflects not "I" singular but the group plural (Fox, 1971). In this type of system, all siblings of the same generation stand in relation to each other. The anthropologist Radcliffe-Brown offers a clear explanation of this system:

> A man is always classed with his brother and a woman with her sister. If I apply a given term of relationship to a man, I apply that same term to his brother. Thus I call my father's brother by the same term I apply to my father, and similarly, I call my mother's sister, mother. The consequential relationships are followed out. The children of any man I call "father" or any woman I call "mother" are my "brothers" and "sisters." The children of any man I call "brother" if I'm a male call me "father," and I shall call them "son" or "daughter." (1931, p. 13)

Needless to say, this type of kinship system has confused travelers, missionaries, and anthropologists in Africa since the time of al-Bakri (Ajayi and Espie, 1972). In fact, most Egyptologists have imposed Western (Indo-European) kinship terminology upon ancient Egyptian civilization by mechanically following Western kinship terms. This type of imposition alters the comprehension and reality of ancient Egyptian terms and social organization. In his *Manual for Kinship Analysis*, E. L. Schusky (1983) states: "A translation of the foreign term into the nearest English distorts the meaning. By proceeding from a Western/European perspective, Egyptologists not only attached Western/European kinship terms on ancient Egyptian society, but they also have imposed their cultural values and connotations to these terms. The ancient Egyptians did not use or have kinship terms such as aunt/uncle, niece/nephew, or cousin as a part of their kinship terminology. And since their marriages were not based on legality/law, then there also does not exist any terminology to classify kinship ties as "in-laws." Ancient Egyptian civilization in this regard is distinctly like that of Black Africa, because these terms also do not appear in any African languages (Obenga, 1992).

The "Instruction Texts" of the ancient Egyptians provide clear advice on marriage, morality, fidelity, and the importance of having a family. From the Old Kingdom, the "Instruction of Prince Hardjedef" advises his son:

> When you prosper, found your household,
> Take a hearty wife; a son will be borne you.

It is for the son you build a house. (Lichtheim,
1975, p. 58)

Likewise, the Old Kingdom sage Ptah-Hotep provides similar instructions:

When you prosper and found your house,
And love your wife with ardor
Fill her belly, clothe her back,
Ointment soothes her body.
Gladden her heart as you live,
She is the fertile field for her lord.
(Lichtheim, 1975, p. 69)

Similar advice is stated in the New Kingdom instructions of Any:

Take a wife while young,
That she make a son for you,
She should bear for you while you are youthful.
It is proper to make people.
Happy the man whose people are many
He is saluted on the account of his progeny.
(Lichtheim, 1976, p. 136)

The ancient Egyptian marriage bond was one of love and respect. A suitable age for a man to marry appears to have been twenty, according to the teachings of the scribe Onkhsheshongy (Lichtheim, 1980), and the bride could be even younger. Advice on how a wife should be treated in the house is also given by Any:

Do not control your wife in her house,
When you know she is efficient;
Don't say to her: "Where is it? Get it!"
When she has put it in the right place.
Let your eyes observe in silence,
Then you recognize her skill;
It is a joy when your hand is with her,
There are many who don't understand this
If a man desists from strife at home'
He will not meet its beginning.
Every man that founds a household
Should hold back the hasty heart. (Lichtheim, 1975, p. 143)

Egyptologists have attempted to use the so-called marriage contracts known from the seventh-century BCE and that continued to be in use through the Late Period into Ptolemaic Egypt to interpret marriage in earlier periods (Robbins, 1993). For example:

> I have taken you as a wife. I have given you (sum of "money" listed here) as your **shep en sehemet.** If I repudiate you as a wife, be it that I hate you, be it that I want another woman as a wife instead of you, I shall give you (sum of money is here listed) apart from (sum of money listed) which I have given you as your *shep en sehemet* . . . And I give you 1/3 (part) of all and everything which will be between you and me from this day onwards. (Pestman, 1961, p. 17)

In most cases, these documents also indicate that any children produced from this union will be heirs to the man's property as well, and he promises to return the value of what the woman has brought with her to his house, regardless of whether she leaves of her own free will or is repudiated by him. These documents, while primarily drawn up by the man, are for the economic protection of the woman and the fair disposition of property. Also, the father of the bride would contribute to the new couple's well being by donating wedding presents of domestic goods and food. He would often continue to supply grain for up to seven years, until the process of living together became a well-established marriage (Briffault, 1927).

Strikingly, we see that in the marriage union it is the man who brings the gift, or compensation, to the woman: *shep en sehemet.* Pestman has translated this Egyptian phrase to mean "price or compensation for marrying a woman." This idea is totally foreign to Semitic and Indo-European cultures, where women were an economic liability and had to provide dowries to secure their marriages (Stone, 1979). However, the idea of the man/husband bringing a gift to the bride's family is typically African and is commonly known to anthropologists and ethnologists as the "bride price" or "marriage payment" (Phillips, 1953).

Similar to marriage in ancient Egypt, African marriage is not the concern of religious or state authorities. The marriage is seen as an alliance between two families (kin groups), based on common interest; that is, it is based on the marriage union and the offspring of that union. The "Bogadi," as it is called among the Bechuana, acts as a safeguard protecting the bride's family in general and the bride particularly. The "marriage payment," whether it is goods, services, or cattle, is an essential part of having the marriage culturally recognized as proper or "legitimate" (Radcliffe-Brown & Forde, 1950). The amount of the "bride price" is determined by several factors, one being the status of the woman's family in the particular community (that is, whether she comes from royalty or a wealthy family). Another factor is the status of the woman to be married; for example, in contemporary African societies, her status may rest upon the level of "formal/western" education she has received. Lastly, another important factor is whether the society is organized with a matrilineal or patrilineal family structure (Dolphne, 1991).

The proper recognition of marriage primarily affects the offspring in regard to status, inheritance, rights, duties, and obligations. In both "Black Africa" and ancient Egypt, the concept of "illegitimate children or bastards" is unknown (Robbins, 1993, p. 66). This is a direct result of the status held by women in the matrilineal family and social organization—along with the fact that in African societies, a child is born into an extended family and therefore does not face the same problems as a child born into the Western nuclear family structure, which is organized patrilineally. In the latter case, the absence of a "biological father" has severe and damaging consequences (Dolphne, 1991). The primary purpose of marriage in ancient Egypt was to produce children and perpetuate the family. Children not only continued the family line but also ensured that correct rituals were conducted and helped to provide a proper burial for their parents. The mother was responsible for the naming of the child at birth. This link between mother and child remained the essential link between family and social organization. The mother's family was so important that children were instructed not to boast, "My mother's Father has a house, a house that lasts" (Lichtheim, 1975, p. 139). The ancient Egyptian sage Any advises on the proper respect that children should have for their mothers:

> Double the food your mother gave you,
> Support her as she has supported you;
> She had a heavy load in you,
> But she did not abandon you.
> When you were born after your months,
> She was yet yoked (to you),
> Her breast in your mouth for three years.
> As you grew and your excrement disgusted,
> She was not disgusted, saying: "What shall I do!"
> When she sent you to school,
> And you were taught to write,
> She kept watching over you daily
> With bread (8,1) and beer in her house
> When as a youth you take a wife,
> And you are settled in your house,
> Pay attention to your offspring,
> Bring him up, as did your mother.
> Do not give her cause to blame you,
> Lest she raises her hands to god,
> And he hears her cries. (Lichtheim, 1975, p. 141)

In addition to nurturing their children, the women in ancient Egypt also provided for their financial well-being. A Middle Kingdom stela illustrates the economic impact that a mother could play in a child's life:

> I was a worthy citizen who acted with his arm, the foremost of his whole troop. I acquired oxen and goats. (3) I acquired granaries of Upper Egyptian barley. I acquired title to a great field. I made a boat of 30 cubits and a small boat that ferried the boatless in the inundation season. I acquired these in (5) The household of my father Itei, but it was my mother who acquired them for me. (Lichtheim, 1975, p. 90)

Women in ancient Egypt were able to obtain material possessions and remained in control of their total assets. This was true in life and death. Women were able to bequeath property to heirs as well as disinherit children (Cerny, 1954). Clearly, the written record left to us by the ancient Egyptians illustrates that the family and social organization was focused around women. Regardless of whether they were wives, mothers, Pharaohs, or daughters, their status remained high. Women were able to manage and acquire property, they were protected in cases of divorce, and they were the crucial link in the family structure. There is no evidence of infanticide, particularly by exposure, or burial in the case of female children in ancient Egypt. Also it is becoming more and more accepted by scholars in Egyptology that social categories such as "concubines" or "harem women" did not exist in ancient Egypt (Ward, 1989).

Even today, with the many gains that were made by women in this society over the last hundred years, we look back and marvel at the brilliance, courage, and freedom that the women of ancient Egypt displayed. Powerful women were a staple of ancient Egyptian society; four women ruled as Pharaohs—Nitocris (6th Dynasty), Sobekneferu (12th Dynasty), Hatchespsut (18th Dynasty), and Twosert (19th Dynasty)—along with women such as Tiye, Nefetari, Ahotep, and Ahmosis-Nefertari (Clayton, 1994; Tyldesley, 1994). Nefertiti had an exceptional place in ancient Egyptian history and wielded great influence in both political and religious arenas (Robbins, 1993; Tyldesley, 1994). Exhibitions of power and prestige could not have happened in a society where the family and social organization were patrilineal. Certainly women in other civilizations in antiquity were as intelligent, creative, and determined as the women of ancient Egypt. However, without social rules or alternatives, there existed no avenues or precedents for women to seek or access power (Hoffman, 1979). Yet in ancient Egypt, women clearly had access to power and status, thanks to the matrilineal family and social organization.

References

Ajayi, J. F. A., & Espie, I. (Eds.). (1972). *A thousand years of west African history.* New York: Humanities Press.

Allen, T. (1998). *Ancient Egyptian kinship: An Afrocentric perspective.* Unpublished dissertation, Temple University, Philadelphia.

Briffault, R. (1927). *The Mothers: A study of the origins and sentiments and institutions* (Vols. 1–3). New York: Macmillan.

Cerny, J. (1954). Consanguineous marriages in Pharaonic Egypt. *Journal of Egyptian Archaeology, 40,* 23–29.

Clayton, P. (1994). *Chronicle of the Pharaohs: The reign-by-reign record of the rulers and dynasties of ancient Egypt.* London: Thames and Hudson.

Diop, C. A. (1974). *African origin of civilization: Myth or reality?* Westport, CT: Lawerence Hill Books.

Diop, C. A. (1978). *The cultural unity of Black Africa.* Chicago: Third World Press.

Diop, C. A. (1981). *Civilization or barbarism: An authentic anthropology.* New York: Lawerence Hill Books.

Dolphne, F. (1991). *The emancipation of women: An African perspective.* Accra: Universities Of Ghana Press.

Erman, A. (1947). *Life in ancient Egypt.* New York: Dover Books.

Eyre, C. (1984). Crime and adultery in ancient Egypt. *Journal of Egyptian Archaeology, 70,* 92–105.

Fischer, H. (1989). *Egyptian women of the Old Kingdom and the Heracleopolitan Period.* New York: Metropolitan Museum of Art.

Forgeau, A. (1996). The survival of the family name and the Pharaonic. In F. Zonabend (Ed.), *History of the family* (p. 135). Cambridge: Belknap Press.

Fox, R. (1971). *Kinship and marriage.* Baltimore, MD: Penguin Books.

Gardiner, A. (1994). *Egyptian grammar* (3rd ed.). England: Griffith Institute.

Hoffman, A. (1979). *Egypt before the pharaohs.* New York: Barnes and Noble Books.

Johnson, P. (1978). *The civilization of ancient Egypt.* New York: Atheneum.

Keesing, R. (1975). *Kin groups and social structure.* Orlando, FL: Holt, Rhinehart, and Winston.

Kemp, B., Trigger, B., O'Connor, D., & Lloyd, A.B. (1983). *Ancient Egypt: A social history.* England: Cambridge University Press.

Lesko, B. (Ed.). (1987). *Women's earliest records: From ancient Egypt and Western Asia.* Atlanta, GA: Scholars Press.

Lichtheim, M. (1975). *Ancient Egyptian literature Volume I: The Old and Middle Kingdoms.* Berkeley, CA: University of California Press.

Lichtheim, M. (1976). *Ancient Egyptian literature Volume II: The New Kingdom.* Berkeley, CA: University of California Press.

Lichtheim, M. (1980). *Ancient Egyptian literature Volume III: The Late Period.* Berkeley, CA: University of California Press.

Murdock, G. (1949). *Social structure*. New York: Macmillan.

Murray, M. (1927). Genealogies of the Middle Kingdom. *Ancient Egypt* (June), 45–51.

Murray, M. (1949). *The splendour that was Egypt: A general survey of Egyptian culture and civilization*. New York: Philosophical Library.

Obenga, T. (1992). *Ancient Egypt and Black Africa: A student's handbook for the study of ancient Egypt in philosophy, linguistics, and gender relations*. London: Karnak House.

O'Connor, D. (1990). *Ancient Egyptian society*. Pittsburgh: Carnegie Museum of Natural History.

Pestman, P. (1961). *Marriage and matrimonial property in ancient Egypt*. Chicago: Third World Press.

Petrie, F. (1924). *Social life in ancient Egypt*. London: Constable and Company.

Petrie, F. (1940). *The wisdom of the ancient Egyptians*. London: Bernard Quaritch LTD.

Phillips, A. (Ed.). (1953). *A survey of African marriage and family life*. London: Oxford University Press.

Radcliffe-Brown, A. (1950). *Structure and function in primitive society: Essays and addresses*. New York: Free Press.

Radcliffe-Brown, A., & Forde, D. (Eds.). (1950). *African systems of kinship and marriage*. New York: Oxford University Press.

Robbins, G. (1993). *Women in ancient Egypt*. Cambridge, MA: Harvard University Press.

Sanderson, S. (1990). *Social evolutionism: A critical history*. Cambridge, MA: Basil Blackwell.

Schusky, E. (1983). *Manual For kinship analysis* (2nd ed.). Lanham, MD: University Press of America.

Simpson, K. (1974). Polygamy in Egypt in the Middle Kingdom? *Journal of Egyptian Archaeology, 60,* 100–105.

Stone, L. (1979). *The family, sex, and marriage in England: 1500–1800*. New York Harper Colophon Books.

Trigger, B. G., Kemp, B. J., O'Connor, D., & Lloyd, A. B. (1983). *Ancient Egypt, a social history*. Cambridge, MA: Cambridge University Press.

Tyldesley, J. (1994). *Daughters of Isis: Women of ancient Egypt*. London: Penguin Books.

Ward, W. (1989). Non-royal women and their occupations in the middle kingdom. In B. Lesko (Ed.), *Women's earliest records: From ancient Egypt and western Asia*. Atlanta, GA: Scholars Press.

Willems, H. (1983). A description of Egyptian kinship terminology of the Middle Kingdom c. 2000–1650 BC. *Bijdragen tot de Taal-Land-en-Volenkunde, 139*(1), 161.

Zonabend, F., et al. (1996). *A history of the family Volume 1: Distant worlds, ancient worlds*. Cambridge, MA: Harvard University Press.

James L. Moore III

James L. Moore III is the director of the student assistance center in the college of engineering at Virginia Tech, where he coordinates tutoring for the entire college. He received his B.A. in English education from Delaware State University, a small, historical Black land-grant university in Dover, Delaware. He earned his master of arts degree in counselor education and is currently completing the final requirements for his Ph.D. in counselor education at Virginia Tech. For his Ph.D., he is writing his dissertation on *The Persistence of African American Males in the College of Engineering at Virginia Tech.*

Mr. Moore has a biography listed in *Outstanding Young Men in America* (1998 edition) and is a member of numerous professional and honor societies, including Alpha Kappa Mu, Phi Kappa Phi, Phi Delta Kappa, Kappa Delta Pi, and Chi Sigma Iota. The Delaware Association of Teachers of English recognized him for his exceptional contribution to English education with its Outstanding Achievement in *English/Language Arts* Award (1995). Perhaps more dear to him than any of his accolades, he was the recipient for Delaware State University's Class of 1995 Outstanding Service Award. Also, while he was at Delaware State University, James was a scholarship college football player for five years. He received many accolades and honors as a student athlete and was team captain during his last year of eligibility (1994).

Over the years, Mr. Moore has actively presented at several state and national conferences. Many of his presentations and papers have been directly or indirectly related to Black males. As a result, James has landed many speaking engagements and potential consulting opportunities related to such topics. In addition to his presentations, papers, and dissertation, Mr. Moore is currently working on several publications and projects. His research areas of interest include but are not limited to multicultural issues, counseling student athletes, counseling adolescents, Black male issues, counseling college students, counseling at-risk youth, mentoring, and community approaches to psychosocial issues.

20

COUNSELING AFRICAN AMERICAN MEN BACK TO HEALTH

James L. Moore III

All black men, if you ask them, can describe the small slights that accumulate to create what I call *invisibility* . . . We are not literally invisible—that might sometimes be preferable. But on the streets, in stores, on elevators and in restaurants, we are seen as potential criminals or as servants, not as ourselves. (Franklin, 1993, p. 34).

The notion of "invisibility," noted by Franklin (1993), is a well-documented phenomenon. Its origins are rooted in racism and racial oppression. The critical point is that African American males face a number of obstacles, and many of these obstacles are predisposed to their experience. Regardless of socioeconomic status, political clout, or reputation, it is virtually impossible for any African American male to escape the daily disregards and insults. These messages, which are communicated loudly and clearly, convey African American males as unmotivated, docile, lazy, and intellectually inferior (Washington, 1987).

From infancy to adulthood, images of inferiority are communicated. These images, which often contribute to social inequities, have a profound effect on the lives of African American males (Blake & Darling, 1994; Elligan & Utsey, 1999; Grier & Cobbs, 1968; Lee & Bailey, 1997; Potts, 1997) Hacker (1995) notes that beginning in this country, African Americans were never given an opportunity to develop as full citizens. As a result, many lost hope in the American system (Hacker, 1995) because there were little indications of equality and justice (Washington, 1987). It is important to note that some are successful and, of course, some are unsuccessful. Regardless of the outcomes, it can be assumed that African American men are less likely to take these challenges they face lightly.

Over the years, negative images have been thought to reflect and impact *only* poor, urban incumbents. On the contrary, Franklin (1993) reports that these images are particularly detrimental to middle-class African American men. Stephen Carter (1991) reminds us that African Americans, especially the educated, are measured along a different continuum: *the first Black, only Black,* and *best Black.* No matter what they do and how well they do it, African American men are constantly reminded that they cannot measure up to White men (Franklin, 1993; Vontress, 1992).

Although African American men are diverse as a group, there are common experiences that link them together (Elligan & Utsey, 1999; Pearson, 1994; Priest, 1991). It is these collective experiences that distinguish them from their White male counterparts and even from African American females. While both African American women and men have been impacted by oppression, Hilliard (1985) articulates the differences by suggesting that historically women have been seen as "sex objects" and men have been seen as "objects of fear." The author explains that the African American man posed a serious threat to the White establishment because he could physically retaliate. Therefore, an assertive effort was made to break his spirit and self-worth in order to contain his physical strength. This was done through various psychological tactics.

Today, popular and scientific literature is overwhelmed with information related to the disenfranchisement of African American males. It projects a message of gloom and doom rather than a message of hope and prosperity. Given recent evidence, some reports (Gibbs, 1984; Parham & McDavis, 1987) even suggest that African American men are an "endangered" species. Perhaps this is a bit extreme, but when examining national statistical data (for example, unemployment, health, crime, education, and so on), the findings reinforce the disenfranchisement of African American men. Research reveals that social institutions (for example, educational system, criminal justice system, mental health system, and social service system) are failing the battle with African American males.

The failures, to a great extent, can be attributed to: (1) African American males' distrust and hesitation toward seeking help from outside the family or fictive kin (Bell, 1990; Harris & Majors, 1992; Willis, 1990), and (2) the social institutions' inadequate training for working with African American males. Despite the reason(s), these institutions are rarely used and are considered a waste of time and energy (Bell, 1990; Madison-Colmore & Moore, 1999; Sue & Sue, 1990; Willis, 1990). The magic question is "What are the requisites for effectively working with African American men?" In this chapter, I will present a short historical overview of African American males. In addition, I will focus on the issues that prevent African American men from utilizing counseling and provide strategies to helping professionals that work with this specific population.

Historical Overview

The formation of "African" and "American" began when Africans were brought against their will to the New World known as "America" (Akbar, 1984, 1997; Madison-Colmore & Moore, 1999). The transport represents the formation of a newly found experience, identity, and struggle. Along with succeeding generations, they inherited racism, discrimination, and racial oppression. Despite the odds, they have remained persistent (Harris, 1993; Howard & Hammond, 1985).

African Americans have made significant gains (for example, emancipation, the right to vote, integration, and so on), since their arrival in the New World. However, many argue that not all of the battles have been won yet (Howard & Hammonds, 1985; Vontress, 1992). Some people even suggest that the causes of African American's indisputable lack of accomplishment can be directly linked to slavery or its residual effects (Akbar, 1982, 1984, 1997; Bell & Peterson, 1992; Elligan & Utsey, 1999; Franklin, 1993; Grier & Cobbs, 1968; Harris & Majors, 1992; June, 1986; Locke, 1992; Madison-Colmore & Moore, 1999; Parham & McDavis, 1987; Priest, 1991; Vontress, 1992; Vontress & Epp, 1997; Willis, 1990).

The predicament of African American males is so complex that to fully understand it, counselors first must grasp the history and culture of African Americans (Akbar, 1997; Hilliard, 1985; Wade, 1994; Willis, 1990). Akbar (1997) suggests that counselors use slavery as the starting point. He also recommends that history be synthesized with psychology to better understand the psyche of African Americans. Such precious information must be used to empower rather than plague. Empowerment refers to using the information to heal broken wounds and hurts rather than using it to oppress and torment (Robinson & Howard-Hamilton, 1994).

Over the years, racism has left many African American males psychologically, emotionally, and socially scarred (Poussaint, 1983). In their clinical practices, Vontress and Epp (1997) noticed a pattern of behavior (for example, hostility, hopelessness, and paranoia) displayed by many African American males, which necessitates a specific conceptual framework for counselors. The pattern of behavior was indefinable from standard pathological labels such as depression, conduct disorders, and personality disorders. As a result, they coined the term *historical hostility* as a way of explaining this cultural phenomenon. Historical hostility, what many authors often refer to as "black rage," was defined as a volatile response to prolonged deprivation and inferior treatment in America. In more detail, Vontress and Epp explain:

> When a people are frustrated across generations by a powerful oppressor, they must strongly repress their anger, the passion of which may slowly ventilate through a manifest hostility. When such anger builds like an expanding balloon that eventually bursts, it may result in the sporadic and explosive release of negative energy in rage, violence, crime, and substance abuse. (1997, p. 172)

After careful examination of the literature, I discovered that other authors (Grier & Cobbs, 1968; Poussaint, 1983; Vontress, 1992; Willis, 1990) have reported the same behavior or at least symptoms of this behavior. The literature is inundated with information related to this topic. For example, Grier and Cobbs (1968) maintained that a potential rage is harbored in "all" African American males. One day they may appear calm and relatively happy, and later they may be frustrated to the point of extreme protest and physical retaliation. No matter how you view it, it is evident that many African American males are in excruciating pain.

Historical hostility is a major contributor to the social breakdown of African American men. When hopeless thoughts and feelings are synthesized with negative experiences, rage escalates either consciously or unconsciously into a negative impulsive state (Poussaint, 1983; Vontress, 1992; Vontress & Epp, 1997). It is critical that counselors recognize that rage has two basic manifestations: (1) *inward rage* and (2) *outward rage.* Inward rage is internalized oppression that is suppressed in the psyche, which often manifests into alcoholism, drug abuse, stress, and other health problems (for example, depression, hypertension, and so on). The difference between outward and inward rage is that outward rage typically manifests into a protest or demonstration of disgust (for example, violence).

Poussaint (1983) and Vontress (1992) point out that certain subcultures are more likely to use violence as an alternative to resolve conflict. They are prone to cast their rage and hostility on other African Americans who often are closest to them (Vontress, 1966, 1992). Given this reality, it is clear that oppression has long-term effects on African American men (Wade, 1994), but perhaps the greatest threat to their existence is hopelessness and life without meaning (West, 1993).

Although West (1993) is not trained in the area of pathology, his perspective is still helpful in examining the problems of African American men. He articulates with eloquence that oppression and exploitation have long existed in America, but somehow, African Americans were still able to find within themselves the drive to persist. Dr. West attributes past persistence and endurance to hope and meaning; without the two, he posits that it is impossible to overcome oppression. West suggests that hope and meaning are difficult to sustain in an era of cutthroat capitalism, declining Black civility, and persistent racism.

More and more, these turbulent times foreshadow the uncertainty of the future for African American males. In the new millennium, counselors will be called upon more to help African American males, so they will need to be familiar with the daily challenges of African American males and how these challenges may affect the counseling process. Therefore, it is imperative that counselors are trained in multicultural education to meet the challenges of African American males.

Perceptions of Counseling

As a way of coping, African American men often exhibit facades to put up with daily assaults on their masculinity (Majors & Billson, 1992; Washington, 1987). These facades are used to protect self-worth and self-esteem (Vontress, 1969; Washington, 1987). Perhaps more importantly, facades help control their resentment and rage toward Whites. Unlike African American females, African American males are socialized not to show emotions and feelings. They operate from a *modus operandi* that requires them to be cool, tough, strong, and fearless (Majors & Billson, 1992; Pollack, 1998). These personas provide an image of control and authority in a world that is constantly trying to undermine both their Blackness and their maleness (Hobbs, 1985; Majors & Billson, 1992).

At an early age, the African American male learns to suppress his feelings of vulnerability. He learns that the political, social, and economic structures provide him little opportunity compared to his White male counterpart. Many take the position that they must work harder than the White male in order to "make it" (Hall, 1981). This particular mindset is nothing new; its origins can be traced back to slavery (Majors & Billson, 1992; Willis, 1990). Grier and Cobbs (1968) state that the slave who demonstrated feelings of resentment was dangerous to himself and the establishment. He learned as a boy to suppress his feelings in order to survive. Even today, this survival strategy seems to be prevalent. It has been passed down from generation to generation (Vontress, 1992).

When experiencing psychological, social, or emotional difficulty, African American men are reluctant to seek and use counseling as means of intervention. Perhaps this is due to negative cultural attitudes and the stigma attached to seeking professional assistance. Tucker, Chennault, and Mulkerne (1981) list several barriers to working with African Americans. The authors imply that the barriers, for the most part, are culturally related. It should be noted that *culture* significantly impacts the way people respond to each other. Vontress (1986) states that acting out, provocativeness, resistance, and blocking are manifestations of the client's reluctance to engage with the counselor (Vontress, 1986).

The essence of counseling is predicated on sharing and engaging. Counseling, like any interpersonal relationship, requires that the involved parties have an atmosphere of trust. The African American male avoids counseling because it is perceived as compromising his manhood. As a result, he attempts to solve his own problems through his own ways (Franklin, 1992; Larrabee, 1986; Lee & Bailey, 1997; Madison-Colmore & Moore, 1999). Hall (1981) states that the African American male is apt to express his repressed feelings with individuals in settings that are considered safe. The person of choice may be one of a number of people: a family member, friend, or minister (Jones & Gray, 1983; Lee & Bailey, 1997; Richardson & Williams, 1990; Washington, 1987; Willis, 1990). Typically, barbershops, social clubs, and sporting events are customary spots where he goes to escape and "clear" his mind (Elligan & Utsey, 1999; Lee & Bailey, 1997).

Research suggests that the African American male is less likely to volunteer for counseling (Franklin, 1992; Jones & Gray, 1983; Willis, 1990). If he uses counseling, there is a high probability that he was referred by some agency (for example, social services and the criminal-justice system), and it was required because the person committed a crime or offense. Washington (1987) states that when the African American male is forced to attend counseling, the therapeutic process is often a negative experience. However, when he enters counseling voluntarily, it is a strong indication that he is in dire need. To facilitate the counseling process with African American males, it is critical that counselors are aware of the social and cultural influences that may potentially affect therapeutic interventions. Such knowledge enhances the counselor-client relationship.

Cultural Influences in Counseling

First and foremost, the African American culture is very diverse in nature (Barnes, 1994; Lee, 1991; Priest, 1991). What is clear about the culture is that it is not monolithic. The culture comprises various subcultures, backgrounds, and experiences. Counselors who operate under stereotypical assumptions risk working effectively with African American males (Lee, 1991; Swartz-Kulstad & Martin, 1999). Counselors need to respond to these clients as unique cultural beings who are shaped by many cultures. In his work, Vontress (1986, 1992) presents the following five cultures:

1. *Universal culture*—a common thread that links all humanity together.

2. *Ecological culture*—conditions that force people to adjust to the natural environment of their respective geographical areas.

3. *National culture*—a unifying force or world view that impacts the values, attitudes, and behaviors (both consciously and unconsciously).

4. *Regional culture*—subtle forces that distinguish people from other parts of the United States.

5. *Racio-ethnic culture*—variables that isolate minority groups from dominant racial group(s).

Vontress' model is a wonderful tool for counselors to use to get an overview of their client's background and experiences. As a way of moving from vague to specific, Bell (1990) presents an excellent conceptual explanation for understanding the subtle nuances within African American culture. His conceptual explanation was divided into six subcultures. It was constructed to help counselors understand that the African American community is very diverse and that it has many world views and identities. Such information is valuable when working with African American males. The six subcultures presented are as follows (Bell, 1990; cited by Madison-Colmore & Moore, pp. 9–10):

1. *Acculturated*—needs and interests are being met primarily by the Caucasian culture. These individuals tend to be more educated and dwell in middle-class settings. It is not uncommon for such individuals to reject or avoid Black establishments. These individuals are usually accustomed to interacting in settings primarily comprised of Caucasians.

2. *Bicultural*—needs are being met by both the Caucasian (for example, survival needs like work experience, political affiliations, and so on) and African American culture (for example, racial identity). Such individuals tend to have a strong racial identity, which is usually defenseless or nonthreatening. In addition, these individuals place a strong emphasis on being successful in the workforce but not at the expense of racial identity.

3. *Culturally immersed conformist*—has a strong racial identity but is usually socially segregated (for example, church, home, and so on) and professionally integrated (for example, high-paying trade occupations, factories, and so on). For example, this person is often born, raised, and lives in predominately Black communities. More specifically, the person usually knows or interacts with the various subgroups.

4. *Culturally immersed Afrocentric*—is very grass-roots-oriented and active in the African American community's political issues. These individuals tend to be educated and well connected in the Black community. Racism and other forms of discriminations are viewed as the primary cause of hardships in the Black community.

5. *Culturally immersed deviant*—is very difficult to deal with and is constantly at war with "self" and others. Such individuals tend to reside in underdeveloped and underserved communities—more often, low-income housing developments in urban areas. These individuals tend to have limited interactions around acculturated Blacks and more specifically Caucasians. In addition, they are often viewed as nihilistic, pathological, and dangerous to themselves and society in general.

6. *Unacculturated traditionalist*—tends to have a strong faith in God and is usually uneducated. These individuals typically reside in the South and are viewed as being very old-fashioned and archaic by acculturated individuals.

When working with African American males, it is critical that counselors are familiar with the different subcultures and that they possess the proper skills when working with them. This determines, in large measure, whether the counselor will establish a therapeutic alliance. What distinguishes the different subcultures are their unique social experiences and how they view and respond to them. Naturally, it can be conceived that the social experiences of the subcultures' individuals will determine how the individuals interact around Black and White counselors (Vontress, 1971).

This proclamation undermines the notion that African American counselors will always produce outcomes of success with African American male clients. In this regard, some counselors (Madison-Colmore and Moore, 1999; Vontress, 1971, 1988) indicate that success rate depends not necessarily on race and ethnicity but the subculture the counselor and client identify with the most. For example, the counselor who identifies with the *acculturated* subculture may find it difficult relating to subculture clients who identify with the *culturally immersed conformist, culturally immersed Afro-*

centric, culturally immersed deviant, and unacculturated traditionalist. Of course, counselors could easily have the same difficulty if subculture roles were switched.

The level of difficulty is related to the individual's different world view and experiences in the United States. Although there is limited research to substantiate this hypothesis, Madison-Colmore and Moore (1999) hypothesized that White counselors will not be able to work with many of the subcultures. The *acculturated* and *bicultural* subcultures are the ones that they will be effective counseling. The two authors suspect that White counselors would feel more comfortable with these subcultures because they are viewed as being more aligned with "Whiteness" than "Blackness."

Implications for Counselors

Warfield and Marion (1985) state that the essence of counseling is the working relationship between the counselor and client. It is most productive when the client surrenders totally to the process (Vontress, 1986) and when the counselor is properly trained (Madison-Colmore & Moore, 1999). Without rapport, trust, and communication, it is impossible to establish a therapeutic relationship with African American males. Once these things are established, even with the most difficult client, the counselor is able to establish a somewhat therapeutic alliance. Many counselors assume that the therapeutic alliance will occur naturally through "small talk" (Vontress, 1971). On the contrary, it typically occurs when the African American male client discovers that the counselor's actions reflect a genuine interest, concern, and, at least moderate understanding of his problems. Listening, empathizing, self-disclosing, and engaging convey these messages.

Over the years, counselors (Elligan & Utsey, 1999; Franklin, 1992; June, 1986; Lee & Bailey, 1997; Vontress, 1992; Washington, 1987) have developed models and strategies that are beneficial for working with African American male clients. However, the HIS *(History, Identity, and Spirituality)* model (Madison-Colmore & Moore, 1999), a condensed version of other models, provides the most simplistic and practical explanation for working with African American males. The model was conceived to help counselors put in context the social experiences of African American males who, in turn, understand how these social experiences may or may not influence the counseling process.

In order for this process to take place, counselors first need to familiarize themselves with the *history* of African American males in the United States.

Without a familiarity of their history, counselors risk minimizing or neglecting historical factors that have been manifested into stereotypes over time. Oftentimes, stereotypes are directly or indirectly related to why African American males are reluctant to seek counseling. By learning the history of African American males, counselors can better serve the client. This information helps the counselor incorporate relevant theories and interventions for African American males (Washington, 1987). The second step to the model is *identity*. As discussed earlier, African American males are segmented into different subcultures (Vontress, 1971). Counselors who are familiar with the different subcultures are more apt to know their own strengths and limitations with certain subcultures; in order words, they are able to make better therapeutic decisions. The goal of counseling is not to help the African American male client move from one subculture to another but to help him identify himself on the subculture continuum and to recognize how the particular subculture is impacting his life (Bell, 1990). The last step to the model is *spirituality*. Many counselors underestimate the importance of spirituality in the life of African American males, which is often a costly mistake.

The essence of African Americans is spirituality. Spirituality and faith in a "higher being" have always been instrumental in helping African Americans get through "hard" times and struggles. At times, their problems are so overwhelming and deep that no ordinary person or thing can help them. As a result, they seek guidance and help from a spiritual leader (for example, elder, minister, and so on). This does not imply that counselors need to be theologically trained, but it does imply that counselors need to be aware of the importance of spirituality in the lives of African Americans (Richardson, 1991). Perhaps more African American males might seek conventional counseling if counselors could connect with them spiritually.

Conclusions

It is evident that racism has impacted the way African American males perceive themselves and counseling. Counselors who work with African American males need to recognize that the group is not monolithic. African American culture is segmented into various subcultures. Like Washington (1987), it is my belief that counseling can be an effective intervention for helping African American males but not until counselors gain the necessary knowledge and skills to work with them. To help counselors become multiculturally trained, the HIS model is an excellent training tool for helping them "counsel African American males back to health."

e

References

Akbar, N. (1982). *From miseducation to "education."* Jersey City, NJ: New Mind Productions.

Akbar, N. (1984). *Chains and images of psychological slavery.* Tallahassee, FL: Mind Productions & Associates.

Akbar, N. (1997). *Breaking the chains of psychological slavery.* Tallahassee, FL: Mind Productions & Associates.

Barnes, M. (1994). Clinical treatment issues regarding black African-Americans. In J. L. Ronch, W. V. Ornum, & N. C. Stilwell (Eds.), *The counseling sourcebook: A practical reference on contemporary issues* (pp. 157–164). New York: Crossroad.

Bell, P. (1990). *Chemical dependency and the African-American: Counseling strategies and community issues.* Center City, MN: Hazelden.

Bell, P., & Peterson, D. (1992). *Cultural pain and African Americans: Unspoken issues in early recovery.* Center City, MN: Hazelden.

Blake, W. M., & Darling, C. A. (1994). The dilemmas of African-American males. *Journal of Black Studies, 24*(4), 402–415.

Carter, S. L. (1991). *Reflections of an affirmative action baby.* New York: Basic Books.

Elligan, D., & Utsey, S. (1999). Utility of an African-centered support group for African American men confronting societal racism and oppression. *Cultural Diversity and Ethnic Minority Psychology, 5*(2), 156–165.

Franklin, A. J. (1992). Therapy with African American men. *Families in Society: The Journal of Contemporary Human Services, 73*(6), 350–355.

Franklin, A. J. (1993). The invisibility syndrome. *Networker,* 33–39.

Gibbs, J. T. (1984). Black adolescents and youth: An endangered species. *American Journal of Orthopsychiatry, 54,* 6–21.

Grier, W. H., & Cobbs, P. M. (1968). *Black rage.* New York: Basic Books.

Hacker, A. (1995). *Two nations: Black and White, separate, hostile, unequal.* New York: Scribner.

Hall, L. K. (1981). Support systems and coping patterns. In L. E. Gary (Ed.), *Black Men* (pp. 159–168). Newbury, CA: Sage.

Harris, S. M. (1993). Where do we go from here? *The Journal of Men's Studies, 1*(3), 287–290.

Harris, S., & Majors, R. (1992). Cultural value differences: Implications for the experiences of African-American men. *The Journal of Men's Studies, 1*(3), 227–238.

Hillard, A. G. (1985). A framework for focused counseling on the African American man. *Journal of Non-White Concerns, 13*(2), 72–77.

Hobbs, S. R. (1985). Issues in psychotherapy with black male adolescents in the inner city: A Black clinician's perspective. *Journal of Non-White Concerns,* 79–87.

Howard, J., & Hammond, R. (1985). Rumors of inferiority. *The New Republic,* 17–21.

Jones, B. E., & Gray, B. A. (1983). Black males and psychotherapy: Theoretical issues. *American Journal of Psychotherapy,* 37(1), 77–85.

June, L. N. (1986). Enhancing the delivery of mental health and counseling services to black males: Critical agency and provider responsibility. *Journal of Multicultural Counseling and Development,* 65, 39–45.

Larrabee, M. J. (1986). Helping reluctant black males: An affirmation approach. *Journal of Multicultural Counseling and Development,* 25–38.

Lee, C. C. (1991). Counseling African Americans: From theory to practice. In R. L. Jones (Ed.), *Black psychology* (3rd ed., pp. 559–576). Berkeley, CA: Cobb & Henry.

Lee, C. C., & Bailey, D. (1997). Counseling African American men and youth. In C. C. Lee (Ed.), *Multicultural Issues in Counseling: New Approaches to Diversity* (2nd ed., pp. 123–154). Alexander, VA: American Counseling Association.

Locke, D. C. (1992). *Increasing multicultural understanding: A comprehensive model.* Newbury, CA: Sage.

Madison-Colmore, O., & Moore, J. (1999, February). *Working with the oppressed and depressed African American male: A counseling model for therapists.* Paper presentation at the meeting of National Association of African American Studies, Houston, Texas.

Majors, R., & Billson, J. (1992). *Cool pose: The dilemmas of Black manhood in America.* New York: Touchstone.

Parham, T. A., & McDavis, R. J. (1987). Black men, an endangered species: Who's really pulling the trigger? *Journal of Counseling and Development,* 66, 24–27.

Pearson, D. F. (1994). The black man: Health issues and implications for clinical practice. *Journal of Black Studies,* 25(1), 81–98.

Pollack, W. (1998). *Real boys.* New York: Henry Holt and Company.

Potts, R. G. (1997). The social construction and social marketing of the "Dangerous black man." *Journal of the African American Men,* 2(4), 11–22.

Poussaint, A. F. (1983). Black-on-Black homicide: A psychological-political perspective. *Victimology,* 8(3–4), 161–169.

Priest, R. (1991). Racism and prejudice as negative impacts on African American clients in therapy. *Journal of Counseling and Development,* 70, 213–215.

Richardson, B. L. (1991). Utilizing the resources of the African American church: Strategies for counseling professionals. In C. C. Lee & B. L. Richardson (pp. 65–75). Alexandria, VA: American Counseling Association.

Richardson, T. M., & Williams, B. A. (1990). *African-Americans in treatment: Dealing with cultural differences.* Center City, MN: Hazelden.

Robinson, T. L., & Howard-Hamilton, M. F. (1994). An Afrocentric paradigm: Foundation for a healthy self-image. *Journal of Mental Health Counseling, 16*(3), 327–339.

Sue, D. W., & Sue, D. (1990). *Counseling the culturally different: Theory and practice.* New York: Wiley.

Swartz-Kulstad, J. L., & Martin, W. E. (1999). Impact of culture and context on psychosocial adaptation: The cultural and contextual guide process. *Journal of Counseling & Development, 77*(3), 281–293.

Tucker, C. M., Chennault, S. A., & Mulkerne, D. J. (1981). Barriers to effective counseling with blacks and therapeutic strategies for overcoming them. *Journal of Non-White Concerns, 68*–76.

Vontress, C. E. (1966). The negro personality reconsidered. *The Journal of Negro Education, 35,* 210–217.

Vontress, C. E. (1969). Counseling the culturally different in our society. *Journal of Employment Counseling, 6,* 9–16.

Vontress, C. E. (1971). Racial differences: Impediments to rapport. *Journal of Counseling Psychology, 18*(1), 7–13.

Vontress, C. E. (1986). Social and cultural foundations. In M. D. Lewis, R. Hayes, & J. A. Lewis (Eds.), *An introduction to the counseling profession* (pp. 215–250). Itasca, IL: Peacock.

Vontress, C. E. (1988). Social class influence on counseling. In R. Hayes and R. Aubrey (Eds.), *New Directions for Counseling and Human Development* (pp. 346–364). Denver, CO: Love.

Vontress, C. E. (1992). The breakdown of authority: Implications for counseling young African American males. In D. R. Atkinson (Ed.), *Counseling American minorities: A cross-cultural perspective* (pp. 457–473). Dubuque, IA: W. C. Brown & Benchmark.

Vontress, C. E., & Epp, L. R. (1997). Historical hostility in the African American client: Implications for counseling. *Journal of Multicultural Counseling & Development, 25,* 170–183.

Wade, J. C. (1994). Substance abuse: Implications for counseling African American men. *Journal of Mental Health Counseling, 16*(4), 415–433.

Warfield, J. L., & Marion, R. L. (1985). Counseling the black male. *Journal of Non-White Concerns, 54*–71.

Washington, C. S. (1987). Counseling black men. In M. Scher, M. Stevens, G. Good, & G. Eichenfield (Eds.), *Handbook of counseling & psychotherapy with men* (pp. 192–202). Newbury Park, CA: Sage.

West, C. (1993). *Race matters.* Boston: Beacon Press.

Willis, J. (1990). *Implications for effective psychotherapy with African American families and individuals.* Matteson, IL: Genesis.

Brian N. Williams

Dr. Brian N. Williams is a native of Thomasville, Georgia, and is a product of the Thomasville city public school system. He holds a bachelor of arts degree in political science, a master of public administration (MPA) degree, and a doctor of public administration (DPA) degree, all from The University of Georgia. Currently, he serves as an assistant professor at the Askew School of Public Administration and Policy at Florida State University.

Dr. Williams' areas of research include community policing, community-oriented governance, and the impact of racial profiling on the coproduction of public safety and public order. His most recent publications include a book titled *Citizen Perspectives on Community Policing: A Case Study in Athens, GA,* which was published by the State University of New York Press, and an article, "Perceptions of Children and Teenagers on Community Policing: Implications for Law Enforcement Leadership, Training, and Citizen Evaluations," published in *Police Quarterly.*

Recently, Dr. Williams has started his own consulting practice, The Williams Consulting Group, which specializes in community building and community policing consulting and training and the development of new performance measures that embrace the community policing philosophy. Dr. Williams is also a public speaker with previous engagements at middle and high schools, as well as universities, churches, civic, and fraternal organizations. He is married to Carla Green Williams, and they are the proud parents of two daughters, Carmen and Camryn. He and his family strive to live their lives by the creed, "to whom much is given, much is required."

21

THE PERSONAL COSTS AND SOCIETAL CONSEQUENCES OF DRIVING WHILE BLACK

IMPLICATIONS FOR THE MINORITY ACADEMIC COMMUNITY

Brian N. Williams

Abstract

Driving while Black (DWB), or racial profiling, is a serious problem that impacts the integration and involvement of minority citizens and communities with law-enforcement agencies. This police tactic adversely influences the perceptions of minority citizens on public-safety and public-order organizations and the nation's criminal-justice system. Highly publicized DWB incidents have resulted in harassment, humiliation, shootings, and deaths of minority citizens in New York, California, Illinois, Florida, and other states. Consequently, the "color of suspicion" has sparked tremendous debate among various segments of our national community, from law-enforcement practitioners, legal scholars, and elected officials, to religious, civil rights, and other grassroots organizations. Nonetheless, more voices need to be heard.

This chapter will provide an overview of racial profiling. To this end, it will highlight the personal costs and societal consequences of these actions on minority communities and will provide a brief discussion that examines the potential inimical effects of this police practice on current efforts to join minority citizens and communities with law-enforcement agencies in the coproduction of public safety and public order. In conclusion, it will discuss the implications of this police strategy for the minority academic community.

Driving While Black—Racial Profiling and Pretextual Traffic Stops

Racial profiling, or the use of pretextual traffic stops using minor traffic violations (either real or imagined) as a reason to stop and search a vehicle and its passengers who fit a particular profile, is one of the hottest topics currently being debated across America. This action, which treats the blackness or brownness of one's skin as a possible indication of criminality, is commonly known as DWB (driving while Black) in the African American community. The tactic of racial profiling has been cited as a byproduct of the Drug Enforcement Agency's (DEA) efforts to impede the flow of drugs, via its couriers, coming into American cities (American Civil Liberties Union [ACLU], 1999). Dubbed "Operation Pipeline," this initiative was developed and implemented during the Reagan administration's War on Drugs. These efforts resulted in the Florida Department of Highway Safety and Motor Vehicles' issuance of guidelines on "The Common Characteristics of Drug Couriers."[1] These guidelines, which portray the typical drug courier as either African American or Hispanic, have been instrumental in spreading the use of pretextual stops in our nation's streets, roads, interstate highways, and airports.

The practice of racial profiling did not begin in 1985 with "The Common Characteristics of Drug Couriers" or in 1986 with the DEA's "Operation Pipeline." The roots that have fed and nourished this police practice reach back to the "founding" of American society, and it has been maintained by the institutionalization of public-safety and public-order organizations via regulative structures and myths, coupled with the subtle support of recent judicial rulings. Moreover, the mass media have nurtured and reinforced this tactic with its attempts to put a black or brown face on crime. A brief discussion of these points follows.

Racial Profiling: Historical Dynamics, Institutionalization, and Organizational Structures

America's history of slavery and race-based discrimination still impacts the development and implementation of crime policy. Hence, racial profiling reflects the historical dynamics of our American society. Skolnick (1998) has noted that the primary areas affected by ongoing discrimination against minorities—African Americans in particular—include the formation of suspi-

---

1. These guidelines were issued in 1985 and cautioned state troopers to be suspicious of specific drug-courier characteristics, including certain "ethnic groups" associated with the drug trade. Consequently, traffic stops were initiated by officers using this race-based description.

cion and the assumption of guilt, especially in drug-related crimes. From the founding of this country as we know it and for many years afterward, people of color were systematically restricted from participating in the mainstream community and were viewed suspiciously. Consequently, people and communities of color were marginalized and targeted for containment by the guardians of the status quo; that is, official law-enforcement agencies and institutions (Williams and Murphy, 1990).

Over the years, the historical policy of suspicion, restriction, and containment of people of color has become institutionalized and embedded in the psyche of public-order and public-safety institutions. These institutions have transferred their logic to officers through training and regulative structures. Consequently, these formal structures of police organizations seem to reflect the myths of their institutional environments instead of their realities (Meyer and Rowan, 1991). And, as noted by Scott (1995), these regulative structures, especially in police organizations, have constrained and regularized police behavior through their rule-setting, monitoring, and sanctioning activities. Consequently, perpetrators of racial profiling transcend race, as in the case of the recent deaths of Robert Russ and LaTanya Haggerty, who were shot by African American police officers in Chicago.

Institutionalization of Racial Profiling— The Systemic Effect

The institutionalization of racial profiling has also been supported by the arbitrators of the U.S. Constitution and legally sanctioned by rulings of the U.S. Supreme Court. In *Whren v. United States* (1996), the Supreme Court required only probable cause of a traffic offense to justify pretextual stops, searches, and seizures. Of particular note, the Court ruled that a police officer's subjective intentions are irrelevant; hence, any traffic offense, either real or alleged, committed by a driver is a legitimate legal basis for a stop.

The Whren decision has been supported by recent Supreme Court rulings, including *Ohio v. Robinette* (1996), *Maryland v. Wilson* (1997), and *Wyoming v. Houghton* (1999). Police power over cars and their passengers has been extended with blatant disregard for the legal protections of the Fourth Amendment. Pretextual traffic stops are an obvious transgression of the equal-protection clause of the U.S. Constitution—the police cannot stop and detain an individual without probable cause or reasonable suspicion—a core principle of the Fourth Amendment. These transgressions often result in extensive collateral damage and victimization of innocent, minority citizens as a by-product of our country's war on drugs (Davis, 1997; Harris, 1997; Maclin, 1998; Sklansky, 1997).

Recently, the Massachusetts Supreme Judicial Court contravened the Whren decision and ruled that the state constitution protects all of its citizens against arbitrary police actions like racial profiling. In particular, it ruled that a Massachusetts police officer must have a reasonable belief that his or her safety or the safety of others is in danger before ordering drivers out of their cars for searches (Ellement, 1999). Even though this ruling hinders the practice of racial profiling in Massachusetts, U.S. Supreme Court decisions like Whren continue to have disastrous consequences on many minority drivers in the United States.

Racial Profiling and the Media: "Black and Brownfacing" Drugs and Crime

The use of racial profiling may be a result of our country's practice of defining our troubling social problems—like crime, drug sales, drug abuse, and public welfare—in black or brownface (Gilens, 1996; Gilliam, Iyengar, Simon, and Wright, 1996). Hence, the controversial tactic of racial profiling reflects social perceptions and public opinion. The latter lead to political or public-policy realities. Similar to the findings of Gilliam et al. (1996) and Gilens (1996), Blendon and Young (1998), Iyengar (1991), and Elias (1994) have noted the significant impact of the electronic and printed media on shaping public perceptions and opinions. Consequently, to understand the roots and branches of American public opinion on racial profiling, one needs to explore and understand Americans' perceptions of the social and political world they inhabit and, in particular, the role of the media in shaping those perceptions (Gilens, 1996).

Even though the coverage of racial profiling incidents has been characterized as fairly accurate and impartial, media institutions have been criticized for failing to acknowledge their own failings or shortcomings, in particular the practice of "media racial profiling," or black and brownfacing our country's social ills (Blendon and Young, 1998; Elias, 1994; Entman, 1990, 1992; Gilens, 1996; Gilliam et al., 1996; Iyengar, 1991; Muharrar, 1998). These actions help to reinforce the stereotypical image of America's "symbolic assailants"—young Black or Brown men—and tend to color the portrait of the drug courier in shades of black and brown (Skolnick, 1998).

The media's color scheme, however, does not reflect the portrait that has emerged in scholarly research. A 1998 survey by the Physician Leadership on National Drug Policy (PLNDP) found that drug users, abusers, and addicts are not principally people of color.[2] This finding parallels the conclusions of

---

2. The Physician Leadership on National Drug Policy revealed that drug addicts are not primarily members of minority groups but are more likely to be affluent, educated Caucasians.

Blendon and Young (1998). Also, it lends support to the findings of other researchers who have revealed that American misperceptions about drug-related problems are by-products of the media's practice of black and brown-facing antisocial behavior.

One of the main culprits in media racial profiling is television coverage of local news. In a study on the impact of the media on public perceptions of crime and criminals, Gilliam et al. (1996) revealed that local news coverage of crime overwhelmingly inferred that criminals were violent and nonwhite. Their research also yielded that viewers were so accustomed to seeing African American crime suspects that even when the race of a suspect was not speci-fied, viewers tended to recall seeing a black person (Gilliam et al., 1996). Sim-ilarly, Iyengar's (1991) study of network news found that crime in minority neighborhoods, especially African American communities, accounted for a sig-nificant share of television news coverage locally and nationally. These find-ings, coupled with the practice of "video wallpapering crime and criminals"— the use of local and national news coverage of crime from big cities that often have high concentrations of persons of color—tend to desensitize American society and may be one factor contributing to public apathy and lack of pop-ular outrage against the discriminatory practice of pretextual traffic stops based on color. Consequently, the news professionals associated with the printed and electronic media have helped to create images of American society that both consistently misrepresent African Americans and other American cit-izens of color and entrench the police practice of racial profiling (Elias, 1994; Entman, 1990, 1992; Gilens, 1996).

Personal Costs of Driving While Black

Many have noted the lack of applying the equal-protection clause of the Fourth Amendment to the discriminatory practice of racial profiling (Davis, 1997; Harris, 1997; Hecker, 1997; Larrabee, 1997; Sklansky, 1997). The trou-bling unanimity of the Whren and more recent Supreme Court decisions reflects a growing insensitivity to the concerns, rights of citizenship, and expe-riences of minority drivers. Moreover, the controversial police practice of racial profiling has ushered in a constitutional crisis with certain personal costs for minority motorists.

Persecution, Humiliation, and Victimization

Anecdotal evidence describes in very visible and tangible terms how these traf-fic stops and searches detain, humiliate, and criminalize law-abiding citizens

(ACLU, 1999; Williams, 1998, 1999).[3] This evidence seems to suggest that age, socioeconomic status, profession, educational background, and so on, are not factors in the equation; only the skin color of the driver is. Regardless of age, socioeconomic status, profession, and other demographic factors, minority drivers and passengers can fall prey to this police practice, which may result in cataclysmic repercussions. Hence, all persons of color are equally likely to be targeted for pretextual traffic stops.

The impact of racial profiling on minorities can be best described in terms of how it persecutes and humiliates innocent people. Victims of this practice have commonly described this police tactic as illegal persecution directed toward persons with black or brown skin (ACLU, 1999; Davis, 1997; Larrabee, 1997; Williams, 1998). More troubling for victims of this practice is the perception it creates for fellow (majority) motorists of the stereotypical criminal. Consequently, driving-while-Black-or-Brown traffic stops and searches may reinforce the misperception of the Black or Brown person as criminal or symbolic assailant held by our society (Skolnick, 1998).

Further compounding the persecution and humiliation of racial profiling is the likelihood that innocent victims will be legally detained or placed under arrest (Davis, 1997; Larrabee, 1997). Often, these detentions and searches of minority citizens, their cars, and their personal possessions can last more than two hours (ACLU, 1999). The amalgamation of persecution, humiliation, and victimization associated with racial profiling reinforces negative perceptions of law enforcement and the U.S. Criminal "Just Us" System by minority citizens. The personal costs of these experiences are significant, but the potential societal consequences that accompany these experiences may be more exorbitant.

Societal Consequences of Racial Profiling
Racial Profiling: Reinforcing the Virtual Wall of Separation and Widening the Perception Divide
Recently, Cheryl King, Camilla Stivers, and others have issued a clarion call to make government "us" by integrating citizens in the production and delivery of public services (King and Stivers, 1998). This call is in response to the current problem of citizen disaffection with government. The use of racial profil-

---

3. Williams (1998, 1999) noted the impact of negative interactions and experiences of African American citizens with the police. Of particular interest were the experiences of African American children and teenagers who had been victimized by this tactic and the lasting negative perceptions of the police that ensued.

ing, however, seems to counter the call of King, Stivers, and other scholars to public-governance integration. In particular, racial profiling seems to present a formidable obstacle in engendering minority support and involvement in public governance, especially partnering efforts with public-safety organizations. Moreover, this practice helps to reinforce the racially polarizing perceptions of crime, law enforcement, and the criminal-justice system (Higgins, 1997).

Researchers have noted a perception gap that reflects America's racial divide. Williams and Murphy (1990), Jacob (1971), Carter (1983), Rossi, Beck, and Edison (1974), and others have found that this divide is more visible and apparent in terms of the disparate views of members of minority and majority groups on law enforcement and the criminal-justice system. Continued use of racial profiling as a police tactic may further widen this gap, reinforce the virtual wall of separation, and ultimately sabotage public-governance efforts directed toward minority citizens (Williams, 1998, 1999).

Racial Profiling: Costs and Consequences of Public Distrust, Mistrust, and Disaffection

The occurrence of pretextual traffic stops and the more recent and highly publicized incidents of police brutality continue to fray the relations between minority communities and the police. Public display of unrest during the Abner Louima trial and the recent deaths in California and Chicago highlight this tension. Consequently, these highly publicized incidents bolster the virtual wall that sequesters minority communities and law enforcement and leads to public distrust and disaffection by minority citizens. This lack of trust and affection has been shown to have a debilitating effect on recruiting minority officers, decreases the likelihood of citizens and police officers partnering in community policing efforts, and deters people of color from cooperating with law enforcement in criminal investigations (Higgins, 1997; Williams, 1998, 1999). Hence, the practice of racial profiling and its harvest of distrust and disaffection impedes the integration of citizens with law enforcement and adversely impacts the coproduction of public safety and public order.

The consequences of racial profiling extend to our nation's criminal-justice system. Anecdotal evidence suggests that the prevalence and pervasiveness of racial profiling both help to cast an ominous shadow of mistrust and disaffection upon the entire criminal-justice system by minorities and affect the willingness of minority citizens to report crime (ACLU, 1999; Williams, 1998). The impact of this consequence may be more obvious and visible in the courtroom. Specifically, those minority jurors who have been victims of pretextual traffic stops or are acquainted with people who have been victimized call into question the testimony of police officers who serve as witnesses (ACLU, 1999).

Responding to the Personal Costs and Societal Consequences

The personal costs and societal consequences of racial profiling tend to further nourish the roots of public discontent in minority communities and call into question the use of pretextual traffic stops. Similar to the findings of the 1967 Kerner Commission, these negative police-minority citizen experiences and interactions continue to segregate law enforcement and the criminal-justice system from ordinary, minority citizens and communities.[4] In an attempt to avoid the often violent past associated with public discontent and unrest over police harassment and persecution, several synergistic efforts are being developed and implemented to curtail and prevent this abusive form of policing.

Executive, Legislative, and Judicial Action to Address Racial Profiling

Racial profiling infringes upon one of the most cherished principles of our American democracy and the U.S. Constitution—individual rights and freedoms. Steps have been taken to thwart this police practice and its potentially harmful effects. Recently, President Clinton ordered all federal law-enforcement agencies to collect information on the race, ethnicity, and sex of people they detain for questioning in an attempt to discourage and stop this highly discriminatory police tactic. Similarly, legislative action has also been undertaken. Congressman John Conyers (D-MI) has introduced the Traffic Stops Statistics Study Act of 1999, which calls for a nationwide study of stops for traffic violations by law-enforcement officers to be analyzed by the Attorney General. Even though the efforts by Congressman Conyers have not been successful in terms of establishing a federal law, they have inspired action at the state level.[5] That notwithstanding, state courts have begun torpidly to reverse their stance on racial pro-

---

4. The Kerner Commission, also known as the National Advisory Commission on Civil Disorders, was ordered to uncover the events that led to the urban riots of the 1960s. It reported, using anecdotal evidence, that the major complaint of African American citizens was racial profiling—the stopping of African American citizens who were on foot or in cars without probable cause.
5. In North Carolina, a bill requiring data collection on all traffic stops was signed into law in April 1999 with similar bills being introduced in other states.

filing (Ellement, 1999). However, governmental actors are not alone in their attempts to end the harrowing, humiliating, and harmful episodes of driving while Black or Brown.

Grass-Roots Efforts to Address Racial Profiling

Numerous grass-roots efforts are also underway to curtail the use of racial profiling. Notable national organizations that represent minority citizens and police practitioners alike, such as the Southern Christian Leadership Coalition (SCLC), the National Urban League (NUL), the National Association for the Advancement of Colored People (NAACP), and the National Organization of Black Law Enforcement Executives (NOBLE), have been instrumental in facilitating the national dialogue and debate on driving while Black. In June of 1999, the Department of Justice sponsored the Police Integrity Conference, which assembled community and civil-rights leaders, police chiefs, and religious and academic groups to discuss racial profiling and its impact on community partnering. These recent efforts are applauded, but the national debate on racial profiling and its inherent focus on overcoming the "color of suspicion" requires the influx of more voices that reflect a greater diversity of life experiences and a continuous stream of research that highlights the personal costs and societal consequences of this tactic.

Racial Profiling—Implications for the Minority Academic Community

The personal costs and societal consequences of driving while Black have become more visible with media attention, executive, legislative, and judicial action, and coalition-building efforts between grass-roots organizations and the law-enforcement community (Higgins, 1997). Yet empirical and anecdotal evidence continue to show that skin color is the predominant factor in highway drug searches and that no person of color is immune to these often harrowing and humiliating experiences (ACLU, 1999; Davis, 1997; Maclin, 1998). Minorities in general and African Americans in particular, ranging from lawyers to letter carriers, professors to policemen, and doctors and dentists to ditch diggers, have been subject to embarrassing roadside stops and searches (ACLU, 1999).

Even though the pervasive practice has stoked public outrage (particularly on the parts of minority citizens), political rhetoric, constitutional debates, judicial jockeying, and even extensive coverage from the "mainstream" media, little meaningful action has resulted. Thus, a substantial policy response needs to be developed and implemented. If not, the incidents of racial profiling will continue to generate widespread public distrust and disaffection on the parts of minority citizens and refortify the virtual wall separating the minority and law-enforcement communities.

The ubiquitous incidents of driving while Black and the negative feelings they engender toward law enforcement and the criminal-justice system require us to listen and learn from our past experiences. A look at the tumultuous 1950s and 1960s reveals the costs and consequences of public distrust and disaffection with law enforcement. The riots of Newark, Detroit, Watts, and, more recently, Los Angeles are tangible reminders of the consequences of unresolved tensions that were created and sustained by rampant negative police-citizen experiences and interactions, as well as questionable rulings by the court. To lessen the likelihood of urban unrest, it is important that more research be done to accent the personal costs and societal consequences of driving while black. Central to this effort are the enlistment and inflow of additional resources to take the debate on racial profiling and pretextual traffic stops to a higher level in hopes of achieving a suitable public policy response.

Akin to the thesis of DuBois, I surmise that only those persons who possess "dual consciousness" can become vital conduits to link the disparate minority, majority, and law enforcement perceptions, experiences, and realities as well as facilitate constructive public-governance efforts. Individuals who possess this level of consciousness are cognizant of the "dual" nature of American society (its disparate perceptions, experiences, and realities) and are more adept at understanding, maneuvering, and manipulating the political whitewater rapids that are part and parcel of our public-policy process. Hence, "dually conscious" scholars are central to any and all attempts to get beyond the current rhetoric on racial profiling and effect substantial policy change.

To expedite the eradication of the practice of racial profiling, more scholars and researchers of color are needed to further reveal and address the personal costs and societal consequences of driving while Black. Toward this end, it is imperative that more minority graduate students, especially African Americans and Hispanic Americans, pursue terminal degrees in the fields of criminal justice, criminology, sociology, political science, public administration, and other disciplines and embark upon research agendas that seek to disclose the various intricacies of racial profiling. In particular, more research is needed on the role of the media in shaping public opinion, public policy, and the performance of law-enforcement officers. Continuous streams of research by scholars who have a vested interest in eradicating this highly discriminatory and abusive tactic are required to ensure that the current dialogue will not be a flash in the pan but will affect our nation's public policy agenda and result in significant governmental action.

References

American Civil Liberties Union. (1999). *Driving while Black—Racial profiling on our nation's highways.* New York: Author.

Blendon, R. J., & Young, J. T. (1998). The public and the war on illicit drugs. *Journal of the American Medical Association, 279*(11), 827–832.

Carter, D. L. (1983). Hispanic interaction with the criminal justice system in Texas: Experiences, attitudes, and perceptions. *Journal of Criminal Justice, 11*(3), 213–227.

Davis, A. J. (1997). Race, cops, and traffic stops. *University of Miami Law Review, 51,* 425–443.

Elias, R. (1994). Official stories: Media coverage of American crime policy. *Humanist, 54,* 3–8.

Ellement, J. (1999). SJC curbs police on car-stop procedure. *Boston Globe.* [Online]. Available: www.boston.com/dailyglobe2/166/m. . ./SJC_curbs_police_on_car_stop _procedure+.shtm.

Entman, R. (1990). Modern racism and images of blacks in local television news. *Critical Studies in Mass Communication, 7*(4), 132–146.

Entman, R. (1992). Blacks in the news: Television, modern racism and cultural change. *Journalism Quarterly, 69*(2), 341–362.

Gilens, M. (1996). Race and poverty in America: Public misperception and the news media. *Public Opinion Quarterly, 60,* 515–542.

Gilliam, F., Iyengar, S., Simon, A., & Wright, O. (1996). Crime in black and white: The violent, scary world of local news. *The Harvard International Journal of Press/Politics, 1,* 6–23.

Harris, D. A. (1997). "Driving while black" and all other traffic offenses: The supreme court and pretextual traffic stops. *Journal of Criminal Law & Criminology, 87*(2), 544–582.

Hecker, S. (1997). Race and pretextual traffic stops: An expanded role for civilian review boards. *Columbia Human Rights Law Review, 28,* 551–604.

Higgins, M. (1997). Looking the part: With criminal profiles being used more widely to spot possible terrorists and drug couriers, claims of bias are also on the rise. *American Bar Association Journal, 83,* 48–50.

Iyengar, S. (1991). *Is anyone responsible?* Chicago: University of Chicago Press.

Jacob, H. (1971). Black and white perceptions of justice in the city. *Law and Society Review, 6,* 646–668.

King, C., & Stivers, C. (1998). *Government is us: Public administration in an anti-government era.* Thousand Oaks, CA: Sage Publications.

Larrabee, J. A. (1997). DWB (driving while black) and equal protection: The realities of an unconstitutional police practice. *Journal of Law & Policy, 6,* 291–328.

Maclin, T. (1998). Race and the fourth amendment. *Vanderbilt Law Review,* *51*(2), 333–393.

Maryland v. Wilson, 117 S. Ct. 882 (1997).

Meyer, J., and Rowan, B. (1991). Institutionalized organizations: Formal structure as myth and ceremony. In W. W. Powell and P. J. DiMaggio (Eds.), *The new institutionalism in organizational analysis.* Chicago: University of Chicago Press.

Muharrar, M. (1998, Sept./Oct.). Media Blackface: Racial profiling in news reporting. *FAIR—Fairness and Accuracy In Reporting.* [On-line]. Available: www.fair.org/extra/9809/media-blackface.html.

O'Day, K. M. (1998). Pretextual traffic stops: Protecting our streets or racist police tactics? *University of Dayton Law Review, 23*(2), 313–335.

Ohio v. Robinette, 117 S. Ct. 417 (1996).

Rossi, P. H., Beck, R. A., & Eidson, B. K. (1974). *The roots of urban discontent.* New York: John Wiley & Sons.

Scott, R. (1995). *Institutions and organizations.* Thousand Oaks, CA: Sage Publications.

Sklansky, D. A. (1997). Traffic stops, minority motorists, and the future of the fourth amendment. *Supreme Court Review, 1997,* 271–329.

Skolnick, J. H. (1998). The color of the law. *The American Prospect, 39,* 90–96.

Whren v. United States, 116 S. Ct. 1769 (1996).

Williams, B. N. (1998). *Citizen perceptions on community policing: A case study in Athens, Georgia.* Albany, NY: State University of New York Press.

Williams, B. N. (1999). Perceptions of children and teenagers on community policing: Implications for law enforcement leadership, training, and citizen evaluations. Unpublished manuscript.

Williams, H., and Murphy, P. V. (1990). The evolving strategy of police: A minority view. *Perspectives on Policing, 13.* Cambridge, MA: Harvard University Press.

Wyoming v. Houghton, 119 S. Ct. 1292 (1999).

C. Keith Harrison

Dr. Keith Harrison studies historical and contemporary effects of sport media and entertainment imagery on student athletes in society. His research is twofold. First, it focuses on mass media images of athletes and how these representations affect identity, self-concept, and career aspirations of student athletes—especially African American males.

Second, he is examining the social and historical context of sport. This research addresses the cultural tendency to value an individual's or group's athletic achievement over educational aspirations and achievements.

Dr. Harrison currently teaches race relations, cultural images and sport, social/historical bases of sport, and a graduate course focusing on leadership and diversity in sport.

Dr. Harrison is currently funded by the associate provost and the Division of Kinesiology. The Robeson Center has also received funds from the Rackham Graduate School, the School of Art, the Undergraduate Research Opportunity Program, and the Summer Research Opportunity Program. Dr. Harrison has participated in several research studies, has delivered over 100 scholarly papers/presentations, has revised two books, and has published more than 10 refereed articles and book chapters. Dr. Harrison has given invited addresses to college campuses, commencement ceremonies, and national and international symposia and has consulted with athletic programs across the country. In 1998, students voted Dr. Harrison to receive the Kinesiology Teaching Excellence Award, the first person to ever receive this honor within one year of service on the faculty.

22

BLACK MALE IMAGES
IN ATHLETICS

C. Keith Harrison

A day does not pass when I do not brood on the negative social profile and bad PR that seem to envelop contemporary images of black
males in America. As an artist and a father, I am filled with urgency
and more than a little anger because I know my own son, now
approaching his twenty-first birthday, and my fourteen-year-old
daughter must negotiate their way through an uncivil public space
soured by the steady bombardment of media images that portray
black people in the worst imaginable ways—as welfare cheats, criminals, incompetent parents, ex-cons, poor students, crackheads, as an
affirmative-action liability in the workplace, and, to put this bluntly,
as the corrupting worm coiled inside the American apple. (Johnson &
McCluskey, 1997, p. 177)

Background

As a young African American male in our society, I am subjected to many of the
stereotypes mentioned above. Often I am asked, "Do you play football or basketball?" When I respond that I am an assistant professor at the University of
Michigan, mouths drop wide open. In fact, people become even more confused
the more they probe and find out that I am a former center on a collegiate football team, have been teaching for six years, and earned my doctorate at age 27.

What is poignant here is the relationship of my personal bombardment of
presumptions, preconceived notions, and flat-out racist conclusions by many
individuals in America. While the "dumb jock" myth affects numerous athletic
people from all backgrounds, I tend to agree with Hutchinson's (1996) thesis:

Racism is subtle in sports, covertly and overtly apparent at times, but problematic to the critical eye. By synthesizing four major themes from Hutchinson's chapter on sport and illuminating preliminary data from a longitudinal study, the realities of the Black male sporting experience can be more closely observed and practically applied into what I am coining *Popular Culture Credo*. This theoretical framework and its analysis will follow the themes of Hutchinson's chapter and will link to the illusions of meritocracy and democracy that race and sport profess as we near the next millennium.

Theme 1: Post-Colonialism Equals Contemporary Capitalism

Hutchinson begins the chapter with the perfect framework, discussing documented racist comments by elites in the sport hierarchy. Hutchinson facetiously observes that Jimmy "the Greek" Snyder being fired was one of the worst things that could have happened. His main point is that when Snyder said that Blacks dominate major sports because they were "bred to be that way by the slave owner," he only said what many of the men who make the decisions in the sports profession really think about Black athletes (Hutchinson, 1996).

There have been other related comments. In 1993, Marge Schott, the owner of the Cincinnati Reds baseball franchise, made several comments behind closed doors that offended Americans of many races and religions (Shropshire, 1996). Statements Schott allegedly made referred to two star Black players as "million-dollar niggers," and she stated that she would "rather have a trained monkey working than a nigger."

The attitudes of the aforementioned eloquently demonstrates just how subtextual racism in sports is, and they raise an important question for future progress in our nation. How much has changed since slavery? Pieterse (1995) reminds us that

> some Blacks have become famous as entertainers or athletes is sometimes presented as an argument to the effect that there is no real discrimination against Blacks, that western societies are integrated and that every opportunity is open to Blacks if only they make an effort. It does not require too much imagination however to realize that this kind of success is a marginal phenomenon and can very well go along with a pattern of discrimination in society at large. (p. 132)

Pieterse guides one in the direction of reality, which is post-colonialism adaptation to a modern world. In other words, the post-slavery period saw segregation and no need for Black athletes except for side acts like the Globetrotters as clowns, buffoons, and "Uncle Toms." As long as they kept away from White women, they were tolerated in boxing since it was considered a sport for brutes anyway. When Jack Johnson (former heavyweight champion) forgot, the sport and country KO'd him fast (Hutchinson, 1996).

From my perspective, the world has no doubt advanced, and while some things are better in terms of racial discrimination, some stay the same. Historically, for their bumps and bruises, the Black bucks got a little better food, an extra set of hand-me-downs, and, if especially lucky, their freedom (Hutchinson, 1996). These Black bucks were the master's prize gladiators, and minimal specialties were provided.

"Conditional integration" has led to Black access to subordinate or participatory roles in sport. This has created a love-hate relationship with the Black male athlete, or what we might call a "post-modern buck." The success of the Black male athlete should always be kept in proper perspective. The racial complexion of *some* sports has changed, but the mentality of many of those who run it, promote it, and broadcast it has not. They are still Black performers employed for the amusement and entertainment of the public and, as always, the bottom-line profit of the men and women who run the sporting industry (Edwards, 1970, cited in Hutchinson, 1996). Frederick Douglass seemed to have captured it when he said, "Only those wild and low sports peculiar to semicivilized people were encouraged." Clearly, Douglass was critical of the promoted subordinate (the Black athlete and physical performance).

Theme 2: Visiting Athletic Scholars

Hutchinson raises the issue of the hypocrisy of collegiate athletics. The fact that Walter Byers (former NCAA executive director for almost 40 years) published a book in 1995 truthfully titled *Unsportsmanlike Conduct: Exploiting College Athletes* should scare all of us concerned. Hutchinson's case in point is the fact that Patrick Ewing made Georgetown an estimated $4.5 million on ticket sales, television, publicity, and promotional revenue. Ewing tangibly got a scholarship worth $48,000 and a degree, plays for the New York Knicks, and makes millions as a superstar. How many Black male student athletes can say the same? Works by scholars such as Harry Edwards, Gary Sailes, Othello Harris, Robert Sellers, Richard Lapchick, Earl Smith, and many others support what Hutchinson argues in this topical debate. Even with the impact of the Black male in sport, Blacks were and still are underpaid, underappreciated, and not accepted as social equals.

Hutchinson focuses on the debate over the years with Edwards and sportswriters and executives as to how much opportunity is really afforded to Black men to receive an education while on athletic scholarship. Sportswriters remind Edwards that slaves don't make millions of dollars, receive a college education, and live in palatial estates in the suburbs. They have always felt that Edwards should shut up and be grateful. From their perspective, if it were not for sports, these guys would be selling hot clothes in Harlem, peddling dope in Watts, or carjacking on Chicago's west side. Eventually, they would all wind up serving hard time in some joint.

Edwards has reminded sportswriters and society as a whole that some Black male student and professional athletes end up in jail anyway once they are dumped from a team because of injury or a run-in with a coach or once they fell from favor with an owner. Edwards has candidly written how even successful Black athletes were often discarded like a dirty jockstrap once their glory days were over. As a norm, Black athletes do not step from the court, gridiron, or cinders into Congress or the Senate like Jack Kemp, Bob Mathias, and Bill Bradley. Edwards today raises the question of how many African American male student athletes are majoring in law, medicine, or engineering? Graduation rates are still known to be a national disgrace for Brothers, and *Emerge* magazine reports the biggest abusers every year (institutions with low graduation rates for Black student athletes).

I want to make one thing clear at this point. Edwards and most of my colleagues mentioned above do not argue that student athletes should be paid. We argue that radical reconstruction of NCAA policies and procedures must come to fruition if true change is ever to take place. Stipends should be increased, freshman should be ineligible, and rewards should be given to those schools who graduate the most players; these are only a few suggestions. In general, we need to construct new priorities and a balance of academics and athletics. Until then, we will have visiting athletic scholars, as Harry Edward's song has lamented for far too many years.

Theme 3: Conditional Acceptance

Grant Hill captures Hutchinson's next argument in his biography, *Change the Game:*

> Bigotry can be blatant and it can be subtle. For example, a magazine
> article appeared that asked, "Can Grant Hill Save Sports?" Most peo-

ple, even my mother, saw it as a positive article. It complimented me for being smart, unassuming, and modest. Along with such praise, though, were some troubling characterizations. The writer of the article described a party I went to. There were some guys wearing fur coats who made a big deal over me, and the writer described me at one point as "the king of the hoodlums." The implication to me and most of my friends was that "hoodlum" equaled "black." Take me out of that scene, a friend pointed out, and it paints an unfair and unflattering picture of African American men. (Hill, 1996, pp. 63–64).

Hill's observation is similar to Hutchinson's discussion of the good and bad Negro in sports. In a perfect narrative, he descibes the Lawrence Phillips incident of a couple of seasons ago (which, in short, was that a star athlete beat up a coed—a White female at that—and got to play anyway). While suspended for several games, Phillips got to play in the national championship game, which his team (the University of Nebraska) won. While Nebraska University got the glory and Coach Osborne the championship, Hutchinson wonders what will happen to Phillips someday. Since his college days, Phillips has been in and out of trouble, was dropped from the team that drafted him, and was picked up by another team at the minimal league salary.

I argue that Phillip's behavior is both accepted and not accepted by the power structure, just because he can run with a football. Take his pads away from him, and he would be seen as just another Brother on the streets. Meanwhile, his stereotypical out-of-control, animalistic behavior reinforces the notion that Black men do not know how to act in a structured society, justifying every conservative politician's head nod of "I told you so."

Hutchinson concludes the section on pseudo-acceptance of Black athletes with two powerful points that he feels Black athletes should internalize if they want to last long: 1) Do not ask for more money, and 2) Never get hurt. Those in control allow Frank Sinatra or Bob Hope to ask for much money long after their best days are over, but the public perception at large is that we have overpaid, arrogant Black superstar athletes. Getting injured opens the door for other criticisms according to Hutchinson. Black men aren't viewed as "normal people." With all that muscle and brawn, Black men are supposed to be impervious to injury and pain. The "injury-prone" label is attached, which is a polite way of saying they're damaged goods. If the Black athlete is smart, he will save his money and plan on a speedy retirement because his days are numbered. Blacks are not allowed to sit on injured reserve lists or be benchwarmers. Those are the quota spots for marginal White players (Hutchinson, 1996). This is why Black athletes are conditionally accepted.

Theme 4: Twisting the Truth—No White Male Error

Hutchinson appropriately cites the Lawrence Phillips ordeal again, but this time he adds to the story Phillips' teammate at the time, Christian Peter. Lapchick (1996) argues that "broadcast and print media are largely responsible for the images that people see and remember" (p. 209). This is important in understanding the disparity between the media's portrayal of Phillips and Peter. Consider the following:

> The critics continued to beat up on Phillips after the Rams made him their first-round draft choice in 1996. Yet they were strangely silent about his white teammate, Christian Peter. The giant defensive tackle apparently did more than sack the opposing teams' quarterbacks. Between 1991 and 1994, Peter was charged with harassing and assaulting a woman in a bar, attacking a former Miss Nebraska, twice raping a Nebraska coed, and threatening the life of a parking-lot attendant. He also faces a federal sex discrimination suit. Peter got brief media mention only after the New England Patriots drafted him and then dropped him because of his sex and violence record. My computer search turned up twenty newspaper articles that specifically mentioned Phillips' off-the-field woes. Despite Peter's misdeeds, there was exactly one on him. Peter is a white athlete with an off-the-field record that made Phillips look like an altar boy. I wonder how the sports establishment missed this? (Hutchinson, 1996, p. 56)

I can answer Hutchinson's last question. To date, White-male error is not seen as "newsworthy" or a story in general. This is why hockey players can fight for hours and NBA and NFL teams get fined astronomical figures for late hits, fights, and flagrant fouls. The summation of Hutchinson's last theme is that the media label and code Black males specifically in terms of performance on and off the field, The Phillips and Peter incidents clearly show a difference between Black and White analysis. It all starts in the broadcast booth with the announcers. Studies such as James A. Rada's (1996) on "Color Blind-Sided: Racial Bias in Network Television's Coverage of Professional Football Games" show strong evidence of Hutchinson's thesis of media bias. Rada's study found that announcers emphasized the athleticism of Black players and the cognitive abilities of White players (p. 231).

Essentially, Black players are given what I call "credit/no credit" for their athletic achievements. This is why the word *athlete* has come to mean *Black*. I always have my students do an assignment on rating announcers and their descriptions, and they are shocked at the biases they hear. I myself have observed hours of athletic contests on television and heard the same biases described. Black athletes have great feet and "natural" ability, while White athletes "know" how to get open or perform a task. This is why the truth gets twisted and White-male error usually gets left out. As Hutchinson says at the end of his chapter, that's why Jackie Robinson said in his autobiography, "I never had it made."

Hutchinson feels that we should bring Snyder back because he made the game so much simpler. Snyder never kept Blacks guessing about where they stood. Snyder was oblivious to twisting the truth (Black-male athletic achievement) and White-male error (his racist beliefs that include negative actions).

Adding Science to McCall's Revolution: Hutchinson's Hypothesis

While Hutchinson has contributed to the body of knowledge on deconstructing mass media images of Black men, another author has added a similar perspective in relation to race and sport. Nathan McCall (1997) in *What's Going On,* describes a contest between Whites and Blacks in his powerful but hilarious chapter "The Revolution is about Basketball":

> Of course, the brothers knew they were being watched. Standing there, dressed in the finest brand-name tennis shoes and athletic gear, they appeared confident, cocky. Like maybe they'd taken too many of those popular sneaker commercials that feed America's myths about their super ball-playing skills. Perhaps they'd bought into that slick Reebok ad, the one where a brother, caught up in a fit of hoops bravado, boasts to the world, this is *my* planet. Or maybe they were inspired by the hip Foot Locker spot, in which a determined dude with a basketball spinning like a crystal on his gleaming bald head turns to Zen meditation to achieve white folks' idea of black men's greatest quest: defying gravity so we can dunk a goddamned basketball. (pp. 4–5)

In American culture, we see primarily three images of Black men: athletes, entertainers, and criminals. And if one were to look closer, one would see that these three images are practically rolled together. That's why Billy Hawkins (University of Georgia) has an excellent article forthcoming titled "Super-Athletes, Super-Heroes, and Super-Criminals," regarding Black masculinity and contemporary images. Hutchinson, McCall, and Hawkins all confirm what I have found in a longitudinal study.

From September of 1995 to the present, I have taped over 350 commercials of advertisements with Black male athletes in them, and I have had two graduate students complete thesis work on sports media advertising and race.

A few themes of these commercials blatantly portray that Black males are "natural" athletes, that education is not a key to being successful, and that the odds of making it professionally are very attainable. McCall's commentary adds to what I am finding, and he concludes his chapter by saying:

> The blind eye that some pro players turn to white America's sham voids them as role models for the young bloods who look up to them. And so youngsters often don't get told—firsthand—that the revolution is *not* about basketball. Instead, they go on, inspired by the commercial hype. They grow up nursing juvenile dreams of being the next Jordan, Shaq, or Hardaway—rich, famous, and above all, loved. You see them in back-yards, on school grounds and city basketball courts, leaping, rising above the stars, descending to the court with flashy thunder-dunks. You see them out there, cocksure as hell, destined to learn the same hard lesson handed those brothers in that Arlington pickup match: that you can have all the natural skills in the world and still lose if you haven't mastered the mental game. (McCall, 1997, pp. 15–16)

Since Jack Johnson and his stardom, too many Black males have felt that the road to success is in a gym, on a football field, or on a baseball diamond.

Conclusion

Nike-sponsored images of Michael Jordan are found around the world. Nike and other corporations have worked hard to sever the Jordan persona from connections with African American experiences. This allows people to comfortably ignore the legacies of colonialism and racism that still affect people's economic, political, and social lives today (Coakley, 1998). Coakley's argument lends immediate support to my theoretical framework, which I call *Popular Culture Credo.*

I have used it recently in papers and keynotes to reach deeper into the psyche of young Black males. Not only have institutions been apathetic about historical racism but so have many Black males who participate in sports. Without a historical perspective, goals are usually directed at athletic achievement. Combine these factors with the exclusion of diverse role-model representation of Black men, and the revolution does become about basketball only. Viewing *point one,* black males must be taught the history of integration, race, and sport. Many of the struggles yesterday are still true today. The problem is that too many Black males treat today's struggles without knowledge of the past and lack proactive strategies for combating and coping with racism.

Point two addresses the notion of stereotypes of the average Black male in society. While less than one percent of the African American male population are professional athletes, society at large assumes the number is much greater (I alluded to this in the opening paragraph of this essay). *Point three* stresses that the salaries of Black athletes channel the goals of many. Many "Brothers" no doubt think, "Why do anything else besides play ball if it pays like that?" Having a limited goal as a professional athlete and the status attached to it can (if achieved) allow an individual to obtain many of the things he wishes to consume (money, women, cars, houses).

Point four relates to the notion of African Americans living in two worlds (homogenous and heterogeneous) and all of the social tensions that are associated with upward mobility. The problem is that many of the Black male role models in institutional roles are not visible to young Black males. And too often when they are visible and present, the desire to become like them is low based on stereotypes of assimilation.

Point five follows that education is seen too often as part of the "sell-out" and assimilation process of being less Black. Early Black male student athletes such as Paul Robeson, Jerome Holland, and William Henry Lewis were all outstanding scholars and athletes—proving this notion to be pathological. *Point six* examines that goals outside of sport appear nebulous, abstract, and a waste of time to many Black males. The assassination of the Black male image in sport becomes more and more complex each day, while seemingly moving farther and farther from equality and reality. Let's hope the next millennium will see more images of Black male super-doctors, super-lawyers, and super-thinkers, thus diffusing the traditional paradigm and becoming more inclusive to holistic realities.

References

Arnold, E. (1997). Personal communication.

Coakley, J. (1998). *Sport in society.* Boston: McGraw-Hill.

Hill, G. (1996). *Change the game.* New York: Warner Books.

Hutchinson, O. (1996). *The assassination of the Black male image.* New York: Simon & Schuster.

Johnson, C., & McCluskey, J. (1997). *Black men speaking.* Bloomington: Indiana University Press.

Lapchick, R. (1996). *Sport in society.* Thousand Oaks, CA: Sage Publications.

McCall, N. (1997). *What's going on.* New York: Random House.

Pieterse, J. (1995). *White on Black.* New Haven, CT: Yale University Press.

Rada, J. (1996). Color blind-sided: Racial bias in network television's coverage of professional football games. *The Howard Journal of Communications, 7,* 231–239.

Shropshire, K. (1996). *In Black and White.* New York: New York University Press.

Charles K. Ross

Dr. Charles K. Ross is an assistant professor of history and Afro-American studies at the University of Mississippi. His teaching interests include 20th-century U.S. history, African American history, and sport history. His responsibilities include research, teaching numerous courses in history and Afro-American studies, as well as advising students, conducting faculty searches, and facilitating off-campus programs. He has also served as acting chair, Afro-American Studies Program, at the University of Mississippi.

Dr. Ross holds a bachelor of arts degree in history from Stillman College. As a senior at Stillman, Dr. Ross received the award for outstanding achievement from the History Department. He has a master of arts degree in Black studies, a master of arts degree in history, and a Ph.D. in history from Ohio State University. Dr. Ross completed his high school education from Mifflin High School in Columbus, Ohio.

Dr. Ross is a member of Kappa Alpha Psi Fraternity Inc., a member of the Association for the Study of Afro-American Life and History (ASALH), North American Society of Sport History (NASSH), American Historical Association (AHA), and the National Council of Black Studies.

Dr. Ross has recently completed his first book, *Outside the Lines: African Americans and the Integration of the National Football League,* which was released by New York University Press in November 1999. Dr. Ross has spoken at numerous high schools, universities, and churches. He has also presented several scholarly papers at conferences throughout the country.

23

A HISTORICAL LEGACY OF BLACK MALE LEADERSHIP: MEDGAR EVERS

Charles K. Ross

When discussing the development and accomplishments of Black male leaders, historically, specific personalities tend to be focused on more so than others. Through no fault of their own, historic black leaders such as Frederick Douglass, Booker T. Washington, W. E. B. DuBois, and of course, Dr. Martin Luther King, Jr. and Malcolm X are prominent figures whose contributions have been well chronicled. However, the environment and conditions in which Medgar Evers was born, lived, and died demand that his name be placed on the same plateau as the aforementioned leaders. There were virtually no parallels to Black life during the postwar period in Mississippi, and whereas Dr. King and Malcolm had organizational support in their struggles against oppression, Evers was largely on his own. In addition, although Dr. King's movement was centered in the South and was met by great resistance in Birmingham, Alabama, it did not compare to the resistance Evers faced in Mississippi. Today Evers' legacy can be seen in many social, political, and economic changes throughout the state. No other Mississippian has done so much to change the racial dynamics specifically for African Americans. Evers' shadow continues to affect Mississippi and America in its seemingly unending struggle with race.

Evers was born in Decatur, Mississippi, on July 2, 1925. When he was eight years old, he witnessed the lynching of one of his father's friends. Willie Tingle was dragged through the streets of town behind a wagon and was hung up to a tree and shot for supposedly looking at a White woman or insulting her. For a long time his bloody clothes were allowed to remain in the field, and Evers and his older brother Charles had to pass them on their long walk to school. Needless to say, the consequences of being a Black male in Mississippi left a lasting impression on young Medgar. By the time he had joined the army and had graduated from Alcorn College, he was well aware of the social, political, and economic boundaries for Blacks in his home state.

For most Blacks in Mississippi, not being able to vote, segregation, and the exposure to violence and death were simply accepted. Between 1880 and 1940, approximately six hundred Mississippi Blacks were lynched, and no jury would convict a White man for killing a Black. In postwar Mississippi, most Blacks were still working at jobs associated with slavery. Nearly two-thirds of the Black male labor force was working in agricultural activities; 80 percent were sharecroppers or day laborers on White plantations. Black women worked as domestics for White women; of the 58,000 Black women in nonagricultural jobs in 1950, two-thirds worked as domestics. And the median yearly family income for Blacks in 1949 was $601; for Whites it was $1,614. More than a third of Black families living in Mississippi reported yearly incomes under $500 (Dittmer, 1994).

Medgar was not atypical of the Black American veterans from the South who fought for the country in World War II, for democratic values as they had been told, and then returned home to find that nothing had changed at all. In 1946 he, Charles, and three friends went to the county courthouse to try to register to vote. While hostile Whites blocked the entrances, they managed to reach the clerk's office—only to be turned away by armed White men. The ironies in this were most abundant, and the litany of them in Mississippi during and after the war was gut wrenching. For example, in a small town in the Mississippi Delta during the war, a decorated Black veteran still nursing an arm wound was not allowed to enter a restaurant where several Nazi prisoners and their security guard from a nearby POW camp were eating. Medgar knew of such instances, and they moved something in his soul (Morris, 1998).

Evers's attempt to register to vote was the first of his many challenges to the White power structure that eventually dominated his life. After graduating from Alcorn College, he took a job with a Black-owned insurance company and moved to the all-Black town of Mound Bayou with his new wife, Myrlie Beasley. Evers's job selling insurance door-to-door in the Delta was in a sense his apprenticeship for his life's work. Distressed by the abject poverty of Delta Blacks, he began to feel guilty about selling policies to people who could barely put food on their tables. Soon he was using his job as a cover for political work, talking up the NAACP on behalf of Dr. Howard (who owned Medgar's company) to Delta sharecroppers and urging their attendance at local mass meetings. At one of these meetings in 1953, Emmett Stringer, state president of the NAACP, asked for a volunteer to attempt to desegregate the

University of Mississippi. When Evers stepped forward and subsequently applied to its law school, his life took a fateful turn. From that point on, national officers of the NAACP had their eyes on Evers, and in December 1954 they offered him the job as field secretary (Dittmer, 1994).

While Evers waited for state Attorney General James P. Coleman—a man who as governor declared that Blacks were not fit to vote—to rule on his application, which was subsequently denied, the historic *Brown* decision was handed down by the U.S. Supreme Court. Whites all across Mississippi feared the implications of the ruling, and a Delta planter whose hobby was writing racist and anti-Semitic pamphlets decided to do something about it. Thus, the White Citizens' Councils, the brainchild of one Robert "Tut" Patterson, were born. The initial goal of these councils was to preserve segregation and block any attempt to enforce the Supreme Court decision, primarily by making Blacks suffer economically. Segregation could be preserved, council leaders always publicly stressed, through legal means. Nevertheless, through its unrelenting attack on human rights in Mississippi, the Citizens' Council fostered and legitimized violent actions by individuals not overly concerned with questions of legality and image (Brown, 1994).

When Blacks in Mississippi stepped out of place by attempting to register to vote or by soliciting support for the NAACP, their names were placed on a list by the Citizens' Council and employers were notified. Black Mississippians lost long-time jobs, failed to get loans from banks, or were violently harassed as a result of their names being placed on council lists. By early 1960, Evers was the most visible and aggressive civil-rights activist in the state, and White supremacists had several reasons for being aware of him:

- He investigated racial murders and beatings, including those of fourteen-year-old Emmett Till from Chicago near the town of Money, who was killed after whistling at or asking a White woman out for a date (Roy Bryant and his half-brother, J. W. Milam, killed the child but were set free after an all-White jury deliberated for 68 minutes and returned a not-guilty verdict); the Reverend George Lee, the NAACP leader in Belzoni who was felled in a downtown neighborhood with shotgun blasts to his face and whose murderers were never arrested (the police claimed the shotgun buckshot pellets were dental fillings); and a farmer named Lamar Smith who was murdered outside the courthouse in Brookhaven while attempting to register to vote.

- He was constantly on the road trying to get Blacks to register to vote. Both Lee and Smith had been murdered for their efforts in this regard, and countless others had been beaten and driven away.

- As early as 1953, he was roaming the Delta and photographing the horrible conditions of Black schools. After the *Brown* decision, he strenuously advocated public-school integration and encouraged local petitions among Blacks to that end.

- He espoused equal access to public facilities and, near the end of his life, organized economic boycotts, mass demonstrations, and lunch-counter sit-ins. Even his more modest pursuits suggested something of the daily life of Mississippi Blacks then: to be able to try on hats in stores, to use public swimming pools and libraries, to have school-crossing personnel at Black schools, and to be addressed as Mr., Mrs., and Miss.

- His most towering accomplishment was his simple presence and his standing up for the idea of racial justice in a time and place where it was extremely dangerous to do so. He publicly kept that idea alive in Mississippi at a time when no one else did. When the Student Non-violent Coordinating Council (SNCC) and other civil-rights leaders came into the state in 1961, they were not carrying their message to virgin territory.

As attractive, college-educated, family-oriented Blacks, Myrlie and Medgar could have easily closed their eyes to the realities of 1950s and 1960s Mississippi and let others lead the struggle; or they could have joined the continuing exodus of Southern Blacks to the North and West. Yet they loved Mississippi and felt its promise. Neither of them set out to be historical figures, but they chose to stay and to lead the fight. "It may sound funny," Medgar once told a reporter from *Ebony*, "but I love the South. I don't choose to live anywhere else. There's land here, where a man can raise cattle, and I'm going to do that someday. There are lakes where a man can sink a hook and fight a bass. There is room here for my children to play, and grow, and become good citizens." When the NAACP offered to send him to California for his own safety, he said, "I belong here" (Morris, 1998).

Shortly after his house was firebombed, he told a reporter, "I may be going to heaven or hell. But I'll be going from Jackson" (Morris, 1998).

In June of 1961, the national office of the NAACP announced the launch of "Operation Mississippi," whose goal was to "wipe out segregation in all phases of Mississippi life." The key strategy was to fight segregation in the courts. But by 1962, the substantial number of young people coming into the state who advocated the use of sit-ins and marches was in stark contrast to the more conservative NAACP legal strategy. Evers initially was ambivalent toward the SNCC, Congress of Racial Equality (CORE), and Southern Christian Leadership Council (SCLC), especially the activities of SNCC workers in organizing voter registration in various counties. However, Evers quickly realized that Mississippi's backlash against civil rights was becoming more violent and that not to work with these groups who all had the same goal would be foolish. Evers decided that the goals of liberation for Blacks in Mississippi warranted working together even if it meant leaving the NAACP altogether. The various civil-rights organizations did, however, find common ground and banded together to form the Council of Federated Organizations (COFO) in 1962 (Brown, 1994).

By late 1962, Evers found himself in a battle facilitated by NAACP activists in Jackson who were mobilizing a campaign against segregated facilities and discriminatory employment practices. Initiated by the Jackson NAACP youth council, a boycott began against downtown merchants, charging them with a broad pattern of discrimination against Black workers and consumers. White merchants in Jackson did not take the boycott seriously, but local Blacks were aware of ongoing protests in Greenwood and in Albany, Georgia, and James Meredith's success in desegregating the University of Mississippi was proof that the White establishment was not invincible (Dittmer, 1994).

By May of 1963, the boycott strategy was reinforced by sit-ins and pickets, transforming it into a mass movement. During a meeting with Black delegates, the mayor of Jackson agreed to several of the demands but later recanted, denying making any concessions. The mayor's actions forced Black leaders into a dilemma, because continued demonstrations were becoming too costly. The NAACP had paid out $64,000 to bail out 640 protesters since the initial boycott. The Black middle-class leadership, specifically ministers and businessmen, opposed mass marches and had become increasingly fearful of White violence. Evers was caught in the middle of both strategies, and instead of taking part in the bitter infighting over tactics, he began to withdraw. Fatigue had also set in, and threats against his life were increasing (Dittmer, 1994).

On the evening of Tuesday, June 11, 1963, President John F. Kennedy made a historic television address, endorsing for the first time federal civil-rights legislation. That night Evers was attending a rally in Jackson at New Jerusalem Baptist Church. Evers looked tired and said little. At 12:20 A.M., he pulled into his driveway and got out of his car carrying a bundle of NAACP T-shirts. As Myrlie and his three children jumped up to meet him, a sniper crouching 150 feet away in a honeysuckle thicket fired one shot from a high-powered rifle, dropped the gun into a patch of weeds, and fled. The slug hit

292 CHARLES K. ROSS

Evers's back just below the shoulder blade. He staggered to his feet, groped toward the kitchen door, and collapsed in a pool of blood. Neighbors rushed him to the hospital, but he died en route from loss of blood and internal injuries. Later police recovered the rifle and identified fingerprints as belonging to a Citizens' Council member from Greenwood named Byron De La Beckwith, who was soon arrested and charged with Evers' murder (Dittmer, 1994).

Beckwith was tried twice in 1964, and in both trials he was represented by politically connected lawyers; even former governor Ross Barnett openly shook his hand in the courtroom during a recess. When Beckwith returned to Greenwood after the second hung jury, he was greeted with "Welcome Home" signs. The prosecution concluded that it would not seek a third trial without significant new evidence. The case, under technicalities of the law, would remain open but dormant. Almost everyone considered it dead, as indeed for all purposes it was. But Myrlie Evers knew the law and knew that there is no statute of limitations on murder, and as she moved her family to California to escape the bitter memories, she waited and kept aware of developments in Mississippi (Morris, 1998).

After the second trial that summer, Beckwith officially joined the White Knights of the Ku Klux Klan. He became an intimate associate of the Imperial Wizard, Sam Bowers. Bowers was the mastermind behind the brutal Neshoba County murders of Michael Schwerner, Andrew Goodman, and James Chaney during the summer of 1964. Eight Klansmen including Bowers were imprisoned on federal charges of conspiracy to commit murder; none served more than six years. The state of Mississippi refused to press charges. Bowers was the key leader in organizing the statewide reign of executions and bombings during the 1960s. Two years after the Neshoba County murders, in 1966, Vernon Dahmer, president of the NAACP in Forrest County, died after a firebomb attack on his home. Thirteen people were charged, and four were convicted of murder. Two cases resulted in mistrials, and the others were dropped. Bowers, accused of organizing the plot, was tried twice for murder and arson; all-White juries refused to convict him (Morris, 1998).

In 1994 Beckwith was retried under new evidence from a reporter of possible jury-tampering in the earlier trials. Many Whites opposed a new trial because of court costs, unfairness to an old man, meaningless political window dressing, and more than anything else, because of the inevitable public airing again of the state's appalling past. The courtroom itself was the same one in which the 1964 trials had been held, but the makeup of the jury was distinctly different. During the 1964 trials, the juries were all White; in 1994, the jury consisted of two White women, two White men, four Black women, and four Black men. Arguably this jury epitomized the changes that had taken place in

Mississippi—changes for which Medgar Evers had been willing to sacrifice his life. After fifteen days of testimony, the jury deliberated for little more than an hour before returning with a guilty verdict. Beckwith was denied bail. "He's been out on bond for thirty years," said one of the prosecutors. Currently there is an appeal by Beckwith's lawyers, but the state Supreme Court has yet to rule on that appeal (Morris, 1998).

Mississippi today has changed dramatically since Medgar Evers lived. No longer do daily lynchings and violent attacks against Blacks by Whites occur; the public school system and higher education institutions are now integrated; Blacks now have the ability to enter many public places that they could not enter under social segregation; and they have the right to participate fully in the political process by voting. Arguably all of these accomplishments were a result of the courage, struggle, demands, and sacrifice of Medgar Evers. Although many other African Americans made similar contributions and paid the ultimate price of dying in the struggle against White supremacy in Mississippi, no other Black leader left such a lasting legacy that is still affecting the state today.

As the first Black applicant to the University of Mississippi, he started the process that facilitated its integration by James Meredith. When Evers applied to the University in 1953, the only Blacks on campus were maids and janitors. Today Black students make up roughly 10 percent of the student population, and African Americans are working as faculty members, staff members, and administrators.

The 1962 boycott of downtown Jackson businesses with which Evers became involved began the process by which many Blacks now keep jobs that were then unattainable. But it is probably the political process that has seen the most change in the state since Evers led the charge for the right to vote. Mississippi has more Black elected officials than any other state in America; these include Black mayors in various cities including Jackson, Black state legislators, a Black congressman, and numerous Black local officials.

Life has vastly changed for Black Mississippians over the past forty years or so.

America in general and Mississippi specifically continue to grapple with their racist past. Once again Medgar Evers's ghost is playing a role in that process. The 1994 trial and murder conviction of Byron De La Beckwith caused the family of Vernon Dahmer to have hope in bringing to justice the killers of their father. They got the case reopened, and in August of 1998, Sam Bowers, former Imperial Wizard of the Ku Klux Klan in Mississippi, was finally convicted for his involvement in the 1966 death of Vernon Dahmer and was sentenced to life in prison. The trial for the last living participant in the firebombing, Charles Noble, is scheduled for July, 2000. In February of 1998, it was reported that Ken Turner, the Neshoba County district attorney, requested the FBI's files on the 1964 civil-rights workers' murder investigation. As they were returning to Meridian, Schwerner, Goodman, and Chaney were stopped around 4:30 P.M. on June 21, 1964, by then-Neshoba County deputy sheriff Cecil Price. The now 60-year-old Philadelphia, Mississippi, resident released the civil-rights workers around 10:30 from the Philadelphia jail. Many have pointed to Price as the organizer of the ambush, and to coconspirator Alton Wayne Roberts as the alleged triggerman in the murders. The state of Mississippi has never filed murder charges in the case, but it may in the near future. This will once again place the state and its past in the national public spotlight, for which it only has itself to blame.

As we enter the twenty-first century, the creation of Black male leaders is of fundamental importance to African Americans. The overt social and political barriers that many Blacks faced during the civil-rights movement have been removed, much like the once familiar signs of "colored" and "white." But the covert economic barriers of the past in many areas of America remain the same. For years the perception was that the quality of life for Blacks outside of the South was much better than for those living in the South. Today I beg to differ. The economic problems of high unemployment, poverty, poor housing, low wages, and access to quality education can be seen clearly in the Mississippi Delta, but also in Compton, California, and the inner cities of Chicago, Detroit, New York, Washington, DC, and various other northern urban areas.

The leaders of the civil-rights movement could easily attack segregation because it was visible in almost every component of that society; arguably the leaders of today and, more importantly, the leaders of tomorrow have a more difficult task ahead. The highly discernible forms of systemic racism have all but disappeared and have been replaced with a new, improved, undiscernible form. After the Civil War and Reconstruction period, there was a White backlash to the ending of slavery and to Blacks gaining limited political rights. It was during this period that W. E. B. DuBois made his historic prediction that "the problem of the twentieth century will be the color line." There is little argument that DuBois' prediction was accurate based on what has happened in America over the last century concerning race. What lies ahead in the twenty-first century in terms of race relations? There is much optimism that the old problems surrounding race relations in America have been solved. Many Blacks and Whites in America today probably would agree. I, however, do not.

In fact, I would argue that "the problem of the twenty-first century will be the unseen color line." Time will tell.

References

Brown, J. (1994). *Medgar Evers.* Los Angeles: Holloway House.

Dittmer, J. (1994). *Local People—The struggle for civil rights in Mississippi.* Urbana, IL: University of Illinois Press.

Morris, W. (1998). *The ghosts of Medgar Evers.* New York: Random House.

Ronald S. Rochon

Dr. Ronald S. Rochon is a native of Chicago, Illinois. He is an associate professor within the Department of Curriculum and Instruction and director of the Masters of Education-Professional Development Program for the School of Education at the University of Wisconsin, La Crosse. He is also co-founder and director of the Research Center for Cultural Diversity and Community Renewal at the university.

Ron obtained his bachelor of science degree in animal sciences from Tuskegee University; he then pursued a master of science degree with an emphasis in reproductive physiology from the University of Illinois at Champaign-Urbana. After working one year at the University of Chicago within its reproductive unit, Ron began developing an interest in teaching and decided to further his formal education by obtaining his Ph.D. in educational policy studies from the University of Illinois at Champaign-Urbana.

He loves teaching. His courses address historical and contemporary perspectives regarding the politics of race and culture within American society. His research agenda is grounded within a historical context, which examines trends among African Americans as it regards their feelings, attitudes, and perspectives toward ethnic versus national identity. His work also investigates the current educational curriculum debate regarding multiculturalism and the role of public schools in addressing questions of ethnic identity.

24

BLACK SUCCESS OR WHITE EMULATION

Who Shall Sit at the Table to Create Effective Solutions That Empower African American Children?

Ronald S. Rochon

When Dr. Lee Jones invited me to submit a reflective piece centered around the issue of African Americans preparing for leadership within this increasingly diverse society, I experienced several personal emotions—humility, excitement, and nervousness. Perhaps a little explication of these feelings will give the reader a better sense of what's behind the argument I'd like to advance. In brief, all three sets of feelings came about because of my commitment to the charge that Malcolm X laid before each of us: "to be a part of the solution." So here I am, humbled by the request to write this chapter, feeling a sense of excitement about the possibility of sharing my thoughts and beliefs, and most importantly, nervous about the remote possibility that sharing my thoughts and beliefs with readers will have a small impact on my community—in particular on "our" children. I have come to learn from family, friends, and teachers that I should always take this kind of opportunity very seriously. In the process of doing so, it is my sincere hope that what I have to say will trigger questions within the reader and thereby encourage reflection on how, together, we will continue to build African American communities.

Often, perhaps too often, society seeks out and becomes dependent upon those who have been identified as successful or as experts. Unfortunately, this is a problem for many who reside in America and is not unique to the Black community. Native, Asian, Latino, Anglo, as well as African American scholars have lamented the way that Americans have become an ineffective public, nearly devoid of the ability to deliberate issues of public policy. The cultural predisposition to defer to experts (for security, half truths, hope, and so on) may be partially to blame for what some see as the slow erosion of character among citizens. The great irony behind this is that the experts who are often sought after for "help" frequently contribute to furthering community suffering. I mention this primarily because I believe that each of us must remain critical of those whom we identify as "successful" or as "expert." Moreover, Black folk must become even more discerning regarding the expert reports and highly touted solutions for the future development of African American communities.

Unfortunately, "we" as a nation in general and as African American people in particular are taught not to—or simply do not—rely upon the "scholars" who reside within our own households and communities. We have become adept at ignoring those whose successes lie in the realm of lives well lived, in favor of those who have acquired certificates or degrees. Most of us respond this way due to the "training" we receive outside of our homes and communities. It is precisely this training that Dr. Carter G. Woodson (1990) identified as "mis-education." Woodson's admonition notwithstanding, we recognize or equate "success" with the initials behind a name, large amounts of money in a bank account, or identifiable faces that the media have etched into our memories.

Rarely, for example, do we seek out our greatest successful resources within the communities in which we live—the parents and extended-community family members that gave and sustained the life of these same "success stories" (including the ones who are being honored in this volume). Generally, these "old school" community contributors do not possess educational credentials, let alone terminal or professional degrees and, therefore, are not highly sought after for the wisdom they possess. These very people, our parents as well as other elders, are the primary reason (if not, in most cases, the sole reason) that university degrees within the African American community exist.

I raise this issue of who is seen and therefore utilized as an intellectual resource, only because I think it's necessary that we examine any discussion regarding African American "success." Surely success must mean more than possession of wealth or a professional degree. This same limited conception is consistently perpetuated at the decision-making level by the media, universities, and other professional settings. Certain voices are simply never heard because they are not invited to participate in assisting with what the quality of life for their children or communities will be. Therefore, we have lives that are directly affected by policy makers—uninformed about the experience, intellect, dreams, desires, aspirations, joys, and pain of those identified as lacking the "business knowledge" needed for policy making. In point of fact, these same experts become so accustomed to not hearing or seeing the "other," that they begin to prescribe remedies that are potentially destructive for the African American community. They repeatedly prescribe, for example, remedies that are designed to keep the policy makers "safe" from those whom Lisa Delpit (1995) has identified in her important book as *Other People's Children*. Prisons, prisons, and more prisons. It is hard to imagine that a committee of parents and other community members, if provided an opportunity to be a part of the "remedy discussion," would repeatedly recommend short-sighted solutions of imprisonment for our children.

As much as possible, we must involve all voices in the quest for solutions to the problems that plague Black communities. In true democratic fashion, we must begin to thoughtfully examine the input of all of our community members. Open democratic dialogue requires serious consideration of the ideas of factory workers as well as professors, maids as well as politicians, mothers as well as company presidents. When we don't have complete representation of the community, we marginalize its members and, at some level, legitimize the stereotyping of White supremacists.

The effect that institutionalized racism has had on the image of African American men is, without argument, immoral and unethical. However, we as Black people should not respond to this propaganda by seeking out only part of the community for solutions—it can only create divisiveness between African Americans. Over centuries, White supremacists have illustrated and continue consistently to illustrate the behavior of what amounts to be less than one percent of the "worst of the worst" of African American outcomes (that is, criminal activity) as Black culture; then we African American academicians illustrate what amounts to be less than one percent of the "best of the best" of African American "successes" as Black intelligentsia.

As we divide African Americans into the invited and the noninvited, we perpetuate the "good Black–bad Black" model and reinforce the power of institutionalized racism. Within his works, Malcolm X often spoke of this "divide and conquer" tactic as he described "massa's" effectiveness at dividing the good house negro from the recalcitrant field negro. His 1960s message conveyed that we, as a people, run a great risk of failing to obtain any form of solidarity if we continue communicating to the world that we believe only in our Black Ph.D. success stories to provide sound leadership for the community. Furthermore, since less than one percent of all African Americans hold doctoral degrees (U.S. Department of Education, 1996), we run an even greater risk of separating the community by conveying a message to Black residents that ninety-nine percent of the community should be governed and the remaining one percent will serve as its governors (Kozol, 1991). Finally, we run the risk of teaching children (in particular African American children), from the poorest to the most affluent, strategies on how ineffectively to eradicate classism while continuing to place future African American children "at risk." In point of fact, we provide children "hands-on" instruction on how to maintain the same social ills we now employ—the "haves" versus "have-nots" within the community.

Examples of these classist beliefs hold true in the year 2000 even as they did throughout the 1980s while I was a student. I can recall several instances when African American university students regarded Black folk "not affiliated" with the university in a destructive way. Some of these students classified community members as valley nigs, townies, country bumpkins, niggas, and so on. Moreover, I also witnessed community members respond to university students with equal disdain: uppity nigga, house nigga, white boy, negro, and so on. (To observe this conflict through the lens of a former African American university student, view Spike Lee's film, *School Daze*.)

Rethinking Success within African American Communities

> Make no distinction in your behavior between those of rank and the common people. Rather choose a person because of his or her skills so that every craft may be carried on. (Karenga, 1984, p. 51)

Let me be clear; I believe in and support the worth of the terminal degree—I hold one myself. However, the existence of African American Ph.D.s should not deter from, but enhance, our lifelong quest and hard work to improve collectively the quality of life for all children. Remember that the majority of our grandparents, parents, and neighbors did not or do not hold a doctorate. We should also remember that many of our well-respected historical leaders (Sojourner Truth, Frederick Douglass, Fannie Lou Hamer, Medgar Evers, Rosa Parks) did not possess this "academic distinction." Nor were they recipients of a Pulitzer or Nobel Peace Prize. However, the majority of our past and present heroines and heroes were, and many still are, experts within the arena of African American liberation. At this point in our history, we can all benefit from the wisdom, guidance, and courage of these African American people.

With greater representation of community members collaborating at the table, both privately as well as publicly, the power of intellectually growing while questioning and challenging one another is limitless. Moreover, it will make our communities and relationships stronger. It will also better serve our children as they prepare not only for participation within their own communities as future productive contributors but also for full participation across the globe. With these examples, our children will not just consume thought and theory; they will produce fruitful, healthy, needed ideas and institutions for the world. I encourage endorsement of the opportunity to have our ideas pushed further and critiqued by many. We can no longer afford to allow the fear of being challenged paralyze us and thereby impede our collective progress toward community betterment.

The Talented Tenth Revisited

In 1903, W. E. B. DuBois published an essay entitled "The Talented Tenth," in which he advocated for a Black leadership of exceptional men via a system that would provide "ten percent" of the men within African American communities an opportunity to seek higher education. DuBois brought forth this plan to create successful leaders who would combat continued problems afflicting Black communities. DuBois commented,

> we shall have only as we make [manhood] the object of the work of the schools—intelligence, broad sympathy, knowledge of the world that was and is, and of the relation of men to it—this is the curriculum of that Higher Education which must underlie true life. On this foundation we may build bread winning, skill of hand and quickness of brain, with never a fear lest the child and [man] mistake the means of living for the object of life. (Gates and West, 1996, p. 133)

His objective was to create a brilliant, politically conscious, selfless group of men who would succeed at educating and leading masses of African American people. DuBois himself did not foresee future criticism of his proposal by his contemporaries, nor, more importantly, did he imagine the unethical and self-promoting response of this new group of highly educated men. In 1948, he wrote another essay regarding his talented tenth idea:

> It has been said that I had in mind the building of an aristocracy with neglect of the masses. This criticism has seemed even more valid because of emphasis on the meaning and power of the mass of people to which Karl Marx gave voice in the middle of the nineteenth century, and which has been growing in influence ever since. There have come other changes in these days, which a great many of us do not realize as revolution through which we are passing. Because of this, it

is necessary to examine the world about us and our thoughts and attitudes toward it. I want then to re-examine and restate the thesis of the Talented Tenth, which I laid down many years ago. (Gates and West, 1996, p. 159)

DuBois, I believe, not only depended upon his contemporaries to understand the needs of the community within an economic and sociopolitical context, but he also expected these men to act productively on behalf of Black communities. Moreover, DuBois expected this action to be carried out with courage and a conviction that was nonnegotiable. In short, he expected an ethical and uncorrupt commitment to social justice. However, years after completing his formal studies and having an opportunity to study Black life among the "professionals" within the community, DuBois began to realize the possible shortcomings of his vision to educate only these select men, the talented tenth, to reverse the ongoing problems facing Black communities. He stated,

> When I came out of college into the world of work, I realized that it was quite possible that my plan of training a talented tenth might put in control and power, a group of selfish, self-indulgent, well-to-do men, whose basic interest in solving the Negro Problem was personal; personal freedom, and unhampered enjoyment and use of the world, without any real care, or certainly no arousing care, as to what became of the mass of American Negroes, or of the mass of any people. My Talented Tenth, I could see, might result in a sort of interracial free-for-all, with the devil taking the hindmost and the foremost taking anything they could lay hands on. (Gates and West, 1996, p. 162)

When parents and educators purport to the world that African American youth "don't know their history," I begin to wonder how many contemporary African American adults know theirs (do we, the "successes" of the Black community, know the works of DuBois and others?). The experiences that Professor W. E. B. DuBois outlined within his essays are poignant historical examples from which we can and should learn regarding a visionary direction to empower all citizens within Black communities. DuBois' insight clearly outlines the negative possibilities that can occur when a nation depends on the "few" to do right by the "many."

We Stand on the Shoulders of Giants

One of the tragedies of Black life in America is that too many Black people never acquire insight into their own existence. They just do not know who they are. And, this confusion about identity and source is at the core of our ignorance.

> The Afrikans have a saying: "If you don't know who you are any history will do." Welcome to America. (Madhubuti, 1990, p. ii)

It is my belief that in order for of us to move an agenda forward that addresses the life circumstances and future liberation of African American minds in general and our children in particular, we must first develop a fundamental understanding of "who we are." When we walk through this world with an understanding of our history, we are able to maintain an intellectual arsenal that not only affirms us as individuals but also allows our collective community to better defend and produce a healthy, inclusive vision for generations to come. It is now, probably more so than ever, apparent that we need to include all people of our community in the effort to empower African American children. Clearly we need historians in every corner of our everyday lives who love, appreciate, and respect the Black experience. Therefore, it is my suggestion that we continue to learn and teach about those who came before us—those with professional credentials as well as those who were barely literate and, in some cases, not literate at all. Let us always remember that we, as a people, are able to work toward personal and collective success only because of the uncompromising visionary sacrifices of our foreparents along with their courage and unwavering belief in us, their children. Finally, with great humility and pride, we should embrace and share with the world the simple fact that we, the African Diaspora, stand on the shoulders of ancestral giants and that we, too, have living giants from all walks of life among us within our communities today.

References

Delpit, L. (1995). *Other people's children: Cultural conflict in the classroom.* New York: W.W. Norton.

Gates, H., & West, C. (1996). *The future of the race.* New York: Random House.

Karenga, M. (1984). *The Husia: Selections from sacred wisdom of ancient Egypt.* Los Angeles: University of San Core Press.

Kozol, J. (1991). *Savage inequalities.* New York: Crown.

Madhubuti, H. (1990). *Black men: Obsolete, single, dangerous? The African American family in transition.* Chicago: Third World Press.

U.S. Department of Education. (1996). *National center for education statistics: Integrated postsecondary education data system, staff survey.* Washington, DC: Author.

Woodson, C. (1990). *The mis-education of the Negro.* Treton, NJ: Africa World Press. (Original work published 1933)

Mark Micaiah Whitaker

Dr. Mark M. Whitaker currently serves as an assistant professor of management in the School of Business at Hampton University. At Hampton University, Dr. Whitaker is responsible for teaching the Business Ethics, Business Law, and Labor-Management Relations courses. In addition, Dr. Whitaker serves as an academic advisor to students in the School of Business. In addition to serving Hampton University, Dr. Whitaker is the assistant pastor at New Bethel Baptist Church in Portsmouth, Virginia, where his father is the pastor and his mother is the minister of music. Furthermore, Dr. Whitaker is the chief executive officer of New Bethel Federal Credit Union, a church-based financial institution providing assistance to the local community.

Prior to his position at Hampton University, Dr. Whitaker served as a business law instructor in the R. B. Pamplin College of Business at Virginia Tech in Blacksburg, Virginia, teaching Business Law and Employment Discrimination courses. While at Virginia Tech, Dr. Whitaker served on the College of Business Multicultural Committee and recruited Black Ph.D. students through the KPMG Peat Marwick Ph.D. Project. Furthermore, Dr. Whitaker assisted many of his African American students in obtaining full scholarships and stipends to MBA and law school programs.

While at Virginia Tech, Dr. Whitaker received many honors, including Dean's List; Who's Who Among American University and College Students; elected President of the Black Students Alliance; inducted into Omicron Delta Kappa National Leadership Honor Society and Order Of Omega National Greek Honor Society; selected as Alpha Phi Alpha College Brother of the Year for 1987 for the State of Virginia; received the National Minority Leadership; and selected for Outstanding Young Men of America.

After Virginia Tech, Dr. Whitaker received his master of business administration in 1989 from The Pennsylvania State University Smeal College of Business. While studying for the MBA, Dr. Whitaker served as a graduate assistant, vice-president of the Black Graduate Student Association, and received the first-place award in the College of Business Executive Panel Presentation.

Dr. Whitaker furthered his education at The Ohio State University College of Law. In 1993, he graduated with the doctor of jurisprudence degree.

25

MARKETPLACE 2000

THE IMPACT ON ETHNIC MINORITIES, BUSINESS ORGANIZATIONS, AND THE GOVERNMENT

Mark Micaiah Whitaker

As our nation becomes more diverse, researchers have speculated about how this diversity will translate into changes in society. Of particular concern has been the issue of how employers will absorb and incorporate ethnically diverse populations into their organizations. Another concern is the influence racial and ethnic employees will have on business organizations. While these concerns are important to examine, very little attention has been devoted to how this growing, diverse labor force will translate into a consumer force and expand the market. This paper examines the impact of Marketplace 2000 on ethnic minorities, organizations, and the government.

Because of the influence of Western Civilization, European perspectives dominate the views in certain areas of our society. As a matter of fact, White males are the reference point from which diversity in our culture is measured. Traditionally, scholars have noted that diversity refers to anyone who is not a White male (Hellriegel, Slocum, & Richard, 1995). In recent years, scholars have devoted much attention to the changing demographic profile of society. Research reveals that the average White woman has 1.7 children, the average African American woman has 2.4 children, and the average Mexican American woman has 2.9 children (Johnston, 1991). Moreover, most of the growth in the world population will be in countries with non-Caucasian populations (Wright, Ferris, Hiller, & Kroll, 1995).

We are demographically a diverse society based on traditional and contemporary notions. One area that illustrates this phenomenon is the American workforce; by the year 2000, researchers estimate that 85 percent of the net additions to the U.S. workforce will be women and non-White men (Cox, Lobel, & McLeod, 1991), as revealed in the study *Workforce 2000* (Johnston & Packer, 1987). Although this workforce metamorphosis has received much attention, based on a review of the literature, sparse research and discussion exist on the implications of new entrants as consumers in the marketplace. The impact of their potential activity deserves a Consumer 2000 examination. The relevancy of examining Marketplace 2000 from a business perspective derives from the concept of competitive advantage. Organizations that understand how rightfully to harness and manage resources gain a sustained competitive advantage and survive (Barney, 1991; Lado, Boyd, & Wright, 1992). Having an understanding of the consumers in the market and addressing their concerns gives an organization a competitive advantage, and this potential understanding merits an analysis of Marketplace 2000. Therefore, this paper analyzes the implications of Marketplace 2000 as it affects ethnic minorities, business organizations, and the government.

The emergence of Marketplace 2000 offers an opportunity for ethnic minorities to reexamine the definition of the marketplace, from consumption of goods to consumption of power. In defining the marketplace, researchers have traditionally defined it as the environment whereby goods and services flow from the producer to the consumer (Kotler, 1984). In order to capitalize on the potential that Marketplace 2000 holds for ethnic minorities individually and collectively, we must redefine the concept of marketplace. First, we must realize that the current definition of "marketplace" is limited; researchers tend to view the marketplace as an arena in which commodities are bought and sold (Williams, 1982). In analyzing the concept of commodities, our definition of commodity tends to be limited to and synonymous with goods and services. To expand our notion of the marketplace, economic empowerment needs to be included as a commodity of Marketplace 2000.

This interpretation of the marketplace moves us beyond a model of consumption to a model of investment. Since the consumers of 2000 will also be the workforce of 2000, it makes sense for these consumers to use their organizations of employment as a source of economic empowerment (Hellriegel, Slocum, & Richard, 1995). Our presence in Marketplace 2000 puts us in a position as ethnic minorities to demand that companies allow for individual compensation plans that provide for employee ownership in the business enterprise. Although profit-sharing and gain-sharing are compensation tools presently used to reward employees for organizational success (Gerhart & Milkovich, 1991), neither of these plans provides an ownership interest. In obtaining ownership interest in the business enterprise, ethnic minorities have a source of influence in numbers. Statistics reveal that the demographic composition of ethnic minorities in America comprises 25 percent of the total population: There are 30 million African Americans, 22.4 million Hispanics, 7.3 million Asians, and 2 million Native Americans (Rossman, 1994). There is power and opportunity in numbers; therefore, as individual consumers in Marketplace 2000, *investment* along with consumption should be a part of our definition of commodity as we expand the notion of marketplace.

As well as offering opportunities for individuals to become empowered, Marketplace 2000 provides an opportunity for organizations to reaffirm commitments to equal opportunity. In the past, executives in most firms found similar human resources to manage—the average worker was a White man with a wife and children at home (Jamieson & O'Mara, 1991). Today, most organizations have not been effective in managing women and non-White men; turnover and absenteeism are usually higher, and job satisfaction levels are lower than they are for White men (Cox and Blake, 1991). Moreover, invisible barriers such as the glass ceiling prevent minorities and women from advancing in an organization (Crosby & Blanchard, 1989; DiTomaso, Thompson, & Blake, 1986; Morrison, White, & Van Velsor, 1987). In other studies, researchers unveiled compensation discrimination against women (Schwartz, 1989; Terborg & Ilgen, 1975); promotion discrimination against women (Cox & Nkomo, 1986); racially motivated job-treatment discrimination (Greenhaus, Parasuraman, & Wormley, 1990); and hiring and promotion discrimination resulting in low minority representation in management (Killingsworth & Reimers, 1983).

These studies depict the climate and culture that exist in most American organizations. Marketplace 2000 will call for changing policies of discrimination to policies of equal opportunity. This reevaluation will not occur out of a framework of ethics or morality but out of the necessity to maintain a competitive advantage. In order to maneuver in Marketplace 2000, the organization must have knowledge and understanding of the consumers (Williams, 1982). Understanding of fundamental cultural values and themes allows for organizations to introduce products acceptable to consumers of varying cultures (Vinson, Scott, & Lamont, 1977). Those organizations that value a diverse workforce will enter Marketplace 2000 with a competitive advantage (Wright, Ferris, Hiller, & Kroll, 1995). If organizations seek to continue and expand their market share or product base and if they wish to survive, Marketplace 2000 will demand that these organizations reevaluate the necessity of equal opportunity.

Beyond the impact on individuals and organizations, Marketplace 2000 will force our government to change, revise, revisit, and reverse some of its fundamental policies and views as the marketplace of 2000 becomes more global. Marketplace 2000 changes the orientation of focus from America to international. As so called third-world nations become developed in the areas of technology, information, transportation, and health, these countries will become a part of Marketplace 2000 (Rossman, 1994). As for the emerging importance of these countries, the visit by President Clinton to parts of Africa signals a gradual change in perspective about African countries from being seen as nonplayers to being seen as players in the markets. The significance to our nation is that if the United States is to remain competitive globally, we must correctly access the opportunities that exist internationally in new markets. Therefore, Marketplace 2000 may call for policies and laws to be significantly changed (Barney, 1980). As for policies, Marketplace 2000 will call for a change in countries that receive Most Favored Nation status by our government. Consumers in Marketplace 2000 will become international shoppers; as products and services become more accessible through Internet purchasing, the consumers of 2000 and beyond will not be limited to the local mall. Such advances in technology and the expanding market will dictate that the government reevaluate its trade and communication policies (Robinson, 1985).

Consumers will increasingly become part of the international workforce. Companies are moving to foreign countries to capitalize on labor cost reductions and to meet the rising demand of products from overseas, and in an effort to keep excellent employees, organizations are offering jobs to individuals in foreign countries. Marketplace 2000 will cause the United States to reevaluate employment laws and tax laws as consumers expand product markets. Therefore, Marketplace 2000 has major implications as the consumers of 2000 participate in the global economy.

In closing, too often when the notion of a new marketplace is discussed in reference to minority communities, researchers tend to focus on how goods and services can be marketed to these communities. As a consequence, new marketing strategies are often instituted that encourage the flow of economic resources outside of minority communities. The changes predicted in the composition of the workforce in the year 2000 will no doubt be an incentive to reintroduce this strategy. The notion of consuming potential economic power in addition to goods and services is an issue that needs to be carefully examined by minorities if we are to build economically sound minority communities in the United States. Furthermore, if organizations are to compete in Marketplace 2000, consumers must perceive and realize equity. Finally, the government must assess the value and needs of consumers of Marketplace 2000 and revise laws and policies as necessary.

References

Barney, G. O. (1980). *The global 2000 report to the president.* Washington, DC: U.S. Government Printing Office.

Barney, J. (1991). Firm resources and sustained competitive advantage. *Journal of Management, 17,* 99–120.

Cox, T. H. & Nkomo, S. (1986). Differential performance appraisal criteria: A field study of Black and White managers. *Group and Organization Studies, 11,* 101–119.

Cox, T. H., & Blake, S. (1991). Managing cultural diversity: Implications for organizational competitiveness. *Academy of Management Executive, 5* (3), 45–56.

Cox, T. H., & Lobel, S. A., & McLeod, P.L. (1991). Effects of ethnic group cultural differences on cooperative and competitive behavior on a group task. *Academy of Management Journal, 34,* 827–847.

Crosby, F. J., & Blanchard, F. A. (1989). Introduction: Affirmative action and the question of standards. In F. A. Blanchard & F. J. Crosby (Eds.), *Affirmative action in perspective* (pp. 37–46). New York: Springer-Verlag.

DiTomaso, N., Thompson, D. E., & Blake, D. H. (1986). *Corporate perspectives on minority advancement in management.* Paper presented at the 4th Annual Meeting of the Academy of Management, Chicago.

Gerhart, B., & Milkovich, G. T. (1991). Employee compensation: Research and practice. In M. D. Dunnette & L. M. Hough (Eds.), *Handbook of industrial & organizational psychology* (2nd ed.). Palo Alto, CA: Consulting Psychologist Press.

Greenhaus, J. H., Parasuraman, S., & Wormley, W. M. (1990). Effects of race on organizational experiences, job performance evaluations, and career outcomes. *Academy of Management Journal, 33,* 64–86.

Hellriegel, D., Slocum Jr., J. W., & Richard, W. (1995). *Organizational behavior* (7th ed.). St. Paul, MN: West Publishing.

Jamieson, D., & O'Mara, J. (1991). *Managing workforce 2000: Gaining diversity advantage.* San Francisco: Jossey-Bass.

Johnston, W. B. (1991). Global workforce 2000. *Harvard Business Review, 69*(2), 115–127.

Johnston, W. B., & Packer, A. (1987). *Workforce 2000: Work and workers for the 21st century.* Indianapolis, IN: Hudson Institute.

Killingsworth, M. R., & Reimers, C. W. (1983). Race, ranking, promotions and pay at a federal facility: A logical analysis. *Industrial and Labor Relations Review, 37,* 92–107.

Kotler, P. (1984). *Marketing management: Analysis, planning, and control* (5th ed.). Englewood Cliffs, NJ: Prentice-Hall.

Lado, A. A., Boyd, N. G., & Wright, P. (1992). A competency-based model of sustained competitive advantage: Toward a conceptual integration. *Journal of Management, 18,* 77–91.

Morrison, A. M., White, R. P., & Van Velsor, E. (1987). *Breaking the glass ceiling.* Reading, MA: Addison-Wesley.

Robinson, G. (1985, January). The FCC in the year 2000. *Federal Communications Law Journal, 37*(1), 156–170.

Rossman, M. L. (1994). *Multicultural marketing: Selling to a diverse America.* New York: American Management Association.

Schwartz, F. (1989). Management women and the new facts of life. *Harvard Business Review, 67*(1), 65–76.

Terborg, J. R., & Ilgen, D. R. (1975). A theoretical approach to sex discrimination in traditional masculine occupations. *Organizational Behavior and Human Performance, 13,* 352–376.

Vinson, D. E., Scott, J. E., & Lamont, L. (1977). The role of personal values in marketing and consumer behavior. *Journal of Marketing, 41,* 44–50.

Williams, T. G. (1982). *Consumer behavior: Fundamentals & strategies.* St. Paul, MN: West Publishing.

Wright, P., Ferris, S. P., Hiller, J., & Kroll, M. (1995). Competitiveness through management of diversity: Effects on stock price valuation. *Academy of Management Journal, 38*(1), 272–287.

Dr. Shuaib Meacham

Dr. Shuaib Meacham currently serves as an assistant professor of secondary English and literacy at the University of Colorado at Boulder. He also serves as a research fellow with CY. SCAN, the Center for Study of Youth in Science, Culture, and New Media. As part of his work at the university, Dr. Meacham co-directs a series of studies that emphasize innovative, community-based approaches to literacy education. The first initiative, the "Study of Literacy for Life," involves community elders and leaders in a supervisory capacity with respect to student teachers working in an urban setting. A second initiative, "CU in the House," connects a cadre of young poets who frequently perform at a local poetry club to middle and high school students to promote literacy as a practice of personal and community well-being. CU in the House also functions in partnership with Brother Jeff's Cultural Center and Cafe, a community landmark that has hosted performances of poets such as Dr. Maya Angelou, Dr. Sonia Sanchez, and Dr. Haki Madhubiti; the Ghandi Hamer King Center, directed by noted scholar and activist, Dr. Vincent Harding; and the internationally renowned Cleo Parker Robinson Dance Troupe. A third study, one that examines a community-based technology initiative, is presently under development. Additionally, Dr. Meacham systematically integrates community organizations and leaders into his literacy methods classes. In addition to his work in the Denver and Boulder, Colorado areas, Dr. Meacham serves on National Committees for the National Council for the Teaching of English.

Dr. Meacham holds a bachelor of arts degree from the University of Michigan in creative writing and literature. He also holds a master of arts degree from the University of Michigan in reading and literacy and a Ph.D. in curriculum and instruction from the University of Illinois. Dr. Meacham completed his high school education at Western Reserve Academy in Hudson, Ohio.

Dr. Meacham is a member of the National Council of Teachers of English, the Phi Beta Kappa educational leadership organization, and the National Reading Conference.

26

THE SPIRIT OF A MAN

Dr. Shuaib Meacham

He that believeth on me, believeth not on me . . .
John 12:44

Introduction

Many discussions of African American men, both in the academy as well as in U.S. society at large, make much of our numerical decline and the various forms of risk we experience as targets of racist energies. Given such a focus, however, it becomes easy to overlook the fact that our presence as African American men in the academy is the function of spirit and thereby contains an important measure of power. In writing of the Spirit of a Man, power must be emphasized. For in contrast to the "at-risk" discourses that perpetually surround us, when we are aware of who we are and whose we are and when we are aware that, as James Baldwin (1985) reminds us, the price of our ticket has already been paid, power becomes the definitive quality of our academic experience. I have drawn from this power throughout my experience in the academy. With it, I feel that I am not only equal to the academic challenges that confront me but also that the particulars of the African experience in America have provided me with an intellectual advantage when compared to my colleagues in the mainstream. But I will speak more of that later.

Notwithstanding the centrality of power, the commonly cited demographic statistics that document the plight of African American males for acceptable levels of representation in the academy in contrast to our overrepresentation in prisons are very real. This begs the question as to how "power" can define our academic presence in the face of such formidable social and demographic odds, traps, and pitfalls. Again, the answer to this question lies in the spirit. This essay attempts to delineate the dynamics of our collective spirit as African American men and the ways in which this spirit manifests itself in our academic identities and practices. This spirit and thus our power manifests itself in three basic areas: (a) our collective, interconnected, and transcendent quality of spirit, (b) the manner in which our presence in the academy represents a calling by that spirit, and (c) the kinetic intellectual energy we embody, which compels us not to replicate but to redefine the standards that characterized the academy prior to our presence there.

Each of these three factors assumes, however, a process and practice of "re-membering." The academy, particularly in its reward structures, constitutes a radically individualistic environment, wherein one's task is to cultivate singularly identifiable intellectual property. Tenure and other forms of basic career survival exert a compelling force of separation, isolation, and individual self-definition apart from any kind of collective framework. Thus, it becomes vital to our ability to remain connected to our spirit to literally "remember" who we are—to reconnect ourselves to this collective heritage, to our personal narratives of overcoming and calling, and to the intellectual orientations that these connections entail. By maintaining these connections, we can feed and sustain ourselves on these irreplaceable cultural resources and cultivate the genuine foundations of our power. This essay is a gesture of "remembering."

The Collective Spirit

The first text assigned to me in my graduate-school experience was Plato's *Republic*. Toward the end of the text, the intellectual and philosophical ideal of the "philosopher king" is proffered for emulation as a prototypical example of intellectual spirit, if you will. The philosopher king deliberately stands apart from community, from relationship, even from personal experience to contemplate more effectively abstract "forms" of perfection. While the philosopher king model is not an articulated ideal in today's academic environment, its basic posture of isolated, individual, intellectual labor is reinforced in the academic reward structure. Individual scholarship receives the highest of rewards, pay increases, and ultimately the Holy Grail of tenure, while commitment and connection to community go wholly unrecognized.

Within such a context, perhaps the most basic act of memory is to recall and reinstitute upon ourselves as African American men the collective and interconnected quality of our relationship to spirit. In contrast to an isolated and individualistic spiritual vision, we exist amidst a "cloud of (spiritual) witnesses," whose lives gave testimony to the power of faith as a guiding force to knowledge and commitment. These witnesses embodied a fury for freedom and changed the shape of this country with their willingness to sacrifice all to redeem ideals stated in foundational documents of this nation. Our relationship to these witnesses is perhaps best stated by Dr. Maya Angelou when, in *And Still I Rise,* she asserts that we are the products of the dreams, visions, and prayers of our ancestors. We are an inseparable outcome of those witnesses who have preceded us, and our presence in academia is a direct result of their sacrifice. As the Bible states so insightfully, "We reap where we have not sown."

In direct contrast to the academic standards to which I am accountable, I have no evidence for these assertions, but I do have experience. In contrast to the philosopher king, I know that when I sit down to write, I am not mentally moving about abstract ideals available through isolation. When I sit down to write, I feel my spirit's relationship to the other witnesses who have preceded me and the manner in which the collective body of wisdom emerges rearticulated in my own language. I know this not by data collected but by the reaction of my mind, soul, and body when I hear the Word accurately rendered in the unspeakable fullness of the John Coletrane tenor sax, in the cutting emotional precision of a James Baldwin sentence, in the revelatory structure of the Toni Morrison novel, and above all, in the defiant strength in weakness of the Word and Person of Jesus Christ. I know that when I sit down to pray, contemplate, and ultimately document my ideas in research, I am moving amidst these and an infinite number of unnamed and unknown personalities, including the participants in this book who have lived out their own witness to this heritage.

This spirit, collectively embodied by the cloud of witnesses, provides us with an unshakeable power, which we bring to our presence in the academy. When faced with the challenges, the labor, the difficult negotiations required to maintain an integrity of presence in the academy, I remember that I am not an isolated presence defined by my physical dimensions. I am a part of that collective presence that has survived the Middle Passage, endured amidst the horrors of slavery—which, in spite of such trials, has produced the most compelling and definitive cultural texts and art forms in the history of the United States—and which has transformed this country and directly inspired similar movements for democracy and freedom around the world. Irish resistance activists, Chinese students on Tiananmen Square, and celebrants along the Berlin Wall all sang out "We Shall Overcome" as they bore witness to the power of this collective spirit and its ability to capture the yearnings in their own hearts.

These examples demonstrate the power available not only for ourselves as African American men but also for the world in the form of this collective spirit that moves us. This power enables us to think beyond the standards and norms of the academy toward a more comprehensive impact on the society and the African American community in addition to our academic environments. This collective, overcoming, freedom-seeking spirit is one of the means by which we experience the academy with power, in spite of the physical circumstances that shape our presence.

The Power of a Calling

It has always been a contention of mine that few people of color in general and African American males in particular arrive in academia as an outcome of a long-term intent to enter the academy. I engaged in an informal test of this proposition while having dinner with some colleagues of color during the most recent meeting of the American Educational Research Association in Montreal. When I asked each of my colleagues whether his presence in the academy was the product of a long-term intention, not one claimed to have harbored such desires. Instead, what they related were powerful narratives and testimonies, some involving the most unlikely circumstances, as a foundation for their academic practice. Two single mothers (one with no academic aspirations) and a fork-lift driver on a California agricultural field represented just a few of the places from which journeys to the academy originated.

Such journeys attest to the spirit's working in our lives and comprise an invaluable resource of certainty regarding our presence in the academy and the authority through which we can engage in practices designed to transform academic norms. After all that it took us to reach the academy, we know that we belong and that there is nothing anyone who holds anything against us can do about it. Our presence in the academy is the function of a calling, a working of the spirit beyond any personal intention or desire.

My journey into the academy actually began aboard a naval aircraft carrier, the U.S.S. Carl Vinson, during an overseas deployment to the Indian Ocean and the Persian Gulf. I actually joined the Navy in an effort to avoid any further experiences in educational institutions by learning a marketable technical skill. I graduated from the University of Michigan utterly bewildered and disconcerted regarding my undergraduate experience. The experience was far more about indoctrination and intellectual socialization than the pursuit of knowledge and truth. I left Ann Arbor vowing to anyone who would listen that with the attainment of my degree, I had completed all personal involvement with formal academic institutions. However, just about the time I left,

Dr. Betty Morrison, one of the first African American tenured professors at the University of Michigan, told me that one day I would be an academic. At the time, that was the most ridiculous idea that I could imagine.

I was stationed aboard the carrier because I had been trained as an aviation electronics technician to repair the electrical systems of airplanes. My professional progress was immediately hampered by the fact that I was not able to secure the "secret" security clearance necessary to work in the field because I had traveled to Saudi Arabia, India, and Pakistan within the last five years and the Navy suspected my involvement with anti-American, potentially terrorist organizations. With no substantive electronics involvement, I eventually found myself more involved with the ship's library and its rather substantial collection of books to the point that I lost interest in electronics. The time period of close to three consecutive months at sea without pulling into port provided me with hours each day to read and contemplate. Consequently, I was almost never to be found without a book in my possession. Eventually, other African American shipmates noticed and began to ask me why I always carried a book with me. Something in my explanation led them to move from asking me to explain why I read so much to asking me to explain the content of the book I happened to be carrying and why I was reading it. I do not remember the specific details of my explanations, but I do remember telling them that I was reading to explore issues and to answer questions that I had about life and that books provided information and insight through which to acquire a deeper level of knowledge. These explanations were seen as Shuaib "dropping science," and they saw how the contents of the books spoke insightfully to their own experiences.

Through my explanations, these Brothers began to identify the possibilities that reading posed, elucidating pathways through the challenges and difficulties that they faced. My African American Brothers, as they connected to the purposes and benefits of reading, began to go to the ship's library themselves, check out books, and bring them to me for discussion. Perhaps the primary topic of reading and discussion involved issues related to racism. I believe that the prominence of this topic related directly to the conditions experienced aboard the ship. On the ship each morning at 5 A.M., a roll call known as "restriction" was undertaken where those who had been subject to the Navy's disciplinary system were ordered to convene as a form of punishment. The percentage of African Americans on these rolls was frequently between 95 and 100 percent on a ship that held up to 6,000 people. In addition to this, the ship's brig was almost exclusively populated by African Americans. African Americans on lock-down in the brig not only lined up for restriction but also had to be escorted to meals by the ship's police (known as

"Masters at Arms") and had to have a circle of empty tables between them and the rest of the ship's population to emphasize their isolation. While those under disciplinary jurisdiction were predominantly African American and dressed in enlisted blue "dungarees," the officers in charge, dressed in khaki, were almost exclusively White. African Americans in khaki were invariably harder on African American personnel than the White officers, in part because they felt compelled to demonstrate to their peers and superiors that they were more loyal to the Navy than to those who shared their common racial background.

African American restriction lines, African American brig inmates being lead to eat by "Masters," and African American officers going out of their way to please metaphorical "Masters" created a context wherein the ship was literally a laboratory of racism. The urgency of the issue was enhanced by the fact that of the seven or so consistent participants in the reading group that emerged, all except one had been incarcerated in the naval prison system at one time in their naval careers. Within these circumstances, these African American Brothers cultivated an ardent desire to read and share their insights with one another. An example of the desire for literacy is captured in the book selection of Andre, a selection I could not fully appreciate until I entered graduate school. Searching for material that would clarify his experiences and validate his perspectives, Andre brought a book to the table called *The Closing of the American Mind* by a writer named Alan Bloom (1987). Andre had not graduated from high school. The metaphor of the closed American mind, one that refused to see him for who he really was, validated this young African American male's experience. He desperately tried to read this text. Only when I entered graduate school and found what *The Closing of the American Mind* was really about did I realize the profound desire underlying Andre's engagement with literacy. The possibilities for personal and social insight posed by the metaphor led Andre to engage in an almost heroic effort to read a text that was far beyond his reading level.

Racism was far from the only topic of discussion. I shared my passion for religious studies and had an unforgettable conversation with several Brothers on the topic of Taoism. Andre became a vegetarian after reading a book on the American diet, "J-Love" read the work of James Baldwin and Malcolm X, and Rashida read books on the drug trade. Collectively the conversations were the most intellectually stimulating that I had had up to that point in my life, significantly more stimulating than those with classmates at the University of Michigan.

From this experience with the Brothers in the Navy, I emerged not only with memories but also with research questions. Why was the insight and brilliance of these young African Americans not cultivated in schools? What was it about the experience that led these young Brothers to engage in reading with such ardor? How did the environment of the ship impact their ability to see the potential significance of books in their lives?

Although I left my naval service commitment with these questions, I had no practical idea how to pursue them in any formal or systematic manner. I held vague ideas related to going into teaching, but I was newly married, had a baby at home, and had no money to pursue the additional education. It was in this context that Dr. Betty Morrison began calling me with suggestions of going to graduate school. Again, I thought that she was crazy. I didn't have money to pursue a teaching certificate in what was little more than a community college in Sacramento, where I was living, let alone graduate school at the University of Michigan. Not knowing anything about fellowships, assistantships, or any of the ways in which such studies were funded, I dismissed the suggestions. Eventually, Dr. Morrison engaged in a practice of what I considered at the time to be "harassment," calling from Ann Arbor on Eastern Standard Time to catch me around 11:00 P.M. Pacific time, up to three times a week trying to get me to apply. Finally, she wore me down, and the day before the submission deadline, I wrote my statement of purpose and completed my application with my one-year-old daughter crying in my lap. I turned the application in with hopes of ending the "harassment." However, I still had not taken the Graduate Record Exam (GRE) and had missed the sign-up deadline. Dr. Morrison harassed me until I agreed to take the test as a "walk on." By that summer, I was not only admitted but was awarded a full tuition waiver and fellowship plus an assistantship.

Such a testimony is the work of the Spirit, who arranged circumstances and forced me into the academy. I was called to be in the academy in spite of myself. Not only did I get into school, but I also arrived with research questions, utterly unaware that there was a field called literacy education, tailor-made for the pursuit of those questions. This testimony of the Spirit's work endowed me with a tremendous confidence. Even though my classmates were former teachers, principals, even school superintendents, I had the conviction of my testimony, and the power of that experience led me to insights and avenues of inquiry that distinguished me from my far more experienced mainstream colleagues. By the end of my tenure in Ann Arbor, I was selected to speak at the University of Michigan School of Education's commencement. My lack of experience in the field of education was more than compensated for by the work of the Spirit. Not only did I not function at a deficit, but I excelled, and the excellence was recognized on academic terms. By the Spirit I had been endowed with the power of a calling that actually provided me with an intellectual advantage regarding the complex educational issues we examined. This power of calling and the understanding of the dynamics that underlie it continue to shape my practice now that I work as a university professor.

The Power of a Spirit-Driven Practice

As I studied toward my master's degree in the field of literacy at the University of Michigan, I was encouraged to pursue my questions by my advisor, William McGinley, through a historical study of African American literacy within the slave community. As I collected material for that study, I came upon a statement of unlimited depth and relevance not only for the study of African Americans and literacy but also for understanding the power of a Spirit-filled engagement with language in general. In Gates' (1987) introduction to the classic slave narratives, I found the following phrase: "the slaves who learned to read and write were the first to run away" (p. ix). The statement speaks of a furious energy, which Dr. Vincent Harding (1992) refers to as a "fury for liberty" (p. 141) that defines, in many ways, the best of the African American cultural tradition and its engagement with literacy in particular. More specifically, the statement effectively articulates a tradition of spiritual, intellectual, and political commitment that has literally transformed the United States and the world. Throughout my career, I have pursued the treasures of that statement. Like a chain wherein each link leads to ever more profound insights and understanding, the statement connects the African American freedom struggle directly to the power of literacy. In addition, the connection between reading and freedom from enslavement, in all of the ways that enslavement may be manifested, has lead me beyond mere academic participation deliberately to the power-filled practice of "witness." Cornel West provides a compelling definition of this practice of academic or intellectual witness when he states:

> To bear witness is to make and remake, invent and reinvent oneself as a person and as a people by keeping faith with the best of such earlier efforts . . . This perennial process of self-making and self-inventing is propelled by a self-loving and self-trusting made possible by overcoming a colonized mind, body and soul. (1996, p. 92)

Within the framework provided by West, literacy itself becomes a practice of witness, particularly the practice of the literacy academic. The study of literacy as a witness becomes "keeping faith the best of such earlier efforts." As suggested above, the connection between reading and runaway speaks to a very specific quality of literacy. As opposed to the mechanical and technical practices of decoding emphasized in back-to-basics literacy approaches and even to the self-centered, nonrelational liberal practices of the "reader response" tradition, the statement constitutes a very different articulation of literacy than what is practiced in schools of education. Within such a statement, knowledge, information, and wisdom are deployed, not for cerebral enjoyment or detached contemplation. Neither are they deployed for individual aggrandizement. "Running away" from enslavement is a metaphor for spiritual transformation and collective liberation.

Frederick Douglass, perhaps the prototypical example of the connection between reading and running away, initially experienced through literacy a personal transformation. Literacy provided him with a language though which to see beyond a life of slavery and to envision the possibility of freedom. However, as one among the cloud of witnesses, his ostensibly personal transformation was actually a collective conception. His own engagement with literacy and the possibilities that emerged compelled him to extend his own insights to as many in the African American community as possible. Within the context of slavery, with severe and painful punishments as a risk, Frederick Douglass created a school in which he simultaneously educated and planned for the escape of up to forty other African Americans. Given the historical model of Douglass, I was able to "re-see" and understand my Naval experience to be a contemporary enactment of that historical and cultural liberating energy. The meetings, hidden among the deepest decks of the ship, were actually a modern-day "bush" school, practiced in Africa and reenacted amidst the dynamics of slavery. Real education is always subject to erasure, and the historical validation of my experience with the Brothers in the Navy attested to the deep cultural power of my literacy work.

As one pursues the chain of possibilities contained in the relationship between reading and running away, one finds that Douglass represents not only an example but also a paradigm of connective political commitments and liberating possibilities. Bearing witness to the possibilities of social transformation merely initiated in his African American experience, Douglass involved himself in the Irish liberation movement (Takaki, 1993). His commitments to liberation lead him to speak out forcefully against racist and exclusionary legislation passed against Asian Americans (Okihiro, 1994). And his work on behalf of the liberation of women lead Angela Davis (1983) to characterize him as the foremost male advocate for women's rights of his generation. This same connection between literacy and liberation can be found in the freedom schools and citizenship schools of the South during the African American freedom struggle in the South, a struggle which, as suggested previously, directly informed freedom struggles throughout the world.

While the connections between reading and running away embody important personal, political, and social implications, Houston Baker (1992) discusses the more subtle intellectual and educational advantages of such a connection. In his fortuitously titled book, *Workings of the Spirit: The Poetics of Afro-American Women's Writing* (1992), Baker delineates what he perceives to be the historical dynamics that have shaped African American intellectual practice. Baker suggests that as an outcome of the conditions posed by slavery, African Americans by necessity developed a strong proclivity for what he refers to as "nonmaterial intelligence" (1992, p. 38):

> Africans uprooted from ancestral soil, stripped of material culture, and victimized by brutal contact with various European nations were compelled not only to maintain their cultural heritage at a meta (as opposed to a material) level but also to apprehend the operative metaphysics of various alien cultures. Primary to their survival was the work of consciousness, of nonmaterial intelligence.

This use of nonmaterial intelligence as a survival strategy produced a norm wherein African Americans learned to process information on at least two levels simultaneously. As Baker suggests, African Americans had to retain contact with an African-based cultural framework while learning the demands of the "alien" American culture simultaneously. Baker adds to this intellectual framework a spiritual disposition, through which multifaceted energies and influences were processed and synthesized for community benefit:

> The primacy of nonmaterial transactions in the African's initial negotiations of slavery and the slave trade led to a privileging of the roles and figures of medicine men, griots, conjurers, priests, and priestesses and musicians. This emphasis (and leadings of the spirit) was embodied in at least one form as the founding institution of African American group life—the church, which in its very name sometimes expresses the spiritual syncretism of its founding: "African Methodist Episcopal." (pp. 38–39)

This cultural emphasis upon the multifaceted and the nonmaterial comprises another important factor through which immersion in the spirit of African American culture constitutes an important preparation for academic work. As the academic constitutes that level of knowledge wherein sophisticated analytical schemes are brought to bear upon complex, multifaceted problems, the ways of knowing demanded by African American survival provide us with a cognitive advantage with respect to academic work. Whereas traditions rooted

in Western European frameworks emphasized ways of knowing aimed at identifying a singular explanatory construct, African American scholars reflected
cultural practices such as jazz and signified multiple ways of knowing. These
multiple ways of knowing work together with the spiritual practice of bearing
witness, with the remaking, reconceptualizing, and reinventing that go along
with such a task.

This spirit of witnessing and remaking enabled me to see a need in literacy instruction for a focus on cultural connections, in contrast to the emphasis on cultural difference that informed most of the multicultural perspectives
on literacy. To conceptualize processes through which such connections may
be understood, I drew upon the connective strengths found in jazz-based musical expression. Murray's (1996) conception of the "blues idiom," of which
jazz is a prototypical expression, is a theoretical treatise on the dynamics associated with jazz. The blues idiom enabled me to document cultural connections within the context of literacy instruction with a degree of clarity and precision yet to be found in academic work on the subject. Through the patterns
and sequences of jazz-based musical connections, I was able to identify more
effectively the patterns that emerged when children connected to one another
across cultures in their reading instruction.

While the research of my dissertation was innovative on an academic
level, in it I tried to enact the spirit of witness and its power on another level.
My dissertation was the first step in a process wherein I attempted to use the
global impact of African American cultural processes such as the blues idiom
(embodied in the social action of the African American freedom movement),
to construct a language of liberating cultural connection. The classroom context of children's elementary-school reading instruction was just a laboratory
through which to view the processes in action, to view the uptake of this language on the part of children. But as Dr. Vincent Harding suggests, children
are the best starting point for such a project.

> Perhaps it is only fitting that a study of human geography that grows
> out of one people's freedom movement should eventually return, via
> the mappings of our hearts, to the higher ground that bears our com-
> mon struggle, our deepest human hope. Even the youngest of our stu-
> dents will likely understand that path. (1992, p. 176)

In concluding this essay, the point of using the concept of spirit within
academic presence was to emphasize the fact that there is power and even
"real" freedom in knowing that we as African Americans are not in the academy of our own design. Remember that each one of us represents only a mere

condensed drop of pure substance that has fallen from an infinitely larger cloud of witnesses. Do not be fooled by apparent separation from that cloud. For that physical appearance has no bearing upon the fact that for all of the time we function in the academic domain, that cloud is in us and we are in the cloud. It shapes our thoughts and ideas; it shapes our practice; it shapes our impact. Do not expect less. Expect more. Our presence in the academy represents the presence of immense power. Prepare to be changed.

References

Angelou, M. (1978). *And still I rise*. New York: Random House.

Baker, H. A. (1992). *Workings of the spirit: The poetics of Afro-American women's writing*. Chicago: University of Chicago Press.

Baldwin, J. (1985). *The price of the ticket: Collected nonfiction, 1948–1985*. New York: Vintage Press.

Bloom, A. (Ed.). (1968). *The republic of Plato*. New York: Basic Books.

Bloom, A. (1987). *The closing of the American mind*. New York: Simon and Schuster.

Davis, A. Y. (1983). *Women, race, and class*. New York: Random House.

Gates, H. L. (Ed.). (1987). *The classic slave narratives*. New York: Mentor.

Harding, V. (1992). *Hope and history: Why we must share the story of the movement*. New York: Orbis Books.

Murray, A. (1996). *The blue devils of nada: A contemporary American approach to aesthetic statement*. New York: Pantheon.

Okihiro, G. Y. (1994). *Margins and mainstreams: Asians in American history and culture*. Seattle: University of Washington Press.

Takaki, R. (1993). *A different mirror: A history of multicultural America*. New York: Little Brown and Company.

West, C. (1996). Black strivings in the twilight of civilization. In H. L. Gates & C. West (Eds.), *The future of the race*. New York: Vintage Books.

CONCLUSION

THE COMMUNITY OF SCHOLARS MODEL: A HOLISTIC APPROACH TO AFRICAN AMERICAN SCHOLARSHIP IN HIGHER EDUCATION

Lee Jones

An African American Scholar is one who contributes original ideas, new insights and information to the existing fund of knowledge— whether or not he/she has a string of academic degrees or executes scholarly activities in a manner appropriate to the traditional and conventions of the existing world of scholarship.

—*Nathan Hare*

Despite the challenges that are before us we know from American history that our plight on the soils of this land has been consistently difficult. We have always had to justify our existence and clarify why we do what we do. It does not matter whether we are talking about sports, education, science, research, or any other profession. We also know from history that we were left a legacy to push forward despite the odds. People like Shem Hotep, John Henry Clark, Harriet Tubman, Fannie Lou Hamer and others have paved the way for every African American or other underrepresented group to achieve personal and collective goals. There will be academicians who will read this book and, perhaps, feel that it is not scholarly enough. I would argue that higher education, more than any other profession, ought to expand from a linear and monolithic view of scholarship.

If we are ever going to move from a place of global acknowledgment of diversity to manifesting this commitment through accepting the unique contributions that ethnic and racial scholarship brings, we must begin to transform the academic enterprise. This paradigm shift will offer quite a challenge to those who have spent a lifetime perpetuating the status quo. My guess is that we will need to continue with our plight. I suggest that Brothers of the academy adopt a model of scholarship development that will continue to support our research interests while continuing to add to the array of research that is conducted. I would also offer that we have to begin developing not only a community of scholars who will broaden higher education's definition of scholarship but a group who will increase the number of African Americans pursuing terminal degrees.

As discussed very thoroughly in previous chapters, high attrition rates and overall underrepresentation of African Americans in higher education graduate programs are issues of critical concern. Therefore, the primary focus of the Community of Scholars (COS) model is to produce African American scholars who will succeed in doctoral studies and within the academy. Previous research has provided linear approaches to examining persistence issues for African American scholars in doctoral programs. One such approach includes simply providing access, recruitment, and retention initiatives within the academy. A comprehensive model that supports, nurtures, and develops African Americans as scholars within the academy is needed. Critical focus is necessary during the doctoral process—a time in which most students are developing their perceptions and beliefs about scholarship.

The COS model proposes a society of scholars who will work collaboratively within the academy and beyond. Aside from incentives that assist in student persistence (i.e., financial assistance and mentoring), the COS model will influence the academic, social, professional, spiritual, and emotional development of scholars. Scholars would be educated in synthetic thinking, which Amen (1990) refers to as thinking from within and from without various systems, while maintaining perspective on all paradigms. The community of scholars seeks to fully utilize and actualize the advantage of the diverse perspectives and approaches of educators. Members literally challenge, encourage, and educate each other to achieve advanced paradigms. Members also incorporate community service and leadership within the academy and greater community. In doing so, members will create a perpetual framework for future generations to achieve excellence in scholarship, community, and humanity.

The Vision

The primary outcomes of the COS model are African American scholars who will revitalize and reshape scholarship and research as they relate to the African American community. This is not the vision itself but a single component. An African American with a degree is not sufficient in light of the quality of life African Americans currently experience. Previous scholarship that has sought to explain African American life has tended to examine it as a negative experience in and of itself. What we need are scholars who will counteract this trend with the intention of elevating the community. The COS vision is a society of African American professionals who nurture subsequent generations of scholars to levels of accomplishment greater than one individual.

Furthermore, the structure of American education does little to include the contributions of all of its constituents. Hence, another component of the COS vision is a relationship among the members that fosters, in the African tradition, synthetic thinking (Amen, 1990). Specifically, this means thinking within and without the system(s) and maintaining the perspective of each item and its relevance to the whole. Members literally challenge, encourage, and educate each other to achieve more advanced paradigms. In doing so, members develop a framework for future generations to have an understanding of scholarship, community, and humanity that is applicable to their time and space.

The vision of the COS also implies a community of scholars who work with the African American community. Woodson (1933) provides an explanation of the afflictions of African American professionals and the implications of a miseducated and unnurturing population. The COS vision requires that all scholars maintain and strengthen their relationships with the African American community and utilize the advantages of an ascent up the socioeconomic ladder beginning from the bottom rung. The COS vision recognizes that one of our most debilitating characteristics is poor solidarity, as evidenced by our political and economic behavior (Kotkin, 1992).

Scholars who participate in the COS model will depart from their degree programs understanding their relative position in society. They will:

1. Receive an academic degree.
2. Possess a holistic paradigm.
3. Work with the African American community.
4. Create scholarship that is central to highlighting and improving the African American community.

Psychological Health Development

African Americans who enter the American educational structure face a system that was not originally designed for inclusive practices. In its evolution, all efforts to accommodate the expanding diversity of the populace have confounded its ability to accomplish the espoused goal of providing all students

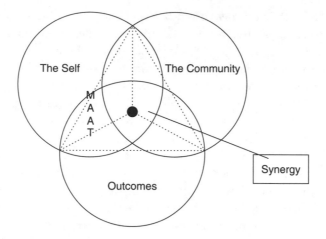

FIGURE 1   The Community of Scholars Model

with the necessary education for a quality life. Though the immediate concern of the COS is higher education completion, the cumulative effects of 0–12 education must not be ignored.

When a student arrives at the college and the community, there is some healing that must be done. Matriculation to the collegiate level is not without psychological influences that may result from experiences such as suppression of identity, education without practical relevance, and saturation of negative images of African Americans. There are also established societal norms, particularly in advanced degree programs, that are culturally different from what many African American students are accustomed.

The community of scholars model has three primary components—the self, the community, and the outcomes—and a fourth component—Maat—that is its structural component (see Figure 1).

The Self

This component primarily deals with what each individual member brings to the graduate school/scholarly experience. This includes readiness for scholarship, readiness for collaborative learning, adjustment issues, individual purpose, and expectations and perceptions of the graduate experience and of the community of scholars. As the self begins to better understand its principal concerns for scholarship, it should open the possibilities for synergistic developments within the community. Following are the competencies of a developing African American scholar:

1. Commitment to a spiritual force higher than life

2. The development of a personal vision statement outlining the multiple steps and strategies needed to accomplish your ultimate vision

3. A thorough assessment of the technical skills needed to excel in your academic discipline

4. An understanding of the social, political, intellectual, academic, and psychological realities of African Americans in America

5. The development of a personal conceptual framework that facilitates the actualization of spiritual balance, mental stability, physical conditioning, and internal peace

6. A personal discipline audit aimed at establishing a proactive teaching, research, and/or administrative commitment to quality

7. A thorough understanding of group dynamics, which leads to meaningful interpersonal communications across ethnic and gender lines

8. A passion and desire to always be willing to "take somebody with you" to the top

The Community

The development of a paradigm that is more suitable to African American intellectual expression and affirmation is a primary concern for the community of scholars. Carter G. Woodson alerted us more than 50 years ago that something was severely wrong with the way African Americans are educated. He provided the principal impetus today for the development of a paradigm that is most suitable for our training and development. The community consists of the coming together of young scholars and mentors from the academic and/or larger community. The community should initially set forth a vision and purpose for the group. Many of the core activities that will occur within this scholarly community will consist of mentoring, scholarly identity development, support and motivation, and professional, personal, and social development.

The critical place of community for self-realization, the centrality of an ethics that reaches beyond individual satisfaction, and the encompassing framework of a relational worldview are all aspects of the community that will resonate as the community develop.

The Outcomes

The primary outcomes of the community of scholars will be degreed profession-als that will effectively use applied and theoretical scholarship for progress. Other primary results should include a well-formed scholarly identity, focused research interest and community interest, a feeling of responsibility to humanity, and an established nurturing cycle to perpetuate the growth of the community of schol-ars. Ultimately, the Community of Scholars will provide a holistic approach to scholarship, which will lead to Ph.D. completion for more African Americans.

The Brothers highlighted within this book are just a few of literally hun-dreds who are earning their way in the academy. I trust that your eyes have been opened, your hearts have been filled, your minds have been expanded, and your arms have been opened to embrace the Brothers of the academy as we seek to continue the long and rich tradition of African Americans in higher education who have taken their seat at the table.

References

Akbar, N. (1985). *Community of self.* Tallahassee, FL: Mind Productions.

Asante, M. (1988). *Afrocentricity.* Trenton, NJ: Africa World Press.

Blackwell, J., & E. (1984). *Increasing access and retention of minority stu-dents in graduate and professional schools.* Paper presented at Educa-tional Testing Service's International Conference on Educational Stan-dards, New York.

Bowen, H., & Schuster, J. (1986). *American professors: A national resource imperiled.* New York: Oxford University Press.

King, R. (1977). *Black dot, melanin, the black experience: A holistic view.* New York: Random House.

Ladner, J. (Ed.). (1973). *The death of white sociology.* New York: Random House.

Myers, L. J. (1988). *Understanding an afrocentric worldview.* Dubuque, Iowa: Kendall Hunt.

Nichols, E. J. (1986). Cultural foundations for teaching black children. In O.M. Ratteray (Ed.), *Teaching mathematics, volume I: Culture, motiva-tion, history and classroom management* (pp. 1–8). Washington, DC: Institute for Independent Education Inc. (Eric Document Reproduction Service No. ED 283 929).

Olsen, D. (1991). Gender and racial differences among research university fac-ulty. *Recommendations for Promoting Diversity, 10,* 123–139.

Staples, R. (1984). Racial ideology and intellectual racism: Blacks in academia. *Black Scholar, 15,* 2–17.

Tierny, W. (1998). *The responsive university: Restructuring for high perfor-mance.* Baltimore, MD: Johns Hopkins University Press.

Page numbers with *f* indicate figures. Page numbers with *t* indicate tables.